Anatomy of LISP

McGRAW-HILL
COMPUTER SCIENCE SERIES

EDWARD A. FEIGENBAUM
Stanford University

RICHARD W. HAMMING
Naval Post Graduate School

Allen **Anatomy of LISP**
Bell and Newell **Computer Structures: Readings and Examples**
Donovan **Systems Programming**
Feigenbaum and Feldman **Computers and Thought**
Gear **Computer Organization and Programming**
Givone **Introduction to Switching Circuit Theory**
Goodman and Hedetniemi **Introduction to the Design and Analysis of Algorithms**
Hamacher, Vranesic, and Zaky **Computer Organization**
Hamming **Introduction to Applied Numerical Analysis**
Hayes **Computer Architecture and Organization**
Hellerman **Digital Computer System Principles**
Hellerman and Conroy **Computer System Performance**
Kain **Automata Theory: Machines and Languages**
Katzan **Microprogramming Primer**
Kohavi **Switching and Finite Automata Theory**
Liu **Elements of Discrete Mathematics**
Liu **Introduction to Combinatorial Mathematics**
Madnick and Donovan **Operating Systems**
Manna **Mathematical Theory of Computation**
Newman and Sproull **Principles of Interactive Computer Graphics**
Nilsson **Problem-solving Methods in Artificial Intelligence**
Rosen **Programming Systems and Languages**
Salton **Automatic Information Organization and Retrieval**
Stone **Introduction to Computer Organization and Data Structures**
Stone and Siewiorek **Introduction to Computer Organization and Data Structures: PDP-11 Edition**
Tonge and Feldman **Computing: An Introduction to Procedures and Procedure-Followers**
Tremblay and Manohar **Discrete Mathematical Structures with Applications to Computer Science**
Tremblay and Sorenson **An Introduction to Data Structures with Applications**
Tucker **Programming Languages**
Watson **Timesharing System Design Concepts**
Wegner **Programming Languages, Information Structures, and Machine Organization**
Wiederhold **Database Design**
Winston **The Psychology of Computer Vision**

McGRAW-HILL SERIES
IN ARTIFICIAL INTELLIGENCE

Consulting Editor
EDWARD A. FEIGENBAUM
Stanford University

Allen **Anatomy of LISP**
Feigenbaum and Feldman **Computers and Thought**
Nilsson **Problem-solving Methods in Artificial Intelligence**
Winston **The Psychology of Computer Vision**

Anatomy of LISP

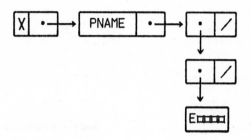

JOHN ALLEN

McGRAW-HILL BOOK COMPANY

NEW YORK/ST. LOUIS/SAN FRANCISCO/AUCKLAND/BOGOTÁ/DÜSSELDORF
JOHANNESBURG/LONDON/MADRID/MEXICO/MONTREAL/NEW DELHI/PANAMA
PARIS/SÃO PAULO/SINGAPORE/SYDNEY/TOKYO/TORONTO

Library of Congress Cataloging in Publication Data

Allen, John, date
    Anatomy of LISP.

    (McGraw-Hill series in artificial intelligence)
(McGraw-Hill computer science series)
    Bibliography: p.
    Includes index.
    1. LISP (Computer program language) I. Title.
QA76.73.L23A44   001.6'424   78-7215
ISBN 0-07-001115-X

Anatomy of LISP

    4 5 6 7 8 9 0 FGRFGR   8 3 2 1

The editor was Peter D. Nalle. and
the production supervisor was Dominick Petrellese.
Fairfield Graphics was printer and binder.

The creation, revision, and styling of this document were performed using the Document
Production System at Stanford's Artificial Intelligence Laboratory; the final pages of this
book are computer-generated. Since higher-quality type was desired and such technology
was not yet readily available, an attempt was made to generate more traditional typeset
output. That attempt finally failed. Thus the production of this book is a uniquely
twentieth-century experience: a result of a nineteenth-century resistance and a twenty-first
century anticipation.

To my parents, John & Esther Allen
To my friend and wife, Ruth E. Davis
To my sons, Christopher & Geoffrey.

Contents

PREFACE   xi

1 SYMBOLIC EXPRESSIONS   1

  1.1   Introduction   1
  1.2   Symbolic Expressions: Abstract Data Structures   5
  1.3   Trees: Representations of Symbolic Expressions   8
  1.4   Primitive Functions   10
  1.5   Predicates and Conditional Expressions   18
  1.6   Sequences: Abstract Data Structures   26
  1.7   Lists: Representations of Sequences   31
  1.8   A Respite   38
  1.9   Becoming an Expert   43

2 APPLICATIONS OF LISP   53

  2.1   Introduction   53
  2.2   Examples of LISP Applications   56
  2.3   Differentiation   57
  2.4   Tree Searching   66
  2.5   Data Bases   69
  2.6   Algebra of Polynomials   75

2.7	Evaluation of Polynomials	79
2.8	The Great Progenitors	91
2.9	Another Respite	92
2.10	Proving Properties of Programs	94

3 EVALUATION OF LISP EXPRESSIONS — 97

3.1	Introduction	97
3.2	S-expr Translation of LISP Expressions	104
3.3	Symbol Tables	107
3.4	λ-notation	110
3.5	Mechanization of Evaluation	114
3.6	Examples of *eval*	118
3.7	Variables	128
3.8	Environments and Bindings	131
3.9	*label*	136
3.10	Functional Arguments and Functional Values	137
3.11	Binding Strategies and Implementations	149
3.12	Special Forms and Macros	154
3.13	Review and Reflection	157

4 IMPERATIVE CONSTRUCTS IN LISP — 184

4.1	Introduction	184
4.2	The *prog*-feature	186
4.3	Alternatives to *prog*	194
4.4	Extensions to *eval*	197
4.5	Non-recursive Control Structures	198
4.6	*eval* with Explicit Access	199
4.7	*eval* with Explicit Control	207
4.8	An Evaluator for *prog*	211
4.9	Alternatives to *eval*	220
4.10	Function Definitions	224
4.11	Rapprochement: In Retrospect	227
4.12	LISP Machines	235

5 THE STATIC STRUCTURE OF LISP — 244

5.1	Introduction	244
5.2	Representation of S-expressions	245
5.3	Representation of LISP Primitives	249
5.4	AMBIT/G	253

5.5   A Few Programming Techniques   254
5.6   Symbol Tables and Property-lists   256
5.7   Property-list Functions   261
5.8   An *eval* for Property-lists   262
5.9   Representation of Property-lists   265
5.10 A Picture of the Atom *NIL*   270
5.11 Input/Output: *read* and *print*   271
5.12 Table Searching: Hashing   275
5.13 A First Look at *cons*   281
5.14 Storage Management: Garbage Collection   282
5.15 A Simple LISP Garbage Collector   284
5.16 A Review of the Structure of the LISP Machine   289
5.17 Implementations of Binding   289
5.18 Stack Implementation of a LISP Subset: Deep Bound   292
5.19 Stack Implementation of a LISP Subset: Shallow Bound   293
5.20 Strategies for Full LISP Implementation   300
5.21 Epilogue   302

6 THE DYNAMIC STRUCTURE OF LISP   304

6.1   Introduction   304
6.2   Primitives for LISP   309
6.3   **SM**: A Simple Machine   312
6.4   Implementation of the Primitives   316
6.5   Assemblers   320
6.6   Compilers for Subsets of LISP   323
6.7   Compilation of Conditional Expressions   325
6.8   One-pass Assemblers and Fixups   329
6.9   A Compiler for Simple *eval*: The Value Stack   332
6.10 A Compiler for Simple *eval*   335
6.11 Efficient Compilation   340
6.12 Efficiency: Primitive Operations   341
6.13 Efficiency: Calling Sequences   343
6.14 Efficiency: Predicates   348
6.15 A Compiler for *progs*   350
6.16 Further Optimizations   352
6.17 Functional Arguments   354
6.18 Macros and Special Forms   355
6.19 Compilation and Variables   356
6.20 Compiling and Interpreting   358
6.21 Interactive Programming   362
6.22 LISP Editors   365
6.23 Debugging in LISP   367

7 STORAGE STRUCTURES AND EFFICIENCY 370

7.1 Introduction 370
7.2 Vectors and Arrays 371
7.3 Strings and Linear LISP 374
7.4 A Compacting Collector for LISP 377
7.5 Bit-tables 380
7.6 Representations of Complex Data Structures 381
7.7 *rplaca* and *rplacd* 382
7.8 Applications of *rplaca* and *rplacd* 385
7.9 Numbers 389
7.10 Stacks and Threading 392
7.11 A Non-recursive *read* 394
7.12 More Applications of Threading 397
7.13 Storage Management and LISP 398
7.14 Hash Techniques 402

8 IMPLICATIONS OF LISP 404

9 PROJECTS 412

9.1 Extensions to *eval* 412
9.2 Pretty-printing 414
9.3 Syntax-directed Processes 417
9.4 Syntax-directed I/O 421

BIBLIOGRAPHY 426

INDEX 443

Preface

"... it is important not to lose sight of the fact that there is a difference between training and education. If computer science is a fundamental discipline, then university education in this field should emphasize enduring fundamental principles rather than transient current technology."

Peter Wegner, *Three Computer Cultures* [Weg 70]

This text is nominally about LISP and data structures. However, in the process it covers much broader areas of computer science. The author has long felt that the beginning student of computer science has been getting a distorted and disjointed picture of the field. In some ways this confusion is natural; the field has been growing at such a rapid rate that few are prepared to be judged experts in all areas of the discipline. The current alternative seems to be to give a few introductory courses in programming and machine organization followed by relatively specialized courses in more technical areas. The difficulty with this approach is that much of the technical material never gets related. The student's perspective and motivation suffer in the process. This book uses LISP as a means for relating topics which normally get treated in several separate courses. The point is not that we *can* do this in LISP, but rather that it is *natural* to do it in LISP. The high-level notation for algorithms is beneficial in explaining and understanding complex algorithms. The use of abstract data structures and abstract LISP programs shows the intent of structured programming and step-wise refinement. Much of the current work in mathematical theories of computation is based on LISP-like languages. Thus LISP is a formalism for describing algorithms, for writing programs, and for proving properties of algorithms. We use data structures as the main thread in our discussions because a proper appreciation of data structures as abstract objects is a necessary prerequisite to an understanding of modern computer science.

The importance of abstraction obviously goes much farther than its appearance in LISP. Abstraction has often been used in other disciplines as a means for controlling complexity. In mathematics, we frequently are able to gain new insights by recasting a particularly intransigent problem in a more general setting. Similarly, the intent of an algorithm expressed in a high-level language like Fortran or PL/1 is more readily apparent than its machine-language equivalent. These are both examples of the use of abstraction. Our use of abstraction will impinge on both the mathematical and the programming aspects. Initially, we will talk about data structures as abstract objects just as the mathematician takes the natural numbers as abstract entities. We will attempt to categorize properties common to data structures and introduce notation for describing functions defined on these abstractions. At this level of discussion we are thinking of our LISP-like language primarily as a notational convenience rather than a computational device. However, after a certain familiarity has been established it is important to look at our work from the viewpoint of computer science. Here we must think of the computational aspects of our notation. We must be concerned with the representational problems: implementation on realistic machines, and efficiency of algorithms and data structures. However, it cannot be over-emphasized that our need for understanding is best served at the higher level of abstraction; the advantage of a high-level language is notational rather than computational. That is, it allows us to think and represent our algorithms in mathematical terms rather than in terms of the machine. It is after a clear understanding of the problem is attained that we should begin thinking about representation.

We can exploit the analogy with traditional mathematics a bit further. When we write $sqrt(x)$ in Fortran, for example, we are initially only concerned with $sqrt$ as a mathematical function defined such that $x = sqrt(x)*sqrt(x)$. We are not interested in the specific algorithm used to approximate the function intended in the notation. Indeed, thought of as a mathematical notation, it doesn't matter how $sqrt$ is computed. We might wish to prove some properties of the algorithm which we are encoding. If so, we would only use the mathematical properties of the idealized square root function. Only later, after we had convinced ourselves of the correct encoding of our intention in the Fortran program, would we worry about the computational aspects of the Fortran implementation $sqrt$. The typical user will never proceed deeper into the representation than this; only if his computation is lethargic due to inefficiencies, or inaccurate due to uncooperative approximations, will he look at the actual implementation of *sqrt*.

Just as it is unnecessary to learn machine language to study numerical algorithms, it is also unnecessary to learn machine language to understand non-numerical or data structure processes. We make a distinction between data structures and storage structures. Data structures are abstractions, independent of *how* they are implemented on a machine. Data structures are representations of information chosen to exhibit certain ordering and accessibility relationships between data items. Storage structures are particular implementations of the abstract ideas. Certainly we cannot ignore storage structures when we are deciding upon the data structures which will encode the algorithm, but the interesting aspects of the representation of information can be discussed at the level of data structures with no loss of generality. The mapping of data structures to storage structures is usually quite machine dependent and we are more interested in ideas than coding tricks. We will see that it is possible, and most beneficial, to structure our programs such that there is a very clean interface between the abstract algorithm and the chosen representation. That is, there will be a set of representation-manipulating programs to test, select or construct elements of the domain; and there will be a program encoding the algorithm. Changes of representations only require changes to the programs which access the representation, not to the basic program.

One important insight which should be cultivated in this process is the distinction between the concepts of function and algorithm. The idea of function is mathematical and is independent of any notion of computation; the meaning of "algorithm" is computational, the effect of an algorithm being to compute a function. Thus there are typically many algorithms which will compute a specific function.

This text is *not* meant to be a programming manual for LISP. A certain amount of time is spent giving insights into techniques for writing LISP functions. There are two reasons for this. First, the style of LISP programming is quite different from that of "normal" programming. LISP was one of the first languages to exploit the virtues of recursive programming and explore the power of procedure-valued variables. Second, we will spend a great deal of time discussing various levels of implementation of the language. LISP is an excellent medium for introducing standard techniques in data structure manipulation. Techniques for implementation of recursion, implementation of complex data structures, storage management, and symbol table manipulation are easily motivated in the context of language implementation. Many of these standard techniques first arose in the implementation of LISP. But it is pointless to attempt a discussion of implementation unless the reader has a thorough grasp of the language.

Granting the efficacy of our endeavor in abstraction, why study LISP? LISP is at least fifteen years old and many new languages have been proposed. The difficulty is that the appropriate combination of these features is not present in any other language. LISP unifies and rationalizes many divergent formulations of language constructs. One might surmise that a new language, profiting from LISP's experience, would make a better pedagogical tool. A strong successor has not arrived, and toy languages are suspect for several reasons. The student may suspect that he is a subject in a not too clever experiment being performed upon him by his instructor. Having a backlog of fifteen years of experience and example programs should do much to alleviate this discomfort. The development of LISP also shows many of the mistakes that the original implementors and designers made. We will point out the flaws and pitfalls awaiting the unwary language designer.

We claim the more interesting aspects of LISP for students of computer science lie not in its features as a programming language, but in what it can show about the *structure* of computer science. There is a rapidly expanding body of knowledge unique to computer science, neither mathematical nor engineering per se. Much of this area is presented most clearly by studying LISP.

Again there are two ways to look at a high level language: as a mathematical formalism, and as a programming language. LISP is a better formalism than most of its mathematical rivals because there is sufficient organizational complexity present in LISP so as to make its implementation a realistic computer science task and not just an interesting mathematical curiosity. Much of the power of LISP lies in its simplicity. The data structures are rich enough to easily describe sophisticated algorithms but not so rich as to become obfuscatory. Most every aspect of the implementation of LISP and its translators has immediate implications to the implementation of other languages and to the design of programming languages in general.

We will describe language translators (interpreters and compilers) as LISP functions. The structure of these translators when exposed as LISP functions aids immensely in understanding the essential character of such translators. This is partly due to the simplicity of the language, but perhaps more due to our ability to go right to the essential translating algorithm without becoming bogged down in details of syntax.

LISP has very important implications in the field of programming language semantics, and is the dominant language in the closely related study of provability of properties of programs. The idea of proving properties of programs has been around for a very long time. Goldstein and von Neumann were aware of the practical benefits of such endeavors. J. McCarthy's work in LISP and the Theory of Computation sought to establish formalisms and rules of inference for reasoning about programs. However, the working programmers recognized debugging as the only tool with which to generate a "correct" program, though clearly the non-occurrence of bugs is no guarantee of correctness. Until very recently techniques for establishing correctness of practical programs simply did not exist.

A recent set of events is beginning to change this.

1. Programs are becoming so large and complex that, even though we write in a high-level language, our intuitions are not sufficient to sustain us when we try to find bugs. We are literally being forced to look beyond debugging.
2. The formalisms are maturing. We know a lot more about how to write "structured programs"; we know how to design languages whose constructs are more amenable to proof techniques. And most importantly, the tools we need for expressing properties of programs are finally being developed.
3. The development of on-line techniques. The on-line system, with its sophisticated display editors, debuggers and file handlers, is the only reason that the traditional means of construction and modification of complex programs and systems has been able to survive this long. The interactive experience can now be adapted to program verifiers and synthesizers.

This view of the programming process blends well with the LISP philosophy. We will show that the most natural way to write LISP programs is "structured" in the best sense of the word, being clean in control structure, concise by not attempting to do too much, and independent of a particular data representation.

Many of the existing techniques for establishing correctness originated in McCarthy's investigations of LISP; and some very recent work on mathematical models for programming languages is easily motivated from a discussion of LISP.

LISP is the starting point for those interested in Artificial Intelligence. It is no longer the "research" language, but has become the "systems" language for A.I. Today's research languages are built on LISP, using LISP as a machine language.

Finally there are certain properties of LISP-like languages which make them the natural candidate for interactive program specification. In the chapter on implications of LISP we will characterize "LISP-like" and show how interactive methods can be developed.

This text is primarily designed for undergraduates and therefore an attempt is made to make it self-contained. There are basically five areas in which to partition the topics: the mechanics of the language, the evaluation of expressions in LISP, the static structure of LISP, the dynamic structure of

LISP, and the efficient representation of data structures and algorithms. Each area builds on the previous. Taken as a group these topics introduce much of what is interesting computer science.

The first area develops the programming philosophy of LISP: the use of data structures in programming; the language primitives, recursion, and other control structures. The second area, involving a careful study of the meaning of evaluation in LISP, gives insights into other languages and to the general question of implementation. The next two areas are involved with implementation. The section on static structure deals with the basic organization of memory for a LISP machine -- be it hardware or simulated in software. The dynamics of LISP discusses the primitive control structures necessary for implementation of the LISP control structures and procedure calls. LISP compilers are discussed here. The final section relates our discussion of LISP and its implementation to the more traditional material of a data structures course. We discuss the problems of efficient representation of data structures. By this point the student should have a better understanding of the uses of data structures and should be motivated to examine these issues with a better understanding.

A large collection of problems has been included. The reader is urged to do as many as possible. The problems are mostly non-trivial; they attempt to be realistic, introducing some new information which the readers should be able to discover themselves. There are also a few rather substantial projects. At least one should be attempted. There is a significant difference between being able to program small problems and being able to handle large projects. Small programming projects can be accomplished in spite of any admonitions about "good programming style". A large project is an effective demonstration of the need for elegant programming techniques. The text is large and covers much more than is recommended for a one-semester course. A typical one semester course on data structures covers:

Chapter 1: all
Chapter 2: without 2.4, 2.5, and 2.10.
Chapter 3: without the mathematical aspects of 3.13
Chapter 4: without 4.7, 4.8, and the mathematical aspects of 4.11
Chapter 5: without 5.8, 5.19, and 5.20
Chapter 6: without 6.8, and 6.12 through 6.20
Chapter 7: without 7.5, 7.6, and 7.10 through 7.14
Chapter 8 is also optional.

If a good interactive LISP implementation is available, then the pace can be quickened and the projects enlarged. However, if only a poor or mediocre implementation is accessible, then the course time is better spent without *any* actual programming, or the course should be augmented to include an implementation laboratory. LISP is an interactive language;

attempts at other modes of operation do a disservice to both the language and the user.

Finally a note on the structure of the text. The emphasis flows from the abstract to the specific, beginning with a description of the domain of LISP functions and the operations defined over that domain, and moves to a discussion of the details of efficient implementation of LISP-like languages. The practical-minded programmer might be put off by the "irrelevant" theory and the theoretical-minded mathematician might be put off by the "irrelevant" details of implementation. If you lie somewhere between these two extremes, then welcome.

Acknowledgments

This book began informally at UCLA in 1970 as an alternative to the data structures course. Any book which takes eight years to complete must have a list of acknowledgements. Between the 1970 manuscript and the present version stretches an incredible list of revisions and rewritings. That task was made possible only by the document preparation system at the Stanford Artificial Intelligence Laboratory. The Artificial Intelligence community is still the superior developer of computer related tools.

The final shape of this book has been guided by many sources, but particularly I would like to mention Michael Burke and the San Jose State Mathematics Department, who allowed me to use my manuscript in their data structures course. To Ruth Davis who read and re-read the enumerable versions of paragraphs, sections, and chapters, trying to make sense out of the author and his material; her reward: to copy-edit the manuscript. Ruth's aid has been both technical and personal; with out her there would be no "Anatomy of LISP." To Nancy Meller of the UCLA Computer Science Department for typing the orginal LISP notes. To Les Earnest of the Stanford A.I. Labs for aid beyond the call of duty. To Paulette for trying to understand. To Richard Manuck of the Stanford Computer Science Library, a most excellent librarian with an exceptional library. To John McCarthy for the insight which led to LISP, and for establishing an environment at Stanford which is staffed so admirably and supplied with so many talented people. To E, PUB, and the XGP, for existing. To Dick Dolan and the staff of the H. P. Journal, who both tolerated and sympathized with my attempts to transform the computer generated text into something which could be typeset.

Particular mention must go to Guy Steele and Gianfranco Prini. Guy reviewed a much inferior version of this text. His insights, comments, and criticisms were invaluable. With comments like: "that's not a compromise, it's a bloody surrender!", the text was bound to improve. Gianfranco, was more fortunate; he reviewed the results of Guy's scoldings.

Many other people have had significant influence on the text. I feel fortunate to be able to acknowledge these individuals: Bruce Anderson, Bob Boyer, Michael Clancy, Bob Doran, Daniel Friedman, Richard Gabriel, Michael Gordon, Patrick Greussay, Anthony Hearn, Freidrich von Henke, Forrest Howard, Bill McKeeman, Peter Milne, J S. Moore, Jorge Morales, Charles Prenner, Steve Russell, Hanan Samet, Vic Scheinman, Herbert Stoyan, Dennis Ting, and Steve Ward. I apologize to any individuals I neglected to mention; I must surely have forgotten someone.

Similarly there are topics related to LISP which I have neglected. The whole area of Artificial Intelligence applications has been slighted, but for every author there must come a time when you have to say "Enough!" I've been saying that for several years. It is particularly difficult to cease when dealing with a topic as dynamic as LISP. Many sections only hint at deeper problems, and surely some errors persist; but "Enough!"

As always, it is the author's responsibility for the final shape of a document; the substantial and textual errors, errors of omission and commission are all mine. Each of the reviewers objected strongly to one or more facets of this book; to some, it was too theoretical; for some, too practical. I must have done something right.

John Allen

CHAPTER 1

Symbolic Expressions

1.1 Introduction

This book is a study of data structures and programming languages; in particular it is a study of data structures and programming languages centered around the language LISP. However, this is not a manual to help you become a proficient LISP coder. We will study many of the formal and theoretical aspects of languages and data structures as well as examining the practical applications of data structures. We will show that this area of computer science is a discipline of importance and beauty, worthy of careful study. How are we to proceed? How do we introduce rigor into a field whose countenance is as *ad hoc* and diverse as that of programming? We must bear in mind that the results of our studies are to have practical applications. We must not pursue theory and rigor without proper regard for practice. Our study is not that of pure mathematics; our results will have applications in everyday programming practice. However, for guidance let's look at mathematics. Here is a well-established discipline rich in history and full of results of both practical and theoretical importance.

One of the more fertile, yet easily introduced areas of mathematics, is that of elementary number theory. It is easy to introduce because everyone knows something about the natural numbers. Number theory studies properties of a certain class of operations definable over the set **N** of

1

non-negative integers also called natural numbers. A very formal presentation might begin with a construction of **N** from more primitive notions, but it is usually assumed that the reader is familiar with the fundamental properties of **N**. In either case the next step would be to define the class of operations which we would allow on our domain.

We shall begin our study of LISP in a similar manner, as an investigation of a certain class of operations definable over a domain of objects, called Symbolic Expressions. Though most people know something about the natural numbers, the term "symbolic expresssions" has no standard interpretation. We must define what we mean by "symbolic expression". If we asked someone to define the domain **N**, the definition we would receive would depend on how familar that individual was with the properties of the natural numbers. [1]

For most people and most purposes, the following characterization of a natural number is satisfactory:

I   A natural number is a sequence of decimal digits.

The definition assumes the terminology of "sequence", "decimal" and "digit" are known. If any of these terms are *not* understood, they can be further elaborated. However, this process of explanation and description must terminate. We must assume that some concepts require no further elaboration. The current definition suffers from a different kind of inadequacy. It fails to illuminate the relationships between natural numbers. The "meaning" of the natural numbers is missing. It is like giving a person an alphabet and rules for forming syntactically correct words but not supplying a dictionary which relates these words to the person's vocabulary.

If pressed for details we might attempt a more elaborate characterization like the following:

    1. *zero* is an element of **N**.
II   2. If *n* is in **N** then the *successor* of *n* is in **N**.
    3. The only elements of **N** are those created by finitely many applications of rules 1 and 2.

Definition **II** appears to be completely at the other end of the spectrum; it tells us very little about the appearance of the integers. It gives us an initial element *zero* and an operation called *successor*, which is to exhibit a new element, given an old one. Unless we are careful about the meaning of *successor*, definition **II** will be inadequate. For example if we define the

---

[1]We will not attempt to arrive at a completely self-contained definition of "natural number". That is a difficult undertaking. See [Goo 57]. We will be satisfied with discussing *some* of their characteristics.

successor of a natural number to be that same number then **II** is satisfied but unsatisfactory.

We can define *successor* as a specific mapping, **S**, which creates new elements subject to the rules that two elements, x and y are equal just in the case that $S(x)$ equals $S(y)$; and $S(x)$ is different from x, for any element x. We select a distinguished element, *0*, as a notation for *zero*; and abbreviate $S(0)$ as *1*, and abbreviate $S(S(0))$ as *2* etc. in the usual manner.

The characterization of decimal digits given in **I** is syntactic. The notation itself tells us nothing about the interrelationships between the numbers, but it does give us a notation for representing them. Thus *2* can be used to represent *two*. One benefit of the S-notation is that it explicitly shows the means of construction. That is, it shows more of the properties of these numbers than just distinguishability. We shall refer to the digit representation as **numerals** and reserve the term, **natural number**, for the abstract object. Thus numerals denote, stand for, or represent the abstract objects called natural numbers; and definition **I** is better stated as: "a natural number can be represented as a finite sequence of digits".

But notation and syntax are necessary and we must be able to give precise descriptions of syntactic notions. Given a choice between the two previous definitions, **I** and **II**, it appears that **II** is more precise. Much less is left to the imagination; given *zero* and a definition of *successor* the definition will act as a recipe for producing elements of **N**. This style of definition is called an inductive definition or generative definition.

The basic content of an inductive definition of a set of objects consists of three parts:

IND

(1) A description of an initial set of objects; the elements of this set are the initial elements of the set we are describing in the inductive definition.

(2) Given the description of some existing elements in the set, we are given a means of constructing more elements.

(3) A termination clause, saying that the only elements in the set are those which gained admittance by either (1) or (2).

Notice that our definition of **N**, in terms of *zero* and *successor*, is an instance of **IND**: we are defining the set of natural numbers: *zero* is initially included in the set; then applying the second phrase of the definition we can say that *one* is in the set since *one* is the successor of *zero*.

We can recast the positional notation description as an inductive definition.

1. A digit is a numeral.
2. If n is a numeral then n followed by a digit is a numeral.
3. The only numerals are those created by finitely many applications of 1 and 2.

In words, "a numeral is a digit, or a numeral followed by a digit".

In this application of **IND**, the initial set has more than one element; namely the ten decimal digits. Again, we assume that the questioner knows what "digit" means. This is a characteristic of all definitions: we must stop *somewhere* in our explication. Notice too that we assume that "followed by" means juxtaposition.

Inductive definitions have been the province of mathematics for many years; however, computer science has developed a style of syntax specification called BNF (Backus-Naur Form) equations which has the same intent as that of inductive definitions. Here is the previous inductive definition of "numeral" as a set of BNF equations:

<numeral>   ::= <digit>
<numeral>   ::= <numeral><digit>
As an abbreviation, the two BNF equations may also be written:
<numeral>   ::= <digit> | <numeral><digit>.

A comparison between the BNF and the inductive descriptions of "numeral" should clarify much of the notation, but we will give a more detailed analysis. The symbol "::=" may be read "is a", the symbol "|" may be read "or". The character strings beginning with "<" and ending with ">" correspond to "numeral" and "digit" in 1 and 2; by convention, components of BNF equations which *describe* elements are enclosed in "<" and ">"; and elements which are given *explicitly* are written without the "< >" fence. Thus "<digit>" is not a numeral but is a description; to make the definition of <numeral> complete we should include an equation like:

<digit>   :: = $0 | 1 | 2 | 3 | 4 | 5 | 6 | 7 | 8 | 9$

Juxtaposition of objects implies concatenation of the syntactic objects. Thus "89" is an instance of "<numeral><digit>".

It will be convenient to have notations for the abstract objects as well as notations for the syntactic representations. The BNF equations describe syntactic classes; for example, the set described by <numeral> is the syntactic class of numerals. [2] When we are talking about a syntactic class of objects we

---

[2]Note we could have written <numeral> ::= <digit> and <numeral> ::= <digit><numeral>, generating the same class, but in a different order. Questions of syntax and grammars will not be stressed in this book. See [Aho 72].

will write <object>; when we are talking about the abstract object we will write **<object>**. For example **<numeral>** is the class of natural numbers.

What should be remembered from the discussion in this section? We need precise ways of describing the elements of our study on data structures. We have seen that inductive definitions are a powerful way of describing sets of objects. We have seen a variant of inductive definitions called Backus-Naur Form equations. We will use BNF equations to describe the syntax of our data structures and our language.

We have also introduced the difference between an abstract object and a representation for that object. This distinction has been well studied in philosophy and mathematics, and we will see that this idea has strong consequences for the field of programming and computer science. Abstract objects and their representations will play crucial roles in this text.

1.2 Symbolic Expressions: Abstract Data Structures

We wish to show that the use of abstraction will benefit the study of data structures and LISP. To begin our study we should therefore characterize the domain of LISP data structures in a manner similar to what we did for numbers.

Our objects are called **Symbolic Expressions**. Our domain of Symbolic Expressions is named **<sexpr>**. Symbolic expressions are also known as **S-expressions** or **S-exprs**.

The set of symbolic expressions is defined inductively over a base set named **<atom>**. The set **<atom>** can itself be defined inductively. We give a set of BNF equations for elements of <atom> below, but the essential character of the domain is that it represents two kinds of objects: the **literal atoms** and the **integers**. The elements of **<atom>** are called **atoms**.

<atom>	:: = <literal atom> | <numeral> | -<numeral>
<literal atom>	:: = <atom letter>
	:: = <literal atom><atom letter>
	:: = <literal atom><digit>
<numeral>	:: = <digit> | <numeral><digit>
<atom letter>	:: = $A \mid B \mid C \ldots \mid Z$ [3]
<digit>	:: = $0 \mid 1 \mid 2 \ldots \mid 9$

A <literal atom> is therefore a string of uppercase letters and digits, subject to the provision that the *first* character in the atom be a letter.

---

[3]We use ellipses here as a convenient abbreviation.

For example: atoms   non atoms

               ABC123   *2A*
               12   *a*
               A4D6   *$$g*
               NIL   *ABD.*
               T   *(A . B)*

The characteristics of atoms which most interest us are their distinguishability: the atom *ABC* is distinguishable from the atom *AB*. That "*AB*" is a part of "*ABC*" is not germane to our current discussion. [4] Similarly, we will seldom need to exploit numerical relationships underlying the numerals; at most we will use simple counting properties. Therefore most of our discussions will deal with non-numeric atoms. Most implementations of LISP do however contain a large arithmetic entourage. Many implementations also give a wider class of literal atoms, allowing some special characters to appear; for most of our discussion the above class is quite sufficient.

The domain of Symbolic expressions, called **<sexpr>** is defined inductively over the domain **<atom>**. [5]

1. Any element of **<atom>** is an element of **<sexpr>**.

2. If α_1 and α_2 are elements of **<sexpr>**, then the pair of α_1 and α_2 is in **<sexpr>**. Pairs are also called **dotted-pairs** since their standard representation in LISP is $(\alpha_1.\alpha_2)$.

Thus **<sexpr>** includes **<atom>** as a proper subset. The notation we chose for the dotted-pairs is the following:

> A dotted-pair consists of a left-parenthesis followed by an S-expr, followed by a period, followed by an S-expr, followed by a right-parenthesis.

For example, let α_1 be *(A . B)* and α_2 be *(1 . T)*; then $(\alpha_1 . \alpha_2)$ is *((A . B) . (1 . T))*.

Greek letters α and β will be used in the text to designate pattern matches. In the current context the pattern matches will involve S-expressions; they can match any well-formed S-expression. For a further example, let *(A . (B . C))* be $(\alpha . \beta)$ then α is *A* and β is *(B . C)*. These variables are called **match-variables** or **meta-variables**.

Finally here's a BNF description of the full set of S-expressions.

$$<sexpr> ::= <atom> \mid (<sexpr> . <sexpr>)$$

---

[4]However, we will discuss such topics in Section 7.3 on string processing.

[5]We will not give the termination clause, but it is assumed to hold.

Notice that if we allow real numbers as atoms then some care would need to be exercised when writing S-expressions. For example, should *(3.1.2)* be interpreted as the dotted pair *(3 . 1.2)*, as the dotted pair *(3.1 . 2)*, or is it just an ill-formed expression? Interpretation of such ambiguous constructs will depend on the implementation; such details are discussed later.

Examples: S-exprs   non S-exprs

A   *A . B*

(A . B)   *(A . B . C)*

(((A . B) . C) . (A . B))   *((A . B))*

The set described by <sexpr> is a *specific* syntactic representation of the domain **<sexpr>**. However, the set <sexpr> will be a convenient notation since it makes explicit the construction of the composite S-expr from its components, [6] and the notation is also consistent with LISP history.

However there is more to the domain **<sexpr>** than syntax, just as there is more to **N** than positional notation. [7] What *are* the essential features of S-expressions? Symbolic expressions are either atomic or they have two components. If we are confronted with a non-atomic S-expression then we want a means of distinguishing between the "first" and the "second" component. The "dot notation" does this for us, but obviously "(", ")", and "." of the dotted-pairs are simply notation or syntax. We could have just as well represented the dotted-pair of *A* and *B* as the set-theoretic ordered pair, *<A,B>* or any other notation which preserves the essentials of the domain **<sexpr>**.

The distinctions between abstract objects and their representation are quite important. As we continue our study of more and more complex data structures the use of an abstract data structure instead of one of its representations can mean the difference between a clear and clean program and a confusing and complicated program. There are similar gains for us when we study algorithms defined over these abstract data structures. The less the algorithm knows about the representation of the data structure, the easier it will be to modify or understand that algorithm. Indeed you may have already experienced this phenomenon if you have programmed. A program written in a high-level language is almost always more understandable than its machine-language counterpart. The high-level program is more abstract whereas the machine-language program knows a

----

[6] Just as the "successor" notation shows the construction of the numbers from *0*. This kind of notation will be much more useful in LISP, since our interest in data structures will focus on the construction process and the interrelationships between components of an S-expr.

[7] 2, II in Roman numerals, 10 in binary, "zwei" in German ... are all representations of the same number.

great deal about representations. Finally, if you still doubt that representations make a difference in clarity, try doing long division in Roman numerals. We will say much more about abstraction and representation in algorithms and data structures as we proceed.

1.3 Trees: Representations of Symbolic expressions

Besides the more conventional typographical notations, S-expressions also have interesting *graphical* representations. S-exprs have a natural interpretation as a structure which we call a LISP-tree or L-tree.

Here are some L-trees:

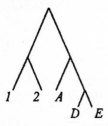
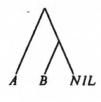

We can give an inductive definition:

1. Any element of <atom> is an L-tree.
2. If n_1 and n_2 are L-trees then

also forms an L-tree. Most important: there are no intersecting branches. Later we will talk about more general structures called list-structures.

You can see how to interpret S-exprs as L-trees. The atoms are interpreted as terminal nodes; and since non-atomic S-exprs always have two sub-expressions we can write the first sub-expression as the left branch of an L-tree and the second sub-expression as the right branch.

For example:

$(A \cdot B)$ $\qquad\qquad$ $(A \cdot (B \cdot C))$ $\qquad\qquad$ $((A \cdot B) \cdot C)$

Other representations of LISP-trees are possible; for example $(A \cdot (B \cdot C))$ can be expressed as:

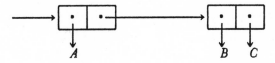

or:

These last two representations are called **box-notation**.

Please keep in mind the distinction between the abstract S-expr and the several representations which we have shown. The question of representation is so important and will occur so frequently that we introduce notation for a representational mapping, $\mathfrak{R}$. To represent domain **D** in domain **E**, we will define a function $\mathfrak{R}_{D \to E}$ which usually will be specified inductively, and will express the desired mapping.

For example a representational mapping $\mathfrak{R}_{<sexpr> \to L\text{-tree}}$ can be given:

$$\mathfrak{R}[\![<atom>]\!] = <atom>$$

and for α and β in <sexpr>:

$$\mathfrak{R}[\![(\alpha \cdot \beta)]\!] =$$

$$\mathfrak{R}[\![\alpha]\!] \qquad \mathfrak{R}[\![\beta]\!]$$

Typically context will determine the appropriate subscript on the $\mathfrak{R}$-mapping; thus we will omit it.

Problems

1. Which of the following are dotted-pairs?
   a. $(X \cdot Y)$ **b.** $((A \cdot (B \cdot C))$ **c.** $A2$ **d.** $(X \cdot Y2 \cdot Z)$

2. Write the following as LISP trees:
   a. $((A \cdot B) \cdot (B \cdot (C \cdot D)))$ **b.** $(((A \cdot B) \cdot C) \cdot E)$
   c. $((X \cdot NIL) \cdot (Y \cdot (Z \cdot NIL)))$ **d.** $(NIL \cdot NIL)$

3. Write the following LISP trees as S-exprs:

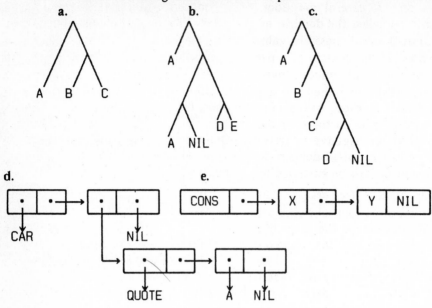

1.4 Primitive Functions

So far we have described the domain of abstract objects called S-exprs and have exhibited several representations for these objects. We will now describe some functions or operations to be performed on this domain. We need to be a bit careful here. We are about to see one of the main differences between mathematics and computer science: mathematics emphasizes the idea of function; computer science emphasizes the idea of algorithm, process, or procedure.

Mathematically a function is simply a mapping such that for any given argument in the domain of the function there exists a unique corresponding value. In elementary set theory, a definition of function f involves saying that f is a set of ordered pairs $f = \{ <x_1, y_1>, ...\}$; the x_i's are all distinct and the value of the function f for an argument x_i is defined to be the corresponding y_i. No rule of computation is given to locate values; with the first definition it is implicit that the internal structure of the mapping doesn't matter; in the set-theoretic definition, the correspondence is explicitly given.

An algorithm or procedure is a process for computing values for a function. The factorial function, $n!$, can be computed by many different algorithms; but as a function it is a set

$$\{<0,1>, <1,1>, <2,2>, <3,6>, ...<n,n!>, ...\}.$$

The **domain** of a function is the set of all values for which the function is defined; the **range** of a function is the set of all values which the function takes on. A careful definition of a function requires specification of a further set called the **domain of discourse**. The domain of discourse, named **D**, consists of all possible values which may occur as the argument to a function. If the domain of a particular function f coincides with **D** then f is said to be a **total function** over **D**; if there are elements of **D** which are not in the domain of f then f is a **partial function** over **D**, and f is said to be **undefined** for those values. For example, the factorial function is typically considered to be partial over the integers: total for the natural numbers, but undefined for negative integers. Thus the concept of "total" or "partial" is relative to a specified domain of discourse. However, a function f total over a domain D_1 can be extended to be total over a domain $D_1 \cup D_2$ by assigning values to $f(d)$ for $d \in D_2 - D_1$. In this way, for example, factorial can be extended to be total over the integers by defining $n!$ to be 0 for n less than 0. We may extend the range of a function when we extend the domain; thus $f(d)$ need not be in the range of the original f. For example, we added 0 to the range when we extended the factorial function. When we extend the range we must specify what additions have been made.

A substantive decision needs to be made on how we are to handle partial functions.[8] Since we are attempting to be reasonably realistic about our modelling of computation we should be as precise as possible in our formalism. We could introduce a class of error values and include them in the range of f; these values would be given as the result of applying f to an argument not in its domain; or we could simply say that the result is "unspecified".[9] We shall pick an intermediate position; we shall introduce *one* new element, $\perp$, called "unspecified" or "undefined", or "bottom".[10] We will define all our functions over domains augmented with this element; thus constructs like $f(\perp) = a$ are allowed. For the moment, think of $\perp$ as covering all anomalous conditions which could be detected and printed as error messages; later we will refine this interpretation.

As we define new data structures we will frequently want to extend our functions to larger domains. For most of our purposes, a function f defined on (an augmented domain) **D** will be extended to a larger domain, $D \cup D_1$, by

---

[8]Partial functions occur naturally in computation. Most programs will fail to give results under some circumstances. The function which that program is computing is a partial function. Some error conditions can produce error messages; some error conditions may cause the program to loop. We will analyze both situations.

[9]How "unspecified" manifests itself on a machine will depend on the implementation. Sometimes error messages are given; sometimes not.

[10]"bottom" is sometimes written $\perp$.

defining $f(d_1) = f(\perp)$ for $d_1 \epsilon D_1 - D$, [11] therefore $f(\perp)$ need not be $\perp$. However many of the functions which we will examine are defined such that $f(..., \perp, ...) = \perp$. Functions which possess this property are called **strict functions**.

To apply this discussion of $\perp$ to S-exprs we will define an extended domain **S** to be:

$$S = \text{<sexpr>} \cup \{\perp\}$$

Then we can talk about functions which are total over **S** or over **<sexpr>**, and we will talk about functions which are partial over **<sexpr>**. When we ask if an S-expr function is partial or total without specifying a domain, we are asking the question over the natural, unextended domain, **<sexpr>**.

We will now move towards a more algorithmic presentation. We will return to the mathematical aspects occasionally, but our main concern in this text is a treatment of algorithms expressed in LISP. We will continue to say "LISP function" or just "function", but what we are expressing or describing is a particular algorithm or procedure, not a function in the mathematical sense. When we wish to stress the distinction we will use "procedure" or "algorithm".

The first LISP function we consider is *cons*. This binary function is used to generate S-exprs from less complicated S-exprs. *cons* is called a **constructor**-function and is a strict function; [12] it is a total function over the domain **S**. More precisely, since *cons* is a **binary** function, each argument of *cons* is free to take on values from **S**. [13] Whenever *cons* is presented with two elements α and β from **<sexpr>**, $cons[\alpha;\beta]$ returns a new S-expr $(\alpha \cdot \beta)$. Interpreted as a LISP-tree, $cons[\alpha;\beta]$ forms a new LISP tree which has a left branch α and has a right branch β.

For example: $cons[A; B] = (A \cdot B)$

$$cons[(A \cdot B); C] = ((A \cdot B) \cdot C)$$

Expressions which can have a value, are called **forms**. S-exprs are forms since they are the constants of our language: the value of a constant is that constant. Function applications are forms: the value is the result of performing the designated function on the designated arguments.

Notice that we are designating function application in LISP by

---

[11]The exception to this extension convention involves the definition of predicates which can tell whether or not an arbitrary element is in a specified domain. These predicates always give true or false when applied to any element other than $\perp$.

[12]For an alternative interpretation of *cons* see [Fri 76a].

[13]We could also say that *cons* is total over the Cartesian product **S×S**.

"function name, followed by a list of arguments delimited by '[' and ']'." [14]
The '[...]'-notation is part of the LISP syntax and we will reserve
'(...)'-notation for the function application of mathematics. In a few places in
our discussions the distinction will be important. Typically the distinctions
will occur when we wish to distinguish between the LISP algorithm and the
mathematical function computed by that algorithm.

A critical distinction has already arisen in discussing forms like
cons[A;B]. The constructor *cons* is actually an algorithm. Since it is a
primitive algorithm it will be represented on a machine by a sequence of
operations which depend on the implementation of S-exprs and depend on
the primitive operations of the hardware machine. The *process* of extracting
a value from the form *cons[A; B]* is called **evaluation**. Evaluation is an
algorithmic idea; there is no idea of evaluation involved with the concept of
"function". To reinforce this algorithmic interpretation we will say things
like " a function returns as value ..." meaning the algorithmic representation
of a function computes and produces a value.

We have two strict, unary **selector** functions, *car* and *cdr*, [15] for
traversing LISP-trees. We already know the meaning of "strict"; a unary
function expects *one* argument; and a selector function is a data structure
manipulating function which will select a component of a composite data
structure. Such LISP functions are called selectors since they will *select*
components of non-atomic elements of **<sexpr>**. Thus *car* and *cdr* are
partial functions over **<sexpr>**: they give values in **<sexpr>** only for
non-atomic arguments; they give $\perp$ whenever they are presented with an
atomic argument.

When given a non-atomic argument, $(\alpha \, . \, \beta)$, *car* returns as value the
first subexpression, α; *cdr* (pronounced could-er) returns as value the second
sub-expression β.

For example:
$$car[(A \, . \, B)] = A$$
$$car[A] = \perp$$
$$cdr[(A \, . \, B)] = B$$
$$cdr[(A \, . \, (B \, . \, C))] = (B \, . \, C)$$
$$car[((A \, . \, B) \, . \, C)] = (A \, . \, B)$$

---

[14]The syntax equations for forms are given on page 17.

[15]These names are hold-overs from the original implementation of
LISP on an IBM 704. That machine had partial-word instructions to
reference the **a**ddress and **d**ecrement parts of a machine location. The *a* of
car comes from "address", the *d* of *cdr* comes from "decrement". The *c* and *r*
come from "contents of" and "register". Thus *car* could be read "contents of
address part of register".

We will include functional composition as a notation for combining LISP expressions. The composition of two unary functions f and g is another function, denoted in mathematics by $f \circ g$. The value of an expression, $f \circ g[x]$, is the value of $f[g[x]]$. That is, the value of $f \circ g[x]$ is a z such that y is the value of $g[x]$ and z is the value of $f[y]$. $f \circ g$ may be undefined for several reasons: $g[x]$ may be undefined and f is strict, or $f[y]$ may be undefined.

Here are some examples of composition:

$$car \circ cdr[(A \cdot (B \cdot C))] = car[cdr[(A \cdot (B \cdot C))]] = car[(B \cdot C)] = B$$

$$cdr \circ cdr[(A \cdot (C \cdot B))] = cdr[cdr[(A \cdot (C \cdot B))]] = cdr[(C \cdot B)] = B$$

$$cdr[cdr[A]] = \perp$$

$$car[cdr[(A \cdot B)]] = \perp$$

$$car[cons[X;A]] = X \qquad cdr[cons[Y;X]] = X$$

All the functions in these examples are strict; for that reason, if $g[x]$ gives $\perp$ then the composition $f \circ g[x]$ also gives $\perp$. That need not be the case if f is non-strict.

The composition of many car and cdr functions occurs so frequently that an abbreviation has been developed. Given such a composition, we select in left-to-right order, the relevant a's and d's in the car's and cdr's. We sandwich this string of a's and d's between a left-hand c and a right-hand r and give the composition this name.

For example: $$cadr[x] \Leftarrow car[cdr[x]]$$

$$caddr[x] \Leftarrow car[cdr[cdr[x]]]$$

$$cdar[x] \Leftarrow cdr[car[x]]$$

These compositions are also called car-cdr-chains, and are useful in traversing LISP-trees. The notation "$\Leftarrow$" is to be read "is defined to be the function ...". This notation is only a temporary convenience and not part of LISP. Soon we will study what is involved in giving and using definitions in LISP (Section 3.4). For the moment intuition will suffice.

It is useful to introduce some terminology for the components of a function definition. Let

$$f[x_1; \dots; x_n] \Leftarrow \xi$$

represent a typical definition. The name of the function is f; the **body** of the function is the expression ξ. The list $[x_1; \dots; x_n]$ appearing after the function name is called the **formal parameter** list. The elements of the formal parameter list are called formal parameters and will play a role similar to that of variables in mathematics. [16] Therefore we will also refer to formal parameters as variables. Lower-case identifiers [17] will be used as variables and function names. So for example Y and CAR are atoms; y and *car* could be used as variables. Be clear on the distinction between LISP variables like x, y or *foo*, and the match variables [18] like α or β. If α and β denote S-expressions then $(\alpha \, . \, \beta)$ denotes a well-formed S-expr. The construction, $(x \, . \, y)$, is *not* well-formed, but *cons*[x;y] is correct.

A function is **applied** using the common notation of **function application**:

$$f[a_1; \,...; \, a_n]$$

The a_i's are called **actual parameters**; for an application to be well formed, the actual parameters must agree in number with the formal parameters of the definition and they are to be associated in a one-for-one order, a_i with x_i. Thus in the expression *car*[*cdr*[(A . B)]] the actual parameter to the *car* function is *cdr*[(A . B)], and the actual parameter to *cdr* is (A . B). The process of associating formal parameters with actual parameters is called **binding**. A large part of our study will involve various aspects of the binding process.

It is convenient to introduce some terminology to distinguish between an algorithmic idea and its mathematical counterpart. The phrase "function call" is used to name the procedural counterpart to "function application". LISP is called an **applicative language** since it is based on the idea of function application. Mathematically speaking, a composition of functions is simply another function -- i.e., a mapping -- and therefore nothing need be said about how to compute composed functions. From a computational point of view, we want to express evaluation of expressions involving composed functions in terms of the evaluation of subexpressions. This would allow us to describe a complex computation in terms of an appropriate sequence of subsidiary computations. One of the more natural ways to evaluate expressions involving compositions is to evaluate the inner-most expressions first, then work outwards. Assume arguments to multi-argument functions are evaluated in left-to-right order. Thus:

cons[*car*[(A . B)];*cdr*[(A . (1 . 2))]]   reduces to *cons*[A;*cdr*[(A . (1 . 2))]]
                                                reduces to *cons*[A;(1 . 2)]
                                                reduces to (A . (1 . 2))

This may seem to be a simple operation but in fact evaluation is a very

---

[16]The behavior of formal parameters and variables is *not* identical. We will say more about the distinction in Section 4.1.

[17]See page 17 for the BNF equations for <identifier>.

[18]also called meta-variables

complex process. The value of an expression may depend on the *order* in which we do things. For example, consider the evaluation of *second*[*car*[*A*]; *B*] where *second*[*x;y*] <= *y*. If we expect *second* to be a strict function, then *second*[*car*[*A*]; *B*] must return ⊥ even though it is reasonable to believe that the value of the computation should be *B* since *second* does not visibly depend on the value of its first parameter. It appears that if we postponed the evaluation of the arguments until those values were actually needed, then at least this problem would be solved. However, the consequences of defining a function to be strict are severe; they cannot be sidestepped by resorting to different schemes for evaluating arguments. There is an alternative, but not particularly attractive, strategy for assigning strictness: we could examine the body of the function; if the function uses all its parameters, then it's strict. If the function doesn't depend on one or more parameters, then it's non-strict. Thus with this interpretation, *second is* non-strict. We prefer the initial interpretation, reasoning that, if a function is passed bad information, then we wish to know about it, even if the function does not use that specious result.

Strictness is closely related to evaluation schemes for parameter passing. Here are two common techniques:

CBV   Evaluate the arguments to a function; pass those evaluated arguments to the function.

This scheme, called Call By Value, is what we were informally using to evaluate the previous examples.

An alternative evaluation process is Call By Name:

CBN   Pass the unevaluated arguments into the body of the function.

Assuming *second* is defined to be strict, then *second*[*car*[*A*]; *B*] yields ⊥ under either **CBV** or **CBN**. However if we define *second* to be non-strict then **CBV** and **CBN** will both give value *B*. With **CBV**, *x* is bound to ⊥; while with **CBN** *x* is bound to *car*[*A*].

Further relationships between evaluation schemes and strictness will be investigated. On page 21 we discuss non-terminating computations. In Chapter 3 we will discuss evaluation techniques and will give a precise characterization of the evaluation of LISP expressions. On page 20 we will introduce a non-strict language construct but, until that time, intuitive application of **CBV** will suffice.

We must exercise care when discussing the process of evaluation; the function we are characterizing by computing its values will often depend on our choice of evaluation scheme.

Before introducing a further class of LISP expressions we summarize the syntax of the LISP expressions allowed so far:

\<form\>	::=	\<constant\> | \<application\> | \<variable\>
\<constant\>	::=	\<sexpr\> (where \<sexpr\> is given on page 6)
\<application\>	::=	\<function-part\>[\<arg\>; ...;\<arg\>]
\<function-part\>	::=	\<identifier\>
\<arg\>	::=	\<form\>
\<variable\>	::=	\<identifier\>
\<identifier\>	::=	\<letter\> | \<identifier\>\<letter\> | \<identifier\>\<digit\>
\<letter\>	::=	$a \mid b \mid c \ldots \mid z$
\<digit\>	::=	$1 \mid 2 \mid \ldots \mid 9$

The use of ellipses in the last equation is an abbreviation we have seen before. The use of ellipses in the \<application\> equation is different. It is an abbreviation meaning "zero or more occurrences". Thus the equation means an \<application\> is a \<function-part\> followed by the symbol "[" followed by zero or more \<arg\>'s followed by the symbol "]". This use of ellipses can always be replaced by a sequence of BNF equations. for example, this instance can be replaced by:

\<application\>	::=	\<function-part\>[\<arg-list\>] | \<function-part\>[ ]
\<arg-list\>	::=	\<arg\> | \<arg-list\>;\<arg\>

To improve readability we will frequently violate these syntax equations, allowing function names containing special characters, e.g. *fact∗*, *fib'* or + ; or writing *x+y* instead of +[*x,y*]. No attempt will be made to characterize these violations; occurrences of them should be clear from context.

Notice that the class \<form\> is a collection of LISP expressions which can be evaluated. A \<form\> is either:

1. a constant: the value is that constant.
2. an application: we've said a bit about evaluation schemes for these constructs.
3. a variable: a variable in LISP will typically have an associated value in some environment.

We will wait to Section 3.4 for a precise description.

An important constraint on LISP forms which is not covered by the syntax equations is the requirement that functions are defined as being n-ary for some *fixed* n. Any n-ary LISP function must have *exactly* n arguments presented to it whenever it is applied. Thus *cons*[*A*], *cons*[*A;B;C*], and *car*[*A;B*] are all ill-formed expressions and therefore denote $\bot$.

Problems

1. Discuss $cons[car[x];cdr[x]] = x$.

2. Discuss $cons[car[\alpha];cdr[\alpha]] = \alpha$.

1.5 Predicates and Conditional Expressions

We cannot generate a very exciting theory based simply on *car*, *cdr*, and *cons* with functional composition. Before we can write reasonably interesting algorithms we must have some way of performing conditional actions. To do this we first need predicates. A LISP predicate is a function returning a value representing truth or falsity. We will represent the concepts of true and false by t and f respectively. Since these truth values are distinct from elements of **S**, we will set up a new domain **Tr** which will consist of the elements, t and f. As usual the extra element $\perp$ is included so that we may talk about partial predicates just as we talked about partial functions on **<sexpr>**. [19]

LISP has two primitive predicates. The first is a strict unary predicate named *atom*; *atom* is total over **<sexpr>**, and is a special kind of predicate called a **recognizer** or a **discriminator**. Recognizers are used to determine the type of an instance of a data structure. Thus *atom* will return t if the argument denotes an atom, and will return f if the argument is a non-atomic S-expr.

$$atom[A] = atom[NIL] = t$$

$$atom[(A . B)] = f$$

$$atom[car[(A . B)]] = t$$

$$atom[\perp] = \perp$$

What should we do about the value of constructs like: $cons[atom[A]; A]$? The evaluation of $atom[A]$ gives t, but t is not an element of **S** and thus is not appropriate as an argument to *cons*. Using our discussion of page 11, we extend the domains of the S-expr primitives to

$$S_1 = S \cup Tr$$

For example, for $s \epsilon Tr : car[s] = car[\perp]$, and $cons[s; A] = cons[\perp; A]$

---

[19] A word for the previous LISP user: our use of t and f marks our first major break from current LISP folklore. The typical LISP trick is to use the atoms T and NIL rather than t and f as truth values. Our convention will disallow some mixed compositions of LISP functions and predicates. We will relax this restriction when we write LISP programs.

Since those primitives are strict with respect to undefined we have:

$$atom[t] = \perp$$

$$cons[\perp; A] = \perp$$

$$cons[A; \perp] = \perp$$

Notice that we now have *two* separate domains: S-expressions and truth values. Since we will be writing functions over several domains we will need a general recognizer for each domain to assure that the operations defined on each abstract data structure are properly applied. Thus we introduce the recognizer *issexpr* which will give t on the domain of S-exprs, f for for any element not in **<sexpr>** and will give $\perp$ for $\perp$.

$$issexpr[(A . B)] = issexpr[A] = t$$

$$issexpr[t] = f$$

$$issexpr[\perp] = \perp$$

Another primitive predicate we need is named *eq*. It is a strict binary predicate, partial over the set **<sexpr>**; it will give a truth value only if its arguments are both atomic. It returns t if the arguments denote the same atom; it returns f if the arguments represent different atoms. *eq* yields $\perp$ if either argument to *eq* denotes an element not in the set **<atom>**.

$$eq[A;A] = t \qquad\qquad eq[A;B] = f$$

$$eq[(A . B); A] = \perp \qquad eq[(A . B);(A . B)] = \perp$$

$$eq[eq[A;B];D] = \perp \qquad eq[\perp;x] = \perp$$

$$eq[car[(A . B)];car[cdr[(A . (B . C))]]] = f$$

Rather than define a version of *eq*, say eq_{Tr}, which is defined over **Tr** and acts like *eq*, we will simply extend the definition of *eq* to S_1 so that it may compare two elements of **Tr**.

$$eq[t;t] = t \qquad eq[f;\perp] = \perp$$

$$eq[f;f] = t \qquad eq[t;f] = f$$

$$eq[A;t] = \perp$$

We need to include a construct in our language to effect a test-and-branch operation. In LISP this operation is indicated by the **conditional expression**. It is written:

$$[p_1 \rightarrow e_1; \ p_2 \rightarrow e_2; \ ... \ ; \ p_n \rightarrow e_n]$$

Each p_i is an expression which takes on values in the set **Tr** or gives $\perp$; each e_i is an expression which will give a value in S_1. We will restrict the conditional expression such that all the e_i must have values in the *same* domain or be $\perp$; i.e. all be in **<sexpr>** or all be in **Tr**.

Assuming that an instance of a conditional expression meets this restriction, the rule for evaluation is given by the following:

We evaluate the p_i's from left to right, finding the *first* which returns value t. When we find such a p_i, we evaluate the corresponding e_i. The value of the conditional expression is the value computed by that e_i; if all of the p_i's evaluate to f then the conditional expression gives $\perp$. The conditional expression also gives $\perp$ if we come across a p_i which has value $\perp$ before we reach a p_i with value t.

For example:

$$[atom \ [A] \to B; \ eq \ [A;(A \ . \ B)] \to C] = B$$

Notice that the p_2 expression is undefined, but the conditional gives value B since p_1 gives value t; this means that conditional expressions are non-strict.

$$[eq \ [A;(A \ . \ B)] \to C; \ atom \ [A] \to B] = \perp$$

Here a reordering makes the evaluation return $\perp$.

$$[atom \ [(A \ . \ B)] \to B;$$
$$eq \ [A \ ; B] \to C;$$
$$eq \ [car[(A \ . \ B)]; \ cdr[(B \ . \ A)]] \to E] \quad = \quad E$$

This example is more complex so, to improve readability, we split the conditional clauses across several lines. This stylistic formatting is called **pretty printing**.

$$[eq \ [A; \ A] \to t; \ atom \ [A] \to f] = t$$
$$[eq \ [A; \ A] \to t; \ atom \ [A] \to B] = \perp$$

Note that non-strictness is relative to a single domain; thus the last example above gives $\perp$ since it contains e_i's of differing domains.

Frequently it is convenient to use a special form of the conditional expression where the final p_n is guaranteed to be true. There are many expressions which always evaluate to t; $eq[1;1]$ is one. The simplest expression is the constant t.

Consider the special form: $[p_1 \rightarrow e_1; ...; t \rightarrow e_n]$

If we know that the previous p_i's are either true or false, [20] the final $p_n \rightarrow e_n$-case is a catch-all or otherwise-case which will be executed if none of the previous p_i's give t. Thus the use of t in this context can be read "otherwise"; and the conditional can be read:

"If p_1 is true then e_1, else if p_2 is true then ..., otherwise e_n"

The introduction of conditional expressions has further widened the gap between traditional mathematical theories and computational theories. Previously we could almost side-step the issue of order of evaluation; it didn't really matter unless $\perp$ was involved. But now the very definition of meaning of conditionals involves an order of evaluation.

The order of evaluation is important from a computational viewpoint: if we are going to give as value the leftmost e_i whose p_i evaluates to t, then there is no need to compute any of the other e_j's; those values will never be used. A more pressing difficulty is that of partial functions. If we did not impose an order of evaluation on the components of a conditional, then frequently we would attempt to evaluate expressions which would lead to undefined results: $[eq[0;0] \rightarrow 1; t \rightarrow car[A]]$ gives 1 using the meaning of conditionals, whereas the expression would be undefined if we were required to evaluate $car[A]$. If we think of an occurrence of $\perp$ being mapped to an error message, evaluating $car[A]$ would cause termination of the computation. But, if we continue to allow $\perp$ as an argument or value, then we can characterize the effect of a conditional expression as a **non-strict** function. Recall, a non-strict function is allowed to return a value other than $\perp$ when one of its arguments is $\perp$; or, put another way, we don't examine the definedness of arguments before applying the function.

For example, let $if(x;y;z)$ be the **conditional function** [21] computed by: $[x \rightarrow y; t \rightarrow z]$. We can define if as a non-strict function such that:

$$if(x;y;z) = \begin{array}{l} y \text{ if } x \text{ is } t \\ z \text{ if } x \text{ is } f \\ \perp \text{ if } x \text{ is } \perp \end{array}$$

However there is more to the "strictness" implied by conditional expressions than just making sure that proper arguments are passed on function calls.

Consider the following algorithm:

$$one[x] \Leftarrow [x=0 \rightarrow 1; t \rightarrow one[x-1]]$$

Assume that *one* is non-strict and assume the domain of discourse is the integers. That means, *one* will try to compute with *any* (integer) argument it

---

[20] We must also know that all the e_i's are elements of the same domain.

[21] Notice we are writing '(...)' rather than '[...]' since we are talking about the function and not the algorithm. See page 12.

is given. The algorithm for *one* defines a function giving *1* for any non-negative integer and is undefined for any other number. From a computational point of view, however, *one*[-1] appears "undefined" in a different sense from *car*[A] being "undefined". The computation *one*[-1] does not terminate and is said to diverge. For a partial function like *car*, we can give an error message whenever we attempt to apply the function to an atomic argument, but we cannot expect to include tests like "if the computation *f*[a] does not terminate then give error No. 15." [22] From the purely functional point of view, *one* still defines the partial function which is *1* for the non-negative integers, but computationally there's an important distinction to be made.

So we see that a computation may be "undefined" for two reasons: it involves a non-terminating computation or it involves applying a partial function to a value not in its domain. [23] Note that the distinction between "undefined" and "diverges" is fuzzy. If we restrict the domain of *one* to the natural numbers, then *one*[-1] denotes ⊥ rather than diverges. Or, put another way, "undefined strictness" is a special case of "divergent strictness" where we are able to predict which computations will not terminate. Those cases can be checked by defining the function to be strict over a domain which rules out those anomalies. Thus a case can be made for identifying divergent computations with ⊥; however there is typically more to non-termination that just "wrong kind of arguments".

We want to extend our discussion of strictness to encompass divergence. Recall the discussion on page 15 of *second*[x; y] <= y. Defining *second* to be strict required that each application of *second* determine whether either argument denoted ⊥. If we want *second* to be strict with respect to divergence, then we must test each argument for divergence. That implies evaluation of each of the arguments, which in turn implies that if a computation of an argument diverges, then the computation of the function application must also diverge. This implies that it is natural to associate "strict with respect to divergence" with **CBV**, since in the process of checking for termination, we must compute values. However if a function is strict then calling style doesn't matter. In contrast, a non-strict function does not check arguments for divergence, and indeed the divergence of a computation may depend on the calling style. Consider the evaluation of *second*[*one*[-1]; B] where *one* is total over the integers. This evaluation will diverge under **CBV** while it converges to B using **CBN**.

We cannot require all our functions to be strict if we expect to do any non-trivial computation. That is, we need a function which can determine its value without computing the values of all of its arguments --a "don't care

---

[22] A discussion of such topics involves a description of the "halting problem" for computational devices. See [Rog 67] for details.

[23] Compare ω-undefined and E-undefined in [Mor 68].

condition"--. The conditional function is such a non-strict function. That is $if(t;q;r)$ has value q without knowing anything about what happens to r. In particular, $if(t;q;\perp) = q$ and $if(f;\perp;r) = r$. Now since if is to be a function and therefore single-valued, if $if(t;q;\perp) = q$ then for any argument x, $if(t;q;x) = q$. Notice that $\perp$ is now carrying an additional "don't-care" interpretation; this is consistent with its previous meaning when we think of the function being computed by the algorithm.

Even given that a computational definition is desired, there are other plausible interpretations of conditionals. Consider the definition: $g[x;y] <= [lic[x] \to 1; t \to 1]$. Assuming that lic is a total predicate, any value computed by g will be 1. But requiring left-to-right evaluation could spend a great deal of unnecessary computation if lic is a *long involved calculation*. One might further request that $g[x;y]$ give 1 even if lic is non-terminating. Questions of evaluation are non-trivial. We will spend two chapters, Chapter 3 and Chapter 4, discussing LISP evaluation and its possible alternatives.

What benefits have resulted from our study of $\perp$ and divergence? We should have a clearer understanding of the difference between function and algorithm and a better grasp of the kinds of difficulties which can befall a computation. We have uncovered an important class of detectable errors. The character of these miscreants is that they occur in the context of supplying the wrong *kind* of argument to a function. This kind of error is called a **type fault**, meaning that we expected an argument of a specific type, that is from a specific domain, and since it was not forthcoming, we refuse to perform any kind of calculation. Thus $atom[f]$ and $cons[t;A]$ are undefined since both expect elements of S as arguments. Divergent computations are equally repugnant but there is no general method for testing whether an arbitrary calculation will terminate.

This discussion concludes the applicative portion of LISP constructs. It may not seem like you can do much useful computation with such a limited collection of operations as those proposed so far for LISP; there are no assignment statements or explicit control constructs. Things are not quite as trivial as they might seem. In elementary number theory all you have is zero and some simple functions, and elementary number theory is far from "elementary." Manipulation of our primitives, with composition, and conditional expressions, coupled with techniques for definition can *also* become complicated.

Let's apply the LISP constructs which we now have, and define a new LISP function. For example: our predicate eq is defined only for atomic arguments. We would like to test for equality of arbitrary S-exprs. What should this more complex equality mean? By equality we mean: as trees, the S-exprs have the same branching structure; and the corresponding terminal nodes are labeled by the same atoms. Thus, we would like to define a predicate, *equal*, such that:

$$equal[(A . B);(A . B)] = t$$

$$equal[A;A] = t$$

$$equal[(A . B);(B . A)] = f$$

$$equal[(A . (B . C));(A . (B . C))] = t$$

$$equal[(A . (B . C));((A . B) . C)] = f$$

Here's an informal description of the *equal* predicate.

1. If both arguments are atomic then see what *eq* says about them. We can test if they are both atomic by using *atom* and a conditional expression.
2. If one is atomic and the other is not they can't be equal S-exprs.
3. Otherwise both are non-atomic S-exprs. Both have two sub-expressions. Look at both first subexpressions. If these sub-expressions are not equal then the original expressions cannot be equal either. If the first subexpressions *are* equal then the question of whether or not the original expressions are equal depends on the equality of the second subexpressions. Thus the following definition:

$$equal[x;y] <= [atom[x] \rightarrow [atom[y] \rightarrow eq [x;y]; t \rightarrow f];$$
$$atom[y] \rightarrow f;$$
$$equal [car[x];car[y]] \rightarrow equal[cdr[x];cdr[y]];$$
$$t \rightarrow f]$$

Notice that the third informal clause translates into a LISP conditional clause which involves applications of the *equal* predicate itself. The use of **recursive** definitions is an important and powerful programming tool.

Notice too that we use nested conditional expressions in *equal*: e_1 is itself a conditional. Also we have used predicates in the e_i positions at e_3 and e_{11}; this is allowable, and in fact expected, since *equal* is a predicate.

Let's show that *equal* does perform correctly for a specific example. This will also show a complicated evaluation of a conditional expression. We will use the call-by-value rules. We will perform the evaluation by substituting the evaluated actual parameters for the formal parameters in the body of the definition. Then we will simplify the resulting expression. [24]

---

[24]This is *not* the method LISP uses to perform call-by value, but it has the same computational effect in most cases. The anomalous cases involve an important area in language design. For example, how should $f[2;3]$ be evaluated when $f[x;y] <= +[x;[y;z]]$?

$equal[(A . B);(A . C)]$ reduces to:

$[atom[(A . B)] \rightarrow [atom[(A . C)] \rightarrow eq[(A . B);(A . C)]; \mathbf{t} \rightarrow \mathbf{f}];$
$atom[(A . C)] \rightarrow \mathbf{f};$
$equal[car[(A . B)];car[(A . C)]] \rightarrow equal[cdr[(A . B)];cdr[(A . C)]];$
$\mathbf{t} \rightarrow \mathbf{f}]$

We find that $\mathbf{p}_1$ (i.e., $atom[(A . B)]$) and $\mathbf{p}_2$ ($atom[(A . C)]$) when evaluated (in order) give $\mathbf{f}$. We must now evaluate $\mathbf{p}_3$, which is: $equal[car[(A . B)];car[(A . C)]]$. This reduces to $equal[A;A]$, and:

$equal[A;A] = [atom[A] \rightarrow [atom[A] \rightarrow eq[A;A]; \mathbf{t} \rightarrow \mathbf{f}];$
$atom[A] \rightarrow \mathbf{f};$
$equal[car[A];car[A]] \rightarrow equal[cdr[A];cdr[A]];$
$\mathbf{t} \rightarrow \mathbf{f}]$

This conditional expression will evaluate to $\mathbf{t}$. So $\mathbf{p}_3$ in the original call of $equal[(A . B);(A . C)]$ is true and we must evaluate the $\mathbf{e}_3$ expression which is $equal[cdr[(A . B)];cdr[(A . C)]]$. That expression simplifies to $equal[B;C]$ and we call $equal$. After substitution and simplification $equal$ will finally return value $\mathbf{f}$. That means that $equal[(A . B);(A . C)]$ gives $\mathbf{f}$. Notice that $eq[(A . B);(A . C)]$ appeared but was never evaluated because of left-to-right evaluation scheme of conditional expressions.

Clearly, evaluation of LISP expressions in this amount of detail is not a process which we wish to do very often by hand. Fortunately the process can be executed by a machine.

Finally, to include conditional expressions in our syntax of LISP expressions, we should add:

<form> ::= <conditional expression>
and <conditional expression> ::= [<form> → <form>; ...; <form> → <form>]
where <form> was defined on page 17.

These syntax equations fail to capture all of our intended meaning. For example, the <form>s appearing in the $\mathbf{p}_i$-position are restricted to be forms taking values in **Tr**, the truth domain. That restriction is not expressed in the equations, and indeed, is difficult to express naturally in such syntax equations. See [Hop 69] for a discussion of expressibility and grammars.

Problems

1. Evaluate the following:

a. $eq[X;Y]$

b. $cons[X;Y]$

c. $car[(X . Y)]$

d. $car[cons[X;Y]]$

e. $cadr[(X .(Y . NIL))]$

f. $cdar[(X .(Y . NIL))]$

g. $eq[cdr[(A . B)];cdr[(C . B)]]$

h. $atom[cons[(A . B);(C . D)]]$

i. $cons[atom[A];atom[(A . B)]]$

j. $eq[atom[ATOM];atom[EQ]]$

k. $[t \rightarrow A; t \rightarrow B]$ l. $[f \rightarrow A; t \rightarrow B]$ m. $[eq[A;B] \rightarrow 4]$

n. $[atom[X] \rightarrow atom[X]; t \rightarrow FOO]$

o. $[eq[EQ; X] \rightarrow A; eq[A; B] \rightarrow B; t \rightarrow C]$

p. $cons[[eq[A; B] \rightarrow 1; t \rightarrow FOO]; cons[A; cadr[(A . (B . C))]]]$

q. $equal[(A . B);(A . B)]$ r. $eq[(A . B);(A . B)]$

2. Consider the following definition:

$$twist[s] <= [atom[s] \rightarrow s;$$
$$t \rightarrow cons[twist[cdr[s]];twist[car[s]]]]$$

a. Is the function partial or is it total? Now evaluate:

b. $twist[A]$ c. $twist[(A . B)]$ d. $twist[((A . B) . C)]$

3. Now try:

$$findem[x;y] <= [atom[x] \rightarrow [eq[x;y] \rightarrow T; t \rightarrow NIL];$$
$$t \rightarrow cons[findem[car[x];y];findem[cdr[x];y]]]$$

a. Is this function total? Now evaluate:

b. $findem[(A . B);A]$ c. $findem[(B .(A . C));A]$

d. $findem[(B .(A . C));C]$ e. $findem[(A . B);(A . B)]$

1.6 Sequences: Abstract Data Structures

In several areas of mathematics it is convenient to deal with sequences of information. For example, a problem domain may be more naturally described as ordered collections of numbers rather than individual numbers. This may either simplify understanding of the problem or simplify the formulation of the functions defined on the domain. Several programming languages include arrays as representations of these mathematical ideas. We should notice that sequences are data structures. We will have to describe constructors, selectors, and recognizers for them. Subsequently we will explore applications of sequences as data structures.

After a certain familiarity is gained in the application of algorithms which manipulate sequences, we will discuss the problems of representation and implementation of this data structure. We will first give an implementation of sequences in terms of S-expressions. That is, we will describe an $\mathfrak{R}$-mapping giving a representation of sequences and their primitive operations in terms of LISP's S-exprs and primitive functions. Still later in Section 7.2 we will discuss low-level implementation of this data structure in terms of conventional machines.

But now we will study sequences as abstract data structures: what are their essential structural characteristics? What properties should be present in a programming language to allow a natural and flexible representation? This discussion will shed light on the important problems of representation and abstraction.

A sequence is an ordered set of elements. [25] For example, (x_1, x_2, x_3), is the standard notation for a sequence of the three elements x_1, x_2, and x_3. The length of a sequence is defined to be the number of elements in that sequence. We will allow sequences to have sub-sequences to an arbitrary finite depth. That is, the elements of a sequence will either be individuals or may themselves be sequences. For example, a sequence of length n, each of whose elements are sequences of length m, is a matrix. Here are BNF equations for sequences and their elements:

<seq>	::= (<seq elem>, ...,<seq elem>) [26]
<seq elem>	::= <indiv> | <seq>
<indiv>	:: = <literal indiv> | <numeral> | -<numeral>
<literal indiv>	:: = <indiv letter>
	:: = <literal indiv><indiv letter>
	:: = <literal indiv><digit>
<numeral>	:: = <digit> | <numeral><digit>
<indiv letter>	:: = A | B | C ... | Z
<digit>	:: = 0 | 1 | 2 ... | 9

Notice that the structure of <indiv> is the same as that for LISP's <atom>; the only difference is in the fonts used for letters and digits. We have made the distinction between LISP atoms and sequence individuals intentionally. Thus (A, (B, C), D, (E, B)) is a sequence of length four, whose second and fourth elements are also sequences whose length is two. We will use "( )" as notation for the empty sequence.

We want to write LISP-like functions operating over sequences, so we will at least need to give constructors, selectors, recognizers, and predicates for sequences. As in the case of S-exprs, we will include the undefined element, and the full domain of sequences will be named

$$\mathsf{Seq} = \text{<seq>} \cup \{\perp\}$$

As on page 18, we extend the primitive LISP operations to include this new domain, by defining:

$$\mathsf{S_2} = \mathsf{S_1} \cup \text{<seq>}$$

and extend each operation appropriately over $\mathsf{S_2}$. For example:

---

[25]For an alternative description of sequences and a discussion of a different view of data structures see page 41.

[26]For the meaning of these ellipses see page 17.

$$atom[A] = \bot$$

$$car[A] = \bot$$

$$car[(A, B)] = \bot$$

$$cons[A; B] = \bot$$

$$issexpr[(A)] = f$$

We need to define some data structure operations specific to sequences. What are the essential characteristics of a sequence? First, a sequence either is empty or has elements. Thus we will want a predicate to test for emptyness. Next, if the sequence is non-empty, we should be able to select elements. Finally, given some elements, we should be able to build a new sequence from them.

Predicates on sequences are like predicates on S-expressions, mapping sequences to truth values in **Tr**.[27] The basic predicate, which tests for emptyness, is called *null*.

$$null[x] \text{ is } \quad \begin{array}{l} t \text{ if } x \text{ is the empty sequence, ( ).} \\ f \text{ if } x \text{ is a non-empty sequence.} \\ \bot \text{ otherwise.} \end{array}$$

$$null[( )] = t$$

$$null[(A, B)] = f$$

$$null[f] = \bot$$

Thus *null* gives usable values only for sequences. Since we intend to operate on domains which contain data structures other than sequences, we will need a recognizer to be sure that *null* is not applied to arguments which are *not* sequences. We will name this recognizer *isseq*.

$$isseq[(A, B, C)] = t$$

$$isseq[A] = f$$

$$isseq[A] = f$$

$$isseq[t] = f$$

$$isseq[( )] = t$$

$$isseq[\bot] = \bot$$

---

[27]The reason for restructuring LISP predicates might now be apparent to previous users of LISP: if we mapped the truth values to the atoms T and NIL as is typically done, then we'd have to map truth values of sequence-predicates to representations as sequence elements, and we would have to perpetuate that decision for every new abstract data structure domain that we wanted to introduce.

The predicate *isseq* is total over all domains, whereas *null* is only partial: total over **<seq>**, but undefined for S-exprs.

While on the subject of predicates, there are a couple more we shall need. The first one is a recognizer, *isindiv*, which will give value t if its argument is an individual, give f if its argument is a sequence, and will give ⊥ otherwise.

The second predicate is the extension of the equality relation to the class of sequence individuals. We shall use the same name, *eq*, as we did for the S-expression predicate. In fact, whenever we define a new abstract data type we will assume that an appropriate version of *eq* is available for the elements of the base domain. One of our first tasks will be to extend that equality relation to the whole domain. We will do so for sequences later in this section. Equality is a basic relation in mathematics so it is not surprising to see it play an important role here. *eq* is one of the few relations which we shall define across all domains. Functions or predicates like *eq*, which are applicable on several domains, are called **polymorphic functions**.

Next, the selectors for a (non-empty) sequence include: *first, second*, etc, where:

$$first[(A, B, C)] = A$$

$$second[(A, B, C)] = B$$

$$third[(A, B)] = \perp$$

It is also convenient to define an "all-but-first" selector, called *rest*.

$$rest[(A, B, C)] = (B, C)$$

$$rest[(B, C)] = (C)$$

$$rest[(C)] = (\ )$$

$$rest[C] = \perp$$

$$rest[(\ )] = \perp$$

In conjunction with *rest*, we shall utilize a constructor, *concat*, which is to add a single element to the front of a sequence.

$$concat[A;(B,C)] = (A, B, C)$$

$$concat[A;(\ )] = (A)$$

$$concat[(A);(B,C)] = ((A), B, C)$$

$$concat[(B,C);A] = \perp$$

$$concat[A; B] = \perp$$

The final constructor is called *seq*; it takes an arbitrary number of sequence elements as arguments and returns a sequence consisting of those elements (in the obvious order). Let $\alpha_1, ..., \alpha_n$ be elements of <seq elem>, then:

$$seq[\alpha_1; \alpha_2; ...; \alpha_n] = (\alpha_1, ..., \alpha_n)$$

One question may have come to mind: how do we know when we have a sufficient set of functions for the manipulation of an abstract data structure? How do we know we haven't left some crucial functions out? If we have enough, how do we know that we haven't included too many? Actually, this second case isn't disastrous, but when implementing the functions it would be nice to minimize the number of primitives we have to program. These problems are worthy of study and are the concern of anyone interested in the design of programming languages. We will say a bit more about solutions to these questions beginning on page 36.

Notice that we have been describing the sequence functions without regard to any underlying representation. We have said nothing about these sequence operations except that they construct, test, or select. We consider sequences as abstract data structures, suitable for manipulation by LISP-like algorithms; we define algorithms over the domain of sequences, using the primitive operations, conditional expressions, and recursion. How sequences are represented as S-exprs or represented on a machine, is irrelevant. Sequences have certain inherent structural properties and it is those properties which we must understand *before* we begin thinking about representation. In the next section we will show how to represent sequences as certain S-expressions and sequence operations as LISP operations on that representation.

Let's develop some expertise in manipulating sequences. The first example will be an extension of the equality relation to sequences. We perpetuate the name *equal* from S-exprs, and the basic structure of the definition will parallel that of its namesake; but the components of the definition will involve sequence operations rather than S-expr operations. It will be of value to compare the two predicates. The S-expr version is to be found on page 24.

$equal[x;y] <= [isindiv[x] \rightarrow [isindiv[y] \rightarrow eq[x;y]; t \rightarrow f];$
$\qquad\qquad isindiv[y] \rightarrow f;$
$\qquad\qquad null[x] \rightarrow [null[y] \rightarrow t; t \rightarrow f];$
$\qquad\qquad null[y] \rightarrow f;$
$\qquad\qquad equal[first[x];first[y]] \rightarrow equal[rest[x];rest[y]];$
$\qquad\qquad t \rightarrow f]$

This *equal* works on sequences and sequence elements as its S-expr counterpart worked on dotted pairs and atoms.

Next, we will write a predicate *member* of two arguments x and y. x is to be an individual; *y* is to be a sequence; *member* is to return t just in the case that *x* is an element of the sequence *y*. What does this specification tell us? The predicate is partial. The recursion should be on the structure of *y*; and termination (with value f) should occur if *y* is the empty sequence. If *y* is not empty then it has a first element; call it *z*. Compare *z* with *x*. If these elements are identical then *member* should return t; otherwise see if *x* occurs in the remainder of the sequence *y*.

Notes:

1. We cannot use *eq* directly to check equality since, though *x* is an individual, there is no reason that the elements of *y* need be. We will introduce a subsidiary predicate *same* to assure that *eq* is applied only to arguments of the correct type.

2. Recall that we can get the first element of a sequence with *first*, and the rest of a sequence with *rest*.

So here's *member*:

$$member[x;y] <= [null[y] \rightarrow f;$$
$$same[first[y];x] \rightarrow t;$$
$$t \rightarrow member[x;rest[y]]]$$

where: $$same[u;v] <= [isindiv[u] \rightarrow eq[u;v]; t \rightarrow f]$$

Next is an arithmetic example to calculate the number of elements in a sequence.

$$length[n] <= [null[n] \rightarrow 0; t \rightarrow plus[1;length[rest[n]]]]$$

1.7 Lists: Representations of Sequences

We can now write LISP-like functions describing operations on sequences; the algorithms are clean and understandable. However, if we wish to run these programs in a LISP environment, then we have to represent the data structures and the algorithms in terms understandable to LISP. [28] This is the problem of representation. Granted, we could have overcome the problem by representing sequences directly as LISP S-expressions and could have written functions in LISP which used *car-cdr*-chains to directly manipulate the representations. However, the resulting programs would be much more difficult to read and debug and understand. More important, the programs would be explicitly tied to a specific representation of the abstract data

---

[28]If we wish LISP to run on a conventional machine we have to represent LISP's data structures and algorithms in a manner understandable to that hardware. This task is the subject of later chapters in the book.

structure. At some later date it might be desired to change the representation; then many programs would have to be rewritten. We will illustrate these difficulties soon. In Section 2.3 we develop a complex algorithm for differentiation on a class of polynomials, moving from an unclear and highly representation-dependent formulation, to a clear, concise, representation-independent algorithm.

Obviously we will always have to supply a representational bridge between the abstract data structures and algorithms, and their concrete counterparts. One aspect of this study of data structures is to understand what is required to build this bridge and how best to represent these requirements in a programming language.

The first decision to be made is how to represent the abstract data structure; how should we represent sequences as S-expressions? How should we choose representations in general? Usually there is not just one "best" representation. Some obvious considerations involve the difficulty of implementing the primitive operations (constructors, selectors, recognizers, and predicates) on the abstract data structure. Also we must keep in mind the kinds of algorithms which we wish to write; computation takes time, and since this is computer science we should give consideration to efficiency.

A reasonable choice for a representation of sequences as S-expressions is the following:

$$\Re [\![\,<\text{indiv}> \,]\!] = <\text{atom}>$$

and for $\alpha_1, ..., \alpha_n$ in **<seq elem>**:

$$\Re [\![\,(\alpha_1, ..., \alpha_n)\,]\!] =$$

The right-hand branch in this LISP-tree representation of a sequence will always point to the rest of the sequence or will be the atom *NIL*. Notice that the description of the $\Re$-mapping is recursive. Thus for example:

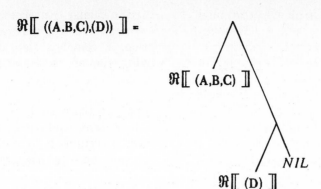

$$\Re[\![\, ((A.B,C),(D)) \,]\!] =$$

which will finally expand to $((A . (B . (C . NIL))) . ((D . NIL) . NIL))$ since $\Re[\![\, (A,B,C) \,]\!]$ is $(A . (B . (C . NIL)))$ and $\Re[\![\, (D) \,]\!]$ is $(D . NIL)$

For convenience sake we will carry over the sequence notation -- (A, B, C) -- to that for the representation in LISP -- (A, B, C) -- [29] thinking of (A, B, C) as an abbreviation for $(A . (B . (C . NIL)))$.

Next, what about a representation for the empty sequence? Looking at the representation of a non-empty sequence it appears natural to take NIL as $\Re[\![\, (\,) \,]\!]$ since after you have removed all the elements from the sequence NIL is all that is left in the representation. To be consistent then:

$$\Re[\![\, (\,) \,]\!] = NIL$$

This gives us a complete specification of the $\Re$-mapping for the domain; we have represented the abstract domain of sequences in a subset of the domain of Symbolic Expressions. The S-expr representation of a sequence is called a list; and we will refer to the abbreviation,

$$(\alpha_1, ..., \alpha_n) \quad \text{for} \quad (\alpha_1 . (\alpha_2 . \ ... \ (\alpha_n . NIL) ...)) \quad \text{as list-notation.}$$

Sequences are the abstract data structure; lists are one of their representations. Since the atom NIL takes on special significance in list-notation it is endowed with the special name list **terminator**.

And a notational point: in graphical interpretation of list-notation it is often convenient to write:

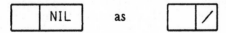

---

[29]Be aware that A is an atom and A is a sequence element; they are *not* the same data structure.

For example $(A, (B, C), D)$ is:

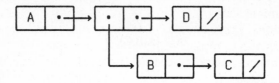

or, in "dotted-pair" notation: $(A . ((B . (C . NIL)) . (D . NIL)))$

Finally, in list-notation the commas can be replaced by spaces [30]

e.g. $(A, (B, C), D) = (A (B C) D)$

but beware: the "dots" in dot-notation are *never* optional!

that is $(A . (B . C)) \neq (A (B C))$

At this point we have an intuitive understanding of what we mean by "sequence"; we have described selectors, constructors, and recognizers, albeit at an abstract level, for manipulating sequences, and we have represented our notion of sequences as a subset of the S-expressions called lists. The final step is to represent our sequence-manipulators as certain LISP functions. Let $first_r$ be a LISP function which will represent the sequence operation $first$. [31] Then for example we might expect:

$$\Re[\![first[(A, B, C)]]\!] = first_r[(A, B, C)] = A$$

The problem is that this line is not quite right. LISP functions expect their inputs to be S-expressions but (A, B, C) is *not* an S-expression. To be correct we *should* have written:

$$first_r[(A . (B . (C . NIL)))] = A$$

It might be argued that (A, B, C) is just a convenient abbreviation for. $(A . (B . (C . NIL)))$, but even so, if we wish the machine to use the abbreviation we must be able to express that translation scheme to the machine. We must therefore examine the implications of the notation. Clearly it is easier to read and write in list notation and, as long as we perform only list-operations on lists, there is no reason to look at the

---

[30]This convention is one of the few instances of a "good" bug. The early LISP papers required full use of commas, but due to a programming error in the LISP output routine, lists were printed without commas. It looked so much better that the bug became institutionalized.

[31]Indeed, once the $\Re$-mapping is defined on the *domain* it is induced on the *operations*.

underlying dotted-pair representation.[32] However, we must keep in mind that list operations are carried out on the machine using the dotted-pair representation. *We* might carry out the "list-to-dotted-pair" transformations implicitly, but a machine which evaluates LISP expressions will have to have an explict transformation mechanism. So a necessary part of our representation of sequences is the specification of transformations between the abstract data structure notation and the notation of the underlying representation. We can give representations for the sequence operations. We should continue to write the subscript $_r$ on the LISP representation of a sequence operation, like *seq* being represented by seq_r. In most circumstances the distinction between abstraction and representation will be clear, so we will usually omit the subscript. The construction of a sequence from an arbitrary number of elements will be represented by a LISP function seq_r. We will use *list* interchangeably with seq_r.

$$\Re[\![\ seq\ ]\!] = list$$

$list[\alpha_1;\ \alpha_2;\ ...\ ;\alpha_n]$ generates a list consisting of the α_i arguments. That is, for

n≥1, *list* is the appropriately nested composition of *cons*es:

$cons[\alpha_1;cons[\alpha_2;\ ...\ cons[\alpha_n;NIL]]\ ...]$, and for n = 0, $list[\ ] = (\ )$

Examples: $list[A;B] = (A\ B)$

$list[A;B;C] = (A\ B\ C)$

$list[A;list[B;C]] = list[A;(B\ C)] = (A\ (B\ C))$

$list[NIL] = (NIL)$

Notice that *list* is *not* strictly a LISP function as we have prescribed them; *list* does evaluate its arguments, but it can take an arbitrary number of them. On page 17 we required that LISP functions be of fixed arity. For the moment, *list* is simply a notational abbreviation for nested applications of *cons*. The representation of the selector functions should be apparent from the graphical representation. We leave it as an exercise for the reader to specify representations for these functions; however, here are a few of the other representations:

---

[32]Indeed, a strong case can be made for *never* allowing any operations on lists *except* list operations! See the discussion of type-faults on page 23 and page 241.

$$\Re[\![\ isindiv\ ]\!] = atom$$

$$\Re[\![\ isseq\ ]\!] = isstrictlist \text{ where:}$$

$$isstrictlist[x] <= \quad [atom[x] \to [eq[x; NIL] \to \mathsf{t}; \mathsf{t} \to \mathsf{f}];$$
$$islistelement[car[x]] \to isstrictlist[cdr[x]];$$
$$\mathsf{t} \to \mathsf{f}]$$

where: $islistelement[x] <= [atom[x] \to \mathsf{t}; \quad \mathsf{t} \to isstrictlist[x]]$

The predicate *atom* does not quite characterize *isindiv*. We have been assuming that:

$$\Re[\![f[t_1; ...; t_n]]\!] = \Re[\![f]\!][\ \Re[\![t_1]\!];\ \Re[\![t_2]\!];\ ...;\ \Re[\![t_n]\!]\ ]$$

but $\Re[\![\ isindiv[(\ )]\ ]\!] \neq \Re[\![\ isindiv\ ]\!][\Re[\![(\ )]\!]]$

Some descriptions of LISP use this strict definition of lists, so that elements of a list are either atomic or are lists themselves. In practice it is often convenient to allow elements of a list to be arbitrary S-expressions. This more liberal interpretation of lists is expressed by the following recognizer:

$$islist[x] <= [atom[x] \to [eq[x; NIL] \to \mathsf{t}; \mathsf{t} \to \mathsf{f}]; \mathsf{t} \to islist[cdr[x]]\ ]$$

Therefore $(A, (A . B), C)$ is a list of three elements. But beware: (A, (A . B), C) is *not* a sequence, and neither is $(A, (A . B), C)$.

Since lists may have dotted pairs as elements, it is natural to extend *list* to handle such cases:

$$list[cons[A;B];car[(A . B)]] = ((A . B)\ A)$$

To summarize the accomplishments of this section, we have in effect added a *new* data structure to the repertoire of LISP. The addition process includes:

1. **The abstract operations.** We give constructors, selectors, and predicates for the recognition of instances of the data structure.

2. **The underlying representation.** We must show how the new data structure can be represented in terms of existing data structures.

3. **Abstract operations as concrete operations.** We must write LISP functions which faithfully mirror the intended meaning of the abstract operations when interpreted in the underlying representation.

4. **The input/output transformations.** We should give conventions for transforming to and from the internal representation.

There is another view of the representability of data structures ([Mor 74]). We use **transfer functions** which are mappings between the abstract structure and its representation. We need two transfer functions; a write-function, **W**, to map the representations into the abstract objects; and a read-function, **R**, to map the abstract objects to their representations.

Consider the problem of representing sequences. We want **R** to map from elements of **<seq elem>** to **<sexpr>** (see page 27 and page 5); and we want **W** to map from **<sexpr>** to **<seq elem>**. Before we give such **R** and **W**, let's see what they will do for us. We could define *first*, such that:

$$first_r[x] = W[car[R[x]]]$$

What the equation says is that given a sequence x, we can map it to the S-expression representation using **R**; the result of this map is an S-expr and therefore suitable fare for *car*; the result of the *car* operation is then mapped back into the set of sequence elements by **W**. The other operations for manipulating sequences can be described similarly. With this introduction, here are appropriate transfer functions:

$$W[e] <= [isnil[e] \rightarrow mknull[];$$
$$atom[e] \rightarrow mkindiv[e];$$
$$t \rightarrow concat[W[car[e]];W[cdr[e]]]]$$

$$R[l] <= [null[l] \rightarrow NIL;$$
$$isindiv[l] \rightarrow atomize[l];$$
$$t \rightarrow cons[R[first[l]];R[rest[l]]]]$$

We have seen all of the functions and predicates involved in **R** and **W** except *atomize*, *mknull* and *mkindiv*. In terms of our current representation of sequences, these three functions are essentially the identity function, $i[x] <= x$. However that is true *only* because of the particular representations that we picked; the functions need not be so simple. A more careful inspection would show that *mkindiv* expects as input an atomic S-expression and outputs a sequence individual; *atomize* acts conversely. If the representations of the atomic S-expressions were different from the representations of sequence individuals, then we would have some work to do.

We review what has transpired since it is a model of what is to come. We developed a new abstract data structure called sequences; discussed notational conventions for writing sequences; described operations and pertinent control structures for writing algorithms; and finally showed that it was possible to represent sequences in the previously developed domain of S-exprs. If we had a machine which could execute S-expr algorithms we could encapsulate that machine within the $\Re$-mapping such that we could write in sequence-notation and have it translated internally to S-expr form; we could write sequence-algorithms and have them execute correctly using the $\Re$-maps of the sequence primitives; and finally it would produce sequence-output rather than the internal S-expr form. For all intents and purposes our augmented LISP machine understands sequences. Indeed, this is the way most LISP implementations are organized; input may either be in S-expr form or list-notation; internally all data structures are stored as S-exprs; all algorithms operate on the S-expr form; and finally, any S-exprs which can be interpreted as lists are output in list-notation.

We will approach the other abstract data structure problems in a similar manner, first developing the data structures independent of their representation, and later showing how to represent this new domain in terms of some previously understood domain. We will see in Section 9.4 that much of the mapping from input through output can be specified in a natural style and LISP can automatically generate the necessary input and output programs.

Problems involving list-notation

1. Discuss $cons[\alpha_1;cons[\alpha_2;\alpha_3]]$

   as opposed to $cons[\alpha_1;cons[\alpha_2; cons[\alpha_3; NIL]]]$

   as a representation for $(\alpha_1, \alpha_2, \alpha_3)$

2. Translate the following lists into S-expr dotted-pair notation.
   a. *(A B C)*   b. *(A)*   c. *((A))*   d. *(A (B (C)))* e. *(NIL)*

   Now go the other way and translate the following S-exprs into list notation.
   f. *((A . (B . NIL)) . ((C . NIL) . NIL))*   g. *(NIL . NIL)*
   h. *(CONS . ((QUOTE . (A . NIL)) . NIL))*

3. Evaluate the following:
   a. *first[(A B)]*   b. *rest[(A B)]*
   c. *concat[A;(B C)]*   d. *concat[A;NIL]*
   e. *concat[eq[A;A];(A B C)]*   f. *first[rest[(A B)]]*

1.8 A Respite

"...I think that one of the chief difficulties is that the general standard of programming is extremely low. ...I think that I would like to suggest again that the general standards of programming and the way in which people are taught to program is abominable. They are over and over again taught to make puns; to do shifts instead of multiplying when they mean multiplying; to multiply when they mean shifts; to confuse bit patterns and numbers and generally to say one thing when they actually mean something quite different. Now this is the standard way of writing a program and they take great pleasure in doing so-'Isn't it wonderful? It saves a quarter of a microsecond somewhere every month'. Now I think we

will not get a proper standard of programming ... until we can have
some proper professional standards about how to write programs;
and this has to be done by teaching people right at the beginning
how to write programs properly ..."

C. Strachey, *Conference on Software Engineering, 1968*

This section summarizes and reflects on the material of this chapter. First a reiteration of a previous admonition: though most of this material may seem quite straightforward, the next chapter will begin to show you that things are not all that trivial. LISP is quite powerful. The preceding material *is* basic and the sooner it becomes second nature to you the better.

A second admonition: besides learning about the basic constructs of the language, the previous material should begin to convince you of the necessity for precise specification of programming languages. In particular we have seen that the process of evaluation of expressions must be spelled out quite carefully. Different evaluation schemes lead to quite different effects. Since evaluation *is* the business of programming languages we should do all we can to make a precise specification.

And a final warning: a major point of this whole book is to instill a respect for abstraction as a tool for controlling complexity in programming, and as a means of writing implementation independent programs. As we begin writing more complex algorithms, the power of abstraction will become more apparent, but the lessons we learned in representing sequences contain the essential ideas of abstraction and representation.

We have now seen two examples of abstract data structures. First, we studied S-expressions without any consideration for their implementation; they were abstract objects of sufficient interest in their own right. We then introduced the operations on the data structures: *car, cdr, cons, eq* and *atom.* Finally the **control structures**, conditional expression and recursion, were given. Control structures are used to direct the flow of the algorithm as it executes. These three components, data, operations, and control, are the main ingredients of any programming language. Most languages have an apparently richer class of control devices; "while"-statements and "DO"-loops are examples. Later we will show how to introduce such constructs into LISP. Most control structures are explicit language constructs like the conditional expression, whereas recursion is typically implicit. [33] The interaction between recursion and the procedure-calling mechanism gives LISP a powerful control structure.

As we introduce each new abstract data structure we add new

----

[33]However some languages do require some kind of declaration to the effect that a procedure is recursive.

operations tailored to its needs. When we introduced sequences we also introduced *first, rest, null,* ...,etc. We did not add any new control structure, though a simpler control structure which operated on sequences, selecting elements and performing operations on those elements, might be useful. There is a natural relationship between data structure and control structure; sometimes we can exploit it to good measure. When we consider abstract data structures in future chapters we will again see the three components: data, operations, and control.

The new feature which we considered in discussing sequences was the problem of representation. We showed how to represent sequences in terms of S-expressions. We will continue this pyramiding of data structures in the future; we will consider our work done as soon as we have a representation of our new data structure in terms of an existing one. Finally we will exhibit a representation of the underlying layer of S-expressions. Later we will discuss different representations of data structures, independent of their possible S-expression representation; there are data structures which are not best represented as S-expressions. A further consideration appears because of the representation issue; even though we have represented a particular data structure as a complex S-expression we should not operate on that representation with S-expression functions. We should refrain from using *car* and *cdr* on lists even though the representation is well-known. In our representation of lists we could find the nth element in a list by using $cad^{n-1}r$. And we know that *cdr* represents the *rest* of the list. Though our representation of sequences is such that *first, rest* and *concat* are identical to *car, cdr,* and *cons* respectively, we should use the names *first, rest,* and *concat* to make it clear that we are operating on lists. These representation-dependent coding tricks [34] are dangerous. They are really type faults as discussed on page 23 and page 241.

For a more practical benefit, consider the problem of program modification. We might wish to change the representation of a data structure. If the programming has been done in terms of abstract operations on abstract data structures then only those functions which relate the abstraction to the representation need be changed. If we had used the representation throughout the program, then every use of the representation must be changed. While we are discussing some of the more practical implications of our work we should discuss how $\perp$ should be understood. As things currently stand, the appearance of $\perp$ in any application of strict functions will immediately cause the termination of the computation. No information other than the fact that $\perp$ did appear results from such an occurrence. If we thought of the evaluation of $\perp$ as resulting in a divergent computation, then no information at all would be forthcoming. In reality, a LISP implementation can handle many computations which involve $\perp$. The

---

[34]called "puns" by C. Strachey

computation might be terminated and an error printed; in an interactive implementation, the user might be given an opportunity to correct the error and have the computation continue; and alas, some implementations just continue computation with some arbitrary piece of information produced by an excursion into the subsconscious of LISP. Divergent computations cannot be detected in such a clear manner and implementations differ in their handling of this interpretation of $\bot$. We will have more to say about the implementation of $\bot$ in Section 6.23.

Later, we will motivate the more traditional studies of data structures by considering the implementations of LISP-related languages. But the path to those studies is at least as important. On the way we will show that we can exploit abstraction as a means for giving a clear specification of evaluation of LISP expressions, and the representational techniques we will use will involve applications of abstract data structures. A more tangible benefit should be an increased awareness of the structure and behavior of programming languages, and the beginnings of a better style of programming.

Another part of our investigation should be to answer the question "What is a data structure?". As we mentioned at the beginning of Section 1.6 there is a different characterization of sequences which will give a different interpretation of data structures. The standard mathematical definition of a sequence is as a function from the integers to a particular domain.

Thus a finite sequence **s** might be given as:

$$s = \{<1, s_1>, <2, s_2>, ...<n, s_n>\}$$

To select components of **s**, we use ordinary function application: $s(i) = s_i$. Indeed, if you have programmed in a language which has array constructs, you will recognize "application" as the style of notation used: A[3] selected the third component for the array A.

However this is quite different from what we did in the section on sequences. For example, if (A, B, C) is a sequence, **s**, then in the new interpretation we should write:

$$s = \{<1, A>, <2, B>, <3, C>\}$$

Thus **s(2)** is B, etc. What has happened is that what was previously considered to be a data structure has become a function, and the selector functions on the data structure have now become static indices on the function. Or to make things more transparent:

$$s = \{<first, A>, <second, B>, <third, C>\}$$

Then we would write **s**(*first*) rather than *first*(**s**). [35] This idea can easily be

_____

[35]The language PPL (Polymorphic Programming Language) lets you do this: *car[s]* and *s[car]* both work.

applied to S-exprs and their functions. In graphical terms we are
representing the structures such that the arcs of the graph are labeled with
the selector indices. With L-trees the labeling was implicit: left-branch was
car; right-branch was *cdr*. With explicit labels on the branches, the trees
need not be ordered. Several languages implement such unordered trees;
they are called *structures* in Algol 68 and EL1, and called *records* in Pascal.
Several formalisms exploit this view of data structures; in particular the
Vienna Definition Language ([Weg 72]), which is a direct descendant of
LISP, represents its data in such a manner.

What then is a data structure? It depends on how you look at it. For
our immediate purposes we will try to remain intuitive and informal. We
will try to characterize an abstract data structure as a domain and a collection
of associated operations and control structures. The operations and control
mechanisms should allow us to describe algorithms in a natural manner but
should, if at all possible, remain representation independent.

A few tricks were embedded in the problem sets. Recall problem **h** on
page 25. The composition *atom[cons[...]]* will always evaluate to f [36] since
the result of *cons* is always non-atomic. In **j**, we used atoms with the same
letter strings as predicate names, *ATOM* and *EQ*. *ATOM* and *EQ* are
perfectly good atoms, and are *not* to be confused with the LISP predicates.
Problem **p** shows that conditional expressions may appear within a
functional composition.

Notice that *twist* in problem 2 is total whereas *findem* is partial.
findem is partial since *y* must be atomic. Both functions build new trees:
twistem reverses left- and right-branches recursively; *findem* builds a tree
with the same branching structure as *x*, but the terminal nodes contain *T* at
the points where the atom *y* appears in the original tree, and *NIL* otherwise.

Be clear on the difference between the representation of the empty list:
NIL, and the list consisting of *NIL*: *(NIL)*; note that *(NIL)* is an
abbreviation for *(NIL . NIL)*, which certainly is not *NIL*. List-notation is
an abbreviation and can always be translated back into a S-expr, but not
every S-expr is the representation of a list.

The distinction between *concat* and *list* is sometimes confusing:

$$concat[\alpha_1; (\alpha_2, ...\alpha_n)] \quad \text{is} \quad (\alpha_1, \alpha_2, ... \alpha_n)$$

$$list[\alpha_1; (\alpha_2, ... \alpha_n)] \quad \text{is} \quad (\alpha_1 (\alpha_2 ... \alpha_n))$$

So *concat* will add a new element to the front of an existing list, whereas *list*
will create a new list whose elements will be the values of the arguments to
list.

---

[36]If it has a value at all! If the computation of the arguments to the
cons does not terminate or gives ⊥ then we won't get f.

1.9 Becoming an Expert

We have already traced the development of a few LISP algorithms, and we have given a few programming hints. It is time to reinforce these tentative starts with a more intensive study of the techniques for writing good LISP programs. This section will spend a good deal of time showing different styles of definition, giving hints about how to write LISP functions, and increasing your familiarity with LISP. For those of you who are impatiently waiting to see some *real* applications of this programming language, we can only say "be patient". The next chapter *will* develop several non-trivial algorithms, but what we must do first is improve your skills, even at the risk of worsening your disposition.

First some terminology is appropriate: the style of definition which we have been using is called **definition by recursion**. The basic components of such a definition are:

REC

> 1. A basis case: what to compute as value for the function in one or more particularly simple cases. A basis case is frequently referred to as a termination case.
>
> 2. A general case: what to compute as value for a function, given the values of one or more previous computations with that function.

You should compare the structure of a REC-definition of a function with that of an **IND**-definition of a set (see **IND** on page 3). Applications of REC-definitions are particularly useful in computing values of a function defined over a set which has been defined by an IND-definition. For example, assume that we have defined a set **A** using **IND** then a typical algorithm for computing a function **f** over **A** would involve two parts: first, an indication of how to compute **f** on the base domain of **A**, and second, given values for some elements of **A** say $a_1, ..., a_n$, use IND to generate a new element **a**; then specify the value of **f(a)** as a function of the known values of $f(a_1), ..., f(a_n)$. That is exactly the structure of **REC**.

Here is another attribute of IND-definitions: Suppose we have defined a set **A** using **IND**, and we wish to prove that a certain property **P** holds for every element of **A**. We need only show that:

PRF

> 1. P holds for every element of the base domain of **A**.
>
> 2. Using the technique we elaborated in defining the function **f** above, if we can show that **P** holds for the new element perhaps relying on proofs of **P** for sub-elements, then we should have a convincing argument that **P** holds over *all* of **A**.

This proof technique is a generalization of a common technique for proving properties of the integers. In that context it is called mathematical induction.

We are seeing an interesting parallel between inductive definitions of sets, recursive definitions of functions, and proofs by induction. As we proceed, we will exploit various aspects of these interrelationships. However our task at hand is more mundane: to develop facility at applying **REC** to define functions over the **IND**-domains of symbolic expressions, **S**, and of sequences, **Seq**.

First let's verify that the functions we have constructed so far do indeed satisfy **REC**. Recall our example of *equal* on page 24. The basis case involves a calculation on members of **<atom>**; there we rely on *eq* to distinguish between distinct atoms. The question of equality for two non-atomic S-exprs was recast as a question of equality for their *cars* and *cdrs*. But that too, is proper since the constructed object is manufactured by *cons*, and *car* and *cdr* of that object select the components.

Similar justification for *length* on page 31 can be given. There the domain is **Seq**. The base domain is the empty sequence, and *length* is defined to give *0* in that case. The general case in the recursion comes from the **IND**-definition of a sequence. [37] Given a sequence *s*, we made a new sequence by adding a sequence element to the front of *s*. Again the computation of *length* parallels this construction, saying that the length of this new sequence is one more than the length of the sequence *s*.

For a more traditional example consider the factorial function, n!.

1. The function is defined for non-negative integers.
2. The value of the function for 0 is 1.
3. Otherwise the value of n! is n times the value of (n-1)!.

It should now be clear how to write a LISP program for the factorial function:

$$fact[n] <= [eq[n;0] \rightarrow 1; \mathbf{t} \rightarrow times[n;fact[sub1[n]]]] \quad [38]$$

The implication is that it is easier to compute (n-1)! than to compute n!. But that too is in accord with our construction of the integers using the successor function.

These examples are typical of LISP's recursive definitions. The body of the definition is a conditional expression; the first few branches involve

---

[37]Note (page 27) that we didn't give an explicit **IND**-definition, but rather a set of BNF equations. The reader should supply the explicit definition.

[38]*times* is a LISP function which performs multiplication, and *sub1* subtracts *1* from its argument.

special cases, called **termination conditions**. Then the remainder of the conditional covers the general case-- what to do if the argument to the function is not one of the special cases.

Notice that *fact* is a partial function, defined only for non-negative integers. When writing or reading LISP definitions pay particular attention to the domain of definition and the range of values produced. The following general hints should also be useful:

1. Is the algorithm to be a LISP function or predicate? This information can be used to double-check uses of the definition. Don't use a predicate where a S-expr-valued function is expected; and don't use an S-expr-valued function where a list-value is expected.
2. Are there restrictions on the argument positions? For example, must some of the arguments be truth values? Similar consistency checking as in 1 can be done with this information.
3. Are the termination conditions compatible with the restrictions on the arguments? If it is a recursion on lists, check for the empty list; if it is a recursion on arbitrary S-exprs, then check for the appearance of an atom.
4. Whenever a function call is made within the definition, are all the restrictions on that function satisfied?
5. Don't try to do too much. Try to be lazy. There is usually a very simple termination case. If the termination case looks messy, there is probably something wrong with your conception of the program. If the general case looks messy, then write some subfunctions to perform the brunt of the calculation.

Apply the suggestions when writing any subfunction. When you are finished, no function will do very much, but the net effect of all the functions acting in concert is a solution to your problem. That is part of the mystique of recursive programming.

As you may have discovered, the real difficulty in programming is writing your own programs. But who says programming is easy? LISP at least makes some of your decisions easy. Its constructs are particularly frugal. So far there is only *one* way to write a non-trivial algorithm in LISP: use recursion. The structure of the program flows like that of an inductive argument. Find the right induction hypothesis and the inductive proof is easy; find the right structure on which to recur and recursive programming is easy. It's easier to begin with unary functions; then there's no question about which argument is to be decomposed. The only decision is how to terminate the recursion. If the argument is an S-expr we typically terminate on the occurrence of an atom. If the argument is a list, then terminate on ( ). If the argument is a number then terminate on zero.

Consider a slightly more complicated arithmetical example, the Fibonacci sequence: 0, 1, 1, 2, 3, 5, 8, ... This sequence can be characterized by the following recurrence relation:

$$f(0) = 0$$
$$f(1) = 1$$
$$f(n) = f(n-1)+f(n-2)$$

The translation to a LISP function is easy:

$$fib[n] <= \quad [eq[n;0] \rightarrow 0;$$
$$eq[n;1] \rightarrow 1;$$
$$t \rightarrow plus[fib[sub1[n]];fib[sub1[sub1[n]]]]]$$

where *plus* is a representation of the mathematical function +.

A few additional points can be made here. Notice that an evaluation scheme may imply many duplicate computations. For example, computation of *fib*[5] requires the computation of *fib*[4] and *fib*[3]. But within the calculation of *fib*[4] we again calculate *fib*[3], etc. It would be nice if we could restructure the definition of *fib* to stop this extra computation. [39] Since we *do* wish to run programs on a machine we should give some attention to efficiency. [40]

We will define another function, called *fib'*, on three variables x, y, and n. The variables, x and y, will be used to carry the partial computations. Consider:

$$fib_1[n] <= fib'[n;0;1]$$

where: $$fib'[n;x;y] <= \quad [eq[n;0] \rightarrow x;$$
$$t \rightarrow fib'[sub1[n];plus[x;y];x]]$$

This example is complicated enough to warrant closer examination. The initial call, $fib_1[n]$, has the effect of calling *fib'* with x initialized to 0 and with y initialized to 1. The calls on *fib'* within the body of the definition, say the ith such recursive call, has the effect of saving the ith Fibonacci number in x and the i-1st in y.

---

[39]An alternative solution is to supply a different evaluation scheme which might be able to remember previously calculated results. [Got 74].

[40]For those readers with some programming experience, the solution may appear easy: assign the partial computations to temporary variables. The problem here is that our current subset of LISP doesn't contain assignment.

For example:

$$fib_1[4] = fib'[4;0;1]$$
$$= fib'[3;1;0]$$
$$= fib'[2;1;1]$$
$$= fib'[1;2;1]$$
$$= fib'[0;3;2]$$
$$= 3$$

Functions like fib', used to help fib_1, are called "help functions" or **auxiliary functions**; variables like x and y in fib' are called **accumulators** ([Moor 74]), since they are used to accumulate the partial computations. The technique of using auxiliary functions and accumulators can also be applied to the factorial example. When viewed computationally, the resulting definition will be more efficient, though the gain in efficiency is not as apparent as that in the Fibonacci example. [41]
Thus:

$$fact_1[n] <= fact'[n;1]$$

where: $fact'[n;x] <= [eq[n;0] \rightarrow x; t \rightarrow fact'[sub1[n];times[n;x]]]$

It appears that the pairs $fact, fact_1$ and fib, fib_1 are equivalent. Perhaps we should prove that this is so. We presented the crucial ideas for the proof in the discussion on page 43 concerning **IND**, **REC** and **PRF**. We shall examine the question of proofs of equivalence in Section 2.10.

Auxiliary functions are also applicable to LISP functions defined over S-exprs:

$$length[n] <= [null[n] \rightarrow 0; t \rightarrow add1[length[rest[n]]]] \quad [42]$$

$$length_1[n] <= length'[n;0]$$

where: $length'[n;x] <= [null[n] \rightarrow x; t \rightarrow length'[rest[n];add1[x]]]$

Again, it appears that $length$ is equivalent to $length_1$.

So far our examples have either been numerical or have been predicates. Predicates only require traversing existing S-exprs; certainly we will want to write algorithms which build new S-exprs. Consider the problem of writing a LISP algorithm to reverse a list x. There is a simple informal computation: take elements from the front of x and put them onto

---

[41]The fib_1 example improves efficiency mostly by calculating fewer intermediate results. The gain in the $fact_1$ example is involved with the machinery necessary to actually execute the program: the run-time environment, if you wish. We will discuss this when we talk about implementation of LISP in Chapter 6. The whole question of: "what is efficient?" is open to discussion.

[42]$add1[x] <= x+1$

the front of a new list y. Initially, y should be $(\ )$ and the process should terminate when x is empty.

For example, reversal of the list $(A\ B\ C\ D)$ would produce the sequence:

x	y
$(A\ B\ C\ D)$	$(\ )$
$(B\ C\ D)$	(A)
$(C\ D)$	$(B\ A)$
(D)	$(C\ B\ A)$
$(\ )$	$(D\ C\ B\ A)$

What follows is *reverse*, where we use a sub-function *rev'* to do the hard work and perform the initialization with the second argument to *rev'*.

$$reverse[x] <= rev'[x;(\ )]$$

$$rev'[x;y] <= [null[x] \rightarrow y;\ t \rightarrow rev'[rest[x];concat[first[x];y]]]$$

This *reverse* function builds up the new list by *concat*-ing the elements onto the second argument of *rev'*. Since y was initialized to $(\ )$ we are assured that the resulting construct will be a list. We will see a "direct" definition of the reversing function in a moment.

The development of an algorithm which constructs new objects may not always be so straightforward. Suppose we require a LISP function named *append* of two list arguments, x and y, which is to return a new list which has x appended onto the front of y. For example:

$$append[(A\ B\ D);(C\ E)] = (A\ B\ D\ C\ E)$$

$$append[A;(B\ C)]\ =\ \perp \text{ since } A \text{ is not a list.}$$

$$append[(A\ B\ C);(\ )] = append[(\ );(A\ B\ C)] = (A\ B\ C)$$

append is a partial function; it should be defined by recursion, but recursion on which argument? If either argument is $(\ )$ then the value given by *append* is the other argument. The next simplest case is a one-element list; if exactly one of x or y is a singleton how does that help us discover the recurrence relation for appending? It doesn't help much if y is a singleton; but if x is a singleton, then *append* could give:

$$concat[first[x];y] \text{ as result}$$

So recursion on x is likely. The definition now follows.

$$append[x;y] <= [null[x] \rightarrow y;\ t \rightarrow concat[first[x];append[rest[x];y]]].$$

Notice that the construction of the result is a bit more obscure than that involved in *reverse*. The construction has to "wait" until we have seen the end of the list x. For example:

$$append[(A\ B\ C);(D\ E\ F)] \quad = concat[A;append[(B\ C);(D\ E\ F)]]$$
$$= concat[A;concat[B;append[(C);(D\ E\ F)]]]$$
$$= concat[A;$$
$$concat[B;$$
$$concat[C;$$
$$append[(\ );(D\ E\ F)]]]]$$
$$= concat[A;concat[B;concat[C;(D\ E\ F)]]]$$
$$= concat[A;concat[B;(C\ D\ E\ F)]]$$
$$= concat[A;(B\ C\ D\ E\ F)]$$
$$= (A\ B\ C\ D\ E\ F)$$

We are assured of constructing a list here because y is a list and we are *concat*-ing onto the front of it. LISP functions which are to construct list output by *concat*-ing *must* concatenate onto the front of an existing *list*. That list may be either non-empty or the empty list, ( ). This is why the termination condition on a list-constructing function, such as the following function, *dotem*, returns ( ).

$$dotem[x;y] <= [\ null[x] \rightarrow (\ );$$
$$t \rightarrow concat[cons[first[x];first[y]];dotem[rest[x];rest[y]]]]$$

The arguments to *dotem* are both lists assumed to contain the same number of elements. The value returned is to be a list of dotted pairs; the elements of the pairs are the corresponding elements of the input lists.

Note the use of both *concat* and *cons*: *concat* is used to build the final list output; *cons* is used to build the dotted pairs. Now if we had written *dotem* such that it knew about our representation of lists, then *both* functions would have been *cons*. The definition would not have been as clear.
Look at a computation as simple as $dotem[(A);(B)]$. This will involve

$$concat[cons[A;B];dotem[(\ );(\ )]]$$

Now the evaluation of $dotem[(\ );(\ )]$ returns our needed ( ), giving

$$concat[cons[A;B];(\ )] = concat[(A\ .\ B);(\ )] = ((A\ .\ B))$$

If the termination condition of *dotem* returned anything other than ( ) then the list-construction would "get off on the wrong foot" and would not generate a list.

As promised on page 48, here is a "direct" definition of *reverse*.

$$reverse[x] <= [null[x] \rightarrow (\ );$$
$$t \rightarrow append[reverse[rest[x]];concat[first[x];(\ )]]]$$

This reversing function is not as efficient as the previous one. Within the construction of the reversed list the *append* function is called repeatedly. You should evaluate something like $reverse[(A\ B\ C\ D)]$ to see the difficulty.

It *is* possible to write a directly recursive reversing function with no auxiliary functions, no functions other than the primitives, and with not much clarity. We shall persist because it is a good example of discovering the general case of the recursion by careful consideration of examples. Let us call the function *rev*.

We consider the general case first, and postpone the termination conditions until later. Consider, for example, *rev[(A B C D)]*. This should evaluate to *(D C B A)*. How can we construct this list by recursive calls on *rev*? Assume *x* has value *(A B C D)*. Now note that *(D C B A)* is the value of *concat[D;(C B A)]*. Then *D* is *first[rev[rest[x]]]* (it is also *first[rev[x]]* but that would not help us since the recursion must reduce the complexity of the argument).

How can we get *(C B A)*? Well:

$$
\begin{aligned}
(C\ B\ A) &= rev[(A\ B\ C)] \\
&= rev[concat[A;(B\ C)]]
\end{aligned}
$$

(we are going after *rest[x]* again,
but first we can get *A* from *x*.

$$
\begin{aligned}
&= rev[concat[first[x];(B\ C)]] \\
&= rev[concat[first[x];rev[(C\ B)]]] \\
&= rev[concat[first[x];rev[rest[(D\ C\ B)]]]] \\
&= rev[concat[first[x];rev[rest[rev[rest[x]]]]]]
\end{aligned}
$$

That is, *rev[x]* looks like   *concat[first[rev[rest[x]]];*
                                                rev[concat[first[x];
                                                               rev[rest[rev[rest[x]]]]]]]

Now, the termination conditions are simple. First *rev[( )]* gives *( )*. But notice that the general case which we just constructed has *two concats*. That means the shortest list which it can make is of length two. So lists of length one are also handled separately: the reverse of such a list is itself. Thus the complete definition should be:

rev[x] <= [*null[x]* → ( );
                null[rest[x]] → *x*;

                t → *concat[first[rev[rest[x]]];*
                           rev[concat[first[x];
                                    rev[rest[rev[rest[x]]]]]]]]

We have only hinted at the issue of efficiency in computation. The question of efficiency involves deeper questions of the evaluation mechanisms. We will return to these issues after we have discussed the LISP evaluation scheme more completely.

Problems

1 Use the following definition:

$$match[k;m] <= [null[k] \rightarrow NO;$$
$$null[m] \rightarrow NO;$$
$$eq[first[k];first[m]] \rightarrow first[k];$$
$$t \rightarrow match[rest[k];rest[m]]]$$

and evaluate:
  a. $match[(X);(X)]$ **b.** $match[(A\ B\ E);(J\ O\ E)]$
  c. $match[(F\ O\ O);(B\ A\ Z)]$

2. Now write your own functions:
    a. $among[x;y] <= ...$: *among* is to be a predicate; x is an atom; y is a list
            of atoms. *among* is to return f if x is not found as an element
            of y; otherwise, *among* is to return t.

  e.g. $among[A;(A\ B\ C)] = among[A;(C\ D\ E\ A)] = t$
      $among[A1;(A2\ B2)] = f.$

    b. $anywhere[x;y] <= ...$: *anywhere* is a predicate; x is an atom; y is an
                arbitrary S-expr or list. *anywhere* is to return t just in the
                case that x appears somewhere in y.

  e.g. $anywhere[A;(A\ B\ C)] = anywhere[A;((A\ .\ B)\ .\ C)] = t$
      $anywhere[A;(B\ C\ D)] = f.$

    c. $collectpair[z;x;y] <= ...$: x and y are atoms; z is an S-expression or list,
                 some of whose subexpressions, may begin $(x\ ...)$ or
                 $(y\ ...)$. *collectpair* is to return a dotted pair whose
                 car-part is a list of all the occurrences of $(x\ ...)$ and
                 whose *cdr*-part is a list of all occurrences of $(y\ ...)$.

  e.g. $collectpair[((A\ 1)\ ((B\ .\ 2)\ (C\ A\ 4)));A;B] = (((A\ 1)\ (A\ 4))\ .\ ((B\ .\ 2)))$

    d. $pred[x] <= ...$: x is a positive integer. *pred* is a function, returning the
             predecessor of its argument. The only arithmetic function you
             may use is *add1*.

  e.g. $pred[3] = 2;$ $pred[0]$ is undefined;
      $pred[add1[x]] = x$ for $x \geq 0$.

    e. $signum[x] <= ...$: x is an integer. *signum* returns $NEGATIVE$, $ZERO$,
             or $POSITIVE$ depending on the sign of x. You may use
             add1 and *sub1* but no comparision function other than *eq*.

f. *maxdepth*[l] <= ... : l is a list. This function is to find the maximum depth of nesting of any element in l. Assume that l is a strict list (see page 36); that is, any sub-element is either atomic or is itself a strict list. For example

maxdepth[( )] = 0; *maxdepth*[(((B) C) A)] = 3

CHAPTER 2

Applications of LISP

"...*All the time I design programs for nonexisting machines and add: 'if we now had a machine comprising the primitives here assumed, then the job is done.'*
... In actual practice, of course, this ideal machine will turn out not to exist, so our next task --structurally similar to the original one-- is to program the simulation of the "upper" machine.... But this bunch of programs is written for a machine that in all probability will not exist, so our next job will be to simulate it in terms of programs for a next lower level machine, etc., until finally we have a program that can be executed by our hardware...."

E. W. Dijkstra, [Dij 72]

2.1 Introduction

There are several ways of interpreting this remark of Dijkstra. Anyone who has programmed at a level higher than machine language has experienced the phenomenon. The act of programming in a high-level language is that of writing algorithms for a nonexistent high-level machine. Typically however, the changes of representation from machine to machine are all done automatically: from high-level, to assembly language, and finally to hardware instructions.

A related view of Dijkstra's remark involves our discussions of abstract data structures and algorithms. We express our algorithms and data structures in terms of abstractions independent of how they may be represented in a machine; indeed we can use the ideas of abstraction *regardless* of whether the formalism will find a representation on a machine. This use of abstraction is the true sense of the programming style called "structured programming". We will see in this chapter how this programming style is a natural result of writing representation-independent LISP programs.

As we have previously remarked, we will see a close relationship between the structure of an algorithm and the structure of the data. We have seen this already on a small scale: list-algorithms tend to recur "linearly" on *rest* to ( ); S-expr algorithms tend to recur "left-and-right" on *car* and *cdr*, finally decomposing the expression to atoms. Indeed, the instances of control structures appearing in an algorithm typically parallel the style of inductive definition of the data structure which the algorithm is examining. [1]

If a structure is defined as:

$$\mathfrak{D} ::= \mathfrak{D}_1 \mid \mathfrak{D}_2 \mid \mathfrak{D}_3$$
e.g.   <seq elem> ::= <indiv> | <seq>

then we can expect to find a conditional expression whose predicate positions are filled by the recognizers for the $\mathfrak{D}_i$'s.

If the structure is defined as:

$$\mathfrak{D} ::= \mathfrak{D}_1 \; ... \; \mathfrak{D}_1$$
e.g.   <seq> ::= (<seq elem>, ..., <seq elem>)

that is, a homogeneous sequence of elements, then we will have a "linear" recursion like that experienced in list-algorithms. [2]

---

[1] The ideas sketched here have more formal explanations in algebraic notions; see [Hen 75].

[2] Indeed there are other forms of control like iteration or *lit* (page 196) which are related to such data structures.

Finally if the structure is defined with a fixed number of components as:

$$\mathfrak{D} ::= \mathfrak{D}_1\, \mathfrak{D}_2\, \mathfrak{D}_3 ... \mathfrak{D}_n$$

e.g.   <sexpr> ::= (<sexpr> . <sexpr>)

then we can expect occurrences of selector functions to extract the components from the structure. [3]

Thus a data-structure algorithm tends to "pass off" its work to subfunctions which will operate on the components of the data structure. Thus if a structure of type $\mathfrak{D}$ is made up of components of types $\mathfrak{D}_1$, $\mathfrak{D}_2$, $\mathfrak{D}_3$, and $\mathfrak{D}_4$, then the structure of an algorithm f operating on $\mathfrak{D}$ typically involves calls on subfunctions f_1 through f_4 to handle the subcomputations. Each f_i will in turn break up its $\mathfrak{D}_i$. Thus the type-structure of the call on f would be:

$$f[\mathfrak{D}] = g[f_1[\mathfrak{D}_1], f_2[\mathfrak{D}_2], f_3[\mathfrak{D}_3], f_4[\mathfrak{D}_4]]$$

This is the essence of level-wise programming: we write f, $f_1, ... , f_4$ independently of the representation of their data structures. f will run provided that the f_i's are available. As we write the f_i's we will probably invoke computations on components of the corresponding $\mathfrak{D}_i$. Those computations are in turn executed by subfunctions which we have to write. This process of elaboration terminates when all subfunctions are written and all data structures have received concrete representations. In LISP this means the lowest level functions are expressed in terms of LISP primitives and the data structures are represented in terms of S-exprs. Thus at the highest level we tend to think of a data structure as a class of behaviors; we don't care about the internal mechanisms which implement that behavior. At the lowest level, machine-language routines simulate *one* of many possible representations.

This process of elaboration of abstract algorithm and abstract data structure may modify the top-level definition of f. In reality, implementation considerations may effect some earlier decisions and require replanning of an earlier strategy. At that time the complete plan should be re-examined; local modifications may have global repercussions. A programming style is not a panacea; it is no substitute for clear thinking. It only helps control the complexity of the programming process.

---

[3]You may have noticed that we are therefore dealing with essentially "context-free" abstract data structures; i.e., those generated by context-free grammars. See [Hop 69].

2.2 Examples of LISP Applications

The next few sections will examine some non-trivial problems involving computations on data structures. We will describe the problem intuitively, pick an initial representation for the problem, write the LISP algorithm, and in some cases "tune" the algorithm by picking "more efficient" data representations.

The examples share other important characteristics:

1. We examine the problem domain and attempt to represent its elements as data structures.
2. We reflect on our (intuitive) algorithm and try to express it as a LISP-like data-structure manipulating function.
3. While performing 1 and 2, we might have to modify some of our decisions. Something assumed to be structure might better be represented as algorithm, or some algorithm might be better repesented as a data structure.
4. When the decisions are made, we evaluate the LISP function on a representation of a problem.
5. We reinterpret the data-structure output as an answer to our problem.

Pictorially in terms of LISP:

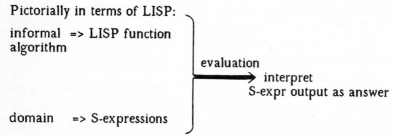

informal => LISP function
algorithm

                   evaluation

                          interpret
                          S-expr output as answer

domain   => S-expressions

Whenever we write computer programs, whatever language we use, we always go through a similar representation problem. The process is more apparent in a higher-level language like FORTRAN or ALGOL, and is most noticeable in a language like LISP which primarily deals with data structures.

When we deal with numerical algorithms, the representation problem has usually been settled in the transformation from real-world situation to a numerical problem. One has to think more explicitly about representation when we deal with structures like arrays or matrices. We are encoding our information in the array. But the preceding diagram occurs within the machine, even for strictly non-structured numerical calculation.

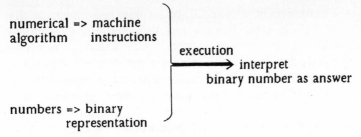

numerical => machine
algorithm   instructions

          execution
                → interpret
                binary number as answer

numbers => binary
        representation

The encodings are done by the input routines. The result of the execution is presented to the external world by the output routines.

However, when we come to data-structure computations, the representation problem really becomes apparent. We have to think more about what we are doing since we lack certain preconceptions or intuitions about such computations. More importantly, we are trying to represent actual problems *directly* as machine problems. We do not attempt to first analyze them into a complex mathematical theory, but try to express our intuitive theory directly as manipulations of data-structures. This is a different kind of thinking, due wholly to the advent of computers. Indeed the field of computation has expanded so much as to make the term "computer" obsolete. "Structure processor" is more indicative of the proper level at which we should view "computers".

We have already seen a simple example of the representation problem in the discussion of list-notation beginning in Section 1.6.

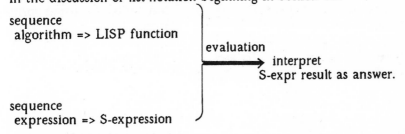

sequence
 algorithm => LISP function

              evaluation
                  → interpret
                  S-expr result as answer.

sequence
 expression => S-expression

The following sections deal with representation of complex data structure problems in LISP.

2.3 Differentiation

This example will describe a rudimentary differentiation routine for polynomials in several variables. We will develop this algorithm through several stages. We will begin by doing a very direct, but representation-dependent, implementation. We will encode polynomials as special LISP lists and will express the differentiation algorithm as a LISP program operating on that representation. When this program is completely specified we will then scrutinize it, attempting to see just how much of the program and data structure is *representation* and how much is essential to the algorithm.

You should recognize two facts about the differentiation algorithm for polynomials: first, the algorithm operates on forms (or expressions) as arguments and returns forms as values. Previously discussed algorithms have operated on simple values and produced simple values. The differentiation algorithm takes expressions as arguments and produces a new expression as value. Second, you should realize that the algorithm for differentiation is *recursive*. The question of differentiating a sum is reduced to the ability to differentiate each summand. Similar relationships hold for products, differences, and powers. There must be some termination conditions. Differentiation of a variable, say x, with respect to x is defined to be the number one; differentiating a constant, or a variable not equal to x with respect to x gives a result of zero. This begins to sound like the **IND**-definitions of sets (in this case the set of polynomials) and the associated **REC**-definitions of algorithms (in this case differentiation of polynomials). If this *is* the mold into which our current problem fits, then we must give an inductive definition of our set of polynomials. Though polynomials can be arbitrarily complex, involving the operations of addition, multiplication, negation, and exponentiation, their general format is very simple if they are described in our LISP-like notation where the operation precedes its operands. We assume that binary plus, times, and exponentiation are symbolized by +, *, and ↑; we will write +[x;2] instead of the usual infix notation x+2. The general term for this LISP-like notation is **prefix notation**.

Here are some examples of infix and prefix representations:

infix	prefix
$x*z+2y$	+[*[x;z]; *[2;y]]
$x*y*z$	*[x;*[y;z]]

We now give an inductive definition of the set of polynomials we wish to consider. The definition will involve an inductive definition of terms.

1. Any term is a polynomial.
2. If p_1 and p_2 are polynomials then the "sum" of p_1 and p_2 is a polynomial.

where:

1. Constants and variables are terms.
2. If t_1 and t_2 are terms then the "product" of t_1 and t_2 is a term.
3. If t_1 is a variable and t_2 is a constant then "t_1 raised to the t_2^{th} power" is a term.
4. If t_1 is a term then "minus" t_1 is a term.

We now give a BNF description of the above set using the syntax of prefix notation:

<poly>   ::= <term> | <plus>[<poly>;<poly>]
<term>   ::= <constant>
            ::= <variable>
            ::= <times>[<term>;<term>]
            ::= <expt>[<variable>;<constant>]
            ::= <minus><term>
<constant> ::= <numeral>
<plus>   ::= +
<times>   ::= *
<expt>   ::= ↑
<minus>   ::= -
<variable> ::= <identifier>

It is easy to write recursive algorithms in LISP; the only problem here is that the domain and range of LISP functions is S-exprs, not the polynomials. We need to represent arbitrary polynomials as S-exprs. We will do the representation in lists rather than S-exprs.

Let $\mathfrak{R}$ be a function mapping polynomals to their representation such that a variable is mapped to its uppercase counterpart in the vocabulary of LISP atoms. Thus:

$$\mathfrak{R}[\![\text{<variable>}]\!] = \text{<literal atom>}$$

Let constants (numerals), be just the LISP numerals; these are also respectable LISP atoms. Thus:

$$\mathfrak{R}[\![\text{<numeral>}]\!] = \text{<numeral>}$$

We have now specified a representation for the base domains of the inductive definition of our polynomials. It is time to develop the termination cases for the recursive definition of differentiation.

We know from differential calculus that if u is a constant or a variable then:

$$du/dx = \quad 1 \text{ if } x = u$$
$$0 \text{ otherwise}$$

We will represent the d-operator as a binary LISP function named *diff*. The application, du/dx will be represented as *diff*[u;x]. Since constants and variables are both represented as atoms, we can check for both of these cases by using the predicate *isindiv*. Thus a representation of the termination cases might be:

$$diff[u;x] <= [isindiv[u] \rightarrow [eq[x;u] \rightarrow 1; \mathfrak{t} \rightarrow 0] \dots]$$

Notice we write the abbreviation, *isindiv* instead of *isindiv$_r$*. You should be a bit wary of our definition already: *diff[1;1]* will evaluate to *1*.

Now that we have covered the termination case, what can be done for the representation of the remaining class of terms and polynomials? That is, how should we represent sums and products?

First, we will represent the operations *, +, -, and ↑ as atoms:

$$\Re[\![\ +\ ]\!] = PLUS$$
$$\Re[\![\ *\ ]\!] = TIMES$$
$$\Re[\![\ -\ ]\!] = MINUS$$
$$\Re[\![\ ↑\ ]\!] = EXPT$$

We will now extend the mapping $\Re$ to occurrences of binary operators by mapping to three-element lists:

$$\Re[\![\ \alpha[\beta_1;\beta_2]\ ]\!] = (\Re[\![\alpha]\!], \Re[\![\beta_1]\!], \Re[\![\beta_2]\!])$$

Unary applications will result in two-element lists:

$$\Re[\![\ \alpha[\beta]\ ]\!] = (\Re[\![\alpha]\!], \Re[\![\beta]\!])$$

For example: $\Re[\![\ +[x;\ 2]\ ]\!] = (PLUS\ X\ 2)$

For a more complicated example, the polynomial

$$x^2 + 2yz + u$$

will be translated to the following prefix notation:

$$+[↑[x;2];\ +[*[2,*[y;z]];\ u]]\qquad [4]$$

From this it's easy to get the list form:

$$(PLUS\ (EXPT\ X\ 2)\ (PLUS\ (TIMES\ 2\ (TIMES\ Y\ Z))\ U))$$

Now we can complete the differentiation algorithm for + and *. We know:

$$d[f + g]/dx = df/dx + dg/dx.$$

Expressing this phrase as part of *diff*,

we would see: $u = \Re[\![\ f + g\ ]\!] = (PLUS, \Re[\![\ f\ ]\!], \Re[\![\ g\ ]\!])$

where: $second[u] = \Re[\![f]\!]$ and, $third[u] = \Re[\![\ g\ ]\!]\qquad [5]$

---

[4]This is messier than it really needs to be because we assume that + and * are binary. You should also notice that our $\Re$-mapping is applicable to a larger class of expressions than just \<poly\>. Look at $(x + y)*(z + 2)$.

[5]As we intimated earlier, we have entered an unwise course here. We have tied the algorithm for symbolic differentiation to a specific representation for polynomials. Believing that much can be learned from seeing mistakes, we will use that representation, and on page 62 we will examine our decision.

The result of differentiating u is to be a new list of three elements:

1. The symbol *PLUS*.
2. The effect of *diff* operating $\mathfrak{R}[\![f]\!]$
3. The effect of *diff* operating $\mathfrak{R}[\![g]\!]$

Thus another part of the algorithm:

$$eq[first[u];PLUS] \rightarrow list\,[PLUS;\ diff[second[u];x];diff[third[u];x]]$$

$d[f*g]/dx$ is defined to be $f*\ dg/dx + g*df/dx$.

So here's another part of *diff*:

$$eq[first[u];TIMES] \rightarrow\ list[PLUS;$$
$$list[TIMES;\ second[u];diff[third[u];x]];$$
$$list[TIMES;third[u];diff[second[u];x]]]$$

Finally, here's an example. We know:

$$d[x*y + x]/dx = y + 1$$

Try:

diff $[(PLUS\ (TIMES\ X\ Y)\ X);\ X]$
$= list[PLUS;\ diff[(TIMES\ X\ Y);\ X];diff[X;X]]$
$= list[\ PLUS;$
 $\quad list[PLUS;$
 $\qquad list[TIMES;\ X;\ diff[Y;X]];$
 $\qquad list[TIMES;\ Y;\ diff[X;X]]];$
 $\quad diff[X;X]]$

$= list[\ PLUS;$
 $\quad list[PLUS;$
 $\qquad list[TIMES;\ X\ ;0];$
 $\qquad list[TIMES;\ Y;1]];$
 $\quad 1\ ]$

$=(PLUS\ (PLUS\ (TIMES\ X\ 0)\ (TIMES\ Y\ 1))\ 1)$

which can be interpreted as:

$$x*0 + y*1 + 1$$

Now it is clear that we have the right answer; it is equally clear that the final representation leaves much to be desired. There are obvious simplifications which would have done before we would consider this output acceptable. This example is a particularly simple case for algebraic simplification. We can easily write a LISP program to perform simplifications like those expected here: like replacing $0*x$ by 0, and $x*1$ by x. But the general problem of writing simplifiers, or indeed of recognizing what is a "simplification", is quite difficult. A whole branch of computer science has grown up around symbolic and algebraic manipulation of expressions. One of the crucial parts of such an endeavor is a sophisticated simplifier. For more details and examples of the power of such systems see [Hea 68], [MAC 74], or [Mos 74].

Points to note

This problem of representation is typical of data structure algorithms regardless of what language you use. That is, once you have decided what the informal algorithm is, pick a representation which makes your algorithms clean. Examine the interplay between the algorithm and the representation, and continue to examine your decisions as you refine your method. In Section 2.6 we will see a series of representations, each becoming more and more "efficient" and each requiring more "knowledge" being built into the algorithm. The remainder of this section will reexamine our representations in the differentiation algorithm.

First, here is the complete *diff* algorithm for + and *:

$diff[u;x] <= [isindiv[u] \rightarrow [eq[x;u] \rightarrow 1; t \rightarrow 0];$
$\qquad\qquad eq[first [u]; PLUS] \rightarrow list[PLUS;$
$\qquad\qquad\qquad\qquad\qquad diff[second[u]; x];$
$\qquad\qquad\qquad\qquad\qquad diff[third[u]; x]];$
$\qquad\qquad eq[first[u]; TIMES] \rightarrow list[PLUS;$
$\qquad\qquad\qquad\qquad\qquad list[TIMES;$
$\qquad\qquad\qquad\qquad\qquad\quad second[u];$
$\qquad\qquad\qquad\qquad\qquad\quad diff[third[u]; x]];$
$\qquad\qquad\qquad\qquad\qquad list[TIMES;$
$\qquad\qquad\qquad\qquad\qquad\quad third[u];$
$\qquad\qquad\qquad\qquad\qquad\quad diff[second[u]; x]]];$

$\qquad\quad t \rightarrow \perp]$ [6]

As we mentioned earlier, the current manifestation of *diff* encodes too much of our particular representation for polynomials. The separation of algorithm from representation is beneficial from at least two standpoints. First, changing representation should have a minimal effect on the structure of the

---

[6]The element $\perp$ is not strictly part of LISP.

algorithm; but *diff* knows that variables are represented as atoms and knows that a sum is represented as a list whose *first*-part is *PLUS*. Second, readability of the algorithm suffers greatly. How much of *diff* really needs to know about the representation and how can we improve the readability of *diff*?

The uses of *first, second,* and *third* are not particularly mnemonic. [7] We used *second* to get the first argument to a sum or product and used *third* to get the second. We used *first* to extract the operator. However *first, second,* and *third* select components of sequences; they know nothing about polynomials. We want to refer to polynomials as abstract data structures. Let's define the selectors:

$$op[x] <= first[x]$$
$$arg_1[x] <= second[x]$$
$$arg_2[x] <= third[x]$$

Then *diff* becomes:

$$diff[u;x] <= [isindiv[u] \to [eq[x;u] \to 1; t \to 0];$$
$$eq[op[u]; PLUS] \to \quad list[PLUS;$$
$$diff[arg_1[u]; x];$$
$$diff[arg_2[u]; x]];$$
$$eq[op[u]; TIMES] \to list[PLUS;$$
$$list[TIMES;$$
$$arg_1[u];$$
$$diff[arg_2[u]; x]];$$
$$list[TIMES;$$
$$arg_2[u];$$
$$diff[arg_1[u]; x]]];$$

$$t \to \perp]$$

Still, there is much of the representation present. Recognition of variables and other terms can be abstracted. We need only recognize when a term is a sum, a product, a variable or a constant. To test for the occurrence of a numeral we shall assume a unary LISP predicate called *numberp* which returns t just in the case that its argument is a numeral. Then, in terms of the current representation, we could define such recognizers and predicates as:

$$issum[x] <= eq[op[x];PLUS]$$
$$isprod[x] <= eq[op[x];TIMES]$$
$$isconst[x] <= numberp[x]$$

$$isvar[x] <= [isindiv[x] \to not[isconst[x]]; t \to f]$$
$$samevar[x;y] <= eq[x;y]$$

---

[7]However, they are more readable than *car-cdr*-chains.

Now we can rewrite *diff* as:

```
diff[u;x] <= [isvar[u] → [samevar[x;u] → 1; t → 0];
             isconst[u] → 0;
             issum[u] → list[PLUS;
                             diff[arg1[u]; x];
                             diff[arg2[u]; x]];
             isprod[u] → list[PLUS;
                              list[TIMES;
                                   arg1[u];
                                   diff[arg2[u]; x]];
                              list[TIMES;
                                   arg2[u];
                                   diff[arg1[u]; x]]];
             t → ⊥]
```

Readability is certainly improving, but the representation is still known to *diff*. When we build the result of the sum or product of derivatives we use knowledge of the representation. It would be better to define:

```
makesum[x;y] <= list[PLUS;x;y]

makeprod[x;y] <= list[TIMES;x;y]
```

Then the new *diff* is:

```
diff[u;x] <= [isvar[u] → [samevar[x;u] → 1; t → 0];
             isconst[u] → 0;
             issum[u] → makesum[ diff[arg1[u]; x];
                                  diff[arg2[u]; x]];
             isprod[u] → makesum[makeprod[arg1[u];
                                          diff[arg2[u]; x]];
                                 makeprod[arg2[u];
                                          diff [arg1[u]; x]]];
             t → ⊥]
```

In the process, *diff* has become much more understandable and, more importantly, the details of the representation have been relegated to subfunctions. Changing representation simply requires supplying different subfunctions. No changes need be made to *diff*. There has only been a slight decrease in efficiency. The termination condition in the original *diff* is a bit more succinct, but speaking precisely it was incorrect. The gain in independence far outweighs the slight efficiency consideration. Looking back, first we abstracted the selector functions: those which selected components; next we abstracted the recognizers: the predicates indicating which kind of term was present; finally we modified the constructors: the functions which make new terms. These three components of programming:

selectors, recognizers, and constructors, will appear again on page 164 in a discussion of McCarthy's abstract syntax.

The *diff* algorithm is much more abstract now, in the sense that the representation of the domain and the representation of the functions and predicates which manipulate that domain have been extracted out. [8] This is our $\Re$-mapping again; we mapped the domain of <poly>'s to lists and mapped the constructors, selectors, and recognizers to list-manipulating functions. Thus the data types of the arguments u and x are <poly> and <var> respectively, *not* list and atom. To stress this point we should make one more transformation on *diff*. We have frequently said that there is a substantial parallel between a data structure and the algorithms which manipulate it. Paralleling the BNF definition of <poly> on page 59, we write:

$$diff[u;x] <= [isterm[u] \to diffterm[u;x];$$
$$issum[u] \to makesum[diff[arg_1[u]; x];$$
$$diff[arg_2[u]; x]];$$

$$t \to \perp]$$

$$diffterm[u;x] <= [isconst[u] \to 0;$$
$$isvar[u] \to [samevar[x;u] \to 1; t \to 0];$$
$$isprod[u] \to makesum[makeprod[arg_1[u];$$
$$diff[arg_2[u]; x]];$$
$$makeprod[arg_2[u];$$
$$diff[arg_1[u]; x]]];$$

$$t \to \perp]$$

To satisfy our complaint of page 59 that *diff*[1; 1] gives a defined result, we should also add:

$$diff'[u; x] <= [isvar[x] \to [ispoly[u] \to diff[u; x]]; t \to \perp]$$

Finally, notice that our abstraction process has masked the order-dependence of conditional expressions. Exactly one of the recognizers will be satisfied by the form u.

Problems

1. Extend the version of *diff* of your choice to handle differentiation of powers such as ↑[x; *3*].
2. Extend *diff* to handle unary minus.
3. Extend *diff* to handle differentiation of the trigonometric functions, *sin* and *cos* and their composition with polynomials. For example it should handle $sin^2x + cos(x^3 + 5x -2)$.
4. Write an algorithm to handle integration of polynomials.

---

[8]To be particularly precise, our references to *0* and *1* should really be *mkconst*[*0*] and *mkconst*[*1*], signifying the functions which make constants.

2.4 Tree Searching

A natural application of LISP's recursive power occurs in tree searching algorithms. These algorithms are the heart of programs which play games. A ubiquitous feature of sophisticated game playing is "a strategy". In a simple game, for example tic-tac-toe, an optimal strategy may be easily computable. In games like checkers and chess, the algorithmic approach would require enormous computational power; heuristic methods are applied to reduce the computational requirements.

The heart of this strategy formation is often a tree structure. That tree will have nodes representing "possible moves". In a single-person game, the evaluation of the tree will result in a "best move"; any move that wins. In a two-person game we must be more careful; the branching structure will represent *both* your moves and those of the opponent, and the position evaluation must take that into account: "Now if I move here, then my opponent will move there, ..."

The tree-structured data and recursive programming style of LISP, allow simple formulations of complex tree strategies. The description involves discussion of the abstract data structures and their representations. The objects are finitely branching trees; that is, we assume that any node in a tree can have any finite number of branches. We will also assume that the trees will terminate on all of their branches. We need a recognizer, named *is_term*, which will return t if the tree is the trivial terminal tree with no branches. A terminal tree may either be a *WIN* or a *LOSS*. If it's a win, we know how to achieve our goal; if it's a *LOSS*, then we look further. That "further" says examine the alternatives the immediate parent of that node; if there aren't any alternatives then back up to the grandparent.

If a tree has branches they are located by the selector *branches*. We will assume those branches are presented as an ordered sequence, perhaps ordered by their plausible value. Therefore we will use the selectors *first* and *rest* to select candidate branches.

$eval\_tree[tr] <= [\; is\_term[tr] \rightarrow [is\_win[tr] \rightarrow tr; \; t \rightarrow LOSS];$
$\qquad\qquad t \rightarrow eval\_branches[branches[tr]]]$

$eval\_branches[l] <= [null[l] \rightarrow LOSS;$
$\qquad\qquad eq[LOSS; eval\_tree[first[l]]] \rightarrow eval\_branches[rest[l]];$
$\qquad\qquad t \rightarrow first[l]]$

The simplicity of the description is pleasing. It encourages us to proceed to more complex tree strategies.

Attempts at exhaustive search of game trees becomes prohibitively expensive when applied to games like checkers and chess. However, computers have had reasonable success at checkers, and are beginning to play passable chess. A recent article, [Sug 77], addresses the feasibility of home chess machines. Those successes are based on more sophisticated analysis of game trees. The ideas involved in that analysis are easily expressed in LISP.

In the following discussions we will make several assumptions.

1. Our opponent is as smart as we are. This assumption allows us to use *our* evaluation function in evaluating the positions of our opponent.

2. We assume that our opponent is also trying to win. Therefore his move will reflect his best attempt to defeat us. Since we are using the same position-evaluator, his "maximal harm" is our "minimal good". We are thus following a "**max-min**" strategy wherein we attempt to find the best move which our opponent cannot turn into a disaster for us.

From these ideas we formulate our position evaluation strategy as follows:

1. Grow a tree of moves. First our possible moves from a position, then his counter moves; then our responses, etc. Continue this until the branch terminates or until a termination condition is forced. [9]

2. Once the tree is built, we evaluate the terminal nodes.

3. The values are propagated back up the tree using the min-max idea. If the preceding node is ours, we assign that node the maximum of the branch values; if the preceding node is his we assign the minimum of the values. We proceed in this fashion, finally returning the value of the "best path".

We will simplify matters somewhat, returning only the "value" of the best path. [10] First, we develop some subfunctions:

$$maxlist[l;f] <= [null[l] \rightarrow -\infty; \; t \rightarrow max[f[first[l]];$$
$$maxlist[rest[l];f]]]$$

$$minlist[l;f] <= [null[l] \rightarrow \infty; \; t \rightarrow min[f[first[l]];$$
$$minlist[rest[l];f]]]$$

The "∞" denotes a number, bigger than any other value our evaluation function f can concoct. The f is a different kind of variable from those we have seen before. It is used as a LISP function within the bodies of the definition, yet passed as a variable. It is therefore called a functional variable. We will discuss such variables in the next chapter, but for now the intent should be clear from some examples:

$$maxlist[(1 \; 3 \; 5 \; 2);add1] = 6 \text{ and } minlist[(1 \; 3 \; 5 \; 2);add1] = 2$$

With those preliminaries, we are ready to present the mini-max strategy:

---

[9]We assume we have methods for determining when a move is already present in the tree.

[10]We should really return the best value *and* a description of the best path.

$maxpos[p] <= [is\_term[p] \rightarrow value[p];$

$\qquad t \rightarrow maxlist[branches[p]; minpos]]$

$minpos[p] <= [is\_term[p] \rightarrow value[p];$

$\qquad t \rightarrow minlist[branches[p]; maxpos]]$

maxpos gives the value of a position for the maximizing player and *minpos* gives the value of a position for the minimizing player.   *value* is the terminal position evaluation function.

What's even more interesting is that there is a simple technique which will allow us to discover the optimal path, usually without having to visit all the nodes. The technique, discovered by John McCarthy in 1958, is called α-β pruning; it is based on the observation that if our opponent is assured that he can force us into an unfavorable position then he won't make a move which would give us a *better* position. That's obvious; what is *not* obvious is that he can often make such decisions on the basis of only a partial evaluation of the tree. Consider:

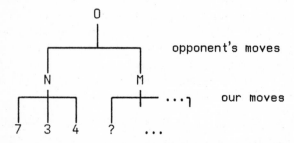

Since we are to evaluate the position at N, we maximize the position, getting 7; that becomes the value of node N. It is up to our opponent to evaluate position O, and he now knows we're going to get a 7 if he moves to N. He looks questioningly at "?"; if that value is greater than 7 then he immediately rejects move M without examining the other possibilities; things can only get worse for him. If "?" is less than 7, then he looks at additional alternatives at M. Once our opponent is finished evaluating the position, then it's our turn to play the game at the position above O, only now we will try to maximize what that stingy individual has left us. We let α be the value which must be exceeded for a position to be desirable by the position about to play; and let β be the value which must *not* be exceeded if the move leading to the position would be made by the opponent; in the above example 7 is the β-value when evaluating M. With that, we modify the min-max algorithms to include α-β pruning.

$maxlist_{\alpha\beta}[l;f;\alpha;\beta] <= [\ null[l] \rightarrow \alpha;$
$$f[first[l]] \geq \beta \rightarrow \beta;$$
$$t \rightarrow maxlist_{\alpha\beta}[\ rest[l];$$
$$f;$$
$$max[\alpha;f[first[l]]];$$
$$\beta]]$$

$minlist_{\alpha\beta}[l;f;\alpha;\beta] <= [\ null[l] \rightarrow \beta;$
$$f[first[l]] \leq \alpha \rightarrow \alpha;$$
$$t \rightarrow minlist_{\alpha\beta}[\ rest[l];$$
$$f;$$
$$\alpha;$$
$$min[\beta;f[first[l]]]]]$$

$maxpos_{\alpha\beta}[p;\alpha;\beta] <= [is\_term[p] \rightarrow max[\alpha;min[\beta;value[p]];$
$$t \rightarrow maxlist_{\alpha\beta}[branches[p]; minpos_1;\alpha;\beta]]$$

$minpos_1[x] <= minpos_{\alpha\beta}[x;\alpha;\beta]$

$minpos_{\alpha\beta}[p;\alpha;\beta] <= [\ is\_term[p] \rightarrow max[\alpha;min[\beta;value[p]];$
$$t \rightarrow minlist_{\alpha\beta}[branches[p]; maxpos_1;\alpha;\beta]]$$

$maxpos_1[x] <= maxpos_{\alpha\beta}[x;\alpha;\beta]$

The process can be initialized with α and β set to $-\infty$ and ∞ respectively. Tighter bounds on "acceptablility" can be enforced by picking different α's and β's. The effect will be to shorten the search time while, perhaps, ignoring some winning moves; *caveat emptor*.

This *not* a trivial algorithm. However its description as a LISP program is about as simple and as compact as you will find; anywhere.

2.5 Data Bases

One of the more intriguing applications of LISP is in the area of data base management. In this section we introduce the ideas and suggest how LISP can be applied to the problems.

A data base is a collection of objects together with a set of functions to pose questions about the objects in the base, to select objects from the base, and to construct new entries in the base. Expressed differently, a data base is an abstract data structure. We need to locate information in the base. We should be able to ask the system for a specific object or we should be able to partially specify our request ("find all books about LISP" or "find all books about LISP published before 1975"). We should be able to add entries and delete entries, but we will postpone these kinds of requests until later.

The representational details of objects will be suppressed as usual, and we will concentrate on the abstract properties. In our first example, the objects in the data base will represent constants: an object will have a name and a collection of properties and values.

prop1	val1
prop2	val2
propn	valn

An object representation

For example, a data base dealing with business supplies might have objects named boxes. Each box has properties like size and contents.

Not all objects need to have the same number of properties. For example in a data base whose objects are bibliographic references, books need not have page references, whereas journal articles require them; journal references don't include a publisher whereas books do. The programs which manipulate the data base must be structured to take changeablility into account.

Here are some examples: the first one was extracted from the side of a Xerox paper box; the second might be a representation of a bibliographic entry for this book.

NAME	4029258
SIZE	8-1/2 × 11
COLOR	WHITE
AMNT	10 REAMS

AUTHOR	ALLEN, JOHN, R.
TITLE	THE ANATOMY OF LISP
TYPE	BOOK
PUBL	MCGRAW-HILL
DATE	1977

Given a data base of objects, we need to be able to manipulate these objects in meaningful ways. We will not address the problems of designing input and output, but will concern ourselves solely with the problems of semantics of data base primitives: how can we use the information in the base?

In requesting information from a data base, we typically specify part of the request and expect the system to come up with a set of possibilities which fit our description. For example, the request: "find all books about LISP", specifies that we are interested only in books, not in journal articles or course notes; the topic is specified to be LISP, but the system is free to select the other components: the author, the title, the publisher and the date of publication. The objects which are specified are called **constants**, the unspecified components are **variables**. A request is a structure called a **pattern** and consists of an ordered collection of constants and variables. The elements in the data base are also patterns; for this example, they contain only constants; such constant patterns are also called records. The process of discovering whether or not a record in the data base matches the request is called **pattern matching**.

We describe a simple pattern matcher named *match*. It expects two arguments. The first argument is a constant pattern called *pat*. The second argument, *exp* represents a request; it may be constant, or it may contain variables. If it does contain variables, then the pattern matching process must establish a match between those variables and components of our data base object. The value returned by *match* will either represent the associations built up to match the constant pattern to the expression, or the value returned will indicate failure if no match is possible.

Patterns will be represented as lists with atoms representing constants, and variables represented as lower-case greek letters. We will represent failure by returning the atom *NO*. In the case that a match is possible, we will return a list of pairs, where each pair is a variable and its matching constant.

For example: $match[(A\ (B\ C));(A\ (B\ \alpha))] = ((\alpha\ C))$

$match[(A\ B\ C);(A\ \alpha\ \beta)] = ((\alpha\ B)\ (\beta\ C))$

$match[(A\ B\ C);(A\ C\ \beta)] = NO$

Pattern matching can become quite complex. For example:

$match[(A\ (B\ C)\ (D\ C));(A\ (B\ \alpha)\ (\beta\ C))] = ((\alpha\ C)\ (\beta\ D))$

$match[(A\ (B\ C)\ (D\ C));(A\ (B\ \alpha)\ (\alpha\ C))] = NO$

The second example fails since once we have associated C with α we must use that association throughout the rest of the pattern match; and $(D\ C)$ does not match $(\alpha\ C)$ when α denotes C. [11]

---

[11] This assumes that the match proceeds in a left-to-right order.

We will write *match* in terms of a subfunction named *match'*. This subfunction carries a third argument, *mlist*, which represents the list of partial matches. Whenever we locate a variable in the expression, we examine the current *mlist*. If the variable appears, then we must check its entry against the corresponding part of the pattern. If the variable does not occur in *mlist*, then we associate the variable with the appropriate part of the constant pattern.

$match[pat;exp] <= match'[pat;exp;(\ )]$

$$match'[pat;exp;mlist] <= [equal[mlist;NO] \rightarrow NO;$$
$$isconst[exp] \rightarrow [\ sameconst[pat;exp] \rightarrow mlist;$$
$$t \rightarrow NO];$$
$$isvar[exp] \rightarrow check[pat;$$
$$exp;$$
$$lookup[pat;mlist];$$
$$mlist];$$
$$t \rightarrow match'[suffix[pat];$$
$$suffix[exp];$$
$$match'[prefix[pat];prefix[exp];mlist]]$$

$$check[var;exp;val;mlist] <= [not[val] \rightarrow concat[mkent[var;exp];mlist];$$
$$sameconst[exp;val] \rightarrow mlist;$$
$$t \rightarrow NO]$$

$$lookup[var;l] <= [null[l] \rightarrow f;$$
$$samevar[var;name[first[l]]] \rightarrow val[first[l]];$$
$$t \rightarrow lookup[var;rest[l]]]$$

To complete our description of *match* we should supply the data structure manipulating functions: *isconst, isvar, prefix, suffix, samevar,* and *sameconst;* and *mkent, name,* and *val.* The first five are related, dealing with the representation of patterns; the final three involve the representation of the match list. Note that we *have* assumed that *mlist* is a list. We will restrict the match algorithm to simple matches on tree structure. We represent *prefix* as *first* and *suffix* and *rest* though much more general interpretations are possible. We leave it to the reader to supply representations of the missing functions.

Given a basic pattern matcher, we can begin to elaborate on a data base management system. We need some means of controlling the matcher. If several entries in the system match the inquiry, then we must decide how to manage the matches. In simple cases we could make a list of all the possibilities. If the number of matches is very large we might want to return a few at a time, remembering where we were in the search of the base. The natural extension of this idea is to allow a potentially infinite set of elements present in the data base. In programming languages we are able to talk about such potentialities by using a procedure.

Instead of having objects explicitly stored in the base, we may allow procedures to occur as data base elements. Such a procedure would generate elements. For example, instead of storing the integers as explicit objects, we could store a procedure to generate the integers. This introduces two problems: how do we store procedures as data objects; and, assuming that we have called such a procedure and it has delivered an explicit object, how do we represent the notion that the *next* time we call that procedure, we want the *next* object? That is, a procedure named *get_next_integer* should return *1* the first time it is called, but know to return *2* the next time it is called in the same context. It must also know to return *1* when it is called in a new context.

Other possible extensions involve the operations on the base. Assume that the base contains "all roses are red" and knows that object O_1 is a rose; if we ask the data base for all red objects, we should expect to see O_1 appear as a candidate. That expectation requires a deductive ability built into the base manipulator. That is, we need not have explicitly stored the information in the base, but we expect to be able to deduce facts from information in the base using some relationships and reasoning ability.

There are at least two ways the "roses are red" problem can be solved. Notice that "all roses are red" is much like a procedure; given an object which is a rose, it generates an object which is red. So, on entering a rose object in the data base, the system could also explicitly add the fact that the rose was red. This is an example of an **input demon**. A demon is a procedure which is not explicitly called but is activated by the occurrence of another event. Whenever an object is added to the base the collection of input demons is checked. If an applicable demon is found, it is activated; its activation might activate other demons.

The activation of a demon is a different kind of procedure call than previously seen. The activation is done on pattern matching rather than by a user-initiated call. Thus the calling style is generally known as **pattern directed invocation** ([Hew 72], [Bau 72]). The demon procedure is stored in the data base along with a pattern which determines conditions for its activation. In the case of an input demon, an input to the base initiates a match of the input demon patterns against the input. If a match is found, the corresponding procedures are executed. The match process can bind variables to parts of patterns and therefore the procedure typically has access to the match information.

Let's establish some notation and give an example. To introduce records to our system we use a unary procedure named *add_item*. The argument to *add_item* is the record we wish to add.

$$add\_item[(ROSE\ O1)]$$

We will use a ternary procedure named *add_demon* to insert demons in the base. The first argument is the type of demon; so far we have discussed demons invoked by adding elements; we will also have demons which are applied when items are removed, or when items are accessed. These three types will be named *ADD*, *REMOVE*, and *FETCH*. The second argument is the pattern which will invoke this demon; and the third argument is the action to be taken if the pattern matches. For example:

$$add\_demon[ADD;(ROSE\ \alpha);add\_item[(RED\ \alpha))]]$$

Demons are also used to monitor the removal of information from the base.

The third use of demons is involved with another possible solution to the "all roses are red" problem. Instead of explicitly adding the fact that *O1* is a red object we might wait until a request for red objects occurs. At that time we could use the "all roses are red" demon *backwards*. That is, we could look for any roses in the data base; the assertion that a "rose" object is also a "red" object allows us to accept "rose" objects as solutions to our inquiry. This feature introduces a certain deductive capability to our system. It also introduces some organizational problems.

We have to recognize when a procedure is capable of producing objects of the desired type. We therefore index these data base procedures by a pattern which tells what the procedure accomplishes. That pattern is called the procedure's goal and the invocation of such a procedure is again pattern-directed, but has an added connotation of being **goal-oriented**.

Again, we introduce some notation and an example. Let the request for a data base item be given by:

$$fetch[\alpha], \text{ where } \alpha \text{ is a pattern.}$$

Since a *fetch* request might discover several possibilities, some being items and some being goal-directed procedures, we need a way of examining the selected information.

We introduce a function named *try_next*, whose single argument is the result of a *fetch*. Each call on *try_next* either produces a new item or signals that no more items exist on the fetch list.

An extension to this basic data base manipulating system has become convenient in artificial intelligence research. Let us assume we wish to derive a plan or scheme for achieving a desired goal. In the derivation process we will make hypotheses and then pursue their implications. A similar behavior can be simulated if we allow the creation of multiple data bases. Each base corresponds to a hypothetical situation or world, and the *fetch*-ing of an object in a world corresponds to asking whether or not a desired state is attainable in that world.

Instead of requiring that all transformations occur in one data base, several systems ([Con 73], [QA4 72]) have implemented a layered data base. In this situation we are able to add, delete and fetch from specified data bases. We add two operations *push_base* and *pop_base* which allow us to manipulate whole data bases as objects.

The control structures necessary for handling such data base manipulations may be very non-structured; some of the implementation ideas for such control will be discussed in Section 4.5. We will discuss some details of the data structure implementation in Section 5.6. For more information see [McD 75] and [Con 73].

Problems

1. Recall our discussion of *match* on page 72. Supply a representation for match lists and supply the eight data structure functions.
2. The *match* routine we developed on page 72 required that *pat* be a constant pattern. Write a more general pattern matcher named *unify* which allows either *pat* or *exp* to contain variables. This more gereral match routine is called a unifier ([Rob 65]).

For example:

$$unify[(A\ (B\ \alpha)\ A);\ (A\ (\beta\ D)\ \delta)] = ((\alpha\ \ D)\ (\beta\ B)\ (\delta\ A))$$

$$unify[(A\ (B\ \alpha)\ A);\ (A\ (\beta\ D)\ \beta)] = NO$$

$$unify[(\alpha\ A\ \alpha);\ (\beta\ \beta\ B)] = NO$$

2.6 Algebra of Polynomials

Assume that we want to perform addition and multiplication of polynomials and further assume that each polynomial is of the form $p_1 + p_2 + ... + p_n$ where each term, p_i, is a product of variables and constants. The two components of each term are a constant part called the coefficient, and the variable part. We shall assume without loss of generality that the set of variables which appear in the polynomials are lexicographically ordered, e.g. $x < y < z$; and assume that each variable part obeys that ordering; thus we would insist that xzy^2 be written xy^2z. We do not assume that the terms are ordered within the polynomial; thus $x + xy$ and $xy + x$ are both acceptable. We further assume that the variables of each p_i are distinct and that no p_i has 0 as its coefficient. The standard algorithm for the addition of $\Sigma^n_{i=1}p_i$ with $\Sigma^m_{j=1}q_j$ indicates that q_j can be combined with a p_i if the variable parts of these terms are identical. In this case the resulting term has the same variable part but has a coefficient equal to the sum of the coefficients of p_i and q_j. We will examine four representations of polynomials, before finally writing any algorithms. To aid in the discussion we will use the polynomial $x^2 - 2y - z$ as our canonical example.

First representation

We could use the representation of the differentiation example. This would result in our example assuming the form:

(PLUS (TIMES 1 (EXPT X 2)) (PLUS (TIMES -2 Y) (TIMES -1 Z)))

The above conventions specify an unambiguous representation for our class of polynomials. Strictly speaking, we did not need to impose the ordering on the set of variables. However, we need to impose some additional constraints before we have data structures which are well-suited to the class of polynomial algorithms we wish to represent.

Second representation

We are really only interested in testing the equality of the variable parts; we will not be manipulating variable parts in any other way. So we might simply represent the variable part as a list of pairs; each pair contains a variable name and the corresponding value of the exponent. Knowing that polynomials are always sums, and knowing the class of algorithms we wish to implement, we write Σp_i as:

((rep of p_1), (rep of p_2), ...)

This representation would make our example appears as:

((TIMES 1 ((X . 2))) (TIMES -2 ((Y . 1))) (TIMES -1 ((Z . 1))))

This representation is sufficient and it does have the flexibility we need, but it is still not terribly satisfying. We are ignoring too much of the structure in our class of polynomials.

Third representation

We know that the occurrence of variables is ordered in each variable part; we can assume that we know the class of variables which may appear in any polynomial. So instead of writing x^2y^3z as

((X . 2) (Y . 3) (Z . 1)),

we could write: *(2 3 1)* assuming x, y, z are the only variables.

In a further simplification, notice that the *TIMES* in the representation is superfluous. We *always* multiply the coefficient by the variable part. So we could simply *concat* the coefficient onto the front of the variable part representation.

Let's stop for some examples.

term	representation
$2xyz$	*(2 1 1 1)*
$2x^2z$	*(2 2 0 1)*
$4z^3$	*(4 0 0 3)*

Thus our canonical polynomial would now be represented as:

$$((1\ 2\ 0\ 0)\ (-2\ 0\ 1\ 0)\ (-1\ 0\ 0\ 1))$$

This representation is not too bad; the *first*-part of any term is the coefficient; the *rest*-part is the variable part. For example, the test for equality of variable parts is now simply a call on *equal*.

Let's start thinking about the structure of the main algorithm.

Fourth representation

The algorithm for the sum must compare terms. Finding similar terms, it will generate an appropriate new term, otherwise it simply copies the terms. When we pick a p_i from the first polynomial we would like to find a corresponding q_j with the minimum amount of searching. This can be accomplished if we can order the terms in the polynomials. A natural ordering can be induced on the terms by ordering the numerical representation of the exponents. For sake of argument, assume that a maximum of two digits will be needed to express the exponent of any one variable. Thus the exponent of x^2 will be represented as *02*, or the exponent of z^{10} will be represented as *10*. Combining this with our ordered representation of variable parts, we arrive at:

term	representation
$43x^2y^3z^4$	$(43, 020304)$
$2x^2z$	$(2, 020001)$
$4z^3$	$(4, 000003)$

Now we can order on the numeric representation of the variable part of the term. One more change of representation, which will result in a simplification in storage requirements:

represent $ax^Ay^Bz^C$ as $(a\ .\ ABC)$

This gives our final representation:

$$((1\ .\ 20000)\ (-2\ .\ 100)\ (-1\ .\ 1))$$

Note that *20000 > 100 > 1*.

Finally we will write the algorithm. We will assume that the polynomials are initially ordered and will write the algorithm so as to maintain that ordering. Each term is a dotted pair of elements: the coefficient and a representation of the variable part.

As in the previous differentiation example, we should attempt to extract the algorithm from the representation.

We shall define:

$$coef[x] <= car[x] \text{ and } expo[x] <= cdr[x]$$

To test the ordering we will use the LISP predicate:

$$greaterp[x;y] \text{ gives } t \text{ if } x \text{ is greater than } y.$$

In the construction of the 'sum' polynomial we will generate new terms by combining coefficients. So a constructor named *mknode* is needed. In terms of the latest representation *mknode* is defined as:

$$mknode[x;y] <= cons[x;y]$$

So here's a graphical representation of our example polynomial:

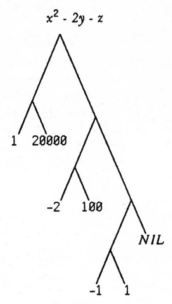

$$x^2 - 2y - z$$

Here's the algorithm:

$polyadd[p;q] <=$
   $[nullpoly[p] \to q;$
   $nullpoly[q] \to p;$
   $greaterp[expo[first[p]];expo[first[q]]] \to concat[first[p];$
                                             $polyadd[rest[p];q]];$
   $lessp[expo[first[p]];expo[first[q]]] \to concat[first[q];$
                                          $polyadd[p;rest[q]]];$
   $zerop[plus[coef[first[p]];coef[first[q]]]] \to polyadd[rest[p];rest[q]];$
   $t \to concat[mknode[plus[coef[first[p]];coef[first[q]]];$
                     $expo[first[p]]];$
                 $polyadd[rest[p];rest[q]]]]$

where: $zerop[x] <= eq[x;0]$
Notice that our algorithm is quite abstract.
   Now for an explanation and example. The form of *polyadd* is:

$$[p_1 \to e_1; p_2 \to e_2; p_3 \to e_3; p_4 \to e_4; p_5 \to e_5; p_6 \to e_6]$$

$p_1 \to e_1$ and $p_2 \to e_2$ check if either polynomial is empty.

$p_3 \to e_3$ and $p_4 \to e_4$ examine the ordering of terms so that the resultant polynomial retains the ordering.

p_5 or p_6 will not be reached unless the variable parts are equal.

$p_5 \to e_5$. Since the variable parts are equal, we can combine terms. However, we must check for cancellations and not include any terms with zero coefficient in our resultant polynomial.

$p_6 \to p_6$. In the final case we must add a new node to our polynomial.

Here's an informal execution of *polyadd:*

$$polyadd[\ x+y+z;\ x^2-2y-z\ ]$$
$$= concat[x^2;polyadd[x+y+z;\ -2y-z]]$$
$$= concat[x^2;concat[x;polyadd[y+z;\ -2y-z]]]$$
$$= concat[x^2;concat[x;concat[node[1+-2;y];polyadd[z;-z]]]]$$
$$= concat[x^2;concat[x;concat[-y;polyadd[z;\ -z]]]]$$
$$= concat[x^2;concat[x;concat[-y;polyadd[(\ );(\ )]]]]$$
$$= concat[x^2;concat[x;concat[-y;(\ )]]]$$
$$= x^2+x-y$$

Extensive work has been done on polynomial manipulating algorithms for efficient storage and fast execution ([Got 76]).

Problem

1. Write an algorithm, *polymult,* to perform the multiplication of two polynomials.

2.7 Evaluation of Polynomials

Though you are undoubtedly quite tired of looking at polynomials, there is at least one more operation which is usefully performed on polynomials. The operation is evaluation. Given an arbitrary polynomial, and values for any of the variables which it contains, we would like to compute its value. First we will assume that the substitutions of values for variables has already been carried out. Thus we are dealing with polynomials of the form: $\Sigma^n_{i=1}p_i$ where p_i is a product of powers of constants. For example:

$$2^3 + 3*4^2 + 5$$

This could be represented as:

$$(PLUS\ (EXPT\ 2\ 3)\ (PLUS\ (TIMES\ 3\ (EXPT\ 4\ 2))\ 5))$$

We have taken this general representation because we have great expectations of generalizing the resulting algorithm.

We describe a LISP function, *value*, which will take such an S-expr representation and compute its value. Input to *value* will be numerals or lists beginning with either *PLUS, TIMES,* or *EXPT* and followed by two numerals or other expressions of the same form.

```
<constexp>::= <constant>
          ::= <sum>
          ::= <prod>
          ::= <expt>
<sum>     ::= (PLUS <constexp> <constexp> )
<prod>    ::= (TIMES <constexp> <constexp> )
<expt>    ::= (EXPT <constexp> <constexp> )
```

The value of a numeral is that numeral; to evaluate the other forms of input we should perform the operation represented. We must therefore assume that operations of addition, multiplication, and exponentiation exist. Assume they are named +, $*$, and ↑, respectively. What then should be the value of a representation of a sum? It should be the result of adding the value of the representations of the two summands or operands. That is, *value* is recursive. It should now be clear how to write *value*:

$$value[x] <= [isconstant[x] \to x;$$
$$issum[x] \to +[value[arg_1[x]];value[arg_2[x]]];$$
$$isprod[x] \to *[value[arg_1[x]];value[arg_2[x]]];$$
$$isexpt[x] \to ↑[value[arg_1[x]];value[arg_2[x]]]]$$

where:

$$isconstant[x] <= numberp[x]$$
$$issum[x] <= eq[first[x];PLUS]$$
$$isprod[x] <= eq[first[x];TIMES]$$
$$isexpt[x] <= eq[first[x];EXPT]$$

Compare the structure of the evaluator with that of the BNF equations.

Problems

1. Show how to extend *value* to handle binary and unary minus.
2. Write an algorithm *instantiate* which will take two arguments, one representing a set of variables and values, the other representing a polynomial. The algorithm is to return a representation of the polynomial which would result from substituting the values for the variables.
3. We would like to represent expressions like 2+3+4 as *(PLUS 2 3 4)* rather than *(PLUS (PLUS 2 3) 4)* or *(PLUS 2 (PLUS 3 4))*; or represent 2*3*4+5+6 as *(PLUS (TIMES 2 3 4) 5 6)*. Write a new version of *value* which can evaluate such n-ary representations of + and $*$.

More on polynomial evaluation

Though it should be clear that the current *value* function does perform the appropriate calculation, it should be equally clear that the class of expressions which *value* handles is not particularly powerful. We might wish to evaluate requests like:

A   "What is the value of *x*y + 2*z* when *x=4, y=2*, and *z=1*?"

Now the function *instantiate*, requested in problem 2 above, offers one solution: make a new copy of the representation of *x*y + 2*z* with the variables replaced by their values. [12] This would result in a representation of *4*2 +2*1*, and this new expression is suitable fare for *value*. Computationally, this is a terrible solution. *instantiate* will go through the structure of the expression looking for instances of variables, and when located, will replace them with the appropriate values. *value* then goes through the structure of the resulting expression performing the evaluation. We desire a function, *value'*, which combines the two processes: the basic structure of *value'* is that of mild-mannered *value*, but when a variable, say *x*, is recognized inside *value'* then *value'* would look at a table like that expected by *instantiate*, find *x* and return the value associated with the entry for *x*.

Let's formalize our intuitions about *value'*. It will be a function of two arguments. The first will be a representation of a polynomial; the second will be a representation of the table of variables and values. You may have noticed that the original version of *value does* handle expressions which are not actually constant polynomials; *(2 + 3)*4* for example. Since we will wish to apply our evaluation functions to more general classes of expressions we will continue, indeed encourage, this generality. Regardless of the class of expressions we wish to examine, it is the structure of the table which should be the first order of business. An appropriate table, *tbl*, will be a set of ordered pairs $<name_i, val_i>$; thus for the above example the table $\{<x, 4>, <y, 2>, <z, 1>\}$ would suffice. Following our dictum of abstraction and representation-independent programming, we will not worry about the representational problems of such tables. We will simply assume that "tables" are instances of an abstract data structure called **<table>**, and we will only concern ourselves for the moment with the kinds of operations we need to perform. We will need two selector functions: *name*, to select the variable-component of a table entry; and *val*, to select the value-component. A complete discussion of such a data structure would entail discussion of constructors and recognizers, and perhaps other functions, but for the current *value'*, these two functions will suffice.

---

[12]We have seen this substitution and simplification process before in discussing *equal* on page 24. It is a useful model for computation, but does not reflect current implementation practice. However, see [Ber 75].

value' will need a table-function, *locate*, to locate an appropriate variable-value entry. The binary function *locate* will take an argument, *x*, representing a variable; and an argument, *tbl*, representing a table. *locate* will match *x* against the *name*-part of each element in *tbl*; if a match is found then the corresponding *val*-part is returned. If no match is found then *locate* is undefined.

So far, little structure has been imposed on elements of **<table>**; tables are either empty or not; but if a table is non-empty then each element is a pair with recognizable components of *name* and *val*. However, the specification of algorithms to examine elements of **<table>** imposes more structure on our tables. If we were dealing with mathematical functions rather than algorithms then a side condition to the effect that a table had no pairs with duplicate first elements would be sufficient (and required). However, we are dealing with algorithms and therefore must describe a method for locating elements.

Recursion is the only method we have for specifying *locate*, and recursion operates by decomposing a structure. Sets are notorious for their lack of structure; there is no order to the elements of a set. But if we are to write a LISP algorithm for *locate*, that algorithm will have to be recursive on the "structure" of *tbl*, and so we impose an ordering on the elements of that table. That is, we will represent tables as *sequences*. We know how to represent sequences in LISP: we use lists.

With this introduction, here's *locate*: [13]

$$locate[x;tbl] <= [eq[name[first[tbl]];x] \rightarrow val[first[tbl]];$$
$$t \rightarrow locate[x;rest[tbl]]]$$

The effect of *locate* is to find the *first* element of *tbl* which has a *name*-component which matches *x*. Having found that match, the corresponding *val*-part is returned. If there were other matches further along in the sequence *locate* would not see them. Other representations of tables are certainly possible. This representation will be useful in later applications. And here's the new more powerful *value'*:

$$value'[x;tbl] <= [isconstant[x] \rightarrow x;$$
$$isvar[x] \rightarrow locate[x;tbl];$$
$$issum[x] \rightarrow +[value'[arg_1[x];tbl];$$
$$value'[arg_2[x];tbl]];$$
$$isprod[x] \rightarrow *[value'[arg_1[x];tbl];$$
$$value'[arg_2[x];tbl]];$$
$$isexpt[x] \rightarrow \uparrow[value'[arg_1[x];tbl];$$
$$value'[arg_2[x];tbl]]]$$

---

[13]The interpretation of *tbl* as a function implies that *locate* represents function application; i.e., *locate[x;tbl]* is *tbl(x)*. This is a very acceptable view of table lookup.

Notice that *tbl* is carried through as an explicit argument to *value'* even though it is only accessed when a variable is recognized. Notice too that much of the structure of *value'* is quite repetitious; the lines which handle sums, products, and exponentiation are identical except for the function which finally gets applied to the evaluated arguments. That is, the basic structure of *value'* is potentially of broader application than just the simple class of polynomials. In keeping with our search for generality, let's pursue *value'* a little further.

What *value'* says is:

1. The value of a constant is that constant.
2. The value of a variable is the current value associated with that variable in the table.
3. The value of a function call is the result of applying the function to the evaluated arguments. It just turns out that the only functions *value'* knows about are binary sums, products, and exponentiation.

Let's clean up *value'* a bit.

value'[x;tbl] <= [isconstant[x] → x;
                 isvar[x] → locate[x;tbl];
                 isfun_args[x] → apply[fun[x];
                                      eval_args[args[x];tbl]];

                 t → ⊥]

The changes are in the third branch of the conditional. We have a new recognizer, *isfun_args* to recognize function application. We have two new selector functions; *fun* selects the representation of the function -- sum, product, or power in the simple case; *args* selects the arguments or parameters to the function -- in this case all functions are binary. We have two new functions to define: *eval_args*, which is supposed to evaluate the arguments finding values for any of the variables; and *apply*, which is used to perform the desired operation on the evaluated arguments.

We are still trying to remain as representation-free as possible: thus the generalization of the algorithm *value'*, and thus the care in picking representations for the data structures. We need to make another data structure decision now; when writing the function *eval_args*, we will be giving a recursive algorithm. This algorithm will be recursive on the structure of the first argument, which is a representation of the arguments to the function. In contrast to our position when writing the function *locate*, there *is* a natural structure on the arguments to a function: they form a sequence. That is $f[1;2;3]$ is typically not the same as $f[3;2;1]$ or f applied to any other permutation of $\{1, 2, 3\}$. Thus writing *eval_args* as a function, recursive on the sequence-structure of its first argument, is quite natural. Here is *eval_args*:

$eval\_args[args;tbl] <= [null[args] \rightarrow ()$;

$\qquad t \rightarrow concat[\ value'[first[args];tbl]$;

$\qquad\qquad\qquad eval\_args[rest[args];tbl]]\ ]$

Notice that we have written *eval_args* without any bias toward binary functions; it will evaluate a sequence of arbitrary length, returning a sequence representing the evaluated arguments.

There should be no real surprises in *apply*; it gets the representation of the function name and the sequence of evaluated arguments and does its job:

$apply[fn;\ evargs] <= [issum[fn] \rightarrow +[\ arg_1[evargs]$;

$\qquad\qquad\qquad\qquad\qquad arg_2[evargs]]$;

$\qquad\qquad isprod[fn] \rightarrow *[arg_1[evargs]$;

$\qquad\qquad\qquad\qquad\qquad arg_2[evargs]]$;

$\qquad\qquad isexpt[fn] \rightarrow \uparrow[\ arg_1[evargs]$;

$\qquad\qquad\qquad\qquad\qquad arg_2[evargs]]\ ]$

If we should desire to recognize more functions then we need only modify *apply*. That would be a satisfactory short-term solution, but we would like a more general function-definition facility. Such a feature would allow new functions to be defined during a computation; then if an application of that function were needed, the *value*-function would find that definition and apply *it* in a manner analogous to the way the pre-defined functions are applied. How far away are we from this more desirable super-*value*? Well *value'* is already well-endowed with a mechanism for locating values; perhaps we can exploit this judiciously placed code. In what context would we be interested in locating function definitions? Here's an example:

B   "What is the value of $f[4;2;1]$ when $f[x;y;z] <= x*y + 2*z$?"

If we have a means of recovering the definition of f, then we can reduce the problem to A of page 81. We will utilize the table-mechanism, and therefore will use *locate* to retrieve the definition of the function f. In our prior applications of *locate* we would find a constant as the associated value. Now, given the name f, we would expect to find the definition of the function. The question then, is how do we represent the definition of f? Certainly the body of the function, $x*y + 2*z$, is one of the necessary ingredients, but is that all? Given the expression $x*y + 2*z$ can we successfully compute $f[4;2;1]$? Not yet; we need to know the correspondence between the values $1, 2, 4$ and the variables, x, y, z. That information is present in our notation $f[x;y;z] <= ...$, and is a crucial part of the definition of f. That is, the *order* of the variables appearing after the function name is an integral part of the definition: $f[y;z;x] <= x*y + 2*z$ defines a different function.

Since we are now talking about *representations* of functions, we are entering the realm of abstract data structures again. We have a reasonable understanding now of the essential components of such a representation.

For our purposes, a function has three parts:

1. A name; f in the current example.
2. A formal parameter list; $[x,y,z]$ here.
3. A body; $x*y + 2*z$ in the example.

We do not need a complete study of representations for functions yet. For our current discussions we can assume a representation exists, and that we are supplied with three selectors to retrieve the components mentioned above.

1. *name* selects the name component from the representation. We have actually seen *name* before in the definition *locate* on page 82.
2. *varlist* selects the list of variables from the representation. We have already seen that the natural way to think about this component is as a sequence. Thus the name *varlist*.
3. *body* selects the expression which is the content of the definition.

Given a function represented in the table according to these conventions, how do we use the information to effect the evaluation of something like $f[4;2;1]$? First *value'* will see the representation of $f[4;2;1]$; it should recognize this as an instance of function-application at the following line of *value'*:

$$isfun\_args[x] \rightarrow apply[fun[x];eval\_args[args[x];tbl]]$$

This should cause an evaluation of the arguments and then pass on the work to *apply*.

Clever *apply* should soon realize that f is not the name of a known function. It should then extract the definition of f from the table; associate (or bind) the evaluated arguments $(4, 2, 1)$ with the variables of the parameter list (x, y, z), making a new table with name-value pairs $(<x, 4>, <y, 2>, <z, 1>)$. Now we are back to the setting of problem A of page 81. We should ask *value'* to evaluate the *body*-component of the function using the new *tbl*. This works fine for x, y, and z; within the evaluation of the body of f we will find the right bindings for these variables. But we might also need some information from the original *tbl*. The evaluation of the body of f might entail the application of some function definition present in *tbl*. For example, the representation of

"what is $g[2]$ where $g[x] <= x+s[x]$; and $s[x] <= x*x$?"

Within the body of g we need the definition of s. Therefore, instead of building a new table we will add the new bindings to the front of the old table. Since *locate* begins its search from the front of the table we will be assured of finding the new bindings; since the old table is still accessible we are assured of finding any necessary previous bindings.

We should be able to create a new *value''* now. Looking at the finer detail of *value'* and *apply*, we can see a few other modifications need to be made. *apply'* will locate the function definition and thus *tbl* should be included as a third argument to *apply'*. That is, inside *apply'* we will have:

$$isfun[fn] \rightarrow apply'[locate[fn;tbl];evargs;tbl];$$

After *locate* has done its work, this line (above) will invoke *apply'* with a function definition as first argument. We should prepare *apply'* for such an eventuality with the following addition:

$$isdef[fn] \rightarrow value''[body[fn];newtbl[varlist[fn];evargs;tbl]];$$

What does this incredible line say? It says

> "Evaluate the body of the function using a new table manufactured from the old table by adding the pairings of the elements of the formal parameter list with the evaluated arguments."

It also says we should write *newtbl*. This LISP function will make a new table by adding new name-value pairs to an existing table. So we'd better name a constructor to generate a new name-value pair:

mkent is the constructor to make new entries. It will take two arguments: the first will be the name, the second will be the value.

Since we have assumed that the structure of tables, variable-lists, and calling sequences to functions are *all* sequences, we will write *newtbl* assuming this representation.

$$newtbl[vars;vals;tbl] <= [null[vars] \rightarrow tbl;$$
$$t \rightarrow concat[mkent[first[vars];first[vals]];$$
$$newtbl[rest[vars];$$
$$rest[vals];$$
$$tbl]]]$$

And finally here's the new *value''-apply'* pair:

$$value''[x;tbl] <= [isconstant[x] \rightarrow x;$$
$$isvar[x] \rightarrow locate[x;tbl];$$
$$isfun\_args[x] \rightarrow apply'[fun[x];$$
$$eval\_args[args[x];tbl];$$
$$tbl]]$$

$$apply'[fn;evargs;tbl] <= [issum[fn] \rightarrow +[arg_1[evargs];arg_2[evargs]]; $$
$$isprod[fn] \rightarrow *[arg_1[evargs];arg_2[evargs]]; $$
$$isexpt[fn] \rightarrow \uparrow[arg_1[evargs];arg_2[evargs]]; $$
$$isfun[fn] \rightarrow apply'[locate[fn;tbl];evargs;tbl]; $$
$$isdef[fn] \rightarrow value''[body[fn]; $$
$$newtbl[varlist[fn]; $$
$$evargs;tbl]] \ ] $$

$$eval\_args[args;tbl] <= [null[args] \rightarrow ( ); $$
$$t \rightarrow concat[value''[first[args];tbl]; $$
$$eval\_args[rest[args];tbl]] \ ] $$

Let's go through a complete evaluation of B of page 84. As before, we will use $\Re$ as a mapping from expressions to representations. Thus we want to pursue:

$$value''[\Re[\![\ f[4;2;1] \ ]\!]; \Re[\![\{ <f, [[x;y;z] \ x*y + 2*z]> \}]\!]].$$

Let us denote the initial symbol table, $\Re[\![\{ <f, [[x;y;z] \ x*y + 2*z]> \}]\!]$ as *init*. This will simplify many of the expressions. Notice that our representation of f in *init* has associated the variable list $[x;y;z]$ with the body of the function. Thus *locate*, operating on this table with the name f, will return a representation of $[[x;y;z] \ x*y + 2*z]$.

The recognizer *isfun_args* should be satisfied and thus the computation should reduce to:

$$apply'[\ fun[\Re[\![\ f[4;2;1] \ ]\!]]; $$
$$eval\_args[args[\Re[\![\ f[4;2;1] \ ]\!]];init]; $$
$$init] $$

or: $apply'[\ \Re[\![\ f \ ]\!] \ ;eval\_args[\ \Re[\![\ [4;2;1] \ ]\!] \ ; init]; init \ ]$

eval_args will build a sequence of the evaluated arguments: $(4, 2, 1)$, resulting in:

$$apply'[\ \Re[\![\ f \ ]\!] \ ;(4, 2, 1) \ ; init \ ]$$

apply' should decide that f satisfies *isfun* giving:

$$apply'[\ locate[\ \Re[\![\ f \ ]\!] \ ; init \ ]; (4, 2, 1) \ ; init \ ]$$

locate will retrieve the definition, and

$$apply'[\ \Re[\![\ [[x;y;z] \ x*y + 2*z] \ ]\!] \ ; (4, 2, 1) \ ; init \ ]$$

should be the result.

Next, *apply″* should realize that $\mathfrak{R}[\![\ [[x;y;z] \ x*y + 2*z] \ ]\!]$ satisfies *isdef* and thus:

$$value″[body[\mathfrak{R}[\![\ [[x;y;z] \ x*y + 2*z] \ ]\!]];$$
$$newtbl[\ varlist[\mathfrak{R}[\![\ [[x;y;z] \ x*y + 2*z] \ ]\!]];$$
$$(4,2,1);$$
$$init]]$$

or: $\quad value″[\ \mathfrak{R}[\![\ [x*y + 2*z] \ ]\!] \ ;newtbl[\ \mathfrak{R}[\![\ [x;y;z] \ ]\!] \ ;(4,2,1);init]]$ after *body* and *varlist* are finished.

$\mathfrak{R}[\![\ [x;y;z] \ ]\!]$ is $(\mathfrak{R}[\![\ x \ ]\!], \mathfrak{R}[\![\ y \ ]\!], \mathfrak{R}[\![\ z \ ]\!])$, and therefore the computation of *newtbl* will build a new table with entries for x, y, and z on the front:

$$\mathfrak{R}[\![\{ \ <x, 4>, <y, 2>, <z, 1>, <f, [[x;y;z] \ x*y + 2*z]> \ \}]\!].$$

Thus we call *value″* with:

$$value″[\mathfrak{R}[\![\ [x*y + 2*z] \ ]\!]];$$
$$\mathfrak{R}[\![\{ \ <x, 4>, <y, 2>, <z, 1>, <f, [[x;y;z] \ x*y + 2*z]> \ \}]\!]]$$

Now we're back at problem A of page 81.

Time to take stock

We have written a reasonably sophisticated algorithm here; we should examine the results quite carefully. Notice that we have written the algorithm with almost no concern for representation. We *assume* that representations are available for such varied things as arithmetic expressions, tables, calls on functions, and even function definitions. Very seldom did we commit ourselves to anything close to a concrete representation, and then only with great reluctance. It was with some sadness that we imposed a sequencing on elements of tables. Variable lists and calling sequences were not as traumatic; we claimed their natural structure was a sequence. As always, if we wish to run these programs on a machine we must supply some representations, but even then the representations will only interface with our algorithms at the constructors, selectors and recognizers.

We have made some more serious representational decisions in the structure of the algorithm. We have encoded a version of the CBV-scheme of page 16. We have seen what kinds of difficulties that can cause. We will spend a large amount of time in Chapter 3 discussing the problems of evaluation. [14]

---

[14]A second decision was implied in our handling of function definitions; namely we bound the function name to a data structure representing the formal parameter list and the function body. This representation gives the expected result in most cases, but involves one of the more problematic areas of programming languages: how do you find the

Finally, our decisions on the data structures and the algorithms were not made independently. For example, there is strong interaction between our representation of tables and the algorithms, *locate* and *newtbl* which manipulate those tables. We should ask how much of this interaction is inherent and how much is gratuitous. For example, we have remarked that our representation can contain pairs with duplicate first elements. It is the responsibility of *locate* to see that we find the expected pair. If we wrote *locate* to search from right to left, we could get the wrong pair. We *could* write *newtbl* to be more selective; it could manufacture a table without such duplications:

$newtbl[vars;vals;tbl]$ <= $[null[tbl] \rightarrow [null[vars] \rightarrow ();$
$$t \rightarrow concat[mkent[first[vars];first[vals]];$$
$$newtbl[\ rest[vars];$$
$$rest[vals];$$
$$(\ )]]];$$
$$member[name[first[tbl]]];vars] \rightarrow newtbl[vars;$$
$$vals;$$
$$rest[tbl]];$$

$$t \rightarrow concat[first[tbl];$$
$$newtbl[vars;vals;rest[tbl]]]\ ]$$

This version of *newtbl* requires much more computation than the alternative. Its advantage is that the "set"-ness of symbol tables is maintained. A disadvantage is that the rebinding process implies a rebuilding of the table. The "set" property is one which we need not depend on for our algorithms; in fact, we will frequently expect that a table is represented as a sequence with the previous values of variables found further along in the sequence.

The main point of this example however is to impress on you the importance of writing at a sufficiently high level of abstraction. We have produced a non-trivial algorithm which is clear and concise. If it were desirable to have this algorithm running on a machine we could code it and its associated data structure representations in a very short time. In a very short time *we* will be able to run this algorithm on a LISP machine.

---

bindings of variables which do not appear in the current variable list? For example, function names belong in this category. Such variables are called non-local variables. The scheme proposed in this section finds the binding which is current when the function was applied. This corresponds to the "latest active" binding made for the variable in question. Some programming languages, in particular LISP, follow this strategy; some other languages follow Algol 60 and use the binding which was current when the function was defined, and some languages allow both. The next two chapters begin a study of binding strategies.

Problem

1. On page 81 we mentioned the possibility of writing the new *value* as a combination of old *value* and *instantiate*. We rejected that scheme. On page 85 we had to save an old table since we might need some previously defined functions. We might not have had this difficulty if we had substituted directly. Write a substitution-type *value* and use it to evaluate the g[2] example.

2.8 The Great Progenitors

The following problems are written (intentionally) with a great deal of the representation built into them.

1. The Great Mother of All Functions (*tgmoaf*)

$$tgmoaf[x] <= [isindiv[x] \rightarrow [eq[x;T] \rightarrow t;$$
$$eq[x;NIL] \rightarrow f;$$
$$t \rightarrow TRYAGAINNEXTWEEK];$$
$$eq[first[x];QUOTE] \rightarrow second[x];$$
$$eq[first[x];CAR] \rightarrow car[tgmoaf[second[x]]];$$
$$eq[first[x];CDR] \rightarrow cdr[tgmoaf[second[x]]];$$
$$eq[first[x];CONS] \rightarrow cons[tgmoaf[second[x]];$$
$$tgmoaf[third[x]]];$$
$$eq[first[x];ATOM] \rightarrow atom[tgmoaf[second[x]]];$$
$$eq[first[x];EQ] \rightarrow eq[tgmoaf[second[x]];tgmoaf[third[x]]];$$
$$t \rightarrow TRYAGAINNEXTWEEK]$$

Evaluate the following:

a. *tgmoaf[T]*
b. *tgmoaf[A]*
c. *tgmoaf[(CAR (QUOTE (A . B)))]*
d. *tgmoaf[(CDR (QUOTE (A B)))]*
e. *tgmoaf[(EQ (CAR (QUOTE (A . B))) (QUOTE A))]*
f. *tgmoaf[(EQ (CAR (QUOTE (A . B))) A)]*
g. *tgmoaf[(ATOM (CAR (QUOTE (A B))))]*

2. The Great Mother of All Functions Revisited (*tgmoafr*)

$$tgmoafr[x] <= [isindiv[x] \rightarrow [eq[x;T] \rightarrow t;$$
$$eq[x;NIL] \rightarrow f;$$
$$t \rightarrow TRYAGAINNEXTWEEK];$$
$$eq[first[x];QUOTE] \rightarrow second[x];$$
$$eq[first[x];CAR] \rightarrow car[tgmoafr[second[x]]];$$
$$eq[first[x];CDR] \rightarrow cdr[tgmoafr[second[x]]];$$
$$eq[first[x];CONS] \rightarrow cons[tgmoafr[second[x]];$$
$$tgmoafr[third[x]]];$$
$$eq[first[x];ATOM] \rightarrow atom[tgmoafr[second[x]]];$$
$$eq[first[x];EQ] \rightarrow eq[tgmoafr[second[x]];tgmoafr[third[x]]];$$
$$eq[first[x];COND] \rightarrow evcond[rest[x]];$$
$$t \rightarrow TRYAGAINNEXTWEEK]$$

$evcond[x] <= [tgmoafr[first[first[x]]] \rightarrow tgmoafr[second[first[x]]];$
$\qquad t \rightarrow evcond[rest[x]]]$

Evaluate the following:

a. *tgmoafr[T]*
b. *tgmoafr[(CDR (QUOTE (A B)))]*
c. *tgmoafr[(EQ (CAR (QUOTE (A . B))) (QUOTE A))]*
d. *tgmoafr[(COND (EQ (CAR (QUOTE (A . B))) (QUOTE A))*
$\qquad$ *(QUOTE FOO)))]*
5. *tgmoafr[(COND ((ATOM (QUOTE (A))) (QUOTE FOO))*
$\qquad$ *(T (QUOTE BAZ)))]*

Coming soon: Son of the Great Progenitor !!

2.9 Another Respite

We have again reached a point where a certain amount of reflection would be beneficial. Though this is not a programming manual we would be remiss if we did not analyze the programming style which we have been advocating.

1. Write the algorithm in an abstract setting; do not muddle the abstract algorithm with the chosen representation. If you follow this dictum your LISP programs will never use *car, cdr, cons,* and *atom,* and rarely use *eq.* All instances of these LISP primitives will be relegated to small subfunctions which manipulate representations.
2. When writing the abstract program, do not be afraid to cast off difficult parts of the implementation to subfunctions. Remember that if you have trouble keeping the details in mind when *writing* the program, then the confusion involved in *reading* the program at some later time will be overwhelming. Once you have convinced yourself of the correctness of the current composition, then worry about the construction of the subfunctions. Seldom does the process of composing a program flow so gently from top-level to specific representation. Only the toy programs are easy; the construction of the practical program will be confusing, and will require much rethinking. But bring as much structure as you can to the process.
3. From the other side of the question, don't be afraid to look at specific implementations, or specific data-structure representations before you

begin to write. There is something quite comforting about a "real" data structure. Essentially data structures are static objects, [15] while programs are dynamic objects. A close look at a possible representation may get you a starting point and as you write the program a distinction will emerge between a dependence on the specific representation and the use of properties of an abstract data structure.

Perhaps the more practical reader is overcome by the inefficiencies inherent in these proposals. Two answers: first, "inefficiency" is a very ethereal concept. Like "structured programming", it is difficult to define but recognizable when it occurs. Hardware development has enabled us to efficiently execute many operations which were quite inefficient on earlier machines. But even at a more topical level, much of what seems inefficient can now be straightened out by a compiler (see Chapter 6). Frequently, compilers can do very clever optimizations to generate efficient code. It is better to leave the cleverness to the compiler, and the clarity to the programmer.

The current problems in programming are not those of efficiency; they are problems of *correctness*. That is, we have a better grasp of techniques for improving efficiency of programs than we do of techniques for guiding the construction of programs which work. How do you write a program which works? Until practical tools are developed for proving correctness it is up to the programmer to certify his programs. Any methodology which can aid the programmer will be most welcome. Clearly, the closer you can write the program to your intuition, the less chance there is for error. This was one of the reasons for developing high-level languages. The original motivation for such languages was a convenient notation for expressing numerical problems. With data structures, we are able to formalize a broader range of domains, expressing our ideas as data structure manipulations rather than as numerical relationships.

There are at least two kinds of errors which are prevalent in data structure programming: errors of omission -- misunderstanding of the basic algorithm; and errors of commission -- errors due to misapplied cleverness in attempting to be efficient.

The occurrences of errors of omission can be minimized by presenting the user with programming constructs which are close to the informal algorithm. Such constructs include control structures, data structures, and representations for operations.

Errors of commission comprise the great majority of the present day headaches. It is here that programming *style* can be beneficial: keep the representation of the data structures away from the description of the algorithm; write concise abstract programs, passing off responsibilities to

---

[15]At least within the program presently being constructed.

subfunctions. Whenever a definition of "structured programming" is arrived at, this advice on programming style will no doubt be included.

The realization that programs *will* have errors or require modification raises some difficulties for highly structured languages. A realistic debugging system must allow program modification and data structure modification; if the language system imposes rigid restrictions on such activities the programmer's productivity will suffer. Most language systems have been designed for the *execution* of programs. LISP systems put a higher premium on *debugging*, perhaps because of the nature of Artificial Intelligence research: the original motivation for LISP. LISP programming systems have a high degree of interactiveness; the result is an effective programming tool. It is a tool with sharp edges; one can either build mediocre tools which can't hurt anyone, or can build a sharp tool and expect that it be applied by knowledgeable users. LISP programmers belong in the second classification. Our discussions of LISP programming style should develop some of the requisite knowledge.

Before closing this discussion of LISP programming style, we can't help but note that in the preceding section, **The Great Progenitors** have completely ignored our good advice. This would be a good time for the interested reader to abstract the *tgmoaf* algorithm from the particular data representation. This detective work will be most rewarding.

Problems

1. Write an abstract version of *tgmoaf*.

2.10 Proving Properties of Programs

People are becoming increasingly aware of the importance of giving convincing arguments for such concepts as the correctness or equivalence of programs. These are both very difficult enterprises. [16] We will sketch a proof of a simple property of two programs and leave others as problems for the interested reader. How do you go about proving properties of programs? In Section 1.9 we noted certain benefits of defining sets using inductive definitions. There was a natural way of thinking about the construction of an algorithm over that set. We have exploited that observation in our study of LISP programming. We need to recall the observation that inductive style proofs (see **PRF** on page 43) are valid forms of reasoning over such domains. Since we in fact defined our data structure domains in an inductive manner,

---

[16]Question of "correctness" reduce to "equivalence" notions in a broad sense, relating perhaps a declarative specification to a procedural specification.

it seems natural to look for inductive arguments when proving properties of programs. This is indeed what we do; we perform induction on the structure of the elements in the data domain.

For example, given the definition of *append* given on page 48 and the definition of *reverse* given on page 49,

$$append[x;y] <= [null[x] \rightarrow y; \; t \rightarrow concat[first[x];append[rest[x];y]]]$$

$$reverse[x] <= \quad [null[x] \rightarrow (\;);$$
$$\qquad\qquad t \rightarrow append[reverse[rest[x]];concat[first[x];(\;)]]]$$

we wish to show that:

$$append[reverse[y];reverse[x]] = reverse[append[x;y]]$$

for any lists, x, and y. The induction will be on the structure of x.

Basis: x is ( ).
We must thus show: $append[reverse[y];(\;)] = reverse[append[(\;);y]]$
But: $reverse[append[(\;);y]] = reverse[y]$ by the def. of *append*
We now establish the stronger result: $append[z;(\;)] = z$ [17]

> **Basis:** z is ( ).
> Show $append[(\;);(\;)] = (\;)$. Easy.
>
> **Induction step:** Assume the lemma for lists, z, of length n;
> Prove: $append[concat[x;z];(\;)] = concat[x;z]$
> Since $concat[x;z]$ is not ( ), then applying the definition of *append* says we must prove: $concat[x;append[z;(\;)]] = concat[x;z]$
> But our induction hypothesis is applicable since z is shorter than $concat[x;z]$.
> Our result follows.

So the Basis for our main result is established.

---

[17]In the following proof several intermediate steps have been omitted.

Induction step: Assume the result for lists, z, of length n; Prove:

(1) $append[reverse[y];reverse[concat[x;z]]]$
    $= reverse[append[concat[x;z];y]]$

Applying the definition of *reverse* to the LHS of (1) yields:

(2) $append[reverse[y];append[reverse[z];concat[x;( )]]]$

Applying the definition of *append* to the RHS of (1) yields:

(3) $reverse[concat[x;append[z;y]]]$

Applying the definition of *reverse* to (3) yields:

(4) $append[reverse[append[z;y]];concat[x;( )]]$

Using our induction hypothesis on (4) gives:

(5) $append[append[reverse[y];reverse[z]];concat[x;( )]]$

At this point we must establish that   (2) = (5).
But this is just an instance of the associativity of *append*:

$$append[x;append[y;z]] = append[append[x;y];z]$$

The structure of the proof is analogous to proofs by mathematical induction in elementary number theory. The ability to perform such proofs is a direct consequence of our careful definition of data structures. Examination of the proof will show that there is a close relationship between what we are inducting on in the proof and what we are recurring on during the evaluation of the expressions. A program written by Boyer and Moore has been reasonably successful in generating proofs like the above by exploiting this relationship. See [Boy 75] or [Moor 75b]. [18]

Problems

1. Prove the associativity of *append*.

2. Analysis of the above proof shows frequent use of other results for LISP functions. Fill in the details. Investigate the possibility of formalizing this proof, showing what axioms are needed.

3. Show the equivalence of *fact* (page 44) and $fact_1$ (page 47).

4. Show the equivalence of *length* and $length_1$ (page 47).

5. Using the definition of *reverse*, given on page 48, prove:

$$reverse[reverse[x]] = x$$

---

[18]There is also a formal system based on a typed λ-calculus which has had significant success in proving properies of programs. [LCF 72], [New 75]. More recently [Car 76] has developed a formal system including rules of inference, a proof checker, and a viable programming language which is based on a "typed LISP".

Evaluation of LISP Expressions

"... I always worked with programming languages because it seemed to me that until you could understand those, you really couldn't understand computers. Understanding them doesn't really mean only being able to use them. A lot of people can use them without understanding them. ..."

Christopher Strachey[Str 74]

3.1 Introduction

In the previous chapters of this text we have talked about some of the schemes for evaluation. We have done so rather informally for LISP; we have been more precise about evaluation of simple arithmetic expressions. Section 2.7 discussed that in some detail. We shall now look more closely at the informal process which we have been using in the evaluation of LISP expressions. This is motivated by at least two desires.

We want to run our LISP programs on a machine. To do so requires the implementation of a translator to turn LISP programs into instructions which can be carried out by a conventional machine. We will be interested in the structure of such implementations. Any implementation of LISP must be grounded on a precise, and clear understanding of what LISP-evaluation entails. Indeed, a deep understanding of evaluation is a prerequisite for implementation of *any* language. [1]

Our second reason for pursuing evaluation involves the question of programming language specification. At a practical level we want a clean, machine independent, [2] "self-evident" language specification, so that the agony involved in implementing the design can be minimized. At a more abstract level, we should try to understand just what *is* specified when we design a language. Are we specifying a single machine, a class of machines, or a class of mathematical functions? Just what is a programming language? The syntactic specification of languages is reasonably well established, but syntax is only the tip of the iceberg. Our study of LISP will address itself to the deeper problems of semantics, or meaning, of languages.

Before we address the direct question of LISP evaluation, we should perhaps wonder aloud about the efficacy of studying languages in the detail which we are proposing. As computer scientists we should be curious about the structure of programming languages because we must understand our tools -- our programming languages. People who simply wish to *use* computers as tools need not care about the structure of languages. Indeed they usually couldn't care less about the inner workings of the language; they only want languages in which they can state their problems in a reasonably natural manner. They want their programs to run and get results. They are interested in the output and seldom are interested in the detailed process of computation. For a simple analogy, consider the field of mathematics. The practicing mathematician uses his tools -- proofs -- in a similar manner to the person interested in computer applications. He seldom needs to examine questions like "what is a proof?" He does not analyze his tools. However not so many years ago such questions *were* raised, and for good reason. Some common forms of reasoning were shown to lead to contradictions unless care was taken.

Our position is more like that of the foundations of mathematics; there the tools of mathematics *are* studied and analyzed. Mathematics has flourished because of it. Though our expectations are not quite that presumptuous, we *do* expect that programming language design cannot help but be improved.

Our study of language implementation will proceed from the abstract to

---

[1] The question of evaluation cannot be sidestepped by basing a language on a compiler. A compiler must produce code which when executed, simulates the evaluation process.

[2] By "machine independent" we mean independent of any specific hardware implementation. A programming language, almost by definition, is a machine specification. What we would like is a "sufficiently high level" machine.

the concrete. Each level will intimately involve the study of data structures. The next two chapters will be the most abstract, building a precise high-level description of an evaluation scheme for LISP. In fact, the discussion is much more general than that of LISP; the text addresses itself to problem areas in the design of any reasonably sophisticated language. In subsequent chapters we probe beneath the surface of this high-level description and discuss common ways of implementing the necessary data structures and control structures. In the process we will not only understand LISP but will develop a firm understanding of virtually any other language.

But how can we begin to understand LISP evaluation? In Section 2.7 we made a beginning, giving an algorithm for a subset of the computations expressible in LISP. This subset covered evaluation of some simple arithmetic expressions. From our earliest grade school days we have had to evaluate simple arithmetic expressions. Later, in algebra we managed to cope with expressions involving function application. Most of us survived the experience. We should now try to understand the processes we used in these simple arithmetic cases, doing our examination at the most mechanical level. The basic intent of the algorithm is fixed: evaluate the expression; but within that general constraint we often have several distinct alternatives. Those places at which we have choices should be remembered. We will make reasonable choices so that the process becomes deterministic and then proceed. Later, we should reflect on what effect our choices had on the resulting scheme. For example, recall the discussion of the representation of symbol tables on page 89. We had several options, but picked one which seemed to satisfy our intuitions and was reasonably efficient. But we should subject that decision to close scrutiny: does it really fulfill our expectations? In absence of absolute standards, these questions are usually answered by examining the behavior of the algorithm.

The first thing to note in reflecting on simple arithmetic examples is that *nothing* is really said about the process of evaluation. When asked to evaluate *(2*3) + (5*6)* we never specified which summand was to be evaluated first. Indeed it didn't matter here. *6 + (5*6)* or *(2*3) + 30* both yield *36*. Does it *ever* matter? Sums and products are examples of arithmetic operations; can we always leave the order of evaluation unspecified for arithmetic operations? What about evaluation of arbitrary functional expressions? If the order doesn't matter, then the specification of the evaluation process becomes much simpler. If it *does* matter then we must know why and where.

We have seen that the order of evaluation *can* make a difference in LISP. On page 15 we saw that CBV, LISP's computational interpretation of function application, requires some care. On page 21 we saw that order of evaluation in conditional expressions can make a difference. Since we are using CBV we must make *some* decision regarding the order of evaluation of the arguments to a function call, say $f[t_1;t_2; ...;t_n]$. We will assume that we will evaluate the arguments from left to right. This second decision about the order of evaluation can also effect the computation.

Consider the example due to J. Morris:

$$f[x;y] <= [x = 0 \rightarrow 0; t \rightarrow f[x-1;f[y-2;x]]]$$

Evaluation of $f[2;1]$ will terminate if we always evaluate the outermost occurrence of f. Thus:

$$f[2;1] = f[1;f[-1;2]] = f[0;f[f[-1;2]-2;1]] = 0$$

However if we evaluate the innermost occurrences [3] first, the computation will not terminate:

$$f[2;1] = f[1;f[-1;2]] = f[1;f[-2;f[0;-1]]] = f[1;f[-2;0]] = ...$$

The choice of evaluation schemes has far reaching consequences. The evaluation scheme, **CBV**, which we chose is called **call-by-value**. It is called applicative order evaluation or **inside-out** style of evaluation, meaning that we evaluate the subexpressions before evaluating the main expression. Alternative proposals exist; call-by-name evaluation, also called normal order evaluation, is another common scheme. We introduced this outside-in scheme on page 16 as **CBN**. From an implementation perspective, call-by-value is favored; these issues will be discussed soon. However those advantages must be weighed against the knowledge that call-by-value may lead to non-terminating computations when call-by-name would terminate. [4]

Informally, call-by-value says: evaluate the arguments to a function before you apply the function definition to the arguments. Let's look at a simple arithmetic example. Let $f[x;y]$ be $x^2 + y$ and consider $f[3+4;2*2]$. Then call-by-value says evaluate the arguments, getting 7 and 4; associate those values with the formal parameters of f (i.e. 7 with x and 4 with y) and then evaluate the body of f resulting in $7^2 + 4 = 53$. This is the scheme we captured in Section 2.7.

Call-by-name says pass the *unevaluated* actual parameters to the function, giving $(3+4)^2 + 2*2$. This expression will simplify to 53. In general, evaluation can be described as "substitution followed by simplification"; the different evaluation schemes involve different choices about the order in which those operations are performed. We will say more

---

[3]The notions of "innermost" and "outermost" evaluation need to be slightly embellished for multiple-argument applications. If the chosen application has several arguments, then we must specify an order for their evaluation. Thus terms like "leftmost-outermost" and "rightmost-innermost" occur. For example, the LISP scheme is an instance of "leftmost-innermost" evaluation.

[4]There are also examples where call-by-value will terminate but call-by-name will not. See page 227.

about call-by-name and other styles of evaluation in Section 3.13 and Section 4.9. Most of this chapter will be restricted to call-by-value.

If you look at the structure of *value''* and *apply'* beginning on page 86 you will see that they encode a call-by-value strategy and have the following interpretation:

1. If the expression is a constant then tne value of the expression is that constant. (The value of *3* is *3*). [5]

2. If the expression is a variable then see what the current value associated with that variable is. Within the evaluation of, say, $f[3;4]$ where $f[x;y] <= x^2 + y$ the current value of the variable x is *3*.

3. The only other kind of arithmetic expression that we can have is a function name followed by arguments, for example $f[3;4]$. In this case we first evaluate the arguments [6] and then apply the definition of the function to those evaluated arguments. When we apply the function definition to the evaluated arguments we associate the formal parameters of the definition with the values of the actual parameters. This process of associating parameters is called **binding** and simulates some form of substitution. We then evaluate the body of the function using this new environment. Notice that we do *not* explicitly substitute the values for the variables which appear in an expression. We *simulate* substitutions by table lookup.

We want to apply this treatment of evaluation to LISP expressions. If the LISP expression is a constant, then the value of the expression is that constant. The constants of LISP are the S-exprs. Thus the value of *(A . B)* is *(A . B)*, just like the value of *3* is *3*. Variables and functional applications appear in LISP and are handled similarly to 2 and 3 above. The additional artifact of LISP is the conditional expression. But its evaluation can also be precisely specified. We did so on page 20.

In more specific detail, here is some of the structure of the LISP evaluation mechanism:

1. If the expression to be evaluated is a constant then the value is that constant.

2. If the expression is a variable find its value in the current environment.

3. If the expression is a conditional expression then it is of the form $[p_1 \rightarrow e_1; p_2 \rightarrow e_2; \dots ; p_n \rightarrow e_n]$. Evaluate it using the semantics defined on page 20.

---

[5]We are ignoring the distinction between the *numeral 3* and the *number 3*.

[6]Here we are using the evaluation process recursively.

4. If the expression is of the form: $f[t_1;t_2; \ldots ;t_n]$ then:

    a. Evaluate the arguments t_1, t_2, ... , t_n from left to right.

    b. Find the definition of the function, f.

    c. Associate the evaluated arguments with the formal parameters in the function definition.

    d. Evaluate the body of the function, while remembering the values of the variables.

We saw in (Section 2.7) that a simple kind of arithmetic evaluation can be transcribed into a recursive LISP algorithm. That algorithm operates on a representation of the expression and produces the value. Most of our work in that example was done without giving explicit details of the representation. We had previously given a detailed representation in Section 2.3.

We have demonstrated an informal, but reasonably precise, evaluation scheme for LISP; our discussion is ready for more formal development. It should be clear that we could write a LISP function representing the evaluation process provided that we can find a representation for LISP expressions as S-expressions. This mapping, $\mathfrak{R}$, of LISP expressions to S-exprs is our first order of business. We will accomplish this mapping by using an extension of the scheme introduced in Section 2.3.

The rationale for mapping LISP expressions onto S-exprs and writing a LISP function to act as an evaluator may seem overly opaque, but the mapping is no more obscure than that in the polynomial evaluation or differentiation examples. It is just another instance of the diagram of page 56, only now we are applying the process to LISP itself. Once the representation is given we will produce a LISP algorithm which describes the evaluation process used in LISP. The effect is to force us to make precise exactly what is meant by LISP evaluation. This precision will have many important ramifications. The first dividend is an abstract, compact, and high level description of a LISP machine.

In terms of the diagrams on page 56 we have:

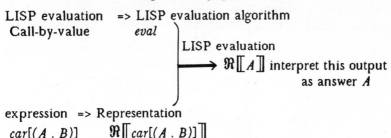

LISP evaluation   => LISP evaluation algorithm
  Call-by-value   *eval*

                          LISP evaluation
                    ───────→ $\Re[\![A]\!]$ interpret this output
                                              as answer A

expression => Representation
  $car[(A . B)]$ $\Re[\![car[(A . B)]]\!]$

The diagram is *almost* circular. We evaluate an evaluation algorithm named *eval*. We break the circle by supplying a lower-level implementation of the original evaluator. That will be the subject of Chapter 5 and Chapter 6. With that, our diagram reduces to:

LISP expression => =>   Representation
  $car[(A . B)]$ $\Re[\![car[(A . B)]]\!]$
                                    ↓↓
                              LISP evaluation
                                  eval
                                    ↓↓
                              Representation of answer
                                  $\Re[\![A]\!]$

This picture reflects two points: we should pick a representation such that the reinterpretation of the answer is easy. We should also pick a representation such that the representation of the expression is easy. If those two conditions are satisfied, then we might as well write our programs in the representation and do the input and output transformations ourselves. With this in mind we can simplify further to:

$$\Re[\![car[(A . B)]]\!] \quad =\text{a LISP evaluation algorithm}=> \quad \Re[\![A]\!]$$

This last diagram reflects the typical LISP programming language. We program using the data structure representation.

We've already seen the evaluation of representations of LISP expressions. The **great progenitor of all functions** is an evaluation algorithm for the LISP primitive functions and predicates, *car, cdr, cons, atom* and *eq* when restricted to functional composition and constant arguments. The representation used there was a list representation, and exemplifies a notation which we will develop further.

In the next section we will give a specific mapping of LISP expressions onto lists and S-exprs. But remember that we should attempt to keep the knowledge of the representation out of the structure of the algorithm. Let's stop for a description of the representation and some examples of translating LISP functions into that representation.

3.2 S-expr Translation of LISP Expressions

We will go through the list of LISP constructs, describing the effect of the representational map, $\Re$, and give a few examples applying $\Re$. The first class of LISP objects we represent are the numerical constants. We will represent numerals just as numerals, e.g.:

$$\Re[\![\text{ <numeral> }]\!] = \text{<numeral>}$$

$$\Re[\![\ 2 \ ]\!] = 2$$

Other simple components of LISP syntax include the identifiers used as variable names and function names; and of course the LISP atoms and S-exprs themselves. We want to represent identifiers and S-exprs as S-expressions. The first request is understandable, but perhaps the second request seems vacuous: LISP S-exprs *are* S-exprs. Both requests are justifiable as we shall now see.

In the evaluator, identifiers are used as variables; therefore we might represent a variable ι as:

$$\Re[\![\iota]\!] = (VAR \ \iota)$$

For example x could be represented as $(VAR \ X)$.

Every LISP expression must have a representation; and the mapping function must be such that we can recover the original object from its representation. From $(VAR \ X)$ we can tell that it is a representation of the variable x. Now consider the representation of the non-numerical LISP constant: atoms and S-exprs. Since $(VAR \ X)$ is a LISP constant, it must have a representation under our mapping. We cannot represent the expression as itself since that would violate our inverse mapping property. Following our discussion of variable representation, we could represent a constant α as:

$$\Re[\![\alpha]\!] = (CONST \ \alpha)$$

This mapping will solve the problems; we can

map the list $(VAR \ X)$ to $(CONST \ (VAR \ X))$

$$\Re[\![x]\!] = (VAR \ X)$$
$$\Re[\![X]\!] = (CONST \ X) \quad [7]$$

When this maping is extended to represent *all* LISP expressions the resulting expressions become very complex. Since we wish to use the mapped expressions as the programming language, human engineering considerations beg for a simplification. Therefore we use the following map:

---

[7]To be consistent, we should represent numerals in this format too.

$$\Re[\![x]\!] = X$$
$$\Re[\![X]\!] = (QUOTE\ X)$$

That is, we will translate identifiers to their upper-case counterpart.

Thus:　　　　　　$\Re[\![<\text{identifier}>]\!] = <\text{literal atom}>$

Examples:　　　　$\Re[\![x]\!] = X$

$$\Re[\![y2]\!] = Y2$$

$$\Re[\![car]\!] = CAR$$

The mapping for LISP constants is:

$$\Re[\![<\text{sexpr}>]\!] = (QUOTE\ <\text{sexpr}>)$$

For example:　　　$\Re[\![X]\!] = (QUOTE\ X)$

$$\Re[\![(A\ .\ B)]\!] = (QUOTE\ (A\ .\ B))$$

$$\Re[\![QUOTE]\!] = (QUOTE\ QUOTE)$$

We must extend the mapping to the other constitutients of the language. We must map applicative expressions of the form $f[e_1 ; ... ; e_n]$ onto S-exprs. Following the style of our initial mapping, we might map $f[x]$ onto something like $(APP\ (VAR\ F)\ (VAR\ X))$ or $(APP\ (FUN\ F)\ (VAR\ X))$, signifying that the list represents an applicative expression. However this leads to cumbersome expressions. We have seen one other mapping for functions in prefix form in Section 2.3. We will use that mapping, called Cambridge Polish, [8] here. That is:

$$\Re[\![f[e_1;e_2;...;e_n]]\!] = (\ \Re[\![f]\!]\ \Re[\![e_1]\!]\ \Re[\![e_2]\!]\ ...\ \Re[\![e_n]\!]\ )$$

Examples:　　　$\Re[\![car[x]]\!] = (\Re[\![car]\!]\ \Re[\![x]\!]\ ) = (CAR\ X)$

$$\Re[\![car[X]]\!] = (\Re[\![car]\!]\ \Re[\![X]\!]\ ) = (CAR\ (QUOTE\ X))$$

$$\Re[\![cons[cdr[(A\ .\ B)];x]]\!] = (CONS\ (CDR\ (QUOTE\ (A\ .\ B)))\ X)$$

---

[8]The name, Cambridge Polish, is derived from two sources: Cambridge, since M.I.T. is in Cambridge Massachusetts, and McCarthy was at M.I.T. while developing his ideas; Polish, since the representation is a dialect of a notation developed by a school of Polish logicians.

The $\Re$-mapping must also handle conditional expressions. A conditional is represented as a list whose first element is *COND* and whose next n elements are representations of the p_i-e_i pairs. The $\Re$-map of such pairs is a list of the $\Re$-maps of the two elements:

$$\Re[\![[p_1 \to e_1; \; ... \; ; p_n \to e_n]]\!] = (COND \; (\Re[\![\; p_1 \;]\!]$$
$$\Re[\![\; e_1]\!])$$
$$...$$
$$(\Re[\![\; p_n \;]\!] \; \Re[\![\; e_n \;]\!]))$$

An example:

$$\Re[\![[atom[x] \to 1; \; q[y] \to X]]\!] = (COND ((ATOM \; X) \; 1)$$
$$((Q \; Y) \; (QUOTE \; X)))$$

Notice that *(COND ...)* and *(QUOTE ...)* *look* like translations of function applications of the form *cond*[...] and *quote*[...]. However since we expect application to be performed using call-by-value, we must handle these constructs in a special manner. Indeed, *quote*[α] stands for $\Re[\![\alpha]\!]$. Similarly the "arguments" to *cond* are not to be interpreted as in function applications; for example, *COND ((ATOM X) 1) ...)* does not represent *cond*[*atom*[x][1]; ...].

Finally, the translations of the truth values t and f will be T and *NIL*, respectively.

$$\Re[\![t]\!] = T$$

$$\Re[\![f]\!] = NIL$$

You might have noticed that these last two applications of the chosen $\Re$-mapping have the potential to cause trouble. They will spoil the 1-1 property of $\Re$:

$$\Re[\![t]\!] = T$$

$$\Re[\![nil]\!] = NIL$$

The usual way to escape from this difficulty is to outlaw t and nil as LISP variables. [9]

Perhaps our concern for the $\Re$-mapping's properties appears heavy-handed where a simple solution seems apparent: t is t and t is t; when we want the truth value we write t and when we want the variable we write t. The answer is that when we write programs for a machine version of

---

[9]In LISP 1.5 T and F were used as the representations of t and f; the atoms T and F were (permanently) bound to values $*T*$ and *NIL*. Note too, that our initial mapping could solve the problem by mapping t to $(VAR \; T)$ and mapping t to $(BOOL \; T)$.

LISP, we will be writing the $\mathfrak{R}$-image, rather than the more traditional syntax. Thus to ask a LISP machine to evaluate $car[(A \cdot B)]$ we present it with $(CAR \; (QUOTE \; (A \cdot B)))$. What this means is that we are presenting our programs to the machine as data structures of the language. [10] It would be like expressing programs in Fortran or Algol as arrays of integers; that is, the data structures of *those* languages. We will explore the implications of this approach to programming in later sections.

In essence, then, there are *two* LISP's: there is the algorithmic language and there is the programming language. The programming language is a data structure representation of the algorithmic language. The algorithmic language is called the **meta-language** or **M-expr LISP**, and for historical purposes, the programming language is called **S-expr LISP**.

Review the *tgm*'s (Section 2.8) now that you understand that they are evaluators for simple subsets of LISP expressions; discover what LISP expressions were encoded in arguments to the *tgm*'s and verify the answers you obtained earlier. Note that the only atoms which the great mothers recognize are T and NIL. Any other atoms elicit an error message. What do other atoms represent? Numerals are atoms and are the $\mathfrak{R}$-maps of numerals. We could extend *tgmoaf* to handle this case. Atoms are also translations of variables and function names. So one task is to include a mechanism in our LISP evaluator to handle evaluation of variables and function names. We have already seen the necessary mechanism in Section 2.7 where we studied tables as abstract data stuctures. The other piece of LISP which did not appear in the evaluator for polynomials was conditional expressions. Conditional expressions *were* handled in *tgmoafr*. The "progenitors" did *not* handle variable references, however. In preparation for that work we reexamine the issues of symbol tables.

3.3 Symbol Tables

One distinguishing feature of computer science is the ubiquity of devices to store and recover information. A notation which addresses itself to computer science must treat this aspect. In hardware oriented languages and some high level programming languages we find the notion of "cell" or "location" and find operations to explicitly deposit and examine information in those cells. Our LISP subset has no such explicit features; it relies on the implementation of binding and variable evaluation to perform similar notions. As part of our examination of evaluation we wish to expose these details to close scrutiny and understand how binding and variable evaluation can be mechanized. The most common notion used to implement these

---

[10]Compare this with the technique of Godel numbering in formal logic [Men 64].

operations is the symbol table.[11] This is the device we used informally in Section 2.7; we will review some of that discussion here.

In its abstract form, a symbol table is a set of ordered pairs of objects; one of the elements of each pair is a name; the other is a value associated with that name. This means that symbol tables can be characterized as relations or perhaps even as functions. This latter characterization is indeed viable. On page 89 we showed that a table could be constructed and maintained in a manner preserving functionality. As an abstract operation, finding an element in a symbol table is also quite simple: given a set of ordered pairs and a name, find a pair whose first element is the same as the given name. This operation can be described as function application where the function being applied is the table and the argument is the name component. That is: $locate[x;tbl] = tbl(x)$.

The maintenance of symbol tables as sets was a bit too abstract; the level of abstraction we implemented viewed a symbol table as a *sequence* of pairs, each pair representing a variable and its corresponding value. The table manipulating algorithms, given in Section 2.7, depended heavily on the implied sequencing of call-by-value and recursion. Since this was consistent with the explicit sequencing used in adding elements to the table, we achieved the desired effect. We found the expected bindings, even though there may have been other candidates in the tables. In the remaining sections of this chapter we will utilize more features of this interplay between representation of data and calling style of algorithm. Symbol tables are just one manifestation of this phenomenon.

Symbol tables are also known as association lists or **a-lists**; thus *assoc* is the traditional name of a LISP function to search a symbol table. More recently symbol tables have been called **environments**; thus we frequently will use the identifer *env* as a variable which is an environment. The binary function *assoc* expects a name and a symbol table as arguments. It will examine the table from left to right, looking for the first pair whose name-component matches the given name. If a pair is found, then that pair is returned; if no such pair is found, the result is undefined. We will need to designate a selector, *name*, to locate the name-component of a pair, and another selector, *value*, to retrieve the value-component.

$$assoc[x;env] <= \quad [eq[name[first[env]];x] \to first[env];$$
$$t \to assoc[x;rest[env]]]$$

If the table is very long and the desired pair is close to the end of the table, then we will be in for a very long search. The search scheme encoded in *assoc* is called **linear search**, and is unnecessarily inefficient for tables of substantial length. However the phenomemona we wish to study now are not

---

[11]Recall, we are *simulating* substitution; see [Ber 75] for an alternative.

directly related to efficiency of searching methods. [12] We will come back to symbol tables in Section 5.6 to study the problems of efficient storage and retrieval of information. It will suffice now simply to think of a symbol table as represented in LISP by a list of dotted pairs: a name dotted with value. In this representation, then, $name[x] <= car[x]$, and $value[x] <= cdr[x]$. For completeness, we should also specify a constructor. Though we won't need the function for a while, we will name it $mkent$; it will take an identifier and a value and return a new symbol table entry. Its representation here is $mkent[x;y] <= cons[x;y]$.

To illustrate the representation and algorithms, assume we wish to represent three variables x, y, and z which were to have values 2, 3, and 4. That fact could be encoded as:

$$((X . 2) (Y . 3) (Z . 4))$$

Then the retrieval of y and u could be encoded as:

$$assoc[Y; ((X . 2) (Y . 3) (Z . 4))] = (Y . 3)$$

$$assoc[U; ((X . 2) (Y . 3) (Z . 4))] = \perp$$

The retrieval of $\perp$ for u could be implemented as an error message or, better yet, could interact with the user to isolate the misconception, correct it, and continue.

We must also represent bindings of variables to non-numeric S-exprs. For example, we must represent information like: "the current value of x is A". We will place the dotted-pair $(X . A)$ in the table. Now this representation is certainly open to question: why not add $(X . (QUOTE A))$? The latter notation is more consistent with our conception of representation espoused on page 56. That is, we map LISP expressions to S-expressions; perform the calculations on this representation, and finally *reinterpret* the result of this calculation as a LISP expression. The representation we have chosen for symbol tables obviates the last reinterpretation step; recall the diagram on page 103. Now it will turn out that for our initial subsets of LISP this reinterpretation step simply would involve "stripping" the $QUOTE$s. The only "values" which a LISP computation can return are constants; however more general evaluation schemes are conceivable; partial evaluation may be useful, simplifying $x+y+2$ to $x+6$ when y has value 4. Perhaps the LISP representation of table entries is a poor one; we will see. In studying any existing language, or contemplating the design of any new one, we must question each detail of representation. Decisions made too early can have serious consequences.

---

[12]At least indirectly the discussion *is* related to search efficiency. LISP implements a dynamic binding or "latest active" binding strategy. A case can be made for static binding on the basis of shorter symbol table searches.

Before continuing we should take stock of our current position. In this section we have recreated the table-lookup mechanism we used in Section 2.7, but now we are paying a bit more attention to representation. We can locate things in a table and we have seen how calling functions can add values to a table. We have said nothing about adding function definitions to the tables. Abstractly we know how to extract the definition from the table and apply it. We must give an explicit representation of the storage of a function. This turns out to be a reasonably non-trivial problem. We have seen that it is possible to mechanize at least one scheme for evaluation of functions -- call-by-value, evaluating arguments from left to right. We have seen that it is possible to translate LISP expressions into S-exprs in such a way that we can write a LISP function which will act as an evaluator for such translations. In the process we have had to mechanize the intuitive devices we might mentally use to recall the definition of functions and to recall the current values of variables. It became clear that the mechanism of symbol tables could be used. To associate a variable with a value was easy. To associate a function name with its definition required some care. That is, part of the definition of a function involves the proper association of formal parameters with the body of the definition. The next section introduces a notation for describing function definitions.

3.4 λ-notation

Recall our discussion of the problems of representation of function definitions. This discussion began on page 84 and our conclusion was that to represent a definition like $f[x;y] <= \xi$ we needed a symbol table entry with name f and a value part which contained the body of the definition, ξ, and the list of formal parameters, $[x;y]$. This view of the content of a definition will have to be revised, but its implementation contains sufficient complexity to support a lively and fruitful discussion. LISP uses a unique notation, called the λ-**notation** to lend precision to our informal discussion of function representation.

The λ-notation is derived from the λ-calculus, a formalism invented by the logician Alonzo Church ([Chu 41]) to model functions which are describable by algorithms. The λ-calculus is useful for discussing the concepts of function and function application. Since many algorithms compute functions and since function application is simulated by procedure calls, the calculus is well suited for a purified discussion of procedures in programming languages. We shall outline the λ-calculus in Section 3.13. The λ-notation was introduced into programming languages by John McCarthy in the description of LISP ([McC 60]). There are several important distinctions between Church's λ-calculus and the λ-notation of McCarthy; we will point out the differences in Section 3.13.

We begin the discussion by exemplifying the need for more precise terminology. We have been informally writing $f[x;y] <= x*y + y$ as a definition of the function f. This notation is supposed to convey the following intent: f is the name of a function or rule; whenever f is supplied with two numeric arguments it is supposed to multiply those arguments and add the result to the second. The resulting sum is the desired answer. Since informality is susceptible to ambiguity, we should analyze the "<="-notation more closely. Though we say f is being defined, it is not f, but $f[x;y]$ which appears to the left of the "<="-symbol. First, $f[x;y]$ does *not* denote a function, f denotes a function. To see what $f[x;y]$ means consider the following example. When we are asked to evaluate $car[(A . B)]$ we say the value is A. $car[(A . B)]$ is an expression to be evaluated; we have called such expressions LISP **forms**. If $car[(A . B)]$ is a form then so is $car[x]$; only now the form references a variable instead of a constant; therefore the value of the form depends on the current value assigned to the variable x. So the **function** is car; the **form** is $car[x]$. Therefore, the function is f; $f[x;y]$ is a form, and so is $x*y + y$. The informal notation has a form on both sides of the "<=". We would like a notation which clearly shows what is being defined and what is given.

Further, our notation has really been specifying more than just the name. The notation specifies the formal parameters (x and y) and the order in which we are to associate actual parameters in a call with the formal parameters of the definition (x with the first, y with the second). More subtly, the notation tells *which* variables in the function body are to be supplied values when the function is called. For example define $g[x] <= x*y + y$; then the expression $g[2]$ specifies that x is to receive a value 2, but leaves unspecified what the value of y should be. [13]

We also wish to have a notation so that function definitions can be inserted into the symbol table as "values" assigned to names. They will be parametric values, but they will be values. The λ-notation performs this task by preceding the function body with a list of variables, called **lambda list**. The lambda list has been previously called the formal parameter list; either term is acceptable. Each parameter in the lambda list is called a lambda variable (or a formal parameter). The resulting construct is preceded by "λ[" and followed by "]". Using the above example, the identifier f denotes exactly the same LISP function as $\lambda[[x;y] x*y + y]$. The λ-notation introduces nothing new as far as our intuitive binding and evaluation processes are concerned; it only makes these operations more clear. To analyze these ideas a bit further, notice that $\lambda[[x;y] x*y + y]$ is the "same" function as $\lambda[[u;v] u*v + v]$. This means in effect that the formal parameters are "place holders" and can be uniformly replaced with other identifiers. Notice to that function names are also place holders.

---

[13]Note also, that the "values" for + and * are also unspecified.

$$one[x] <= [x=0 \rightarrow 1; t \rightarrow one[x-1]]$$

is the same function as:

$$fxy[x] <= [x=0 \rightarrow 1; t \rightarrow fxy[x-1]]$$

There are certain restrictions on the replacement of identifiers; the precise description of that algorithm requires care. The implementation of that algorithm will be part of this chapter.

One benefit of the λ-notation is that we need not give explicit names to functions in order to perform the evaluation. Evaluation of expressions involving such anonymous functions, also called **open lambdas**, is within the province of LISP. Currently, we will restrict our discussion to λ-expressions which are function constants, just like A is an S-expr constant. Since a λ-expression is a constant, its value is itself. LISP will evaluate an application involving a λ-expression in two stages; first, it will bind the evaluated actual parameters to the λ-variables, and then it will evaluate the function body.

Consider, for example:

$$\lambda[[x;y] \; x^2 + y][2;3]$$

We associate 2 with x and 3 with y and evaluate the expression:

$$x^2 + y$$

This calculation will give 7.

To evaluate the more complex:

$$\lambda[[x] \; cdr[car[x]]][((A \cdot B) \cdot C)]$$

we bind x to the S-expression $((A \cdot B). C)$ and evaluate the function body. The evaluation procedure first evaluates $car[x]$ with the current binding of x; this result, $(A \cdot B)$, is passed to cdr; and that calculation finally returns B.

The λ-notation can be used anywhere LISP expects to find a function, for example:

$$\lambda[[x] \; first[x]]$$
$$[\lambda[[y] \; rest[y]][(A \; B)]]$$

This expression equivalent to writing:

$$f[g[(A \; B)]] \quad \text{where } f[x] <= first[x] \quad \text{and} \quad g[y] <= rest[y]$$

Though the second form is perhaps easier for us to comprehend, the first form *is* equivalent and will be acceptable to the evaluator. In fact, the evaluation of the second formulation will effectively reduce to the first formulation on its way to final evaluation.

$$\lambda[[x] \; first[x]][\lambda[[y] \; rest[y]][(A \; B)]] = \lambda[[x] \; first[x]][(B)] = B$$

LISP evaluation requires care. For example the LISP function $\lambda[[x]2]$ is *not* the constant function which always gives value 2. The evaluation of an expression involving this function requires the evaluation of the actual parameter associated with x. That computation may not terminate. For example, consider $\lambda[[x]2][fact[-1]]$ where *fact* is the LISP implementation of the factorial function given on page 44.

Since we intend to include λ-expressions in our language we must include an $\Re$-mapping into S-expression form for them. The character λ will be translated to *LAMBDA* and the formal parameters will be translated into a list:

$$\Re[\![\lambda[[x_1; \ldots; x_n] \, \xi]\,]\!] = (LAMBDA \, (X_1 \ldots X_n) \, \Re[\![\xi]\!])$$

Here are some examples of λ-expressions and their $\Re$-translations:

$$\Re[\![\lambda[[x;y] \, x^2 + y]\,]\!] = (LAMBDA \, (X \, Y) \, (PLUS \, (EXPT \, X \, 2) \, Y))$$

$$\Re[\![\lambda[[x;y] \, cons[car[x];y]]\,]\!] = (LAMBDA \, (X \, Y) \, (CONS \, (CAR \, X) \, Y))$$

To complete our introduction of λ-expressions, our LISP syntax equations will be augmented to include:

<function> ::= λ[<varlist><form>]

<varlist>   ::= [<variable>; ... ; <variable>]   [14]

Besides giving a clear notation for function definitions, the λ-notation is a useful computational device. Consider the following sketch of a function definition:

$$g <= \lambda[[x][\pi[lic[x]] \rightarrow lic[x]; \ldots x \ldots]]$$

where *lic* may be a *long involved calculation*, and π is a predicate.

We certainly must compute *lic[x] once*. But as g is defined, we would compute *lic[x] twice* if p_1 is true: once in the calculation of p_1, and once as e_1. Since both calculations of *lic[x]* will give the same value, [15] this second calculation is unnecessary. Instead, we could write:

$$g <= \lambda[[x] \, f[lic[x];x]]$$

where: $f <= \lambda[[u;v][\pi[u] \rightarrow u; \ldots v \ldots]]$

In this scheme *lic* will only be evaluated once; its value will be passed into f. This solution requires introduction of a new function name. Using λ-expressions, in a style called **internal lambdas** we can improve g without adding any new function names to our symbol tables.

Replace the body of g with:

LAM $\lambda[[y][\pi[y] \rightarrow y; \ldots x \ldots]][lic[x]]$

---

[14]Recall that this use of ellipses means "zero or more occurrences of <variable>".

[15]Our current LISP subset has no side effects. That means there is no way for a computation to affect its surrounding environment. The most common construct which has a side-effect is the assignment statement.

Call this new function g':

$$g' <= \lambda[[x] \, \lambda[[y][\pi[y] \to y; \dots x \dots]][lic[x]]]$$

Now when g' is called we evaluate the actual parameter, binding it to x, and evaluate **LAM**. Evaluation of **LAM** involves only one calculation of $lic[x]$, binding the result to y. We then evaluate the body of the conditional expression as before. If p_1 *is* true, then this definition of g' involves one calculation of $lic[x]$ and two table look-ups (for the value of y), rather than the two calculations of $lic[x]$ in g. More conventional programming languages can obtain the same effect as this use of internal lambdas by assignment of $lic[x]$ to a temporary variable. We will introduce assignment statements in LISP in Section 4.2. [16]

Problems

1. What is the difference between $\lambda[[\ ]\ x*y + y]$ and $x*y + y$?

3.5 Mechanization of Evaluation

We first gave plausibility arguments for the existence of an evaluator for LISP; and then picked a representation for LISP expressions; finally we introduced a precise notation for discussing functions. It is now time to write an evaluator for representations of LISP expressions. The evaluator will be the final arbiter on the question of the meaning of a LISP construct. The evaluator is thus a very important algorithm. We will express it and its related functions in a representation-free form, but we will keep our Cambridge Polish representation in mind.

As we have discovered, the great progenitors (Section 2.8) are evaluators for subsets of LISP. With our symbol-table mechanism we could now extend those algorithms to handle variable look-ups. Rather than do this we will make a total revision of the structure of the evaluators. In making the revision, the following points should be remembered:

---

[16]This technique is also related to the ideas of common sub-expression recognition in compiling algorithms (Section 6.16).

1. Expressions to be evaluated can contain variables, both simple variables and variables naming λ-expressions. Therefore, evaluation must be done with respect to an environment or symbol table. We wish to recognize other function names besides *CAR, CDR, CONS, EQ,* and *ATOM* in our evaluator, but explicitly adding new definitions to the evaluator in the style of the recognizers for the five primitives is not an attractive approach. That scheme would require rewriting sections of the evaluator every time a new definition was introduced. An alternative solution is to hold the definitions in a symbol table. Our symbol table should hold the function definitions and the evaluator should contain the general schemes for finding the definitions, binding variables to values, and evaluating the function body.

2. All **function** calls are to be evaluated "by-value." However, there are some **special forms** which are not evaluated in the normal manner. Conditional expressions, quoted expressions, and lambda expressions are handled differently, and the evaluator will recognize these constructs specially.

The primary algorithm in the evaluator will be named *eval*. It will take two arguments; the first will be a representation of an expression to be evaluated, and the second will be a representation of a symbol table. The evaluator will recognize numbers, and the constants *T* and *NIL*, and if presented with a variable, will attempt to find the value of the variable in the symbol table using *assoc* (Section 3.3).

eval will also recognize the special forms *cond* and *quote*. When *eval* recognizes a conditional expression (represented by *(COND ...)*), the body of the *COND* will be passed to a subfunction named *evcond*. *evcond* embodies the conditional expression semantics as described on page 20. The representation, *(QUOTE α)*, signifies the occurrence of a constant, **α**, which is simply returned. Any other expression is a call-by-value application. The argument-list evaluation is handled by *evlis* in the authorized left-to-right ordering. This calculation is performed by recurring on the list representing the arguments. Finally, we **apply** the function to the list of evaluated arguments. This is done by the function *apply*.

With this introduction we will now write a more general evaluator which will handle a larger subset of LISP than the *tgms*.
Here's the new *eval*:

$$
\begin{aligned}
eval <= \lambda[[&exp;environ] \\
&[isconst[exp] \rightarrow denote[exp]; \\
&\ isvar[exp] \rightarrow lookup[exp;environ]; \\
&\ iscond[exp] \rightarrow evcond[arg_c[exp];environ]; \\
&\ isfunc+args[exp] \rightarrow apply[func[exp]; \\
&\hspace{5em} evlis[arglist[exp];environ]; \\
&\hspace{5em} environ]]]
\end{aligned}
$$

and:

lookup <=λ[[*var;env*] *value*[*assoc*[*var;env*]]]

denote <= λ[[*exp*][*isnumber*[*exp*] → *exp;*
          istruth[*exp*] → *exp;*
          isfalse[*exp*] → *exp;*
          issexpr[*exp*] → *rep*[*exp*];
          islambda[*exp*] → *exp*]]

where:

rep knows how to extract the S-expr from the representation. In our scheme
      the selector *rep* is given by *cadr*.
The other selectors, constructors and recognizers which relate this abstract
definition to our particular S-expression representation are grouped on
page 117.

evcond <= λ[[*e;environ*]
          [*eval*[*ante*[*first*[*e*]];*environ*] → *eval*[*conseq*[*first*[*e*]];*environ*];
          t → *evcond*[*rest*[*e*];*environ*]]]
and,

evlis <= λ[[*e;environ*] [*null*[*e*] → ( );
          t → *concat*[*eval*[*first*[*e*];*environ*];
          evlis[*rest*[*e*];*environ*]]]]

The subfunctions, *evcond* and *evlis*, are simple. *evcond* appeared before in
tgmoafr in a less abstract form; *evlis* constructs a new list consisting of the
results of evaluating the elements of *e* from left to right, using the symbol
table, *environ*, where necessary. Since *evcond* and *evlis* are LISP functions,
they are subject to the left-to-right evaluation rule. Thus *evlis* embodies the
left-to-right rule. If *evlis* were evaluated under a right-to-left rule then *evlis*
would evaluate expressions in right-to-left order. It is possible to write a
version of *evlis* which only depends on being evaluated **CBV**, and which
does embody the left-to-right rule:

evlis <= λ[[*e;environ*] [*null*[*e*] → ( );
          t → λ[[*x*] *concat*[*x;evlis*[*rest*[*e*];*environ*]]]
          [*eval*[*first*[*e*];*environ*]]]]

     To continue, the function *apply* takes three arguments: a representation
of a function, a representation of the evaluated arguments, and a
representation of a symbol table. *apply* explicitly recognizes the
representations of the five primitive functions *CAR, CDR, CONS, EQ,* and
ATOM. If the function name is a variable, the definition is located in the

symbol table by *eval* and applied to the arguments. Otherwise the function must be a λ-expression. Things now get interesting; we must evaluate the body of the λ-expression after binding the formal parameters of the λ-expression to the evaluated arguments. We add variable-value pairs to the front of the current symbol table. We will define a subfunction, *mkenv*, to perform the binding; then pass the function body and the new symbol table to *eval*.

Here is *apply*:

$$apply <= \lambda[[fn;args,environ]$$
$$[iscar[fn] \to car[arg_1[args]]];$$
$$iscons[fn] \to cons[arg_1[args];arg_2[args]];$$

$$\cdots \qquad \cdots$$

$$isvar[fn] \to apply[eval[fn;environ];args;environ];$$
$$islambda[fn] \to eval[body[fn];$$
$$mkenv[vars[fn];args;environ]]]]$$

$$mkenv <= \lambda[[vars;vals;environ] pairlis[vars;vals;environ]]$$

$$pairlis <= \lambda[[vars;vals;environ]$$
$$[null[vars] \to environ;$$
$$t \to concat[mkent[first[vars];first[vals]];$$
$$pairlis[rest[vars];$$
$$rest[vals];$$
$$environ]]]]$$

Some of the functions and predicates which will relate these abstract definitions to our specific S-expression representation of LISP constructs are given below.

Recognizers

$$iscar <= \lambda[[x] eq[x;CAR]]$$
$$isSexpr <= \lambda[[x] eq[first[x];QUOTE]]$$
$$istruth <= \lambda[[x] eq[x;T]]$$
$$islambda <= \lambda[[x] eq[first[x];LAMBDA]]$$
$$isfun+args <= \lambda[[x] t]$$

Selectors

$$func <= \lambda[[x] first[x]]$$
$$arglist <= \lambda[[x] rest[x]]$$
$$body <= \lambda[[x] third[x]]$$
$$vars <= \lambda[[x] second[x]]$$

$$args_c <= \lambda[[x] rest[x]]$$
$$arg_1 <= \lambda[[x] first[x]]$$
$$arg_2 <= \lambda[[x] second[x]]$$
$$ante <= \lambda[[x] first[x]]$$
$$conseq <= \lambda[[x] second[x]]$$
$$rep <= \lambda[[x] second[x]]$$

Constructor

$$mkent <= \lambda[[x;y] cons[x;y]]$$

Another application of the left-to-right property occurs within *apply*, in the symbol table search and construction process. Notice that *lookup* uses *assoc* to look from left to right for the latest binding of a variable. Thus the function which *augments* the table must add the latest binding to the *front*. New bindings occur when the function *mkenv*, using *pairlis*, builds an augmented symbol table with the λ-variables bound to their evaluated arguments. The functions *lookup* and *mkenv* operate together. We will see representations of these functions other than *assoc* and *pairlis*. The actual search and construction operations will change, but the critical relationship that *mkenv* always builds a table compatible with the search strategy of *lookup* will be maintained.

To summarize then: the evaluation of an expression $f[a_1; \ldots ;a_n]$, where the a_i's are S-exprs, consists in applying *eval* to the $\Re$-translation, $(\Re[\![f]\!] \; \Re[\![a_1]\!] \ldots \Re[\![a_n]\!])$. This behavior is again an example of the diagrams of page 56. In its most simple terms, we mapped LISP evaluation onto the LISP *eval* function; mapped LISP expressions onto S-expressions; and executed *eval*. Notice that in this case we do not reinterpret the output since the structure of the representation does this implicitly. We have commented on the efficacy of this already on page 109.

The specification of the evaluation of LISP expressions using *eval* and *apply* is one of the most interesting developments of computer science.

Problems

1. Compare our version of *eval* and *apply* with the version given in [McC 65]. Though the current version is much more readable, how much of it *still* depends on the representation we chose? That is, how abstract is it really?
2. Complete the specification of the selectors, constructors, and recognizers.

3.6 Examples of *eval*

We will demonstrate the inner workings of the evaluation algorithm on a couple of samples and will describe the flow of control in the execution in a couple of different ways. The examples will be done in terms of the image of the $\Re$-mapping rather than being done abstractly. We do this since the structure of an actual LISP evaluator will use this representation. [17] It is important that you diligently study the sequence of events in the execution of the evaluator. The process is detailed, but it must be done at least once.

Let's evaluate $f[2;3]$ where $f \mathrel{<=} \lambda[[x;y]\; x^2 + y]$. That is, evaluate:

$$eval[\; \Re[\![f[2;3]]\!] \;]; \Re[\![\{ <f, \lambda[[x;y]\; +[\uparrow[x;2];\; y]]> \}]\!]]$$

After appropriate translation this is equivalent to evaluating:

$$eval[(F\;2\;3);\; ((F\;.\;(LAMBDA\;(X\;Y)\;(PLUS\;(EXPT\;X\;2)\;Y))))]$$

_____

[17] Recall that we will be programming in the $\Re$-image.

Notes:

1. *((F . (LAMBDA (X Y) ...)))* = *((F LAMBDA (X Y) ...))* This is mentioned because most LISP implementations will print the latter even if you write the former.

2. Since the symbol table *((F ...))* occurs so frequently in the following trace, we will abbreviate it as st. We have no mechanism yet for permanently increasing the repertoire of known functions. We must therefore resort to subterfuge and initialize the symbol table to get *f* defined.

3. For this example we must assume that + and ↑ (exponentiation) are known functions. Thus *apply* would have to contain recognizers for *PLUS* and *TIMES*:

$$... atom[fn] \rightarrow [\ isplus[fn] \rightarrow +[arg_1[args];arg_2[args]];$$
$$isexpt[fn] \rightarrow ↑[arg_1[args];arg_2[args]];$$
$$...]$$

$$...$$

So *eval*[(F 2 3);st]

    = *apply*[*func*[(F 2 3)];
           evlis[*arglist*[(F 2 3)];st];
           st]

    = *apply*[F ;*evlis*[(2 3);st];st]
    = *apply*[F ;(2 3);st]

    = *apply*[*eval*[F ;st];
          (2 3);
          st]
    = *apply*[(LAMBDA (X Y) (PLUS (EXPT X 2) Y));
          (2 3);
          st]

    = *eval*[*body*[(LAMBDA (X Y) (PLUS (EXPT X 2) Y))];
        mkenv[*vars*[(LAMBDA (X Y) (PLUS (EXPT X 2) Y))];
             (2 3);
             st]]

    = *eval*[(PLUS (EXPT X 2) Y);
        pairlis[(X Y);(2 3);st]]

    = *eval*[(PLUS (EXPT X 2) Y);
        ((X . 2)(Y . 3)(F LAMBDA (X Y) ...))]

    = *apply*[PLUS;
          evlis[((EXPT X 2) Y);((X . 2)(Y . 3)..)];
          ((X . 2)...)]

Let's do a little of: *evlis*[((*EXPT X* 2) *Y*);((*X* . 2)(*Y* . 3)...)]

$$= \textit{concat}[\textit{eval}[(EXPT \ X \ 2);((X \ . \ 2)(Y \ . \ 3) \ ...)];$$
$$\textit{evlis}[(Y);((X \ . \ 2) \ ...)]]$$

$$= \textit{concat}[\textit{apply}[\ EXPT;$$
$$\textit{evlis}[(X \ 2);((X \ . \ 2)...)];$$
$$((X \ . \ 2) \ ...]$$
$$\textit{evlis}[(Y); \ ...]]$$

$$= \textit{concat}[\textit{apply}[\ EXPT;$$
$$(2 \ 2);$$
$$((X \ . \ 2);$$
$$...];$$
$$\textit{evlis}[(Y); \ ...]]$$

$$= \textit{concat}[\ \uparrow[\textit{arg}_1[(2 \ 2)];\textit{arg}_2[(2 \ 2)]];$$
$$\textit{evlis}[(Y); \ ... \ ]]$$

$$= \textit{concat}[\uparrow[2;2];\textit{evlis}[(Y); \ ... \ ]]$$
$$= \textit{concat}[4;\textit{evlis}[(Y);((X \ . \ 2)(Y \ . \ 3) \ ....)]]]$$
$$= \textit{concat}[4;\textit{concat}[\textit{eval}[Y;((X \ .2) \ ...)]; \ \textit{evlis}[(\ );((\ ...))]]]]$$
$$= \textit{concat}[4;\textit{concat}[3;(\ )]]$$
$$= (4 \ 3)$$

Now back to *apply*:

$$= \textit{apply}[\ PLUS;$$
$$(4 \ 3);$$
$$((X \ . \ 2) \ (Y \ . \ 3) \ ... \ )]$$

$$= +[4;3]$$
$$= 7$$

It should now be clear that *eval* does perform as you would expect, at least for this example. It is not clear that a simpler scheme might not do as well. In particular, the complexity of the symbol table mechanism which we claimed was so important has not been exploited. The next example will show that a scheme like ours is necessary to keep track of variable bindings.

Let's sketch the evaluation of *fact[3]* where:

$$fact <= \lambda[[x][x = 0 \rightarrow 1;\ t \rightarrow *[x;fact[x-1]]]]$$

that is, *eval[(FACT 3);st]* where st names the initial symbol table:

```
((FACT .  (LAMBDA (X) (COND((ZEROP X) 1)
                      (T (TIMES X
                                (FACT (SUB1 X))))))))) 18
```

In this example we will assume that the binary function $*$, the unary predicate *zerop* $<= \lambda[[x]\ x = 0]$ and unary function *sub1* $<= \lambda[[x]\ x-1]$ are known and are recognized in the evaluator as *TIMES*, *ZEROP* and *SUB1* respectively.

Then *eval[(FACT 3);st]*
```
    = apply[FACT;
              evlis[(3);st];
              st]
    = apply[(LAMBDA (X) (COND ...));
              (3);
              st]
    = eval[(COND ((ZEROP X) 1) (T ( ...)));((X . 3) . st)]
    = evcond[((((ZEROP X) 1) (T (TIMES X (FACT (SUB1 X))))));
              ((X . 3) . st)]
```
Now, let st1 be *((X . 3) . st)*
```
    = eval[(TIMES X (FACT (SUB1 X))); st1]
    = apply[TIMES;
              evlis[(X (FACT (SUB1 X))); st1];
              st1]
    = apply[TIMES;
              concat[3;
                        evlis[((FACT (SUB1 X))); st1]];
              st1]
```

---

[18]We have split the *COND* across several lines in an indented fashion to improve readability. Such techniques are common in LISP. The idea is called "pretty printing" and is discussed further on page 274 and in Section 9.2.

Now things get a little interesting inside *evlis*:

   evlis[(((*FACT* (*SUB1 X*)));st1]
             = *concat*[*eval*[((*FACT* (*SUB1 X*)); st1];
                          ( )]
        and *eval*[((*FACT* (*SUB1 X*));st1]
                       = *apply*[*FACT*;
                                evlis[(((*SUB1 X*));st1];
                                st1]
                       = *apply*[*FACT*; (2);st1]
                       = *apply*[(*LAMBDA* (*X*) (*COND* ...));
                                (2);
                                st1]

                       = *eval*[((*COND* ((*ZEROP X*) 1) ...));((*X* . 2) . st1)]
               . . .

Within this latest call on *eval* the symbol-table-searching function, *lookup*, will find the pair (*X* . 2) when looking for the value of *x*. This is as it should be. But notice also that the older binding, (*X* . 3), is still around in the symbol table st1, and will become accessible once we complete this latest call on *eval*. It will become accessible because this earlier manifestation of the table was saved by the λ-binding process as we entered the inner call on *eval*; as we leave this inner evaluation, the previous incarnation of the table is restored.

As the computation continues, the current symbol table appears as follows:

            ((*FACT LAMBDA* (*X*) (*COND* ...))) = st
                ((*X* . 3) . st) = st1
                ((*X* . 2) . st1) = st2
                ((*X* . 1) . st2) = st3
                ((*X* . 0) . st3)

Thus each new level of the table builds on the prior table; each prior table is saved by the following line from *apply* (page 117):

   islambda[*fn*] → *eval*[*body*[*fn*];*mkenv*[*vars*[*fn*];*args*;*environ*]

The call on *eval* is performed with the augmented table; when we leave that inner *eval* we return to an environment which contains the prior table.

Using *mkenv* to concatenate the new bindings onto the front of the symbol table as we call *eval*, generates the required environment. The tricky part occurs when we leave that particular call on *eval*; the old table is automatically restored by the recursion mechanism. That is, concatenating things onto the front of a table doesn't change the table, but if we call *eval* or *apply* with a symbol table of say:

$$concat[(X \ . \ 2);concat[(X \ . \ 3); \ st]]$$

then in *that* call on *eval* or *apply* we have access to *2* as the value of *x*, rather than *3*.

In this representation, the search function *lookup* always proceeds from left to right through the table and, since the table entry function *mkenv* always adds pairs onto the left of the table before *eval* is called, we will get the expected binding of the variables.

The structure of *mkenv* should be analyzed further: it takes a formal parameter list, an evaluated actual parameter list, and an environment, as its arguments; it allocates a new block to contain the name-value pairs and proceeds to send each name-value pair to its proper slot in the block. The value of *mkenv* is the newly constructed environment formed by linking the new block onto the front of the old environment. It turns out that *pairlis* is able to combine the action of making the new block and filling the slots.

A more accurate picture of the abstract behavior of *mkenv* is:

$$mkenv <= \lambda[[vars;vals;env] \ mkenv'[vars;vals;alloc[vars];env]]$$

$$mkenv' <= \lambda[[vars;vals;block;env] \ [null[vars] \to link[block;env];$$
$$t \to mkenv'[\ rest[vars];$$
$$rest[vals];$$
$$send[\ first[vars];$$
$$first[vals];$$
$$block];$$
$$env] \ ]]]$$

Our current implementation of *pairlis* is equivalent to:

$$alloc <= \lambda[[x] \ (\ )] \ [19]$$

$$send <= \lambda[[var;val;block] \ concat[mkent[var;val];block]]$$

$$link <= \lambda[[block;env] \ append[block;env]]$$

The computational behavior of *pairlis* is slightly different: here the name-value pairs are added to the environment in an order reverse to that used in *pairlis*. Since the variables in the λ-list must be distinct from one another, this alternative environment is equivalent to the previous one.

Symbol table manipulation is very important, so let's look at it again in a slightly different manner. In this example, expressions and table entries will be written more informally. Since the evaluator is operating on the list representation of expressions we should continue to present these arguments to *eval* as lists. However, the object being represented might be more

---

[19]*alloc* is defined as a unary function even though its argument is ignored here. This generality is in anticipation of future binding implementations.

understandable and readable [20] than the representation of that object. Thus, initially, we will write $\mathfrak{R}[\![\xi]\!]$ rather than the explicit $\mathfrak{R}$-image of ξ; for example, write $\mathfrak{R}[\![fact[3]]\!]$ rather than *(FACT 3)*. Later we will simply write ξ where no confusion is likely. With similar motivation, we represent the symbol table between vertical bars, "|", in such a way that if a table, t_1, is:

$$\left|\begin{matrix} b_n \\ ... \\ b_1 \end{matrix}\right|$$ then *concating* a new element, b_{n+1} onto t_1 gives:

$$\left|\begin{matrix} b_{n+1} \\ b_n \\ ... \\ b_1 \end{matrix}\right|$$

The elements of the table should also be presented as $\mathfrak{R}$-images, but we will represent the entries in a more transparent form. For example:

$eval[\mathfrak{R}[\![fact[3]]\!]$; $|\, fact : \lambda[[x][x=0 \rightarrow 1; \mathfrak{t} \rightarrow *[x;fact[x-1]]]] \,|\,]$

$= eval[\mathfrak{R}[\![[x=0 \rightarrow 1; \mathfrak{t} \rightarrow *[x;fact[x-1]]]]\!]$; $\left|\begin{matrix} x : 3 \\ fact : \lambda[...] \end{matrix}\right|$ $]$

$= *[3;eval[\mathfrak{R}[\![[x=0 \rightarrow ...]]\!]$; $\left|\begin{matrix} x : 2 \\ x : 3 \\ fact : \lambda[...] \end{matrix}\right|$ $]$

$= *[3; *[2;eval[\mathfrak{R}[\![[x=0 \rightarrow ...]]\!]$; $\left|\begin{matrix} x : 1 \\ x : 2 \\ x : 3 \\ fact : \lambda[...] \end{matrix}\right|$ $]$

---

[20] Readability of LISP expressions is a subject of heated between LISP users and non-users. Since we program using the list representation there is an initial period in which the representation is "difficult to read". However that phemononon is short lived; the regularity of LISP expressions, the minimality of syntax, the use of formatting programs called "pretty printers", and several abbreviational devices soon overcome any supposed disadvantages. This text presents LISP expressions in the meta-language since we wish to stress the notions of representation independence, rather than LISP's programming behavior.

$$= *[3; *[2; *[1; eval[\Re[\![[x=0 \rightarrow ...]]\!]]]; \qquad \begin{array}{|c|c|} x:0 &] \\ x:1 & \\ x:2 & \\ x:3 & \\ fact:\lambda[...] & \end{array}$$

$$= *[3; *[2; *[1;1]]] \quad \text{with:} \qquad \begin{array}{|c|c|} x:1 &] \\ x:2 & \\ ... & \end{array}$$

$$= *[3; *[2;1]] \qquad \text{with:} \qquad \begin{array}{|c|c|} x:2 &] \\ ... & \end{array}$$

$$= *[3;2] \qquad\qquad \text{with:} \qquad \begin{array}{|c|c|} x:3 &] \\ ... & \end{array}$$

$$= 6 \qquad\qquad\quad \text{with:} \qquad |\; fact:\lambda[...]\;|$$

$$= 6$$

Notice that after we went to all the trouble to save the old values of x we never had to use them. However, in the general case of recursive evaluation we must be able to save and restore the old values of variables. For example, if we had defined *fact* as:

$$fact <= \lambda[[x][x=0 \rightarrow 1; \mathfrak{t} \rightarrow *[fact[x-1];x]]],$$

then we *would* have to access the old binding of x.

For further example, recall the definition of *equal*:

$$equal <= \lambda[[x;y][atom[x] \rightarrow [atom[y] \rightarrow eq[x;y]; \mathfrak{t} \rightarrow \mathfrak{f}];$$
$$atom[y] \rightarrow \mathfrak{f};$$
$$equal[car[x];car[y]] \rightarrow equal[cdr[x];cdr[y]];$$
$$\mathfrak{t} \rightarrow \mathfrak{f}]]$$

If we were evaluating:

$$equal[((A . B) . C);((A . B) . D)],$$

then, reading across the page, our symbol table structure would change as follows:

$$|equal:\lambda[[x;y]...]\;| ==> \quad \begin{array}{|c|} x:((A . B) . C) \\ y:((A . B) . D) \\ equal:\lambda[[x;y]...] \end{array} ==>$$

$$\begin{vmatrix} x:(A\,.\,B) \\ y:(A\,.\,B) \\ x:((A\,.\,B)\,.\,C) \\ y:((A\,.\,B)\,.\,D) \\ equal:\lambda[[x;y]\,...\,] \end{vmatrix} \quad ==> \quad \begin{vmatrix} x:A \\ y:A \\ x:(A\,.\,B) \\ y:(A\,.\,B) \\ x:((A\,.\,B)\,.\,C) \\ y:((A\,.\,B)\,.\,D) \\ equal:\lambda[[x;y]\,...\,] \end{vmatrix} \quad ==>$$

$$\begin{vmatrix} x:B \\ y:B \\ x:(A\,.\,B) \\ y:(A\,.\,B) \\ x:((A\,.\,B)\,.\,C) \\ y:((A\,.\,B)\,.\,D) \\ equal:\lambda[[x;y]\,...\,] \end{vmatrix} \quad ==> \quad \begin{vmatrix} x:C \\ y:D \\ x:((A\,.\,B)\,.\,C) \\ y:((A\,.\,B)\,.\,D) \\ equal:\lambda[[x;y]\,...\,] \end{vmatrix} \quad ==>$$

$$|\,equal:\lambda[[x;y]\,...\,]\,|$$

This degree of complexity is necessary, for while we are evaluating *equal[car[x];car[y]]*, we rebind *x* and *y* but we must save the old values of *x* and *y* for the possible evaluation of *equal[cdr[x],cdr[y]]*. It is *not* clear that this implementation is optimal. The search for the values of *x* and *y* is short, but the evaluation of any subexpressions involving *equal* must retrieve the definition of *equal*. That search is proportional to the depth of the initial arguments to *equal*.

Before continuing, we should examine *eval* and *apply* to see how they compare with our previous discussions of LISP evaluation. The spirit of call-by-value and conditional expression evaluation is maintained. λ-binding seems correct, though our current discussion is not complete. At least one preconception is not maintained here. Recall the discussion on page 17. We wanted n-ary functions called with exactly n arguments. An examination of the structure of *eval* and *apply* shows that if a function expecting *n* arguments is presented with fewer, then the result is undefined; but if it is given *more* arguments than necessary then the calculation is performed. For example:

eval[(CONS (QUOTE A) (QUOTE B) (QUOTE C));NIL]
        reduces to   *eval[(CONS (QUOTE A) (QUOTE B));NIL]*
        reduces to   *(A . B)*

This example shows one of the pitfalls in defining a language by an evaluator. If the intuitions of the language specifiers are faulty or incomplete then either we must maintain that faulty judgement, or we must lobby for a "revised report". [21]

The definition of a language by an evaluator written in that language is subject to other criticisms. The troublesome areas of our description of LISP's evaluation included λ-binding, calling styles in general and call-by-value in particular, and left-to-right order of evaluation. We wrote *eval* to explicate the meaning of these constructs, yet within *eval* we often relied on exactly these constructs to convey our intent. Now, our description in not entirely circular; *eval* does convey much of our intention to the reader, but the discussion of *how* these constructs operate is either implicit or is explained by using the same kind of constructs. In gaining a clearer understanding of what LISP constructs mean, *eval* is exemplary. Indeed many of the details of how these constructs work are irrelevant to such an understanding. When we attempt to implement a language feature we cannot assume the existence of that feature; the implementation must be prepared from a combination of more primitive components. As we proceed through the text we will introduce the mechanisms which are necessary to implement LISP and, indeed, implement the constructs of most other languages. In Section 4.4 we give several alternative algorithms for *eval*. The algorithms will evolve to an *eval* which makes explicit most of the mechanisms we need. In Chapter 5 we will begin to discuss efficient representations for LISP's data structures, control structures, and primitive operations. The remainder of the current chapter will explicate further features of LISP in preparation for that discussion.

Problems

1. Which parts of the evaluator allow the evaluation of functions applied to too many arguments?

2. Find other anomalies in the evaluator. That is, find places where unexpected results are obtained?

3.7 Variables

Let's look more closely at λ-binding in *eval*. The scheme presented seems reasonable, but as with "cons[A;B;C]", there may be more expressed here than we anticipated.

If we asked *eval* to compute $f[2]$, given a representation for $f \mathrel{<=} \lambda[[x] x + y]$ but no representation for the value of y it would complain. It would find f, bind 2 to x, and begin the evaluation of the body of f. It

---

[21]For example the LISP 1.6 system ([Qua 72]) gives $(A . A)$ for $cons[A]$; the MacLISP system ([Moo 74]) gives $(A . \text{"missing-arg"})$; and InterLISP ([Int 75]) gives (A).

would find x's value, but it would find no value for y. However, if we asked it to evaluate the form $\lambda[[y]\,f[2]][1]$ it *would* work. It would find the value of y to be 1 and would get a final answer of 3. You should convince yourself of this assertion.

Within the evaluation of $f[2]$ in $\lambda[[y]\,f[2]][1]$ the variable y has a different character from that of x. The value of x is found within the latest λ-binding, whereas y was bound in a dynamically surrounding λ-binding. That is, the λ-expression which bound y took effect before the binding of x and is still in effect when the binding of x is made. We do have access to y's binding in this case; the *lookup* routine will locate y's value. There is a third kind of name-value association present in these examples: we expect that the symbol "+" is recognized during the evaluation as denoting a procedure for computing the sum of two numbers. In previous discussions we have assumed that "+" was pre-defined inside *apply* and therefore explicitly recognized. Finally, in the first example, a fourth kind of variable usage occurred. The variable y had no associated value when the computation expected one. In this section we wish to examine these properties of variables.

The implementation of λ-bindings described in *pairlis* (page 116) is slightly misleading. There, the new λ-bindings are *concat*-ed onto the front of the existing table. They go on in a one-at-a-time fashion even though they are to be thought of as a logical unit: at the language level they all go on together, and they all come off together. It is the structure of this table which we should also examine. To these ends we now introduce some terminology.

Consider the evaluation of the expression:

$$\lambda[[y]\ equal[\lambda[[x]\ cons[x;y]][(A \cdot B)];x]][A]$$

in an environment where the definition of *equal* is known.

We evaluate the main argument A, and perform the λ-binding of A to y. This operation of λ-binding creates what we call a **local symbol table** and the variables bound in that local table are called **local bindings** for the body of the λ-expression. We now begin the evaluation of the arguments to *equal*. The first argument is itself an expression requiring λ-binding. We evaluate it's argument and bind $(A \cdot B)$ to x. This creates a local binding for x. In the process of making x local what happens to y? Notice that the binding process has not made y inaccessible: we can compute $cons[x;y]$ even though y is not local. Variables like y which are accessible, but not local, we call **non-local** variables. Thus both y and *cons* are non-local variables in our evaluation of $cons[x;y]$. There is a further distinction between y and *cons*: We expect *cons* to be a predefined function; indeed *cons* has not been λ-bound any where in our computation. Variables like *cons* we will call **global variables**.

Global variables include predefined function names, *car*, *cdr*, etc., and variables like t and *nil*. A useful interpretation of global variables is that

they are bound in the initial symbol table, also called the **global table**. [22]
Non-local variables which are λ-bound somewhere in the symbol table we
call **free variables**, and variables which have some accessible binding at the
current point in the computation are called **bound variables**. [23]

Finally the first argument to *equal* is evaluated giving *((A . B) . A)*. As
we complete that evaluation the local binding for *x* becomes inaccessible, and
y becomes local again. We examine the second argument to *equal*, which is *x*,
and now find there is no binding for that variable. Variables which have no
binding of any kind at the time we ask for a value are called **unbound
variables**. The local, free, and global variables make up the class of **bound
variables**.

For a computation to be meaningful, each variable which that
computation references must be bound when we ask for its value. The
computation of our current example would fail; it would fail even before we
asked for the definition of *equal* since we are doing call-by-value. One of our
tasks will be to discuss where definitions such as that for *equal* should be
kept.

Here is a diagram of our characterization of variables:

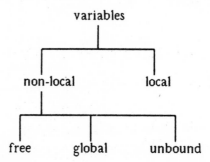

Notice that a variable which is initially global may become local and then
free by virtue of λ-bindings.

The binding strategy for local variables is reasonably uniform in
programming languages: bind some form of the actual parameters [24] to the
formal parameters and evaluate the body of the definition. One of the
difficulties in programming languages is deciding what value to associate

---

[22]This analogy breaks down somewhat in that usual implementations
of LISP allow this global table to be augmented; for example, by function
definitions using a version of "<=". Thus the global table can be enlarged
whereas a true λ-binding involves a fixed number of variables.

[23]Our notion of free and bound variables has a decidedly
computational flavor, in contrast to the mathematical definitions of "free"
and "bound" given on page 170. For example a variable may be both free
and bound in our terminology.

[24]The parameters may either be evaluated or unevaluated, however.

with a non-local variable. In LISP, it is clear *how* values get associated; it happens through λ-binding or by virtue of an initial entry in the symbol table. The scheme which LISP uses for discovering the value of any variable is to proceed linearly down the symbol table, looking for the *latest active* binding. This scheme is called **dynamic binding**. It *usually* results in uncovering the value that is expected; but not always as we will see in Section 3.10. Conceptually, the dynamic binding scheme corresponds to the physical replacement of the function call with the function body and then an evaluation of the resulting expression. Free variables whose bindings are determined dynamically are called **fluid variables**.

In review, the evaluation of a typical function-call will involve the evaluation of the arguments, the binding of the λ-variables to those values, the addition of these new bindings to the front of the symbol table, and finally the evaluation of the body of the function. That segment of the symbol table which we have just added by the λ-binding will be called the **local symbol table** or local environment. The variables which appear in that segment are the local variables. The remainder of the symbol table makes up the **non-local table**. Variables which appear in the global table but not in any local table are the **global variables**. Free variables are bound somewhere between the local table and the global table. Variables which are local to a form-evaluation are those which were present in the λ-binding. We first wish to develop a useful notation for describing bindings before delving further into the intricacies of binding strategies. That discussion will be the content of Section 3.11.

Problems

1. Write a LISP predicate, *non* <= λ[[x;e] ...], which will give **t** just in the case that x and e represent a variable and a λ-expression respectively, and x is non-local to e.
2. Give an example showing that the phrase "latest binding" is not a proper characterization of dynamic binding.

3.8 Environments and Bindings

This section will introduce one more notation for describing symbol tables or environments. This notation, due to J. Weizenbaum ([Wei 68]), only shows the abstract structure of the symbol table manipulations during evaluation. Its simplicity will be of great benefit when we introduce the more complex binding schemes necessary for function-valued functions in Section 3.10.

In the previous discussions it has been sufficient to simply think of a symbol table as a sequence of pairs; each pair was a variable and its associated value. This sufficed because we dealt only with λ-variables; we ignored the possibility of free variables. As long as we added the λ-bindings to the *front* of the sequence representing the symbol table we showed that expected evaluation would result. Local values were found in the table; global values were found by explicit recognizers in *eval* and *apply*. With the advent of free variables, however, it will be necessary to examine the structure of environments more closely. We will describe our environments in terms of a local symbol table augmented by a description of where to look for the non-local values.

Instead of having one amorphous sequential symbol table, we envision a sequence of tables. One is the local table, and its successor in the sequence is the previous local table. The information telling where to find the previous table is called the **access chain** or **access link**. Thus if tables are represented by E_i and the access link by → then we might represent a symbol table as:

$$(E_n \rightarrow E_{n-1} \rightarrow \ ...\rightarrow E_1 \rightarrow E_0)$$

where E_n is the local or current segment of the table. We reserve E_0 to name the global table.

LISP finds local bindings in the local table and uses the access chain to find bindings of non-local variables. If a variable is not found in any of the tables, then it is unbound.

An environment will be described as:

$$
\begin{array}{l}
\textbf{Form} \\
E_{local} \\
\mid E_i \\
\hline
\text{var}\mid \text{value} \\
v_1 \mid \text{val}_1 \\
v_2 \mid \text{val}_2 \\
\quad \cdot\cdot\cdot \\
v_n \mid \text{val}_n \\
\mid
\end{array}
$$

Form is the current form being evaluated. E_{local} is the name of the current environment or symbol table. Let x be a variable appearing in **Form**. If x is not found among the v_j's, then entries in the table named E_i are examined. If x is not found in E_i then the environment mentioned in the upper right-hand quadrant of E_i is searched. The search will terminate if x is found as a v_j; the value of x is the corresponding val_j. If x is not found in a local table, and the symbol "/" appears in the right-hand quadrant, then x is unbound.

The notation is used as follows: when we begin the evaluation of a form, the initial table E_0 is set up with "/" in its access field. The execution of a function definition, say $f <= \lambda[[x;y]\ x^2 + y]$, will add an appropriate entry to the table, binding f to its lambda definition. [25] Now, consider the evaluation of the form $f[2;3]$. When the λ-expression is entered, i.e., when we bind the evaluated arguments (2 and 3) to the λ-variables (x and y), a new local table (E_1) is set up with an access link to E_0. Entries reflecting the binding of the λ-variables are made in E_1 and evaluation of the λ-body is begun.

The flow of symbol table creation is:

$$f[2;3] \qquad\qquad x^2 + y$$
$$E_0 \qquad\qquad\qquad E_1 \qquad\qquad\qquad E_0$$
$$|/ \qquad\qquad\qquad\ |\ E_0 \qquad\qquad\qquad |/$$

$$\underline{\quad\quad} \Rightarrow \qquad \underline{\quad\quad} \Rightarrow \qquad \underline{\quad\quad} \quad \text{return with value 7}$$

$$f\ |\ \lambda[[x;y]\ x^2 + y] \qquad x\ |\ 2 \qquad\qquad f\ |\ \lambda[[x;y]\ ...\ ]$$
$$y\ |\ 3$$

Compare this sequence to the example on page 120.

The sequence of tables corresponds to the evaluation sequence:

$$eval[\Re[\![\,f[2;3]\,]\!];\ \Re[\![\,\{<f,\ \lambda[[x;y]\ x^2 +y]>\}\,]\!]]$$
$$\downarrow$$
$$eval[\Re[\![\,x^2 + y\,]\!];\ \Re[\![\,\{<x,\ 2>,\ <y,\ 3>,\ <f,\ \lambda[[x;y]\ x^2 +y]>\}\,]\!]]$$
$$\downarrow$$
$$7$$

You should realize that the Weizenbaum environments are just another abstract data structure with associated constructors, selectors, and recognizers. They may be expressed as LISP data structures without much difficulty. The only difference here is that the environments happen to be more meaningful when described graphically than if they were specified by their manipulating functions. See the problem on page 135. Graphical representations and languages are an important tool in data structure programming; we will say a bit more about this in Section 5.4.

---

[25]Note that we really mean "representation of lambda definition".

The execution of *fact[3]* on page 122 results in a more interesting example. The following discussion should be read in conjunction with that description. [26]

```
    fact[3]             [x=0→ ...]        *[x;fact[x-1]]          ↦ 6
    E₀                  E₁                E₁                    ⎫
    | /                 | E₀              | E₀                  ⎬  ↑
         _____           _____           _____  =>        2
  fact  | λ[[x][x=0→1;...]   =>   x  | 3     =>    x  | 3            ↑

    fact[2]             [x=0→ ...]        *[x;fact[x-1]]          ⎫
    E₁                  E₂                E₂                    ⎬  ↑
    | E₀                | E₁              | E₁                      
=>       _____     =>     _____    =>     _____  =>        1
      x  | 3               x  | 2              x  | 2               ↑

    fact[1]             [x=0→ ...]        *[x;fact[x-1]]          ⎫
    E₂                  E₃                E₃                    ⎬
    | E₁                | E₂              | E₂                      
=>       _____     =>     _____    =>     _____  =>        
      x  | 2               x  | 1              x  | 1               ↑
                                                                   1
    fact[0]             [x=0→1; ...]                              ↑
    E₃                  E₄                                      
    | E₂                | E₃              send                     
=>       _____     =>     _____  => 1       1               
      x  | 1               x  | 0           back up
```

At the end of the first line we are faced with the evaluation of *[x;fact[x-1]]. This requires the evaluation of the arguments to *; this is done by *evlis*. First *x* is evaluated and saved, [27] then the evaluation of *fact[x-1]* is begun using environment E_1. In E_1, *x-1* gives 2 and we find the definition of *fact* in E_0. In the second line we set up E_2 and evaluate *fact[2]*. Analogous situations occur until the fourth line; at this time we suddenly find ourselves in E_4 with *x* bound to 0. The expression *x=0* is satisfied and we start back up the right margin to conclude the nested evaluations of *[x;fact[x-1]]*. This process finally terminates at the top, returning a value 6. Notice that we will get the

---

[26]The layout of this example is due to R. Davis.

[27]This saved information is not explicitly represented in these pictures or in the Weizenbaum diagrams.

correct binding of x locally. It is important to note that the occurrence of *fact* within the body of the definition of *fact* is *global*. [28] We find the correct binding for *fact* by searching the access chain. We must search the access chain even though *fact* is global. We cannot shortcut the search by simply looking in E_0. A variable might have been rebound in an enclosing environment and it would be that binding we should discover.

As a final example showing access to non-local variable bindings consider $f[3]$ where $f <= \lambda[[x]\ g[2]]$ and $g <= \lambda[[y]\ x+y]$.

```
   f[3]                    g[2]                   x + y
   E₀                      E₁                     E₂
   | /                     | E₀                    | E₁
 _____   =>          _____      =>          _____
 f| λ[[x] g[2]]           x | 3                    y | 2
 g| λ[[y] x+y]
```

Notice that when we evaluate $x + y$ we find y has a local value, but we must look down the access chain to find a binding for x.

The scheme for using Weizenbaum environments for the current LISP subset is:

When preparing a λ-binding, set up a new E_{new} with the λ-variables as the local variable entries and add the values of the arguments as the corresponding value entries. The access slot of the new E_{new} points to the previous access environment. The evaluation of the body of the λ-expression takes place using the new table; when a local variable is accessed we find it in E_{new}; when a non-local variable occurs, we chase the access chain to find its value.

When the evaluation of the body is completed, E_{new} disappears and the previous environment is restored.

You should verify that the current access- and binding-scheme espoused by LISP is faithfully described in these diagrams.

Problem

1. Environments really are a class of abstract data structures: they include constructors, selectors, and recognizers. To help discover what a set of such functions might be, give a representation for Weizenbaum environments and write new versions of the symbol table manipulating functions, *lookup* and *mkenv*, which will operate on Weizenbaum environments. See page 124.

---

[28] Notice that *eq*, +, and * are also global.

3.9 *label*

Placing "λ" and a list of λ-variables in front of an expresson designates the variables which appear in the λ-list as local variables. All other variables appearing in the expression are non-local. For example, f is non-local in the following:

$$f <= \lambda[[x][zerop[x] \to 1; t \to *[x;f[x-1]]]]$$

Clearly our intention is that the f appearing to the right of "<=" is the same as the f appearing to the left of "<=".

This has not been a problem for us. We have simply pre-loaded the symbol table, binding f to its definition; see page 122. LISP has a more elegant device for this binding. It is called the *label* operator and is written:

$$label[<identifier>;<function>]$$

Its evaluation has the effect of binding the <identifier> to the <function>. The value constructed by executing a *label*-expression is a representation of a function with name <identifier> and body <function>.

For example, a proper definition of *fact* is:

$$label[fact; \lambda[[x][eq[x;0] \to 1; t \to *[x;fact[sub1[x]]]]]]$$

To include *label* in the LISP syntax add:

$$<function> ::= label[<identifier>;<function>]$$

and the S-expr translation of the *label* construct should naturally be:

$$\Re[\![label[f;fn]]\!] = (LABEL \; \Re[\![f]\!] \; \Re[\![fn]\!])$$

Note that *label* is a special form, not a call-by-value function.

Since the *label* operator creates a function, it should appear in the function position of a function application. A typical application of the *label* construct, say $label[f;\lambda[[x] \; \xi[x]]][\epsilon]$, results in the following environmental picture when we get ready to evaluate $\xi[x]$:

$label[f;\lambda[[x] \; \xi[x]]][\epsilon]$	$\xi[\epsilon]$
E_0	E_1
| /	| E_0
——————— =>	———
|	f | $\lambda[[x] \; \xi[x]]$

Notice that $label[f;\lambda[[x]\xi]][\epsilon]$ is equivalent to $\lambda[[x]\xi[\epsilon]][quote[\epsilon]]$; notice too that the definition does not appear in the global table E_0. We use *label* to create temporary function definitions. Such definitions disappear when the environment in which the *label* was executed is no longer accessible to the computation. Thus within the evaluation of the body $\xi[x]$ a recursive call on f will refer to the definition of f located in E_1 so long as f is not rebound in

ξ; once we have completed the computation initialized in E_0 the definition of f will disappear. If f is not recursive, then the use of *label* is unnecessary; an anonymous function application will suffice.

What about statements like "evaluate $g[A;B]$ where $g <= \lambda[[x;y] \dots f[u;v] \dots]$ and $f <= \lambda[[x;y] \dots]$?" *label* defines only one function; we may not say $label[f,g; \dots]$. What we *can* do is embed the *label*-definition for f within the *label*-definition for g. [29] Thus:

$$label[g; \lambda[[x;y] \dots label[f; \lambda[[x;y] \dots]][u;v] \dots]]$$

Several languages allow a simpler notation for giving mutually recursive definitions; see [Rey 72], [Hew 74], or [Sus 75].

It can be shown that the *label* operator is superfluous; the same effect can be obtained by a complicated λ-binding. However our point here is not to be "minimal", but to be "useful". Implementations of LISP offer other definitional facilities, with "<=" having the effect of permanently establishing the definition in E_0.

The apparent simplicity of the *label* operator is partly due to misconception and partly due to the restrictions placed on the current subset of LISP. The following sections will illuminate some of these difficulties.

Problems

1. Show one way to change *eval* to handle *label*.
2. Express the definition of *reverse* given on page 48 using *label*.
3. Evaluate the following:

$$\lambda[[y] \ label[fn;fn_2][f]] \ [f]$$

where: $fn_2 <= \lambda[[x][y \to 1; x \to 2; t \to fn_1[t]]$

and: $fn_1 <= \lambda[[y] \ fn[y]]$

3.10 Functional Arguments and Functional Values

Recall our discussion of :

$$eval[(F \ 2 \ 3);((F \ . \ (LAMBDA \ (X \ Y) \ (PLUS \ (EXPT \ X \ 2) \ Y))))]$$

We now know this is equivalent to:

$$eval[((LABEL \ F \ (LAMBDA \ (X \ Y) \ (PLUS \ (EXPT \ X \ 2) \ Y))) \ 2 \ 3);(\ )]$$

In either case, the effect is to bind the name f to the λ-expression. Binding also occurs when f is called: we bind x to 2, and y to 3. In the latter case we

---

[29] Indeed *every* occurrence of f must be replaced by the $label[f; \dots]$ construct.

are binding simple values; in the former we are binding functions as values. We have decided that the necessary ingredients to characterize a functional value [30] are a representation of the formal parameters, and a representation of the expression described in the body of the function. In this section we will examine the adequacy of that decision. We begin informally with a few examples.

Assume we have a list l of dotted-pairs α_1 ,..., α_n, and we wish to form a new list of the form $(car[\alpha_1] ... car[\alpha_n])$. That is we wish to apply car to each of the elements of l. Such a function is easy to write:

$$carfirst <= \lambda[[l][null[l] \rightarrow (\ ); \mathbf{t} \rightarrow concat[car[first[l]];carfirst[rest[l]]]]]$$

Now suppose we wish to write a more general function, which instead of being specific to car, will take an *arbitrary* unary function f and apply it to each of the elements of l, generating $(f[\alpha_1], ..., f[\alpha_n])$. Such a function could plausibly be defined as follows:

$$mapfirst <= \lambda[[fn;l][null[l] \rightarrow (\ );$$
$$\mathbf{t} \rightarrow concat[fn[first[l]];mapfirst[fn;rest[l]]]]]$$

Thus the first calculation we requested above could be expressed as:

$$mapfirst[car;l] \ .... \ \text{or could it?}$$

Recalling LISP's penchant for call-by-value evaluation, we might believe that the computation would not be done as expected. We do *not* want the argument car evaluated to produce an S-expr value; rather, we want its evaluation to produce a representation of a primitive function, suitable for application. There are two ways out of this dilemma. One solution is to suppress the evaluation of car, postponing it until the *apply* function can recognize that a function name has been seen. We have seen one artifact in LISP to subdue evaluation: we can make it a constant by *quote*-ing it. Indeed, $mapfirst[quote[car];l]$ or $mapfirst[CAR;l]$ will work. You should convince yourself that $mapfirst[CAR;l]$ will compute $carfirst[l]$; that exercise requires examining the details of *eval*.

A second solution exists and is the one we will pursue. We say that the "value" of car *is* the description of the program which computes car. Since car is a primitive, that description is machine code for this specific implementation.

Before going on to more complex examples it would be well to note that $mapfirst$ is a different kind of LISP function from those we have seen before. The first argument to $mapfirst$ is expected to represent a function. Notice that the argument fn appears in the body of $mapfirst$ in a position reserved for functions. Therefore any parameter bound to fn is expected to be a function. Such a use of a function is called a **functional argument**.

---

[30]It would be better to call these constructs "procedure values" since we will take a decidedly algorithmic interpretation of them.

　　　The first trick we used above, representing the functional argument *car* as a constant *CAR*, can be applied to other instances of functional arguments. Thus the functional argument:

$$\lambda[[x]\,f[g[x]]$$

could be represented as,　　　$(LAMBDA\ (X)\ (F\ (G\ X)))$

The trick is called *QUOTE*-ing the functional argument since the S-expr representation of an instance of such a construct is a *QUOTE*-ed expression. *QUOTE*-ing is not strictly necessary if we follow the second alternative above and use the evaluator described in Section 3.5. Worse yet, *QUOTE*-ing is also not sufficient to capture the intended meaning in all cases of functional parameters. To understand why *QUOTE*-ing is not sufficient we need a slightly more complex set of examples. First we try:

$$mapfirst[\ \lambda[[x]\ concat[x;(\ )]];(A\ B\ C\ D)] \qquad {}^{31}$$

which we expect to evaluate to $((A)\ (B)\ (C)\ (D))$

$$
\begin{array}{ll}
mapfirst[\ \lambda[[x]\ concat[x;(\ )]];\ ...\ ] & [null[l]\ ...\ ] \\
\qquad E_0 & \qquad E_1 \\
\qquad |\,l & \qquad |\,E_0 \\
\underline{\hspace{4cm}} \ \ \Rightarrow & \underline{\hspace{3cm}} \ \ \Rightarrow\ ... \\
mapfirst\ \ |\,\lambda[[fn;l][null[l]\ ...\ ]] & l\ \ |\,(A\ B\ C\ D) \\
 & fn\,|\,\lambda[[x]\ concat[x;(\ )]]
\end{array}
$$

Since *null[l]* is false, the problem reduces to:

$$
\begin{array}{l}
concat[fn[first[l]];mapfirst[fn;rest[l]]]. \\
\qquad E_1 \\
\qquad |\,E_0 \\
\underline{\hspace{3cm}} \\
\qquad l\ \ |\,(A\ B\ C\ D) \\
\qquad fn\ \ |\,\lambda[[x]\ concat[x;(\ )]]
\end{array}
$$

Since we are using call-by-value we have to evaluate the arguments to *concat*; that requires evaluating *fn[first[l]]*. The value of *l* we find locally and evaluate *first[l]*, getting *A*. The value for *fn* is also found locally, and since it is the representation of a λ-definition, we set up a new environment in which to evaluate the body of *fn*, binding the λ-variable *x* to *A*:

---

[31]Note that we do not use *quote*. Some implementations do not support this notation. Some require *quote*, and still others give a different interpretation to unembellished functions appearing as actual parameters.

$$concat[x;(\ )]$$
$$E_2$$
$$|\ E_1$$

_____

$$x\ |\ A$$

The expected evaluation takes place: (A) is computed and returned to environment E_1 so that we may continue the evaluation $mapfirst[fn;rest[l]]$.

However, consider the following variant of this last example. Define:

$$foo\ <=\ \lambda[[l]\ mapfirst[\ \lambda[[x]concat[x;l]];\ (A\ B\ C\ D)]$$

It would seem that $foo[(\ )]$ should also give $((A)\ (B)\ (C)\ (D))$ since l will be bound to $(\ )$ and therefore the l in the functional argument will effectively be $(\ )$.

$$foo[(\ )] \qquad mapfirst[\ \lambda[[x]\ concat[x;l]]];...] \qquad [null[l]\ ...\ ]$$
$$E_0 \qquad\qquad\qquad E_1 \qquad\qquad\qquad E_2$$
$$|\ / \qquad\qquad\qquad |\ E_0 \qquad\qquad\qquad |\ E_1$$

_____   => _____   =>   _____   => ...

$foo\quad|\ \lambda[[l]...\ ]$ $l\quad|(\ )$ $l\quad;(A\ B\ C\ D)$

$mapfirst\ |\ \lambda[[fn;l][null[l]...]]$ $fn\ |\ \lambda[[x]\ concat[x;l]]$

$null[l]$ is false since l is $(A\ B\ C\ D)$, so we evaluate $concat[fn[first[l]]\ ...\ ]$. This involves evaluating $first[l]$ in E_2, giving A. We evaluate fn in E_2 and, finding a representation of a λ-definition, we make a new environment E_3 in which to evaluate the body of fn.

As we make E_3, we add an entry binding x to A and we settle down in E_3 to evaluate $concat[x;l]$:

$$concat[x;l]$$
$$E_3$$
$$|\ E_2$$

_____

$$x\ |\ A$$

Since l is non-local to E_3, we follow the access chain to find its value in E_2 to be $(A\ B\ C\ D)$. But that's not the expected value! We expected to find $(\ )$, which was hidden away in E_1.

The trouble here is that l was rebound in the interim. The first thing to note is that the problem is caused by free variables and dynamic binding: l is free in the functional argument. Local variables aren't problematic; neither are global variables. The desired binding for l is the one which was current when we were binding the functional argument to the formal parameter fn. A plausible solution then is to replace all non-local variables with their values at the time we recognize the functional argument. This will not always suffice. See page 145 for a counterexample. A more promising solution associates the name of the current environment with the function and use that pair as the value to be given to the formal parameter. When we want to apply the functional argument we set up a new environment, introducing a local table with the λ-variables bound to their values; only *now* we use the saved environment as the beginning of the access chain. The values of any non-local variables which we encounter in the process of applying the functional argument will be searched for in the saved environment.

To initialize this process we must be able to recognize the occurrence of a functional argument. To that end, we introduce a new operator called *function*. This operator takes one argument: a representation of the function. The effect of *function* will be to construct a value representing that argument and the environment which was current when the *function*-instance was evaluated.

In the current example, we would recognize the *function*-construct while evaluating the arguments to *mapfirst*; the environment which was current then was E_1. Therefore as we build E_2 we want to associate the pair $\lambda[[x]\ concat[x;l]]$ - E_1 with the formal parameter *fn*. Whenever we apply *fn* we want to use $\lambda[[x]\ concat[x;l]]$; and within that context, whenever we want l, we want the value of l in E_1.

The function-environment pair is called a **closure** or **funarg**. In our diagrams we will designate the pair as:

$$<function>:<environment>.$$

Therefore, in our example we should designate the value of the functional argument as:

$$\lambda[[x]\ concat[x;l]]:E_1$$

We must also extend the manipulation of Weizenbaum environments to handle such constructions. The process which recognizes λ-definitions and sets up new environments must now watch for funargs. When it sees one it uses the associated environment as the access environment. Let's do the example again.

```
foo[( )]    mapfirst[function[λ[[x] concat[x;l]]; ..]  [null[l] ... ]
    E₀                      E₁                           E₂
    | /                     | E₀                          | E₁
 _____     =>   _____      =>   _____      => ...
   foo | λ[[l]...           l |( )           l |(A  B  C D)
 mapfirst  | λ[[fn;l][null[l]...]]           fn | λ[[x] concat[x;l]]:E₁
```

Things are as before except now *fn* is bound to the funarg pair in E_2. We look up *fn* in E_2 and, finding a λ-definition, we make a new environment E_3 in which to evaluate the body of *fn*. As we make E_3, we add an entry binding x to A. But now since the λ-definition is a funarg we make the access environment E_1 as saved with *fn*. Thus we settle down in E_3 to evaluate $concat[x;l]$:

$$concat[x;l]$$
$$E_3$$
$$|\ E_1$$

$$x\ |\ A$$

Since l is non-local to E_3, we follow the access chain to find its value in E_1 to be ( ) as desired. Thus instead of simply tracing back to the previous environment we detour around E_2:

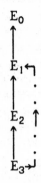

However, there is still some information which we must make explicit if these Weizenbaum diagrams are to faithfully represent the process of evaluation. Namely, after we have finished the evaluation of $concat[x;l]$ we are to restore a previous environment. Which one is it? It isn't E_1, it's E_2! That information is not available in our diagram, so we must correct the situation.

In the left-hand quadrant of our diagram we place the name of the environment which we wish restored when we leave the current environment. That environment name will be called the **control environment**, and will head a chain of environments, called the control chain. [32] Here's the correct picture:

$$concat[x;l]$$
$$E_3$$
$$E_2 \quad |\ E_1$$

$$x\ |\ A$$

So after we have finished the computation in E_3 we return control to E_2. Thus the general structure of an environment is as follows:

---

[32]In Algol, the access chain is called the static chain, and the control chain is called the dynamic chain.

$$
\begin{array}{c}
\text{Form} \\
E_{current} \\
E_{control} \quad | \; E_{access}
\end{array}
$$

$E_{control}$	E_{access}
var	value
x_1	...
x_2	...
...	...
x_n	...

Consider another example, involving a function to produce the composition of two unary functions. We will call the function *compose*. The value returned by *compose* will be a function; that means *compose* will produce a functional value:

$$compose[function[car];function[cdr]] = cadr$$

with a plausible definition as:

$$compose <= \lambda[[f;g] \; \lambda[[x]f[g[x]]]]$$

This definition of *compose* is almost right. The value returned by *compose* is to be a function. Indeed it is an instance of a **functional value**, so, as with functional arguments, it needs to be decorated with *function* so that the evaluator will save the environment which contains the right bindings for f and g. That environment is the one which was current when the *function*-construct was recognized. So we write:

$$compose <= \lambda[[f;g] \; function[\lambda[[x] \; f[g[x]]]]]$$

Now try: $app[cons[A;(B . C)];compose[function[car];function[cdr]]]$

where: $app <= \lambda[[y;f] \; f[y]]$

As usual we evaluate the arguments to *app*, bind the results to y and f and evaluate the body of *app*.

$$app[cons[A;(B . C)];compose[function[car];function[cdr]]]$$
$$E_0$$
$$/ \mid /$$

$$app \mid \lambda[[y;f] \; f[y]]$$
$$compose \mid \lambda[[f;g] \; function[\lambda[[x] \; f[g[x]]]]]$$

Evaluation of the first argument to *app* brings no surprises; we get $(A . (B . C))$. We begin evaluating the second argument; we find the definition of *compose* in the environment and since it is a λ-definition we set up a new environment, E_1, and evaluate the body $function[\lambda[[x] \; f[g[x]]]]$:

$$function[\lambda[[x] \ f[g[x]]]]$$
$$E_1$$
$$E_0 \mid E_0$$

___

$$f \mid car{:}E_0$$
$$g \mid cdr{:}E_0$$

Again, the recognition of the *function*-construct says return a funarg-pair as value. The environment we associate is the current one, E_1. We now go back to E_0, using the control chain. Since both arguments to *app* are now evaluated, we find the definition of *app* and set up a new environment E_2. Thus:

$$f[y] \qquad\qquad f[g[x]]$$
$$E_2 \qquad\qquad\quad E_3$$
$$E_0 \quad \mid E_0 \qquad\qquad E_2\mid E_1$$

___   => ___

$$y \quad \mid (A \cdot (B \cdot C)) \quad x \ \mid (A \cdot (B \cdot C))$$
$$f \quad \mid \lambda[[x] \ f[g[x]]]{:}E_1$$

The form to be evaluated in E_2 is $f[y]$; we find y and f both locally. We evaluate the argument y, then since f is a λ-definition, we set up a new environment binding the λ-variable x to the value $(A \cdot (B \cdot C))$. But the λ-definition is also a funarg; therefore the access environment stored in E_3 is E_1. The control component of E_3 is set to the prior environment, E_2; and we begin evaluation of the body $f[g[x]]$.

Now in E_3 we find x locally but have to resort to the access chain to find f and g; using funargs, we have set up the appropriate environments. From E_3 we have access to E_1:[33]

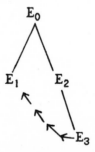

The rest of the evaluation goes without incident: we finish the evaluation in E_3 and return to E_2 and finally to E_0 following the control evironments.

Notice that f and g in the body of *compose* are free variables and therefore their bindings are not to be found in the local environment. Since the interesting applications of such functions usually involve free variables,

___

[33]We can go from there to E_0 if it were needed.

we must deal with them. In particular, the *label* operator will typically involve free variables. We remarked that *f* in:

$$f <= \lambda[[x][zerop[x] \rightarrow 1; \mathbf{t} \rightarrow *[x;f[x-1]]]\ ]$$

is free. But we want the occurrence of *f* on the right to be synonymous with the *f* being defined on the left. We can do this by "tying a knot" in the access environment chain. Therefore, we should modify the diagram for *label* to be:

$$label[f;\lambda[[x]\ \xi[x]]][\epsilon] \qquad \xi[\epsilon]$$

$$\begin{array}{ccc} E_0 & & E_1 \\ |\ / & & |\ E_0 \end{array}$$

$$\underline{\qquad\qquad} \quad => \quad \underline{\qquad}$$

$$\qquad\qquad\qquad f\ \ |\ \lambda[[x]\ \xi[x]]{:}E_1$$

Notice that the effect of *label* is to build *function*$[\lambda[[x]\ \xi]]$ and associate that with *f*. If we attempted to implement *function*$[\Phi]$ by replacing all non-local variables in Φ by their current values we wouldn't always get what we expect.

Consider $fact <= \lambda[[x][x=0 \rightarrow 1; \mathbf{t} \rightarrow *[x;fact[x-1]]]]$

If the current environment is E_i:

$$\begin{array}{ccc} & E_i & \\ E_c & | & E_a \end{array}$$

$$\underline{\qquad\qquad\qquad}$$

$$fact|\ foo$$

then executing <= should give something like:

$$\begin{array}{ccc} & E_i & \\ E_c & | & E_a \end{array}$$

$$\underline{\qquad\qquad\qquad}$$

$$fact|\ \lambda[[x]\ ...fact[x-1]]\ {:}E_i$$

rather than:

$$\begin{array}{ccc} & E_i & \\ E_c & | & E_a \end{array}$$

$$\underline{\qquad\qquad\qquad}$$

$$fact|\ \lambda[[x]\ ...foo[x-1]]$$

Our final step is to include a data structure representation of the *function* construct. The translation scheme is simple: represent *function*$[\xi]$ as $(FUNCTION\ \Re[[\xi]])$.

Thus: $function[\lambda[[x]\ f[g[x]]]]$

has an $\Re$-image of $(FUNCTION\ (LAMBDA\ (X)\ (F\ (G\ X))))$

We must also develop new sections of *eval* to deal with *FUNCTION*. The device LISP used to associate environments with functions is called the

FUNARG device. [34] When *eval* sees the construction (*FUNCTION* fn) it returns as value the list:

$$(FUNARG \quad fn \quad "saved")$$

where "saved" represents a pointer to the current symbol table. This representation, as a list of three objects, is called a **funarg triple**. It is *apply* that recognizes (*FUNARG* fn "saved"). When we are *calling fn*, we use the "saved" symbol table for accessing non-local variables.

Thus there are *two* environments involved in the proper handling of functional arguments. First there is the environment which is saved with the *FUNARG*. This is called the **binding environment** since it is the environment current at the time the functional argument was constructed or bound. The second environment, called the **activation environment** or application environment, is the environment which is current immediately before the functional argument is *applied* or activated.

It is the duty of *eval* and *apply* to use the *FUNARG* device to maintain the proper control of the activation and binding environments.

Finally, we should update our description of the usage of Weizenbaum environments given on page 135:

When the *function* construct is recognized, we manufacture a *FUNARG* triple consisting of the atom *FUNARG*, the function described in the instance of *function*, and the current environment. This triple is the value of the *function* construct and may be bound to any LISP variable; typically the LISP variable will appear in an expression in a position reserved for functions.

When doing a λ-binding, set up a new E_{new} with the λ-variables as the local variable entries and the values of the arguments as the corresponding value entries. The control slot of E_{new} always points to the previous symbol table. The access slot also points to the previous environment unless the function being applied is a *FUNARG*. If it is a *FUNARG*, then set the access slot to the environment which was saved with the *FUNARG*.

The evaluation of the body of the λ-expression takes place using E_{new}; when a local variable is accessed we find it in E_{new}; when a non-local variable occurs, we chase the access chain to find its value. When the evaluation of the body is completed, the previous environment is restored. E_{new} disappears unless it has been saved in a functional object constructed during the evaluation of the body, and that object is returned as a functional value. [35]

Notice that there is a certain asymmetry about access and control. The

---

[34]More is said about implementations of *FUNARG* in Section 6.17.

[35]In fact, LISP will allow the retention of environments in more general ways since funarg triples can be manipulated as data structures.

control slot always points at the previous environment, while the access slot may vary. It may follow control, as is the case on simple function calls; it may point to an environment earlier in the control chain, as is the case for functional arguments; it may point to an environment which control cannot return to, as is the case for functional values; or it may point to itself as is the case for *label*'s revised implementation.

There is another asymmetry in the properties of access and control. The access environment is a self-sufficient data structure; it can be described and manipulated as such using the usual constructors, selectors, and recognizers. Typically such environments come into existence as a part of a computation; they are constructed during the λ-binding process. We can implicitly save such an environment through the *FUNARG* device; and we can explicitly build such environments using the data structure operations and pass them to *eval* as a symbol table. But symbol tables are independent of the method used to create them. In particular, once a table has been captured by a *FUNARG* we need not retain any information about the computation which created that table. However the idea of "control" and "state of computation" is integrally tied to access structure. The state of the computation involves the expression currently being evaluated, the history of those computations which are suspended and waiting for the completion of the current computation, and it also involves the access environment since that is necessary for the correct evaluation of variables. To "save the state of computation" implies saving the partial computation to that point, saving the expression being evaluated, and saving the current access environment.

To a large extent, "control environment" is a misnomer. What we are intending to capture is the idea of a suspended computation: suspended until the subsidiary computation has been completed. Part of the suspended computation *is* the "control environment", but there's more. The Weizenbaum diagrams show part of the information; they show the environments and the expressions being evaluated. However they leave implicit the dynamics of the computation: which argument is being evaluated, and where the partial results are being stored, and where in the expression we are to continue when the subsidiary computation is completed. In Section 4.4 we will develop a different *eval* family which will make much of this information explicit. Also in Section 4.4 we will examine the possibility of expanding the behavior of control slots. That is, allowing environments other than the predecessor to appear in the control slot of an environment.

We have already remarked that functions are parametric values; to that we must add that functions may also be tied to the environment in which they were created; they cannot be evaluated *in vacuo*. What does this say about "<="? It *still* appears to act like an assignment statement. It is taking on more distinct character since it must associate environments with the function body as it does the assignment.

The implementation of *function* seems like a lot of work to allow a moderately obscure construct to appear in a language. However constructs like functional arguments appear in several programming languages under different guises. Usually the syntax of the language is sufficiently complex that the true behavior and implications of devices like functional arguments is misunderstood. Faulty implementations usually result. In LISP the problem and the solution appear with exceptional clarity. [36]

Here is a sketch of the abstract structure of the current *eval*.

$eval \Leftarrow \lambda[[exp;environ]$
$\qquad [isvar[exp] \to lookup[exp;environ];$
$\qquad isconst[exp] \to denote[exp];$
$\qquad iscond[exp] \to evcond[args_c[exp];environ];$
$\qquad isfun[exp] \to mkfunarg[exp;environ];$
$\qquad isfunc+args[exp] \to apply[func[exp];$
$\qquad\qquad\qquad\qquad\qquad evlis[arglist[exp];environ];$
$\qquad\qquad\qquad\qquad\qquad environ]] \ ]$

where:
$apply \Leftarrow \lambda[[fn;args;environ]$
$\qquad [isfunname[fn] \to ...;$
$\qquad islambda[fn] \to eval[body[fn];$
$\qquad\qquad\qquad\qquad mkenv[vars[fn];args;environ]];$
$\qquad isfunarg[fn] \to apply[func_1[fn];$
$\qquad\qquad\qquad\qquad args;$
$\qquad\qquad\qquad\qquad evn[fn]];$
$\qquad ... \qquad\qquad ... \ ]]$

The reader is encouraged to complete the definitions, supplying appropriate constructors, selectors and recognizers.

Now for some specific examples. Most implementations of LISP include a very useful class of mapping functions.

maplist is a function of two arguments: *fn*, a unary function; and *l*, a list. *maplist* applies the function *fn* to the list *l* and its tails (*rest[l]*, *rest[rest[l]]*, ..) until *l* is reduced to *( )*. The value of *maplist* is the list of the values returned by *fn*. Here's a definition of *maplist*:

$maplist \Leftarrow \lambda[[fn;l][null[l] \to (\ ); \mathbf{t} \to concat[fn[l];maplist[fn;rest[l]]]]]$

Thus:
$maplist[function[reverse];(A \ B \ C \ D)] = ((D \ C \ B \ A) \ (D \ C \ B) \ (D \ C) \ (D))$
The use of *function* is not strictly necessary since *reverse* does not reference free variables.

The mapping functionals can be generalized. For example ([Moo 74])

---

[36]LISP was the first programming language which allowed functional values.

an application $mapfirst[fn;l_1; ...; l_n]$ would expect fn to be an n-ary function to be applied to consecutive members of each l_i, building a list of the results of each application.

An interesting and non-trivial use of functional arguments is shown on page 196 where we define a new control structure suitable for describing algorithms built to operate on lists.

Problems

1. What changes should be made to the LISP syntax equations to allow functional arguments?
2. Use *app* on page 143 to define a function which computes factorial without using *label* or explicit calls on the evaluator.
3. Extend *eval* and friends to handle functional arguments.
4. An interesting use of functional arguments involves self-applicative functions. An application of a function f in a context $f[...;f;...]$ is an instance of self application.[37] Self-applicative functions can be used to define recursive functions in such a way that the definition is not *statically* self-referential, but is *dynamically* re-entrant. For example, here is our canonical example, written using a self-applicative function:

$$fact <= \lambda[[n] \, f[function[f]; \, n]]$$

$$f <= \lambda[[g;n][n=0 \to 1; \, t \to *[n; \, g[g; \, n-1]] \,]]$$

   Use Weizenbaum's environments to show the execution of $fact[2]$.
5. Write a LISP function to find the permutations on a set of n elements. For example $perm[(A \ B \ C)]$ gives

$$((A \ B \ C) \, (A \ C \ B) \, (B \ C \ A) \, (B \ A \ C) \, (C \ A \ B) \, (C \ B \ A))$$

6. Write a generalized form of the *diff* algorithm (Section 2.3) to handle n-ary sums and products.

3.11 Binding Strategies and Implementations

After the discussion of variables in Section 3.7 and the intervening discussions of environments, it should now be clear that the root of the binding problem is free variables. We don't want to restrict the use of free variables too precipitously since they are a very useful programming technique. For example, the possible alternative of passing all global information through as extra parameters in calling sequences is overly

---

[37]Provided the designated argument position is a functional argument.

expensive; [38] often the most natural formulation of a problem involves free variables.

Handling of free variables varies from programming language to programming language. The solution advocated by Algol-like languages is called **static binding** or **lexical binding** and dictates that all non-local references be fixed in the binding environment; thus free variables aren't really free in the sense that we have a choice to make. LISP at least gives you a choice. [39] Using *quote* you will get the dynamic binding on free variables in a functional argument; using *function* gives the static interpretation. [40] There are no questions about Algol's interpretation of functional values: the construct is not allowed. When we discuss implementation of binding strategies in Chapter 5 we will see why.

The binding strategy determines *when* the variables will receive values; the implementation determines *how* those bindings are to be accomplished and therefore, how the lookup of values is to be accomplished. We have seen one implementation in the *assoc - pairlis* pair (Section 3.5, page 124), and on page 135 suggested a related implementation using Weizenbaum environments. Now we examine another implementation.

The most general environment structure which LISP creates is a tree of local symbol tables, rooted in the global table. The typical LISP computation generates a single branch, but functional arguments and values can generate additional branches. Locating a variable n involved searching the current branch from tip to root, looking for the first occurrence of n. If n was bound very deep, the search could be long. Indeed the time is proportional to the depth of the branch; recall our sample evaluation of *equal* on page 124. It has been noted [Wegb 75] that variables tend to be rebound rather seldom; there are few occurrences of any given variable on any particular branch. If this is the case, then the search will examine many environment blocks which do not contain the desired variable. If the number of bindings of any variable is small compared to the number of environment blocks which have to be searched to find those bindings, then we would like a viable alternative to the *assoc - pairlis* implementation of *lookup - mkenv*. That is, a scheme whose search is proportional to the number of bindings for a variable, rather than proportional to the depth of the tree. There is such an alternative.

---

[38]Though much of that expense can be mitigated by a clever compiler.

[39]However [Ste 76b] shows that dynamic binding can be simulated in a statically bound LISP-like language.

[40]A case can be made for even more flexibility in the interpretation of free variables. We could ask that the binding be done on a per variable basis. That is we could declare which free variables are to be captured statically and which are to be captured dynamically. We could also ask that *both* bindings be available and supply selectors which would access either the dynamic or the static binding.

Namely, we associate *all* the values possessed by n with n itself. To signify which environment created the binding, we associate pairs consisting of the value and the environment name. Thus the new *mkenv[vars;vals;env]* application must name a new environment, call it *new*, and attach it to the tip of the current branch in the environment tree. Also, for each entry in *vals*, *mkenv* must associate a value-*new* pair with each name in *vars*.

The *lookup* procedure is given the name n and a branch in the environment tree. Assume that the tip node of the tree is named Env. If n has an attached value pair whose environment component is Env, then the associated value is returned by *lookup*. Otherwise the environment branch is searched recursively by *lookup* for the first node in that branch which has an associated value attached to n.

Here's a graphical description of this reorganized symbol table:

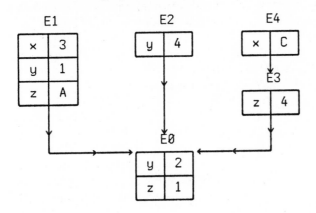

The *assoc-pairlis* structure

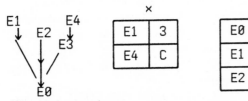

The new structures

Using the discussion of *mkenv* on page 124, we define:

alloc <=λ[[x] *gensym*[]]

link <= λ[[block;env] *concat*[block;env]]

send <= λ[[n;v;blk] *addval*[n;mkent[first[blk];v]]]

The function *gensym* is to generate a new environment name which *alloc* makes into a new tip node on the end of the current environment branch.

The function *addval* adds a new entry to the variable *n*. The value of *addval* is *env*.

The new *lookup* is more complicated than the simple *assoc*. Given a node in the environment branch, we must see if there is a related binding for *n*. If there is, then that's the binding we want. If no binding is found we look at the next deeper node on the tree, and check its bindings.

lookup <= λ[[n;env] λ[[z] look'[z;z;env]][getval[n]]]

look' <= λ[[l;ll;env] [null[l] →look'[ll;ll;rest[env]]
              eq[name[first[l]];first[env]] → value[first[l]]
              t → look'[rest[l];ll;env]]]

This new scheme is called **shallow binding**, and the *assoc-pairlis* scheme is called **deep binding**. The essential differences between these two binding implementations is that a deep binding search is keyed on the name of the variable, whereas a shallow binding strategy is keyed on the environment name. These requirements have corresponding implications for the organization of the symbol tables. [41]

A further elaboration of the shallow scheme is possible. The essential aim of shallow binding is the reduction of the search time for values of variables. The current scheme improves the situation, but if a variable is bound several times we still may have to search the table of values associated with the atom. The next modification arranges that the correct binding is always found in a fixed location associated with the atom. As with any scheme, the benefits are not without penalty; we will discuss some of the tradeoffs after we describe the implementation.

With each variable *n* we associate a *single* entry called the **value cell**. The binding and unbinding mechanisms will maintain the correct value of the variable in the value cell. The scheme is a mixture of the two previous implementations.

The *lookup* routine is similar to the shallow lookup:

lookup <= λ[[x;env] *getval_cell*[x]]

Notice that *env* is ignored in *lookup*.

---

[41]The table organization discussed in this section was also used in a language named LC^2 ([Mit 70]). In their terminology, "deep table" was called "scope oriented organization" and "shallow table" was called "name oriented organization".

The binding routine is a bit more complex. When binding n we have to replace the current value cell with the new binding. We also have to save the old binding so that it may be restored when the sub-computation is completed; this part of the implementation is like deep binding. We perform most of the *mkenv* operations as given on page 124, but require a new version of *send*. Instead of placing the new bindings in the block built by *send*, we place the current bindings there as we place the new bindings in the value cell. The new definition of *send* follows:

$$send <= \lambda[[var;val;block]\; concat[mkent[var;swp\_val\_cell[var;val]];block]]$$

where *sw_val_cell* places *val* in the value cell of *var* and returns the old value.

The unbinding operation is even more complicated. When we leave an environment we expect the prior environment to be re-established. That is done automatically by recursion in the deep implementation and in the previous shallow binder. See page 117; the recursive call on *eval* with the new binding of *environ* will lose its effect as we leave *eval*.

However, the new scheme requires more; we must restore the saved values to the value cells, and recursion will not do that automatically. We will discuss more of the details of this process in Section 3.11 and Section 5.19, but the basic idea is to swap the contents of the saved block back into the value cells as we leave the inner call on *eval*. Notice that we cannot simply throw away the old bindings since a call on *function* may have occurred. The *funarg* triple can be built as before: saving the current environment name (*not* saving the current contents of all the value cells). The application of *funargs* is therefore more problematic. In the previous binding implementations, all we needed to do was establish the saved environment name as the evironment to be used for non-local searches. In this latest binder, we must *re-establish* the value cells which were current when *function* was recognized. We will postpone this discussion until Section 5.19 and Section 5.20.

This latest implementation of binding is by far the most complex we have seen. It gives fast access to values of variables, but requires more effort in changing environments; that is particularly evident in the discussion of *function* constructs. We will discuss the relative merits of these implementations in more detail in Chapter 5. Be clear on the distinction between a binding strategy and a binding implementation. The two strategies we have discussed are called "dynamic" and "static"; the two implementations are called "deep" and "shallow". Either implementation technique can be used with either binding strategy.

Problems

1. Suggest an implementation of *addval* which will improve the search efficiency of *lookup*.

2. Analyze *lookup* in a manner similar to that performed on *mkenv* on page 124. Identify the parts of *lookup* which are independent of the binding implementation. Rewrite the shallow and deep versions of *lookup* in this more general setting.

3.12 Special Forms and Macros

We have remarked that the evaluation scheme for LISP functions is call-by-value and, for functions with multiple arguments, left-to-right evaluation of arguments. We have also seen, in *quote* and *cond*, that not all forms to be evaluated in LISP fall within this category. The purpose of *quote* was to *stop* evaluation; and the "argument list" to *cond* is also handled differently. Since *quote* and *cond* were rather anomalous we have called them **special forms**. Now we would like to discuss special forms as a general technique.

Consider the predicates *and* and *or*. We might wish to define *and* to be a binary predicate such that *and* is true just in case *both* arguments evaluate to t, and define *or* to be binary and false just in case both arguments evaluate to f. Notice two points. First, there is really no reason to restrict these predicates to be *binary*. Replacing the words "binary" by "n-ary" and "both" by "all" in the above description has the desired effect. Second, if we evaluate the arguments to these predicates in some order, say left-to-right, then we could immediately determine that *and* is false as soon as we come across an argument which evaluates to f; similarly a call on *or* for an arbitrary number of arguments can be terminated as soon as we evaluate an argument giving value t. But if we insist that *and* and *or* be LISP *functions* we can take advantage of neither of these observations. Rather we will define *and* and *or* as special forms and handle the evaluation ourselves. Presently, the only way to handle special forms is to make explicit modifications to *eval*. [42]

----

[42]On page 212 and in Section 4.10 we will discuss simple ways to add such forms without modifying *eval*.

Recognizers for the predicates must be added to *eval*:

$isand[e] \rightarrow evand[arglist[e];environ];$
$isor[e] \rightarrow evor[arglist[e];environ];$

where:

$evand <= \lambda[[l;a] \; [null[l] \rightarrow t;$
$\qquad\qquad\qquad eval[first[l];a] \rightarrow evand[rest[l];a];$
$\qquad\qquad\qquad t \rightarrow f] \;]$

$evor <= \lambda[[l;a] \; [null[l] \rightarrow f;$
$\qquad\qquad\qquad eval[first[l];a] \rightarrow t;$
$\qquad\qquad\qquad t \rightarrow evor[rest[l];a]] \;]$

Or, exploiting the duality of *and* and *or* ([Ste pc]):

$isand[e] \rightarrow evandor[arglist[e];environ;t];$
$isor[e] \rightarrow evandor[arglist[e];environ;f];$
$evandor <= \lambda[[l;a;d] \; [null[l] \rightarrow d;$
$\qquad\qquad\qquad\qquad xor[d;eval[first[l];a]] \rightarrow not[d];$
$\qquad\qquad\qquad\qquad t \rightarrow evandor[rest[l];a;d]]]$

$xor <= \lambda[[a;b][a \rightarrow not[b]; t \rightarrow b]]$

In either formulation there are explicit calls on *eval*. [43] This seems expensive, but the arguments must be evaluated.

Special forms have been used for two purposes: one is to control the evaluation of arguments; conditional expressions, quoted expressions, *and*, and *or* are examples. The second application area is to create the effect of call-by-value functions with an indefinite number of arguments *all* of which are to be evaluated; the LISP functions, *list*, *append*, and *plus* are examples in this category.

Even though we wish to define these functions as if they had an arbitrary number of arguments, when we *call* the function, the number of arguments to be applied *is* known. [44]

Assume, for example, we wish to define *plus* as a function with an indefinite number of arguments such that:

$$plus[4;5] = 9$$
$$plus[4;5;6] = 15$$
$$plus[4;add1[2];4] = 11$$

---

[43] Also notice that the abstract versions of *evand*, *evor* and *evandor* *know* that the arguments are represented as a sequence and the structure of the recursion implies a left-to-right evaluation.

[44] For example, at compile time the number of arguments is known, and the compiler can often generate more efficient code than just calls on *eval*.

We can define *plus* in terms of a *binary* addition function, **plus*.

$$plus[4;5] = *plus[4;5] = 9$$
$$plus[4;5;6] = *plus[4;*plus[5;6]] = 15$$
$$plus[4;add1[2];4] = *plus[4;*plus[add1[2];4]] = 11$$

We expand calls on *plus* into a composition of calls on **plus*. *plus* is being used as a **macro** and the expansion process in terms of **plus* is called **macro expansion**. The macro expansion generates a composition of calls on **plus*.

A macro definition is a λ-expression of *one* argument. The call on a macro looks just like an ordinary function call, but what is bound to the λ-variable is the whole call on the macro. [45] The task of the macro body is to expand the macro call and return this expansion as its value. This expanded form is passed back through *eval* to complete the computation. In Section 4.10 we will discuss the additional mechanisms which evaluators must possess for execution of macros.

Let's define $<_m=$ to mean " is defined to be the macro ...". Then a simple macro definition of *plus* might be:

$$plus <_m= \lambda[[l] \; [eq[length[l];3] \to concat[*PLUS;rest[l]];$$
$$t \to list[*PLUS;$$
$$second[l];$$
$$concat[PLUS;rest[rest[l]]]]]]$$

Thus a call *(PLUS 3 4 5)* would bind *l* to *(PLUS 3 4 5)* and the evaluation of the body would result in *(*PLUS 3 (PLUS 4 5))*. Evaluation of this expression would result in another call on the macro. This time *l* would be bound to *(PLUS 4 5)*. Now *eq[length[l];3]* is true and the value returned is *(*PLUS 4 5)*. This will be evaluated, giving *9*; finally the outermost call on **PLUS* has all its arguments evaluated, and we get the final answer, *12*.

A more general macro expander can be described as:

$$expand <= \lambda[[fn;l][null[rest[l]] \to l;$$
$$t \to list[\; fn;$$
$$first[l];$$
$$expand[fn;rest[l]]]]]$$

Then we can define *plus* $<_m= \lambda[[l] \; expand[*PLUS;rest[l]]]$.
In a similar manner,

$$append <_m= \lambda[[l] \; expand[*APPEND;rest[l]]]$$

where **append* is the binary version of *append*.

Since the body of a macro has available all of the evaluation mechanism of LISP, and since the program structure of LISP is also the data structure, we can perform arbitrary computations inside the expansion of the macro.

---

[45]A similar device, called "meta composition", is used in [Bac 73].

The idea of macro processing is not recent. Some of the earliest assemblers had extensive macro facilities. Lately macros have been used as a means of extending so-called high level languages. One of the most simple kinds of macros is **textual substitution**. That is, when a use of a macro is detected we simply replace the call by its body. A slightly more sophisticated application is the **syntax macro**. Everytime we come across an application of a syntax macro the expander processes it as if it had never been seen before even though much of the expansion is repetitious. That is, syntax macros have no memory.

Computational macros are an attempt to reduce some of this repetition. In this scheme a certain amount of processing is done at the time the macro is *defined*. For example a computational subtree reflecting the body of the macro might be formed. Then whenever the macro is *used* we can simply make a copy of this subtree and "glue" this subtree into the parse-tree which we are building. This computational subtree is commonly formed by passing the body of the macro through the language processor in a slightly non-standard way. The main problem with the computational macro is that there are many desirable macros which have no such subtree, or there is other information necessary to process the macro. There are solutions to this problem, one of which closely parallels the abstract syntax ideas of McCarthy. All of these styles of macros are subsets of the LISP macros.

Problems

1. What is the difference between a special form and call-by-name evaluation? Can call-by-name be simulated in LISP without redefining *eval*?

2. *select* is a special form to be called as: *select*$[q;q_1;e_1; ... ;q_n;e_n;e]$ and to be evaluated as follows: q is evaluated; the q_i's are evaluated from left to right until one is found with the value of q. The value of *select* is the value of the corresponding e_i. If no such q_i is found the value of *select* is the value of e. The *select* operator is a precursor of the **case statement**; see page 193. Add a recognizer to *eval* to handle *select* and write a function to perform the evaluation of *select*.

3. Define *list* as a macro.

4. Extend the *eval-apply* pair of Section 3.5 to handle macros.

3.13 Review and Reflection

"I think that it is important to maintain a view of the field that helps minimize the distance between theoretical and practical work."

Saul Amarel, [Ama 72]

By way of review we sketch the basic LISP evaluator of Section 3.5: *eval* plus the additional artifacts for *label* and *function*.

There are two arguments to *eval*: a **form**, [46] that is, an expression which can be evaluated; and an association list or **symbol table**. If the form is a constant, return that form. If the form is a variable, find the value of the variable in the current environment. If the form is a conditional expression, then evaluate it according to the semantics of conditional expressions.

The form might also be a functional argument. In this case evaluation consists of associating the current environment with the function and returning that construct as value; in LISP this is done with the *funarg* device. Any other form seen by *eval* is assumed to be an application, that is, a function followed by arguments. The arguments are evaluated from left-to-right and the function is then applied to these arguments.

The part of the evaluator which handles function application is called *apply*. *apply* takes three arguments: a LISP function, a list of evaluated arguments, and a symbol table. If the function is one of the five LISP primitives then the appropriate action is carried out. If the function is a λ-expression then bind the formal parameters (the λ-variables) to the evaluated arguments and evaluate the body of the function. The function might also be the result of a functional argument binding; in this case apply the function to the arguments and use the saved environment, rather than the given environment, to search for non-local bindings. If we are applying the *label* operator, we build a *funarg*-triple and new environment such that the environment bound in the triple is the new environment. We then apply the function to the arguments in that environment.

If the function has a name we look up that name in the current environment. We expect that value to be a λ-expression, which is then applied. However, since function names are just variables, there is no reason that the value of a function name could not be a simple value, say an atom, and *that* value can be applied to the arguments. Examination of *apply* on page 117 will show that $apply[X; ((A\ B)); ((X\ .\ CAR)\ ...\ )]$ *will* be handled correctly. A generalization of this idea is possible. If the function passed to *apply* is not recognized as one of the preceding cases, then continue to evaluate the function-part until it is recognized. Such functions are called **computed functions**.

For example, we will allow such forms as:

$$((CAR\ (QUOTE\ (CAR\ (A\ .\ B))))\ (QUOTE\ (A\ .\ B)))$$

---

[46]Throughout this section we will say "form", "variable", "λ-expression", etc. rather than "a representation of a" ... "form", "variable", "λ-expression", etc. No confusion should result, but remember that we *are* speaking imprecisely.

The introduction of computed functions modifies *apply* (page 117) slightly:

$$apply <= \lambda[[fn;args;environ]\ [iscar[fn] \rightarrow car[arg_1[args]];$$
$$iscons[fn] \rightarrow cons[arg_1[args];arg_2[args]];$$

$$...\qquad\qquad ...$$

$$islambda[fn] \rightarrow eval[\ body[fn];$$
$$pairlis[vars[fn];$$
$$args;$$
$$environ]];$$

$$t \rightarrow apply[eval[fn;environ];$$
$$args;$$
$$environ]\ ]]$$

The subset of LISP which is captured by this evaluator is a strong and useful language even though it lacks several of the more common programming language features. [47] This subset is called the **applicative subset of LISP**, since its computational ability is based on the mathematical idea of function application. We have persistently referred to our LISP procedures as LISP functions, even though we have seen some differences between the concept of function in mathematics and the concepts of procedure in LISP. It is the mathematical idea of "function" which the "procedures" of our applicative programming language approximate. Regardless of differences in syntax and evaluation schemes, the dominant characteristic of an applicative language is that a given "function" applied to a given set of arguments *always* produces the same result: either the computation produces an error, or it doesn't terminate, or it produces a specific value. The applicative subset of LISP uses dynamic binding and therefore the occurrence of free variables calls the environment into play. But still, we have no way to destructively change the environment. Constructs which do have such an ability are said to have **side-effects** and are discussed in the next chapter.

LISP was the first language to exploit procedures as objects of the

---

[47]It is "strong", both practically and theoretically. It is sufficiently powerful to be "universal" in the sense that all computable functions are representable in LISP. In fact the *eval-apply* pair represents a "universal function", capable of simulating the behavior of any other computable function. The usual arguments about the halting problem ([Rog 67] and page 181) and related matters are easily expressed and proved in this LISP. Indeed, the original motivation for introducing the M-to-S expression mapping was to express the language constructs in the data domain so that universality could be demonstrated. "S-expression LISP" was used as a programming language only as an afterthought. It was S. Russell who convinced J. McCarthy that the theoretical device represented in *eval* and *apply* could in fact be programmed on the IBM 704.

language. The idea has been generalized substantially in the intervening years. A concise statement of the more general principle appears in [Pop 68a].

> "...This brings us to the subject of items. Anything which can be the value of a variable is an item. *All items have certain fundamental rights.*
>
> 1. All items can be the actual parameters of functions
> 2. All items can be returned as results of functions
> 3. All items can be the subject of assignment statements [48]
> 4. All items can be tested for equality.
>   ..."

LISP performs well on the first two principles, allowing LISP functions to be the arguments as well as the results of functions. The fourth principle is more difficult; that is, test for the equality of two LISP functions. In can be shown ([Rog 67]) that no algorithm can be constructed which will perform such a test for arbitrary functions. However in more selective settings, program equality can be established, both theoretically ([Man 74]), and practically ([Boy 75], [Dar 73], [Car 76]).

The language POP-2 ([Pop 68]) has also generalized the notion of function application in a slight, but significant, way. The generalization is called **partial application**. Given a function

$$f <= \lambda[[x_1; \dots ;x_n] \, \xi]$$

we compute a new function of $n-m$ arguments by applying f to m arguments and obtain a function of the remaining arguments x_{m+1} through x_n:

$$\lambda[[x_{m+1}; \dots x_n] \, \xi'] = f[t_1; \dots; t_m]$$

where ξ' results from ξ by binding x_1 through x_m to t_1 through t_m respectively. [49] Further generalizations of partial application are imaginable ([Sta 74]).

We have pointed out several "procedural" differences. Our treatment of conditional expressions differs from the usual treatment of function application: our standard rule for function application is "call by value" which requires the evaluation of all arguments before calling the LISP function; only some of the arguments to a conditional expression are evaluated. Note that the whole question of "evaluation of arguments" is a procedural one; arguments to functions aren't "evaluated" or "not evaluated", they just "are".

We have seen different algorithms computing the same function; for example *fact* (page 47 and page 149) and *fact*₁ (page 47) all compute the

---

[48]This issue will be postponed until Chapter 4.
[49]POP-2 actually binds the *last m* arguments.

factorial function. If there are different algorithms for computing factorial, then there are different alorithms for computing the value of an expression, and *eval* is just one such algorithm. Just as the essence of *fact* and $fact_1$ is the factorial function, we should capture the essence expressed in *eval*. Put another way, when applications programmers use *sqrt* or π they have a specific mathematical concept in mind. The implementation of the language supplies approximations to these mathematical entities, and assuming the computations stay within the numerical ranges of the machine, the programmers are free to interpret any output as that which the mathematical entities would produce. More importantly, the programmers have placed specific interpretations or meanings on symbols. We are interested in doing the same thing; however we wish to produce a *freer* interpretation, which only mirrors the essential ingredients of the language constructs. That is, *sqrt* represents a *function* and π represents a *constant*. The *eval-apply* pair gives one interpretation to the meaning of functions and constants, but there are different interpretations and there are different *eval-apply* pairs. The remainder of this section will resolve some of the tension between function and procedure.

What does this discussion have to do with programming languages? Clearly the order of evaluation or reduction is directly applicable. Our study will also give insights into the problem of language specification. Do we say that the language specification consists of a syntactic component and some description of the evaluation of constructs in that language? Or do we say that these two components, syntax and a machine, are merely devices for describing and formalizing notions about some abstract domain of discourse? A related question for programmers and language designers involves the ideas of correctness and equivalence of programs. How do we know when a program is correct? This requires some notion of a standard against which to test our implementations. [50] If our algorithms really are reflections of functional properties, then we should develop methods for verifying that those properties are expressed in our algorithms. Against this we must balance the realization that many programs don't fit neatly into this mathematical framework. Many programs are best characterized as themselves. In this case we should then be interested in verfying equivalence of programs. If we develop a new algorithm we have a responsibility to demonstrate that the algorithms are equivalent in very well defined ways. [51]

The study of formal systems in mathematical logic offers insight into

---

[50]"Unless there is a prior mathematical definition of a language at hand, who is to say whether a proposed implementation is *correct*?" [Sco 72].

[51]Current theory is inadequate for dealing with many real programming tasks. However the realization that one has a responsibility to consider the questions, *even informally*, is a sobering one which more **programmers should experience.**

many of these questions. In logic, we are presented with a syntax, and a system of axioms and rules of inference. Most usually we are also offered a "model theory" which gives us interpretations for the objects of the formal system; the model theory supplies additional methods for giving convincing arguments for the validity of statements in the formal system. The arguments made within the formal system are couched in terms of "provability" whereas arguments of the model theory are given in terms of "truth". For a discussion of formal systems and model theory see [Men 64].

C. W. Morris ([Mor 55]) isolated three perspectives on language, syntax, pragmatics, and semantics:

Syntax: The synthesis and analysis of sentences in a language. This area is well cultivated in programming language specification.

Pragmatics: The relation between the language and its user. Evaluators, like *tgmoaf*, *tgmoafr* and *eval*, come under the heading of pragmatics. Pragmatics are more commonly referred to as operational semantics in discussions of programming languages.

Semantics: The relation between constructs of the language and the abstract objects which they denote. This subdivision is commonly referred to as denotational semantics.

Put differently, syntax describes appearance; pragmatics describes implementation; and semantics describes meaning. [52] Though there is a strong concensus on the syntactic tools for specifying languages, [53] there is no consensus on adequate pragmatics, and even less agreement on the adequancy of semantic descriptions. We will first outline the pragmatics questions and then discuss a bit more of the semantics issues. In this discussion we will use the language distinctions of Morris even though the practice is not commonly followed in the literature. Typically, syntax is studied precisely and semantics is "everything else"; however the distinction between computation (pragmatics) and truth (semantics) is important and should not be muddled.

One thought is to describe the pragmatics of a language in terms of the process of compilation. That is, the pragmatics is specified by a specific

---

[52]This division of language reflects an interesting parallel between mathematical logic and programming languages: in mathematical logic we have deduction, computation, and truth; in programming language specification we have three analogous schools of thought: axiomatic, operational, and denotational. See [Men 64] for the mathematical logic and [Dav 76] for a study of the interrelationships; see [Hoa 69] for a discussion of the axiomatic school; we will say more about the operational and denotational schools in this section.

[53]But see [Pra 73] for a contrary position.

standard compiler producing code for some well-defined simple machine. The meaning of a program is the outcome of an interpreter interpreting this code. But then, to understand the meaning of a particular construct, this proposal requires that you understand the description of a compiler and understand the simple machine. Two problems arise immediately. Compilers are not particularly transparent programs. Second, a very simple machine may not adequately reflect the actual mechanisms used in an implementation. This aspect is important if the description is to be meaningful to an implementor.

A more fundamental difficulty is apparent when we consider the practical aspects of this proposal. When asked to understand a program written in a high-level language you think about the *behavior* of that program in a very direct way. The pragmatics is close to the semantics. You think about the computational behavior as it executes; you do not think about the code that gets generated and then think about the execution of that code.

A more natural pragmatics for the constructs is given in terms of the execution of these constructs; thus *eval* is the pragmatic description of LISP. The *eval* function describes the execution sequence of a representation of an arbitrary LISP expression. That description has a flavor of circularity which some find displeasing. However some circularity in description is inevitable; we must assume that something is known and does not require further explication. If language L_1 is described in terms of a simpler language L_2 then either L_2 is "self evident" or a description L_2 must be given.

So, realistically, the choice is where to stop, not whether to stop. The LISP position is that the language and data structures are sufficiently simple that self-description is satisfactory. Attempts have been made to give non-circular interpreter-based descriptions of semantics for languages other than LISP. There is a Vienna Definition Language ([Weg 72]) description of PL/1, and a description of ALGOL 68 ([Alg 75]) by a Markov algorithm. Both these attempts result in a description which is long and unmanageable for all but the most persistent reader.

There are some compelling reasons for deciding on direct circularity. First, you need only learn one language. If the specification is given the source language, then you learn the programming language and the specification language at the same time. Second, since the evaluator is written in the language, we can understand the language by understanding the workings of the single program, *eval*; and if we wish to modify the pragmatics, we need change only one collection of high-level programs. If we wished to add new language constructs to LISP we need only modify *eval* so that it recognizes an occurrence of that new construct; and we must add a function to describe the interpretation of the construct. Those modifications may be extensive, but they will be controlled revisions rather than a complete reprogramming effort.

There is another common method for specifying the pragmatics of a programming language. The Algol report ([Alg 63]) introduced a standard for syntax specification: the BNF equation. It also gave a reasonably precise description of the pragmatics of Algol statements in natural language. The style of presentation was concise and clear, but suffers from the imprecision of natural language. Regardless, this style of description is quite common and is very useful. A recent report ([Moor 76]) on the pragmatics of InterLISP used this descriptive style. If the language is quite complex, then a formal description can be equally complex. In Section 4.8 we will see that our interpreter definition will extend nicely to richer subsets of LISP.

Regardless of the descriptive method used, a language description should not attempt to explain everything about a language. It need only explain what needs explaining. You must assume that your reader understands something ... . McCarthy: 'Nothing can be explained to a stone' [McC 66]. A description of a language must be natural and must match the expressive power of the language. That is, it should model how the constructs are to be implemented. What is needed is a description which exploits, rather than ignores, the structure of the language. Mathematical notation is no substitute for clear thought, but careful formulations of semantics will lead to additional insights in the pragmatics of language design. [54] The task requires new mathematical tools to model the language constructs, and requires increased care on the part of the language designer.

Let's look at the issue of syntax for a moment. A satisfactory description of much of programming language syntax is standard BNF. The BNF is a generative, or synthetic grammar since the rewriting rules specify how to *generate* well formed strings. An evaluator, on the other hand, executes the already existing program. This implies that our evaluator is *analytic* rather than synthetic; it must have some way of analyzing the structure of the given program.

In [McC 62], John McCarthy introduced the concept of abstract analytic syntax. The idea is directly derivable from the LISP experience. The syntax is analytic, rather than synthetic, in the sense that it tells how to take programs apart -- how to recognize and select subparts of programs using predicates and selector functions. [55] It is abstract in the sense that it makes no commitment to the external representation of the constitutents of the program. We need only be able to recognize the occurrence of a desired construct. For example:

---

[54]R. D. Tennent has invoked this approach in the design of *QUEST* ([Ten 76]).

[55]We will deal with abstract *synthetic* syntax when we discuss compilers.

isterm <= λ[[*t*] *or*[*isvar*[*t*];
                          isconst[*t*];
                          and[*issum*[*t*];*isterm*[*addend*[*t*]];*isterm*[*augend*[*t*]]]]]

and the BNF equation:

<term> ::= <var> | <const> | <term> + <term>

issum, addend, and *augend,* don't really care whether the sum is represented
as x+y, or +[x;y] or *(PLUS X Y)* or xy+. The different external
representations are reflections of different concrete syntaxes; the BNF
equation above gives one. Parsing links a concrete syntax with the abstract
syntax.

Since the evaluator must operate on *some* internal representation of the
source program, a representation reflecting the structure of the program is
most natural. This representation is more commonly known as a parse tree.
We can describe the evaluation of a program in terms of a function which
operates on a parse tree using the predicates and selectors of the analytic
syntax. Abstract syntax concerns itself only with those properties of a
program which are of interest to an evaluator.

The Meta expression LISP constitutes a concrete syntax. [56] The
M-to-S-expression translator is the parser which maps the external
representation onto a parse (or computational) tree. The selectors and
predicates of the analytic syntax are straightforward. Recall the BNF for
LISP:

<form>   ::= <constant>
         ::= <variable>
         ::= <function>[<arg>; ... ;<arg>]
         ::= [<form> → <form>; ... ;<form> → <form>]
         ....

We need to write a parser which takes instances of these equations onto an
internal representation. Much is known about parsing techniques ([Aho 72],
also see Section 9.4 and Section 9.3) so we will concentrate on the
post-parse processing.

Our evaluator will operate on the parse tree and will therefore need to
recognize representations of constants, variables, conditional expressions, and
applications. We need to write a function in some language expressing the
values of these constructs. Since the proposed evaluator is to manipulate
parse trees, and since the domain of LISP functions *is* binary trees, it should
seem natural to use LISP itself. If this is the case, then we must represent
the parse tree as a LISP S-expr and represent the selectors and recognizers as
LISP functions and predicates.

---

[56]The S-expr notation is also a concrete syntax, but one which is more
closely related to the abstract syntax.

Perhaps:

$isconst$ <= $\lambda[[x]$ $or[numberp[x];$
$\qquad\qquad\qquad and[atom[x];eq[x;NIL]];$
$\qquad\qquad\qquad and[atom[x];eq[x;T]];$
$\qquad\qquad\qquad and[not[atom[x]];eq[first[x];QUOTE]$

$isvar$ <= $\lambda[[x]$ $and[atom[x];$ $not[isconst[x]]]]$

$iscond$ <= $\lambda[[x]$ $eq[first[x];COND]]$

There are really two issues here: a representation of the analytic syntax of a language, and a representation in terms of the language *itself*. In conjunction, these two ideas give a natural and very powerful means of specifying languages. If this style of specification is really effective, then we should be able to specify other languages in a similar fashion. One of the weak points of LISP as a programming language is the insistence on binary tree representations of data. [57] Many applications could profit from other data representations. What we would then like is a language which has richer data structures than LISP but which is designed to allow LISP-style semantic specification. We would be able to write an evaluator, albeit more complex than *eval*, in the language itself. The evaluator would operate on a representation of the program as a data structure of the language, just as *eval* operates on the S-expr translation of the LISP program. The concrete syntax would be specified as a set of BNF equations, and our parser would translate strings into parse trees.

In outline, to specify a construct we must have at least the following:

1. A concrete production.
2. An abstract data type.
3. A mapping from 1 to 2.
4. An evaluator for the abstract type.

In Chapter 8 we will sketch a recent LISP-like language, EL1, which *does* apply these principles. [58]

From a discussion of syntax we have returned to evaluation. After we reduce the questions of syntax of programming languages to questions of abstract syntax and stripped way the syntactic differences, how many *real* differences between languages are there? Semantics addresses this issue.

---

[57]Many 'production' versions of LISP have array, string, and even record structures available. However the programmer must explicitly request and manipulate such storage structures. We would rather develop techniques in which the storage structures are *implied* either by the types of operations desired, or by the specification of the abstract data struture, or by interaction between the programming system and the user.

[58]Compare steps 1 through 4 with those on page 36.

Many of the semantic ideas in applicative programming languages can be captured in λ-calculus ([Chu 41]). The λ-calculus was developed to supply a formalism for discussing the notions of function and function application. Rather than develop the syntax of λ-calculus, we will use LISP-like syntax and show how we can abstract from the procedural LISP function to a mathematical function.

Most of the description of LISP which we have given so far is classified as operational. That means our informal description of LISP and our later description of the LISP interpreter are presented in terms of "how does it work or operate". Indeed the purpose of *eval* was to describe explicitly what happens as a LISP expression is evaluated. We have seen (page 100) that discussion of evaluation schemes is non-trivial; and that order of evaluation can effect the outcome (page 21).

However, many times the order of evaluation is immaterial. [59] We saw on page 127 that *eval* will compute a value for an application $f[a_1; ...; a_n]$ even though f was defined for fewer arguments. How much of *eval* is "really" LISP and how much is "really" implementation? On one hand we have said that the meaning of a LISP expression is by definition what *eval* will calculate using the representation of the expression. On the other hand, we claim that *eval* is simply *an implementation*. There are certainly other implementations; i.e, other LISP functions *eval*$_i$ which have the same input-output behavior as our *eval*. The position here is not that *eval* is wrong in giving values to things like *cons[A;B;C]*, but rather we want to know what is it that *eval* implements.

This other way of looking at meaning in programming languages is exemplified by denotational or mathematical semantics. This perspective springs from the philosophical or logical device of distinguishing between a *representation* for an object, and the object itself. The most familiar example is the numeral-number distinction. Numerals are notations (syntax) for talking about *numbers* (semantics). thus the Arabic *numerals 2, 02,* the Roman numeral II, and the Binary notation *10,* all *denote* the same number denoted by the word "two." In LISP, *(A B), (A . (B)), (A , B)* and *(A . (B . NIL))* all are notations for the same S-expr. That is, an object transends its representations. We want to say that a LISP form *car[(A . B)]* denotes the same object denoted by *A*, or *car[A]* denotes undefined just as we say in mathematics that 2+2 denotes 4 or 1/0 is undefined.

---

[59]"One difficulty with the operational approach is that it (frequently) specifies too much": C. Wadsworth.

Similarly, we say that the denotational counterpart of a LISP function is a mathematical function defined over an appropriate abstract domain. Before proceeding, we introduce some conventions to distinguish notation from *de*notation. We will continue to use italics:

$$A, B, ..., x, ..., car, ..., (A . B)$$

as notation in LISP expressions.

Gothic bold-face: **A, B, ..., x, ..., car, ..., (A . B)**

will represent denotations.

Thus A is notation for **A**; the expression $car[cdr[(A . (B . C))]]$ denotes **B**; the mapping, **car** is the denotation of the LISP function *car*.

Several areas of LISP must be subjected to an abstraction process. In particular, the operations involved in the evaluation process must be abstracted away. These involve an abstraction from LISP's call by value evaluation and its left to right order of evaluation of arguments. For example, the operation of composition of LISP functions is meant to denote mathematical composition; in LISP, $car[cdr[(A . (B . C))]]$ means apply the procedure *cdr* to the argument $(A . (B . C))$ getting $(B . C)$; apply the procedure *car* to $(B . C)$ getting B. Mathematically, we have a mapping **car∘cdr**, which is a composition of the **car** and **cdr** mappings; the ordered pair **<(A . (B . C)) , B>** is in the graph of this composed mapping. At this level of abstraction, any LISP characterization of a function is equally good; the "efficiency" question has been abstracted away. Many important properties of real programs *can* be discussed in this mathematical context; in particular, questions of equivalence and correctness of programs are even more tractable.

As we remove the operational aspects, we discover a few critical properties of functions which must be reconciled with LISP's procedures. We must treat the ideas of binding of variables, and we must handle the notion of function application.

We know that there are at least two binding strategies available: static binding and dynamic binding; we know that the choice of strategy can effect the resultant computation. This computational difference must be studied. To illuminate the problem we take an example in LISP.
Consider:

$$\lambda[[z]$$
$$\quad \lambda[[u]$$
$$\quad\quad \lambda[[z] \, u[B]][C]]$$
$$\quad\quad [\lambda[[x] \, cons[x;z]]] \,]$$
$$\quad [A]$$

The dynamic binding strategy will bind z to A; then bind u to the functional argument, $\lambda[[x] \, cons[x;z]]$; next, z is rebound to C, and finally $u[B]$ is evaluated. That involves binding x to B and evaluating $cons[x;z]$. Since we are using dynamic binding, the *latest active* bindings of the variables are used. The latest active bindings for x and z are B and C respectively, and the final value is therefore $(B . C)$.

We can obtain static binding by replacing $\lambda[[x] \, cons[x;z]]$ by $function[\lambda[[x] \, cons[x;z]]]$. This has the effect of associating the variable z with the atom A. As we know, the final result of this computation will be $(B . A)$.

Before discussing binding strategies further, we must strengthen our understanding of the ideas underlying function application. It is this notion which a binding strategy is implementing. This involves a more careful study of the notion of λ-notation as the representation of a function. We shall restrict out discussion to unary λ-expressions, since n-ary functions can be represented in terms of unary functions:

$$\lambda((x \ y) \ \xi) = \lambda((x) \ \lambda((y) \ \xi))$$

What properties do we expect a function, denoted by a λ-expression, to possess? For example, we expect that a systematic renaming of formal parameters should not effect the definition of a function.

$\qquad \lambda[[y] \, x] \qquad$ should denote the same function as $\qquad \lambda[[w] \, x]$

But

$\qquad \lambda[[x] \, \lambda[[y] \, x]][w] \quad$ is not the same as $\qquad \lambda[[x] \, \lambda[[w] \, x]][w]$

This example shows that we need to be careful in defining our substitution rules. Closer examination of the last example shows that the result $\lambda[[w] \, w]$ would occur if the substitution changed a non-local name (x) into a local name (w). The expected result would have been obtained if we had recognized the clash of names and replaced the formal parameter y with a new name, say u, and then performed the substitution, getting $\lambda[[u] \, w]$ which is the same as $\lambda[[y] \, w]$. Before giving a substitution rule which accounts for such changes of name we will introduce some new terminology.

First, the "same as" relation will occur frequently in the discussion; we should establish some properties of this notion. We introduce $\equiv$ to denote "is the same as"; we could therefore say

$$\lambda[[y] \, x] \equiv \lambda[[w] \, x]$$

We expect that $\equiv$ obey the rules of equality, being a reflective, transitive and symmetric relation. It should also "substitutive" in the following sense:

(σ):
$\qquad$ if $f \equiv g$ then $f[a] \equiv g[a]$
$\qquad$ if $f \equiv g$ then $\lambda[[x] \, f] \equiv \lambda[[x] \, g]$
$\qquad$ if $a \equiv b$ then $f[a] \equiv f[b]$

Next, we need to talk about the bindings of variables more carefully. We will refer to well formed components of the statically bound λ-calculus as "terms"; we will continue to refer to components of the dynamically bound language LISP as "expressions". Thus, a variable, x, is a **free variable** [60] in an term, ξ if:

ξ is the variable, x.

ξ is a term $f[A]$, and x is free in f or x is free in A.

ξ is a term $\lambda[[y] M]$, and x is free in M and x is distinct from y. Thus w is free in $\lambda[[x] w]$.

We can define a LISP predicate to test for free-ness:

$isfree <= \lambda[[x;z] [is\_var[z] \rightarrow samevar[x;z];$
$\qquad\qquad\qquad is\_app[z] \rightarrow [isfree[x;func[z]] \rightarrow t;$
$\qquad\qquad\qquad\qquad\qquad t \rightarrow isfree[x;arg_1[arglist[z]]]];$
$\qquad\qquad\qquad samevar[\lambda\_var[z];x] \rightarrow f;$
$\qquad\qquad\qquad t \rightarrow isfree[x;body[z]]]]$

An occurrence of variable is a **bound occurrence** in a term ξ if it occurs in ξ and the occurrence is not free in ξ. For example, w is bound in $\lambda[[w] w]$. A variable may have both bound and free occurrences; consider $w[\lambda[[w] w]]$.

Using our new terminology, we can say that a substitution of the actual parameter for free occurrences of the formal parameter can be made provided no free variables in the actual parameter will become bound variables as a result of the substitution.

Here is an appropriate substitution rule:

$subst^\bullet <= \lambda[[x;y;z] [is\_var[z] \rightarrow [eq[y;z] \rightarrow x; t \rightarrow z];$
$\qquad\qquad\qquad is\_app[z] \rightarrow mk\_app[subst^\bullet[x;y;func[z]];$
$\qquad\qquad\qquad\qquad\qquad\qquad subst^\bullet[x;y;arg_1[arglist[z]]]];$
$\qquad\qquad\qquad eq[y;\lambda\_var[z]] \rightarrow z;$
$\qquad\qquad\qquad not[isfree[y;body[z]]] \rightarrow z;$
$\qquad\qquad\qquad not[isfree[\lambda\_var[z];x]] \rightarrow mk\_\lambda[\lambda\_var[z];$
$\qquad\qquad\qquad\qquad\qquad\qquad\qquad subst^\bullet[x;$
$\qquad\qquad\qquad\qquad\qquad\qquad\qquad\qquad y;$
$\qquad\qquad\qquad\qquad\qquad\qquad\qquad\qquad body[z]]];$
$\qquad\qquad t \rightarrow \quad \lambda[[u]mk\_\lambda[u;$
$\qquad\qquad\qquad\qquad\qquad subst^\bullet[x;$
$\qquad\qquad\qquad\qquad\qquad\qquad y;$
$\qquad\qquad\qquad\qquad\qquad subst^\bullet[u;$
$\qquad\qquad\qquad\qquad\qquad\qquad \lambda\_var[z];$
$\qquad\qquad\qquad\qquad\qquad\qquad body[z]]]]]$
$\qquad\qquad [genvar[ ]]]]$

---

[60]Compare this definition of free with that in Section 3.7.

where *genvar* is to supply a new identifier for use as a variable name.

The substitution rule, *subst"*, is used to express the β-rule of the λ-calculus:

(β): $app \equiv subst"[arg_1[arglist[app]];\lambda\_var[func[app]];body[func[app]]]$

where *app* is an anonymous λ-application.

There is another basic rule of the λ-calculus called the α-rule. The α-rule captures the notion that $\lambda[[y] \ x]$ denotes the same function as $\lambda[[w] \ x]$; that is, subject to certain restrictions, we can change the formal parameter. The α-rule says:

(α): $fun \equiv \lambda[[u] \ mk\_\lambda[u;subst"[u;\lambda\_var[fun];body[fun]]][var]$
          provided that $not[isfree[var;body[fun]]]$

To summarize then, the λ-calculus is a formalism. The α and β rules are transformation rules, and σ expresses properties of the relation $\equiv$ as rules of inference. To complete the description, axioms which govern the behavior of $\equiv$ as an equivalence relation must be given. The α and β-rules are called **conversion rules**; they express the essential behavior of functions and their applications. The α rule formalizes the notion that a function denoted by a λ-term is unchanged if we change the formal parameters of the λ-term. that is:

$$\lambda[[x] \ f[x]] \equiv \lambda[[y] \ f[y]]$$

We know that such a rule is not valid in LISP; for example x may occur free in the definition of f. We can insure that a programming language will satisfy the α-rule by requiring that the free variables be bound to the values which were available at the time the definition was made. This is the effect of the *function* construct of LISP. A language which satisfies these notions is called **referential transparency**. Thus dynamic binding violates referential transparency. The difficulty again is the treatment of free variables.

The λ-calculus *does* possess referential transparency. Referential transparency is not simply a worthwhile theoretical property; its corollary, static binding, is a very useful practical property. In programming terms, referential transparency means that to understand a particular progam we need only understand the effect of the subprograms rather than understand the implementation of those subprograms. For example, we need not concern ourselves with the naming conventions used internal to the programs. These ideas are expressed in the philosophy of **modular programming**. That programming style encourages the construction of program segments as self-contained boxes, or modules, with well-defined input and output specifications. The intent is to manufacture larger programs by systematic combination of smaller modules. We will discuss some further implications of static binding in Section 5.21.[61]

The β-rule expresses the intent of function application. We would then expect that a model of the λ-calculus would have a domain consisting of functions; and require that the β-rule be reflected in the model as function application. The equality preserving properties of the $α$ and $β$ rules would require that if f and g are terms such that if $f(a) = g(a)$, then any $α$ or $β$ manipulations of f, g or a yielding f', g' and a', the relation $f'(a') = g'(a)$ holds.

We are now in a position to relate binding strategies with the ideas of substitution and $β$ reduction. Static binding is an implementation of the ideas expressed in the $β$ rule. We can implement the notions using *subst'* and do explicit substitutions, or we can simulate the substitutions using a symbol table device as LISP does for dynamic binding. No problems should arise if we use *subst'*; however this solution is not terribly efficient. Particular care is needed if *subst'* is to be simulated. The difficulty arises in adequately modelling the substitution of values for variables which are free in functional arguments or functional values. From LISP, we know one solution to this problem: use the *function* construct. We could simulate the effect of *subst'* by using a LISP symbol table and requiring that every functional argument or value be *funarg*-ed.[62]

From this standpoint, dynamic binding is simply an incorrect implementation of substitution. Attempts to legitimize dynamic binding by supplying formal rules lead to difficulties. The simple properties expressed in *subst'* and the $β$ rule do not hold for dynamic binding. However, dynamic binding is a very useful programming tool. Its ability to postpone bindings is particularly useful in interactive programming environments where we are creating program modules incrementally. The final word on binding strategies has not been heard.

So far the discussion has concentrated on binding strategies. We now wish to discuss the implications of calling style. We have discussed two calling styles: call-by-value and call-by-name; these computational devices should have mathematical interpretations. The conversion rules contain no instructions for their order of application. If the hypotheses for a rule is satisfied, then it may be applied. In the reduction of a λ-expression there may be several reductions possible at any one time. This is as it should be; we are extracting the procedural aspects, and certainly calling style is procedural. The order of application of rules expresses a particular calling algorithm. If we design a λ-calculus machine, we might specify a preferred order, but the machine reflects "*procedure*"; the calculus reflects "*function*".

An interpretation of the conversion rules as rules of computation

---

[61]There have been several recent investigations ([Hew 76], [Sus 75], [Ste 76b], [Ste 76c]) of statically bound LISP-like languages.

[62]Of course, such a claim should be proved.

requires the establishment of a notion of what is to be computed. The conversion rules simply state equivalences between expressions; however the β rule can be applied in a manner analogous to LISP's λ-binding. That is, it can be used to replace an application with the appropriately substituted body. In this context the β rule is called a **reduction rule**; and the application of the rule is called a reduction step. There are two common strategies for choosing a reduction step: applicative order and normal order.

Applicative order reduces right most term; normal order reduces the left most term. We will say that a λ-term is in **normal form** if it contains no term reducible by the β rule. Not all terms have normal forms: let Δ name $\lambda[[x]\ x[x]]$; then $\Delta[\Delta]$ does not have a normal form. Every β transformation of Δ produces a new term which is also β reducible. Not all reduction sequences yield a normal form: when $\lambda[[x]\ y][\Delta[\Delta]]$ is reduced in normal order, a normal form results; whereas applicative order will not yield a normal form.

The application of the reduction rules can be considered a computation scheme. The process of reducing a term is the computation, and a computation terminates if that reduction produces a normal form. With this interpretation, some computations terminate and some don't. A term has a normal form just in the case that some reduction sequence terminates. A λ-calculus machine ([Lan 64]) can simulate the reduction rules in several ways since no order of application is specified by the rules. Also, a machine might perform the substitutions directly or might simulate the substitutions in a manner similar to LISP. Finally we note the close relationships between reduction orders and calling styles: applicative order is most naturally associated with call-by-value, and call-by-name is reflected in normal order reduction. [63]

These discussions suggest some interesting problems. First, there may well be two or more sequences of reductions for a λ-expression; assuming they both terminate, will they yield the same normal forms? In fact, if both reduction sequences terminate then they result in the same normal form. This is called the Church-Rosser theorem ([Cur 58], [Ros 71], [Mil 73], [Wad 74a], [Leh 73]).

Second, if we have two λ-terms which reduce to distinct normal forms, are they "inherently different" terms? This requires some explanation of "inherently different". We might say that by definition, terms with different normal forms are "inherently different". But thinking of λ-terms as denoting functions, to say two λ-terms are "different" is to say we can exhibit arguments such that the value of application of one function is not equal to the value of the other function application. C. Boehm has established this for λ-terms which have normal forms ([Wad 71]).

---

[63]There is more to normal order reduction that just call-by-name; normal order reduction also performs "partial evaluation" of function bodies.

The situation changes when we examine λ-terms which do not have normal forms. Recalling the intuitive relationship between non-termination and "no normal form", we might expect that all expressions without normal form are "equivalent". However, it can be shown that such an identification would lead to contradictions. We might also expect that terms without normal forms are "different" from terms which do have normal forms. This is also not true; [Wad 71] exhibits two expressions, I and J with and without normal form, respectively such that $I \equiv J$. These two terms are the "same" in the sense that 3 and 2.99999 ... are the "same"; J is the limit of a sequence of approximations to I. In fact for any term with normal form there is an equivalent term without normal form. Also, we can exhibit two λ-terms, Y_1 and Y_2, both without normal form, which are distinct in that no reduction sequence will reduce one to the other; but they are "the same function" in the sense that, for any argument, a we supply, both reductions result in the same term. That is $Y_1[a] \equiv Y_2[a]$. [64] The reduction rules of the λ-calculus cannot help us. The resolution of the idea of "same-ness" requires stronger analysis. [65]

We can give an interpretation to the λ-calculus such that in that interpretation the pairs I and J, or Y_1 and Y_2, have the same meaning. This should be a convincing argument for maintaining that they are the "same function" even though the reduction rules are *not* sufficient to display that equivalence. [66] D. Scott *has* exhibited a model or interpretation of the λ-calculus, and D. Park has shown the equivalence in this model of Y_1 and Y_2, and C. Wadsworth as shown the equivalence of I and J.

As we said at the beginning of the section, this calculus was intended to explicate the idea of "function" and "function application". There is a reasonably subtle distinction between Church's conception of a function as a rule of correspondence, and the usual set-theoretic view of a function as a set of ordered pairs. In the latter setting we rather naturally think of the elements of the domain and range of a function as existing *prior* to the specification of the function:

"Let **f** be the function {<x,1>, <y,2>, ...}"

When we think of a function given as a predetermined set of ordered pairs we do not expect functions which can take themselves as arguments like **f(f)**.

---

[64]Note that $f[a]$ may have a normal form even though f does not.

[65]The interpretation of "same-ness" which we have been using is that of extensional equality. That is, two functions are considered the same function if no differences can be detected under application of the functions to any arguments.

[66]This demonstration also gives credence to the position that the meaning transcends the reduction rules. Compare the incompleteness results of K. Godel ([Men 64]).

Such functions are called **self-applicative**. Several languages, including LISP, allow the procedural analog of self applicative functions. They are an instance of functional arguments (Section 3.10). The LISP function discussed in the problem on page 149 is an instance of a self-applicative LISP function. Since we can deal with self-application as a procedural concept at least, perhaps some of this understanding will help with the mathematical questions.

The λ-calculus is an appropriate tool for studying self-application since any λ-term may be applied to any λ-term including itself. Compare this with the condition in LISP when we think of the S-expression representation of the language as the language itself. For example, in the *programming language* LISP, we can evaluate expressions like:

$$((LAMBDA\,(X)\,\xi)\,(LAMBDA\,(X)\,\xi))$$

That is, the distinction between program and data disappears, just as it does in the λ-calculus.

As we move again from procedural notions to more denotational concepts we remark that denotational interpretations have been introduced before. When we said (page 118) that:

$$f[a_1;\, ...;\, a_n]\ \text{was the same as}\ \ eval[(F\ A_1\ ...\ A_n);(\ )]$$

we were relating a denotational notion with an operational notion. The left hand side of this equation can be interpreted denotationally. The right hand side is operational, expressing a procedure call. A proper mathematical theory should allow us to state such an equation precisely and should contain methods which allow us to demonstrate the correctness of the assertion. Recent research ([Sco 70], [Sco 73], [Wad 71], [Gor 73], [Gor 75]) has begun to develop such mathematical methods.

This denotational-operational distinction is appropriate in a more general context. When we are presented with someone's program and asked "what does it compute?" we usually begin our investigation operationally, discovering "what does it *do*?" [67] Frequently, by tracing its execution, we can discover a denotational description: E.g., "ah! it computes the square root".

When *great mother* was presented it was given as an operational exercise, with the primary intent of introducing the LISP evaluation process without involving complicated names and concepts. Forms involving *great mother* were evaluated perhaps without understanding the denotation, but if asked "what does *great mother* do?" you would be hard pressed to give a comprehensible and purely operational definition. However, you might have discovered the intended nature of *great mother* yourself; then it would be

---

[67] Another common manifestation of this "denotation" phenomonon is the common programmer complaint: "It's easier to write your own than to understand someone else's program."

relatively easy to describe her behavior. Indeed, once the denotation of *great mother* has been discovered questions like "What is the value of *tgmoaf*[(*CAR* (*QUOTE* (*A . B*)))]? " are more easily answered by using the denotation of *tgmoaf*: "what is the value of *car*[(*A . B*)]?"

In discussing models for LISP, we will parallel our development of interpreters for LISP since each subset, *tgmoaf, tgmoafr*, and *eval*, will also introduce new problems for our mathematical semantics. Our first LISP subset considers functions, composition, and constants. Constants will be elements of our domain of interpretation. That domain will include the S-expressions since *most* LISP expressions denote S-exprs; since many of our LISP functions are partial functions, it is convenient to talk about the undefined value, ⊥. We wish to extend our partial functions to be **total** functions on an extended domain. As before (page 12), we shall call this extended domain **S**.

$$\mathsf{S} = \mathsf{<sexpr>} \cup \{\bot\}$$

Before we can discuss the properties of mathematical functions denoted by LISP functions, we must give more careful study to the nature of domains. Our primitive domain is **<atom>**. Its intuitive structure is quite simple, basically just a set of atoms or names with no inherent relationships among them. Another primitive domain is **Tr**, the domain of truth values. The domain **<sexpr>** is more complex; it is a set of elements, but many elements are related. In our discussion of **<sexpr>** on page 6 we made it clear that there is more than syntax involved. We could say that for s_1 and s_2 in **<sexpr>** the essence of "dotted pair" is contained in the concept of the set-theoretic ordered pair, $\langle s_1, s_2 \rangle$. Thus the "meaning" of the set of dotted pairs is captured by Cartesian product, **<sexpr> x <sexpr>**.

Let's continue the analysis of:

$$\text{<sexpr> ::= <atom> | (<sexpr> . <sexpr>)}$$

We are trying to interpret this BNF equation as a definition of the domain **<sexpr>**. Reasonable interpretations of "::=" and "|" appear to be equality and set-theoretic union, respectively. This results in the equation:

$$\mathsf{<sexpr>} = \mathsf{<atom>} \cup (\mathsf{<sexpr>} \times \mathsf{<sexpr>})$$

This looks like an algebraic equation, and as such, may or may not have solutions. This particular "domain equation" has at least one solution: the S-exprs. There is a natural mapping of BNF equations onto such "domain equations", and the solutions to the domain equations are sets satisfying the abstract essence of the BNF. The mapping process is also applicable to the language constructs. Consider the BNF equations for a simple applicative subset of LISP:

$$\text{<form> ::= <variable> | } \lambda[[\text{<variable>}] \text{ <form>}] | \text{ <variable>[<form>]}$$

We would like to describe the denotations of these equations in a style similar to that used for <sexpr>'s. The denotations of the expressions, <form>, of applications, <variable>[form]], and of the variables, <variables>, are just elements of S. Expressions of the form "λ[[<variable>] <form>]" denote functions from S to S. Write that set as $S{\to}S$. Then our domain equation is expressed:

$$S = (S{\to}S) \cup S$$

This equation has no *interesting* solutions. A simple counting argument will establish that unless a domain C consists of a single element, then the number of functions in $C{\to}C$ is greater than the number of elements in C. This does *not* say that there are no models for this LISP subset; it says that our interpretation of "$\to$" is too broad.

What is needed is an interpretation of functionality which will allow a solution to the above domain equation; it should allow a natural interpretation such that the properties which we expect functions to possess are true in the model. D. Scott gave one interpretation of "$\to$" for the λ-calculus, defining the class of "continuous functions" ([Sco 70], [Sco 73]). This class of functions is restricted enough to satisfy the domain equation, but broad enough to act as the denotations of procedures in applicative programming languages. We will use the notation "$[D_1 \to D_2]$" to mean "the set of continuous functions from domain D_1 to domain D_2". It is the continuous functions which first supplied a model for the λ-calculus and it is these functions which supply a basis for a mathematical model of applicative LISP ([Gor 73]).

We can assume that the LISP primitives denote specific continuous functions. For example, the mathematical counterpart to the LISP function *car* is the mapping **car** from S to S defined as follows:

car: $[S \to S]$

$$\textbf{car(t)} \quad \begin{array}{l} \text{is } \bot \text{ if } t \text{ is atomic} \\ \text{is } t_1 \text{ if } t \text{ is } <t_1, t_2> \\ \text{is } \bot \text{ if } t \text{ is } \bot \end{array}$$

Similar strategy suffices to give denotations for the other primitive LISP functions and predicates. For example:

atom: $[S \to S]$

$$\textbf{atom(t)} \quad \begin{array}{l} \text{is } f \text{ if } t \text{ is not atomic} \\ \text{is } t \text{ if } t \text{ is atomic} \\ \text{is } \bot \text{ if } t \text{ is } \bot \end{array}$$

Notice that these functions are strict: $f(\bot) = \bot$

Corresponding to *tgmoaf*, we will have a function, Δ_{tg}, which maps expressions onto their denotations. Since Δ_{tg} is another mapping like $\mathfrak{R}$, we will use the "$[\![$" and "$]\!]$" brackets to enclose LISP constructs. We need to introduce some notation for elements of the sets <sexpr> and <form>.

Let s be a meta-variable ranging over <sexpr> and e range over <form>, then we can write:

$$\Delta_{tg}[\![s]\!] = s$$

$$\Delta_{tg}[\![car[e]]\!] = car(\Delta_{tg}[\![e]\!])$$

with similar entries for *cdr*, *cons*, *eq*, and *atom*. The structure of this definition is very similar to that of *tgmoaf*.

Now we continue to the next subset of LISP, adding conditional expressions. As we noted on page 23, a degree of care need be taken when we attempt to interpret conditional expressions in terms of mappings. We can simplify the problem slightly: it is easy to show that the conditional expression can be formulated in terms of the simple *if*-expression: $if[p_1;e_1;e_2]$. We will display a denotation for such *if* expressions. It will be a mathematical function, and therefore the evaluation order will have been abstracted out. [68]

Let *if* denote **if** where:

$$\textbf{if: } [Tr{\times}S{\times}S \rightarrow S]$$

$$\begin{array}{ll} & \text{is } y \text{ if } x \text{ is } t \\ \textbf{if}(x,y,z) & \text{is } z, \text{ if } x \text{ is } f \\ & \text{is } \perp, \text{ otherwise} \end{array}$$

This interpretation of conditional expressions is appropriate for LISP; other interpretations of conditionals are possible. For example:

$$\textbf{if}_1\textbf{: } [Tr{\times}S{\times}S \rightarrow S]$$

$$\begin{array}{ll} & \text{is } y \text{ if } x \text{ is } t \\ \textbf{if}_1(x,y,z) & \text{is } z, \text{ if } x \text{ is } f \\ & \text{is } \perp \text{ if } x \text{ is } \perp \text{ and } y \neq z \\ & \text{is } y \text{ if } x \text{ is } \perp \text{ and } y = z \qquad [69] \end{array}$$

Neither **if** nor **if**$_1$ are strict mappings.

---

[68]Recall the comment of Wadsworth (page 167). Indeed, the use of conditional expressions in the more abstract representations of LISP functions frequently is such that exactly one of the p_i's is t and all the others are f. Thus in this setting, the order of evaluation of the predicates is useful for "efficiency" but not necessary to maintain the sense of the definition. See page 64.

[69]Basing conditional expressions on **if**$_1$ would give a value of 1 to $[car[A] \rightarrow 1; t \rightarrow 1]$.

To add *if* expressions to Δ_{tg}, yielding Δ_{tgr} we include:

$$\Delta_{tgr}[\![\,if[e_1;\ e_2;\ e_3]\,]\!] = if(\Delta_{tgr}[\![\,e_1\,]\!],\ \Delta_{tgr}[\![\,e_2\,]\!],\ \Delta_{tgr}[\![\,e_3\,]\!])$$

The next consideration is the denotational description of LISP identifiers. Identifiers name either S-exprs or LISP functions. Thus an identifier denotes either an object on our domain S or denotes a function object. Let Fn name the set of continuous functions: $\Sigma_{n=1}[S^n \rightarrow S]$, and Id be **<identifier>**$\cup\bot$. We know that the value of a LISP <identifier> (page 17) depends on the current environment. Then we might characterize the set of environments, **env**, as:

$$[Id \rightarrow S \cup Fn]$$

That is, an element of **env** is a continuous function which maps an identifier either onto a S-expr or onto an n-ary function from S-exprs to S-exprs. This is the essence of the argument used in introducing *assoc* (Section 3.3). Note that $assoc[x;l] \equiv l[x]$ is another instance of a operational-denotational relationship.

For example, given a LISP identifier x and a member of **env**, say the function consisting of $\{<x,2>,<y,4>\}$, together with all pairs $<z,\bot>$ for any z other than x or y, then Δ should map x onto 2. This is an intuitive way of saying that Δ should map a member of <identifier> onto a *function*. This function will map a member of **env** onto an element of S. Introducing i as a meta-variable to range over <identifier>, then for $I \in$ **env** we have:

$$\Delta[\![\,i\,]\!](I) = I(i)$$

The *denotation* of an identifier is a function; whereas the *value* of an identifier is an element of $S \cup Fn$.

The treatment of identifiers leads directly into the denotional aspects of function application. We shall maintain the parallels between evaluation and denotation, by giving Δ_e and Δ_a corresponding to *eval* and *apply*. Let f be a member of <function> and e be a member of <form>, then for a given element of **env**, Δ_a maps f onto an element of Fn, and Δ_e maps e onto an element of S.

For example: $\Delta_a[\![\,car\,]\!](I) =$ **car** for all I in **env**.

Similar equations hold for the other LISP primitive functions and predicates. In general, then:

$$\Delta_a[\![\,f\,]\!](I) = I(f)$$

To describe the evaluation of a function-call in LISP we must add an equation to Δ_e:

$$\Delta_e[\![\,f[e_1, ..., e_n]\,]\!](I) = \Delta_a[\![\,f\,]\!](I)(\Delta_e[\![\,e_1\,]\!](I), ..., \Delta_e[\![\,e_n\,]\!](I))$$

We must also make consistent modifications to the previous clauses of Δ_{tgr} to account for environments. That is, the value of a constant is independent of the specific environment in which it is evaluated.

$$\Delta_e [\![s]\!](I) = s \text{ for all } I \text{ in } \mathbf{env}.$$

We must also extend our equations to account for conditional expressions.

To discuss function application we must give a mathematical characterization of function definitions. In this section we will handle λ-notation without free variables, postponing more complex cases to Section 4.11.

Assuming the only free variables in ξ are among the x_i's, the denotation of $\lambda[[x_1; ...; x_n] \xi]$ in a specified environment should be a function from $\mathbf{S}^n$ to $\mathbf{S}$ such that:

$$\Delta_a [\![\lambda[[\mathbf{v}_1; ... ;\mathbf{v}_n] \, e]]\!](I) =$$
$$\boldsymbol{\lambda}((x_1, ..., x_n) \, \Delta_e [\![e]\!](I : <x_1,\mathbf{v}_1>, ..., <x_n,\mathbf{v}_n>))$$

where λ is the LISP λ-notation and $\boldsymbol{\lambda}$ is its mathematical counterpart and $\mathbf{v}_i$ is the denotational counterpart of $\mathbf{v}_i$, and $(I : ...)$ means a new environment which coincides with I except for the explicitly given pairs.

That is, $(I : <x_1,\mathbf{v}_1>, ..., <x_n,\mathbf{v}_n>)$ is a variant of I such that each $\mathbf{v}_i$ is bound to the corresponding x_i:

$$(I : <x,v>)(v_1) \text{ is:if}(v = \bot,$$
$$\bot,$$
$$\text{if}(v_1 = \bot,$$
$$\bot,$$
$$\text{if}(v_1 = x,$$
$$v,$$
$$I(v_1))))$$

In more detail: $\boldsymbol{\lambda}((x_1, ... ,x_n) \, e(x_1, ... ,x_n))$ is a function $f: [\mathbf{S}^n \to \mathbf{S}]$ such that:

$$\text{is } e(t_1, ... ,t_n) \text{ if } m{\geq}n \text{ and for every } i, t_i \neq \bot \quad {}^{70}$$
$$f(t_1, ..., t_m)$$
$$\text{is } \bot \text{ otherwise}$$

Given this basic outline, we can more accurately describe the "equation" of page 175:

$$f[a_1; ...; a_n] \equiv eval[(F \; A_1 \; ... \; A_n)],$$

Namely;

$$\Delta_e [\![eval[\Re[\![f[e_1; ... e_n]]\!]; \Re[\![a]\!]]]\!](I_{init}) =$$
$$\Delta_a [\![f]\!](I_{new})(\Delta_e [\![e_1]\!](I_{new}), ..., \Delta_e [\![e_n]\!](I_{new}))$$

where I_{init} is the initial symbol table and I_{new} is I_{init} augmented with the entires from $\mathbf{a}$.

---

[70]Note that this equation models the LISP trick of supplying too many arguments. Other anomalies of LISP, including dynamic binding, are describable using these techniques ([Gor 73], [Gor 75]).

One of the major difficulties in supplying models for applicative languages is caused by the type-free requirement. [71] Self-application is one indication of this. We can show that imposing a type structure on our language will solve many problems. In a typed λ-calculus a term will always have a normal form ([Mor 68]). Computationally this means that all the programs will terminate. Also, models for typed λ-calculus are much more readily attained ([Mil 73]). However the type free calculus is a stronger system; requiring all terms to have a consistent type structure rules out several useful constructs; in particular, the λ-calculus counterpart to the LISP *label* operator cannot be consistently typed.

From the practical side, a typed structure is a mixed blessing. Language delarations are a form of typing and can be quite helpful in pinpointing programming errors. Declarations can also be used by compilers to help produce optimized code. However, a type structure can be a real nuisance when trying to debug a program. It is frequently desirable to examine and modify the representations of abstract data structures. Those kinds of operations imply the ability to ignore the type information.

As a final bridge between theory and practice we will use LISP to introduce one of the fundamental results in recursion theory: a proof of the non-existence of an algorithm to determine whether or not a LISP function is a total function. This is also called the unsolvability of the halting problem, since the existence of such an algorithm would tells us whether a LISP function would terminate for all inputs. [72] That algorithm does not exist. [73]

The proof depends on our knowledge of the function *apply*. The fundamental relationship is:

For a function f and arguments $a_1, ... , a_n$ we know

that if $f[a_1; ... ; a_n]$ is defined in *env*

then $f[a_1; ...; a_n] = apply[\Re[\![f]\!];list[\Re[\![a_1]\!]; ... ;\Re[\![a_n]\!]];env]$

Compare this equation with the equation on page 180. This property of *apply* makes it a universal function for LISP in the sense that if *apply* is given an encoding of a function, of some arguments to be applied, and an environment which contains the definition of f and all the necessary subsidiary definitions needed by f, then *apply* can simulate the behavior of f.

We will assume that the representation of *env* is the standard a-list of dotted pairs: representation of name dotted with representation of λ-expression. Given a function named g, together with its λ-definition we will designate the S-expr representation of the dotted pair as g^R.

---

[71]It was not until 1969 that a model for the λ-calculus was discovered by D. Scott even though the formalism was invented in the late 1930's.

[73]Again, we use "LISP function" as a synonym for "algorithm". To complete the halting argument we would have to show that every algorithm is expressible in LISP.

[73]The argument is adapted from [Lev un].

For example, given

$$fact <= \lambda[[x][x = 0 \rightarrow 1; \mathfrak{t} \rightarrow *[x;fact[x-1]]]]$$

Then $fact^R$ is:

$(FACT . (LAMBDA (X)$
$\qquad (COND ((ZEROP X) 1)$
$\qquad\qquad (T (TIMES X$
$\qquad\qquad\qquad (FACT (SUB1 X)))))))$

Next, if f refers to f_1 through f_n in its evaluation, we will represent the environment as:

$$list[f^R;f_1^R;... ;f_n^R]$$

Finally, we will identify such an environment structure as the representation of the definition of the *first* function in that environment. For example, a complete definition of *fact* would be an environment beginning with $fact^R$ and followed by $zerop^R$, $times^R$, or $sub1^R$ if any of these functions were not considered primitive.

Now assume the existence of a unary predicate *total* such that:

$\qquad$ gives $\mathfrak{t}$ if x is a representation of a total unary function. [74]
$total[x]$

$\qquad$ gives $\mathfrak{f}$ in all other cases

Notice that if $total[list[f^R; ...]]$ is true, then for arbitrary a the evaluation of $apply[name[f^R];list[a]; list[f^R; ...]]$ will terminate and give value $f[a]$.

Now we define a function:

$$diag <= \lambda[[x][total[x] \rightarrow list[apply[name[first[x]];list[x];x]]; \mathfrak{t} \rightarrow \mathfrak{f}]]$$

Note that $diag$ is total. Now consider $diag^R$:

$(DIAG . (LAMBDA$
$\qquad (X)$
$\qquad (COND ((TOTAL X) (LIST (APPLY (NAME (FIRST X))$
$\qquad\qquad\qquad\qquad\qquad\qquad (LIST X)$
$\qquad\qquad\qquad\qquad\qquad\qquad X)))$
$\qquad\qquad (T NIL))))$

Form $list[diag^R; total^R; apply^R; ...]$, and call the resulting list *denv*. That list will be the representation of *diag* and all its necessary functions.

---

[74]This discussion will nominally concern unary functions, but the generalization to n-ary functions is immediate.

Now consider the evaluation of $diag[denv]$. Since $diag$ is total, then $total[denv]$ is true, and we can reduced the problem to:

$$list[apply[name[first[denv]];list[denv];denv]]$$

but $name[first[denv]] = DIAG$; and therefore the call on $apply$ reduces to $apply[DIAG;list[denv];denv]$. But that's just $diag[denv]$, and we've shown $diag[denv] = list[diag[denv]]$. That's just not possible. Thus the assumption of the existence of $total$ must be in error.

The usual proof of this result is given in number theory and involves encoding the functions into the integers and then expressing the equivalent of the $apply$ function as an algorithm in number theory. The encoding in the integers is analogous to what we did in encoding in the S-expressions. This is the problem of representation again. LISP *is* more than a programming language; it is also a formalism for discussing computation.

To return to our denotational analysis of LISP, the next addition to Δ will involve recursion and function definitions: *label* and "<=". We know that the LISP *label* operator is similar to "<=", but *label* builds a temporary definition, while "<=" modifies the global environment. Programming language constructs which modify the environment are said to have **side-effects**. Side-effects are usually introduced into programming languages using imperative constructs. Since our main interest lies in the programming aspects of LISP, we will postpone the mathematics until we have discussed the procedural aspects of imperative constructs and side-effects.

Problems

1. Recall the problem on page 149, dealing with the following factorial algorithm:

   $$fact <= \lambda[[n] \, f[function[f]; n]]$$

   where: $f <= \lambda[[g;n][n=0 \rightarrow 1; t \rightarrow *[n; g[g; n-1]]]]$

   Rewrite $fact$ in terms a unary function τ:

   $$\tau <= \lambda[[x] \, function[\lambda[[n][n=0 \rightarrow 1; t \rightarrow *[n; x[n-1]]]]]].$$

   Show that $fact = \tau[fact]$.

2. The λ-calculus described by the α and β rules doesn't look particularly rich, similar in power to LISP with just function application but without conditional expressions. That is only an illusion. Show that we can represent a simple *if* function $if[p;then;otherwise]$. Hint: show that the term $\lambda[[x;y] \, y]$ is a good representation for f and the term $\lambda[[x;y] \, x]$ is a good representation for t.

Imperative Constructs in LISP

4.1 Introduction

All of the language constructs we have introduced so far are based on a computational interpretation of function application. We therefore call the language, applicative LISP. [1] Though this applicative subset is rich and powerful, it is often convenient to have access to another type of language constuct called the **imperative**.

An imperative construct has the intent of a command. For that reason imperative commands are called statements rather than expressions since it is the *effect* of the command which is important; and its *value*, if it has one, is of secondary importance. [2] For example, most programming languages have sequencing commands: "first do S_1, then do S_2"; that might be written "$S_1; S_2$", where S_1 and S_2 are statements. The nature of imperatives is somewhat illusory, since sequencing can be expressed in our applicative subset:

---

[1] It is also referred to as "pure LISP".

[2] Some programming languages insist that statements do *not* have value. The imperatives of LISP *do* have values; they may be used or ignored as the programmer desires.

$$S_1;S_2 \quad \text{is} \quad \lambda[[] \ S_2][S_1] \qquad 3$$

Here we depend on LISP's call by value evaluation. Since S_1 is the argument, it is evaluated first; then S_2 is evaluated. The value of the sequence is the value of S_2. LISP calls this sequencing operation *prog2*.

An area which is thought to be the province of imperatives is that of the assignment statement. We will discuss assignment statements further in Section 4.2, but the intent of such a statement, written:

<identifier> ← <expression>

is to think of the <identifier> as a "box" and the intent of the assignment is to put the value of the <expression> in the "box". Yet, function application can encompass many of the traditional uses of assignment.

Recall our definitions of *length* and *length₁*:

$$length[l] <= [null[l] \rightarrow 0; \ t \rightarrow add1[length[rest[l]]]]$$

$$length_1[l] <= length'[l;0]$$

$$length'[l1;c] <= [null[l1] \rightarrow c; \ t \rightarrow length'[rest[l1];add1[c]]]$$

The variable c is being used as a "box" or "accumulator" [Moor 74] to accumulate length of the list. We will show in Section 4.2 that *length₁* can be translated into a program using several imperative features: statements, sequencing, assignments, and an imperative control regime called **iteration**. We will study iterative control in Section 4.2 and Section 4.3 but it can be shown that iterative control can be translated into recursive control ([McC 60], [Sam 75]).

In many instances the most important implication of imperatives is "convenience". There are algorithms which are most naturally described in terms of sequences of statements and iteration; and there are many lessons to be learned by careful analysis of natural implementations of imperative constructs. We are not looking for a minimal language, we are looking for a useful programming tool. One of the most useful places for imperative constructs is in area of non-local variables, using assignment statements to pass information across applicative boundaries. This technique is called using side-effects. It may very well be that the most distinctive features of imperative constructs are involved with their side-effect aspects.

For example, LISP implementations include a unary primitive named *print* whose effect is to print the value of its argument on the current output device. This function also returns its evaluated argument as the value of the *print* statement. Thus mathematically, *print* acts like an identity function, but its execution certainly affects the programmer's environment. [4]

---

[3]Or better perhaps, $\lambda[[dummy] \ S_2][S_1]$ where *dummy* is a variable not occurring free in any function called within S_2.

[4]Whether the act of printing is a side-effect or the fact that *print* returns a value is a side-effect depends on your point of view.

Side-effects can also spoil some of the theoretical properties of languages. In our earlier discussions, we have implied that call-by-value is a subset of call-by-name in the sense that whenever a call-by-value computation terminates, the corresponding call-by-name computation will as well. In the presence of side-effects, this is *not* true. We give an example on page 227.

4.2 The *prog*-feature

Though recursion is a significant tool for constructing LISP programs, there is another technique for defining algorithms in LISP. It is an iterative style of programming which is called the *prog* or *program* feature.

Many algorithms are presented more naturally as iterative schemes. For example, the recursive algorithms *length* and *length*$_1$, given on page 185, compute the length of a list. Compare those schemes with the following:

1. Set a variable ll to the given list. Set a variable c to zero.
2. If the list is empty, return the current value in c as value of the computation.
3. Otherwise, increment c by one.
4. Set ll to the *rest* of ll.
5. Go to line 2.

Here is a LISP version of the algorithm:

$length <= \lambda[[l]prog[[ll;c]$
$\qquad\qquad ll \leftarrow l;$
$\qquad\qquad c \leftarrow 0;$
$\qquad a\ [null[ll] \rightarrow return[c]];$
$\qquad\qquad c \leftarrow c+1;$
$\qquad\qquad ll \leftarrow rest[ll];$
$\qquad\qquad go[a]]\ ]$

We have introduced several new symbols, formats, and functions in this example. These innovations must be explained before the example is complete. First, the basic syntax of a *prog* is given by:

```
<prog>        ::= prog[[<prog variables>]<prog body>]
<prog body> ::= <prog element><prog body> | <prog element>
<prog element>     ::= <label> | <prog form>;
<label>       ::= <identifier>
<prog form> ::= <application>
              ::= <conditional statement>
              ::= <assignment statement>
              ::= <return statement>
              ::= <go statement>
```

<conditional statement>::= <conditional expression>
<assignment statement>::= <identifier> ← <form>
<return statement>   ::= *return*[<form>]
<go statement> ::= *go*[<form>]

In the example, the variables, ll and c, are called *prog* variables. They are local variables, similar in behavior to λ-variables; in most implementations the *prog* variables are initialized to ( ) and we will assume this convention throughout the text. [5] This behavior of *prog* variables can be expressed as:

$$prog[[x_1; ...; x_n] \, \xi] \equiv \lambda[[x_1; ... x_n]\xi][( ); ... ( )]$$

The body ξ contains the imperative behavior. The *prog* body is a sequence of *prog* forms and labels. Each *prog* form is evaluated in the usual LISP manner, and since the *prog* body can consist of a sequence of *prog* forms, the *prog*-body is evaluated from left-to-right.

If the intent of the *prog* was simply to execute the sequence of *prog* forms, in left-to-right order, then *prog* could be replaced by a much simpler construct like *progn*:

$$progn <= \lambda[[x_1; ...; x_n] \, x_n]$$

However we will add constructs to LISP which will allow us to vary the flow of control within the *prog* body. It is to this end that we use labels, like a in the example. [6] Before we discuss control structures, we give more details on LISP's assignment statement.

As with all LISP constructs, the assignment statement returns a value, but we identify it as a statement since it is executed more for effect than for value. The value of the assignment is the value of the form on its right-hand-side. In our example of *length*, we used an assignment to bind ll to the value of l and to bind c to 0. To evaluate an assignment, we first evaluate the form; then the identifier is located by searching the access chain. Thus the identifier may be a non-local variable. When the identifier is located its current value is *replaced* by the value of the form. Notice that this is a different kind of binding than that previously done by λ-binding. In λ-binding we always associated a new value with a newly created local symbol table as we entered the λ-body. We never destroyed the old binding of a variable. The assigment statement involves a destructive change to the binding. This is important since assignments to non-local variables can have effect outside the *prog* while a λ-rebinding cannot. This is how an

---

[5]A useful alternative is to initialize them to some "unbound" value. In that way the system can recognize attempts to select the value of a *prog* variable before is has been assigned to.

[6]Labels are also known as "tags".

188 Imperative Constructs in LISP

assignment statement can achieve a more permanent side-effect. However, since *prog* variables are created like λ-bindings, assignments to local *prog* variables cannot effect bindings of these variables which were made outside the scope of the current *prog*. This behavior makes *prog*s suitable as components in recursive definitions. For example, a function to reverse a list and all of its sublist can be described as:

$$bigrev <= \lambda[[l] \ prog[[x]$$
$$a \quad [null[l] \to return[x]];$$
$$x \gets concat[bigrev[first[l]];x];$$
$$l \gets rest[l];$$
$$go[a]]]$$

As the examples have intimated, *prog* introduces some new control structures so that the *prog* body need not be executed in simple left-to-right order. The control structures are: the conditional statement, the *return* statement, and the *go* statement.

Though conditional statements in *prog*s have the same syntax as conditional expressions, their semantics is slightly different. A conditional statement is executed in the usual manner unless none of the predicate alternatives is satisfied. Recall that a conditional expression is undefined in this case; a conditional statement however is defined, returns ( ), and executes the next statement in the *prog* body. In our *length* example, the expression, [null[ll] → return[c]]   indicates that if *ll* is not empty the *prog* body continues at the next statement with the assignment of *rest[ll]* to *ll*; the assignment destroys the old value of *ll*. If *ll* is empty, then the statement *return[c]* is executed.

There is a useful interplay between the λ-binding of *l* and the assignment binding of *ll*. We could have dispensed with the *prog* variable *ll*, and used *l* throughout the *prog* body. Even the assignment *l ← rest[l]* would not have effected the binding of the original argument passed to *length*. This is assured because the λ-binding saves that value and the effect of the assignment is only to change the contents of a "box" whose current content is a "pointer" to the value. None of the LISP operations we have discussed can alter a value "pointed to" in this fashion. We will discuss such operations in Section 7.7.

The *return* statement is a *prog* construct similar in effect to exiting a λ-expression. It is used to leave a *prog* body and return to the caller of the *prog*. As we leave the *prog*, the bindings of the *prog* variables are removed as are any λ-bindings made on entry to the *prog*. The value returned is the value of the argument to the *return* statement. The *return* statement may be nested within other LISP computation, as for example:

$$concat[A;return[list[B]]]$$

The effect of the *return* is immediate; the *concat* would never complete its operation. We would return *(B)* to the caller of the enclosing *prog*. A bit of care is needed in describing the meaning of *return*: we look for the latest instance of an entrance to a *prog* and return from that *prog*. To visualize this, we use the Weizenbaum environments (page 142). We search the **control chain**, looking for the first **Form** which is *prog*[[...] ...]. We then restore using the access and control information found in that diagram. We will give a comprehensive example after discussing the *go* statement.

The *go* statement is used in conjunction with labels to divert the implied left-to-right execution of the *prog* body. Labels really aren't executed; they are used to name statements in a *prog*. It is the *go* statement which uses the label as a destination for transferring control. Labels may be in conflict with the λ-variables or *prog* variables since the evaluator for *prog*s can resolve the conflicts by context. Any identifier occurring by itself in a *prog* body is a label. Any identifier occurring in an application other than a *go* statement is a variable and its value is searched for in the access chain, whereas an identifier appearing in a *go* statement is interpreted as a label and searched for in a *prog* body.

The *go* statement is a little more complicated than the *return* statement. If the argument to *go* is an identifier then it is interpreted as a label; otherwise, the argument is *evaluated* and the result of the evaluation examined. This process continues until a label has been uncovered as the result of an evaluation. At that time we must locate a statment in a *prog* which has a matching label attached to it. Our intention is to transfer control to that statement. We locate the labeled statement as follows: we look through the control chain for the first *prog* which contains the label. When the label is found we transfer control to that labeled statement, restoring the access and control environments of the *prog* which contain that statement. Thus there is a double search involved: we search the control chain for *prog* forms, and search the *prog* forms for the label. Labels need not be local; we find the closest dynamically surrounding *prog* which contains the required label.

The non-local *go* and *return* differ from the usual procedure exit in that they do not restore the enclosing control environment, but escape further back the control chain.

Finally, as an example covering the new features of *prog* consider:

$$f <= \lambda[[y;z]\ prog[[l;x]$$
$$l \leftarrow 2;$$
$$l\ u \leftarrow g[y;x;z]$$
$$...\ ]]$$

$$g <= \lambda[[x;y;z]\ prog[[\ ]$$
$$...$$
$$go[l]$$
$$...$$
$$return[first[x]]$$
$$...\ ]]$$

In f, l is both a label and a *prog* variable. Notice in g that we have no *prog* variables; and since we assume that l is not a label in g we have a non-local *go*.

Consider the evaluation of $f[(A\ B);3]$.

```
f[(A B);3]              prog[[l;x]...]     [l ← 2; l u ← g[y;x;z];...]
E₀                      E₁                 E₂
 /   //                 E₀ | E₀            E₁ | E₁
_____     =>      _____   =>     _____   =>
f  | λ[[y;z] prog[...]]  y  |(A B)         l  |( )
g  | λ[[x;y;z] prog[...]] z  |3            x  |( )
```

At this point we have done the λ-binding and initialized the *prog* variables. As we begin the execution of the *prog* body, we assign 2 to l and, since labels have no computational effect, begin the evaluation of the assignment statement: $u \leftarrow g[y;x;z]$:

```
[... l u ← g[y;x;z];...]        [...u ← g[y;x;z]; ...]
E₂                              E₂
E₁  | E₁                        E₁| E₁
_____      =>            _____
l  | 2                          l  | 2
x  | ( )                        x  | ( )
```

We evaluate $g[y;x;z]$:

```
prog[[ ] ...]                   [...go[l]; ... return[first[x]]; ...]
E₃                              E₄
E₂  | E₂                        E₃| E₃
_____      =>            _____
x  | (A B)
y  | ( )
z  | 3
```

The $go[l]$ will search the control chain; it looks in the *prog* form of E_3 but finds no label l. It examines the *prog* of E_1 next, and there it does find the label *l*. Thus execution would be continued at the assignment statement using E_2, the environment which bound the *prog* variables. In general, we continue in the environment which was created on entry to the *prog* body.

Notice that once we have left E_4 there is no way to jump back into it. We can only search down the control chain, and the entry to *g* is not below that of *f* on that chain. An extension of the semantics of LISP could allow such generalized control and we will develop some of those ideas in Section 4.4.

If we executed the *return[first[x]]* in E_4 an action similar to that of *go* would transpire. We would evaluate *first[x]*, getting *A*. We would search the control chain for the *latest prog* expression; here found in E_3; and then return control to the environment designated in the control quadrant; here E_2. Thus we return *A* as the value of *g[y;x;z]*. Since the call on *g* was a component of the assignment $u \leftarrow g[y;x;z]$, we must complete that assignment. We search the access chain for *u*. Since *u* is not found we make a global assignment in E_0:

$$E_0$$
$$/ | /$$

$$
\begin{array}{c|l}
f & \lambda[[y;z] \ldots] \\
g & \lambda[[x;y;z] \ldots] \\
u & A
\end{array}
$$

The ability to evaluate the argument to *go* results in a useful programming trick. Let *l* be a list of dotted pairs, each of the form, (object$_i$. label$_i$). At each label$_i$ we begin a piece of program to be executed when object$_i$ has been recognized. Then the construct:

UGH   *go[cdr[assoc[x;l]]]*

can be used to "dispatch" to the appropriate code when *x* is one of the object$_i$. This is an instance of **table-driven** programming. The blocks of code dispatched to can be distributed throughout the body of the *prog*. Each block of code will usually be followed by a *go* back to the code involving equation UGH (above). In fact the argument *l* in UGH may be *global* to the *prog*-body. The effect is to make a *prog* which is very difficult to understand. The LISP *select* (page 157) will handle many of the possible applications of this coding trick and result in a more readable program. The case-statement (page 193) present in some other languages is also a better means of handling this problem.

The *go* statement is useful if used with discretion. It is a building block for constructing more complex control regimes, particularly since the label need not be local to the *prog* but only need be accessible through the control chain. We will examine some more complex kinds of control behavior in Section 4.4.

Now to the problem of translating a *prog* into an S-expression representation: the construct,

$$prog[[v_1; ...; v_n] ...] \text{ will be translated to:}$$

$$(PROG(V1 ... VN) ...)$$

The body of the *prog* must be handled specially by a new piece of the evaluator since *prog* is a special form.

We must also be careful about the interpretation of ←. We will write $x \leftarrow y$ in prefix form as: $setq[x;y]$. We will map this to:

$$(SETQ \ X \ Y)$$

The assignment, *setq*, is also a special form. For if x and y have values 2 and 3, for example, then the call-by-value interpretation of $setq[x;y]$ would say $setq[2;3]$. This was not our intention. We want to evaluate the second argument to *setq* while stopping the evaluation of the first argument.

LISP has another assignment-like operator called *set*. Both arguments of this binary operator are evaluated; the value of the first argument is expected to be a representation of a variable; that is, the first argument evaluates to a literal atom. The second argument is a LISP form and using the value of that form, an assignment is made to the variable represented by the first argument. Thus $setq[x;y]$ is synonymous with $set[quote[x];y]$.

As a more complex example, consider $set[z; \ plus[x;1]]$. If the current value of variable z is an identifier, then $set[z; \ plus[x;1]]$ makes sense. Assume the current value of z is A; and assume the current value of x is 2; since A represents the identifier a, the effect of the *set* statement is to assign the value 3 to a. Normally when making assignments, we want to assign to a *name* and not a *value*; thus we will tend to use the *setq* form.

Finally, here is a translation of the body of the *prog* version of *length:*

```
(LAMBDA (L)
        (PROG (L1 C)
            (SETQ L1 L)
            (SETQ C 0)
        A   (COND ((NULL L1) (RETURN C)))
            (SETQ C (ADD1 C))
            (SETQ L1 (REST L1))
            (GO A) ))
```

Now that assignment statements have been described, let's re-examine "<=". We already know (page 147) that "<=" does more than simply associate the right hand side with a symbol table entry of the left hand side; it must also associate an environment with the function body, and this environment is to be used for accessing non-local variables. This operation of associating environments is called forming the **closure**. We thus might be tempted to say:

$$f <= \lambda[[...] ...] \text{ is } f \leftarrow function[\lambda[[...] ...]] \ ]$$

Alas, this implementation is still not sufficient as we will see in Section 4.11.

Problems involving *prog*

1. Write *prog*-versions of the following functions (or predicates).
   a. *member* <= λ[[x;y] ...]: x is atomic; y is a list of atoms. *member* is to return t just in the case that x is one of the elements in y.
   b. The factorial function.
   c. delete <= λ[[x;y] ...]: x is atomic; y is a list of atoms. *delete* is to return a list which looks like y, except all occurrences of x have been deleted.
   d. The *append* function.
   e. *last* <= λ[[x] ...]: x is a non-empty list. *last* is to return the last element in x.
   f. Now write the S-expr translations of each of your functions.

2. What is necessary to extend the evaluator to recognize *prog* and friends?

3. The *go*[*cdr*[...]]-construct on page 191 is better handled with a **case** statement. A typical syntax for such might be:

$$\text{case<index>of <form}_1\text{>; ... ;<form}_n\text{>}$$

   <index> is to evaluate to an integer, i. Where 0<i≤n. The ith <form> of the case-statement is executed, and is the value of the statement. Give a representation for the case statement and extend the evaluator to recognize it.

4. Some languages allow constructs like:

   (if p(x) then x else y) ← exp, which is to mean the same as:

   if p(x) then x← exp else y ← exp

   Can such a construct be written in LISP?

5. Compare the *prog* version of *length* on page 186 with *length*$_1$ on page 47. Do you see any interesting relationships?

6. Give a macro definition of an extended *SETQ*, which is called as $(SETQ \ var_1 \ exp_1 \ ... \ var_n \ exp_n)$. Each var_i is a name; each exp_i is an expression to be evaluated and assigned to var_i. The assignments should take effect from "left-to-right". Thus *(SETQ X 2 Y (TIMES 2 X) X 3)* when executed should assign *3* to *X* and *4* to *Y*.

7. Express *setq* as a macro over *set*.

8. Write a *prog* which will terminate if call-by-value evaluation is used, but will not terminate under call-by-name.

9. Use your *prog* version of *fact* (prob 1, b) and evaluate *fact*[2] using Weizenbaum diagrams. Note the difference between the internal structures used here and the structures used in the recursive version. This difference in implementation overhead is a quantitive measure of the expense of recursion versus the expense of iteration.

4.3 Alternatives to *prog*

The *prog* feature of LISP is an effective means for encoding iterative algorithms, however it suffers from a few draw-backs. For example, The label-and-*go* style of control is only a slight elaboration of the control mechanisms which are typically used to control a hardware machine, and thus the level of description which is required tends to obscure the actual flow of the algorithm unless the programmer is careful. A slight extension to conditional expressions and conditional statements can alleviate some of the confusion which is likely when constucting complex *progs*.

Conditional expressions are currently defined such that each e_i must be a single expression. With the introduction of side effects, it is convenient to extend conditionals to include components of the form: $p_i \rightarrow e_{i1}; ... ; e_{in}$. This extended component is to be evaluated as follows: if p_i is true, then evaluate the e_{ij}'s from left to right, with the value of the component to be the value of e_{in}. [7]

For example, this feature, used in *progs* would allow us to replace:

$$\begin{array}{ll} & .... \\ & [p_1 \rightarrow go[l]] \\ m & \\ & ... \\ & return[t]; \\ l & e_1; \\ & e_2; \\ & ... \\ & go[m]; \end{array}$$

with:

$$... [p_1 \rightarrow e_1; e_2; ...] \quad ...; return[t]]$$

The improved readability is largely do to the localizing or "packaging" of the actions with their initiators; we need not scan an arbitrarily long piece of text to discover what the computation will be when the predicate is true.

Several languages have included more "packaged" versions of iterative control. The motivation is similar to that which we used in justifying recursive control: we didn't care *how* recursion was implemented, all we wished to discuss was the *effect* or *behavior* of recursion. [8]

An iterative unit must allow the programmer a reasonable degree of freedom and naturalness in expression. What should also be recognized is

---

[7] This extended conditional expression ([Bob 69]) is available in several versions of LISP: LISP 1.6 [Qua 72], MACLISP [Moo 74], and INTERLISP [Int 75].

[8] We *could* have replaced recursive control with an appropriate combination of label-and-*go*'s. and a simulated stack. We will do so shortly.

that the structural unit should be amenable to analysis to the same degree as that allowed in recursion. We must be able to state precise properties of algorithms which use these constructs, and we should be able to prove properties of such algorithms. With the control of the loop structure in the language rather than in the hands of the programmer, the static text and the dynamic flow of the execution have a close relationship. General use of label-and-*go*'s and assignments does not maintain such properties. Our iterative control construct should therefore capture all of the essential ingredients of an iteration, and its semantics should be restricted such that its static text does indeed reflect its dynamic flow.

Our first example is based on the MacLISP *do* [Moo 74]. With some inessential changes, its syntax is:

$$do [<\text{var}_1> <\text{init}_1> <\text{step}_1>;$$
$$<\text{var}_2> <\text{init}_2> <\text{step}_2>;$$
$$...$$
$$<\text{var}_n> <\text{init}_n> <\text{step}_n>;$$
$$[<\text{pred}> \rightarrow <\text{exit}>]$$
$$<\text{body}>]$$

The construct captures the ideas of intialization and updating of variables nicely. Each $<\text{var}_i>$ is initialized to its $<\text{init}_i>$-value simultaneously. Each $<\text{step}_i>$ is a form which will be evaluated simultaneously upon proper completion of each cycle of the *do*. The $<\text{pred}>$ is evaluated, and on giving value t the loop will terminate, returning the value of $<\text{exit}>$. If $<\text{pred}>$ gives f then $<\text{body}>$ is executed. This component of the *do* is a *prog* body; when the last statement in $<\text{body}>$ is executed, the $<\text{step}_i>$ forms are evaluated and assigned to the $<\text{var}_i>$'s, and another cycle of the *do* is begun.

Since the $<\text{body}>$ of the *do* is a *prog* body, the *return* statement may appear. This feature allows the dynamic flow to diverge from the static text. [9] But consider the *do* version of *member*:

$$member <= \lambda[[a;l] do [x \; l \; rest[x];$$
$$[null[x] \rightarrow f]$$
$$[eq[first[x];a] \rightarrow return[t]] \;]$$

This algorithm could be expressed without *return* but the resulting program is unnecessarily complex.

An alternative iterative construct was proposed in [Wis 75].

$$repeat[<\text{st-list}_1>;while <\text{pred}_1>; <\text{st-list}_2>; until <\text{pred}_2>; <\text{st-list}_3>]$$

where $<\text{pred}_i>$ is a predicate, and $<\text{st-list}_i>$ is a list of statements. The list may be empty, but may not contain *returns* or *gos*.

[9] Compare this to the behavior of free variables under dynamic binding. From a programming point of view, being able to escape from the static text, either for variable reference or for control may be convenient. Whether either feature is "good practice" is a matter of taste.

The semantics is as follows: <st-list$_1$> is executed; <pred$_1$> is then evaluated and if false we exit the *repeat* with f̵. If <pred$_1$> is true, then we execute <st-list$_2$> and test <pred$_2$>; if <pred$_2$> is true we exit with t̵, otherwise we execute <st-list$_3$> and iterate the loop beginning again at <st-list$_1$>.

For example we could write *member* as:

member <= λ[[a;l]
      repeat[*while*
          not[*null*[l]]];
         until
          equal[a;*first*[l]];
         l ← *rest*[l]]]

The difficulty which we encountered with the MacLISP *do* has been alleviated, however the *repeat* construct has several shortcomings of its own. In particular, we have no means for designating what variables are to be initialized and incremented within the loop. Such variables must be declared and initialized external to the *repeat*; also the stepping of the loop variables must be done using the assignment statement. Similarly the power of expression on leaving the *repeat* is limited; we cannot explicitly declare what values are to be returned. The value is that of the appropriate <pred$_i$>.

Problems

1. Some of the generality of *prog*s can be controlled by the use of a new control structure for list operations. The construct is called *lit*. [10] *lit* takes three arguments: a binary function f, a list l, and a value v. If l is empty, give v; otherwise apply f to the first element of l and the effect of applying *lit* to the remainder of l.
   For example *append* could be expressed as:
           append <= λ[[x;y] *lit*[*function*[*concat*];x;y]]
   Give a non-*prog* definition for *lit*.
2. Here is another useful extension to LISP: Instead of requiring that the body of a λ-definition be a single expression: ξ in λ[[...] ξ], allow bodies of the form: ξ$_1$; ...; ξ$_n$, giving rise to λ-definitions like λ[[...] ξ$_1$; ...; ξ$_n$]. The application of such a definition means: bind the λ-variables as usual, then evaluate the ξ$_i$'s from left to right returning as value, ξ$_n$. Extend the evaluator of Section 3.5 to handle such constructs.
3. Give an S-expr representation for the *repeat* expression and add *repeat* to *eval* of Section 3.5.

---

[10]Named for *list iterator* [Bar 66]

4.4 Extensions to *eval*

The introduction of the *prog*-feature completes our syntactic description of the language constructs of LISP. We would like to give a new version of *eval* which describes the semantics of *prog*s in a manner which accurately reflects the techniques used in implementations. We could simply simulate *prog* behavior using recursive techniques, but the iterative control expressed in *prog*s is an important idea in its own right and is a simple instance of non-recursive control. A mechanism which faithfully implements such control structures leads easily to the idea of **generalized control structures**.

The second interesting feature introduced with *prog*s was the assignment statement. Again, we could mirror most of the behavior of assignments by careful use of the techniques of recursion and symbol tables, but such modelling would not adequately reflect the intent of the construct or give insight into the techniques used in implementing such constructs. We could describe such implementations in a low-level machine language, but such practice would only introduce unnecessary details. Rather, we will describe an evaluator in LISP using the techniques we have been developing. In the process we will elucidate much more than just *prog*s and assignments; we will lay bare much more of the behavior which was implicit in the previous evaluators. Those evaluators used recursion in the explication of recursion, frequently depended on call-by-value in the explanation of call-by-value, and suppressed much of the detail of binding and look up. The Weizenbaum environments added more detail, but failed to describe an explicit mechanism for the handling of partial computations, neither showing where partial results were maintained nor how the evaluator was to remember where it was in an expression when it had to evaluate a sub-expression. All of this detail will come out in the new evaluator. Since the structure of the new *eval* is quite different from those we have seen before, and since the level of detail is more intense, we will proceed in several steps.

First we discuss some generalizations of the label-and-*go* control structures. These ideas have importance in their own right when we discuss actual interactive implementations of LISP. Next we develop an *eval* in which the handling of access structures is explicit. The innovations in this evaluator will form the basic blocks which we will use to model parameter passing and assignments. This evaluator will still be recursively described, and will not handle the *prog* feature. In the final step we replace the recursion with explicit control and with this change we have the basis for adequate treatment of non-recursive control. Finally we present an evaluator which handles all of the *prog*-related constructs.

4.5 Non-recursive Control Structures

On page 189 we discussed the *go* construct. In that discussion we noted that the scope of the *go* was not restricted to the current *prog*; we need only locate an appropriate label in a *dynamically* surrounding expression. Thus we could jump out of an expression, passing through many intervening expressions, whereas strict recursive control requires that we exit functions in a level-by-level fashion. This ability to exit across many levels of computation finds applications at the system level in interactive LISP implementations and is also a useful programming feature. For example, if some extraordinary condition occurs within a computation we might wish to abort that whole endeavor. As things currently stand we would have to supply an additional value in the range of each function which could occur in that computation. Each function would have to test for that exception-value and when it is found, return that value to the caller. This is an effective, but not elegant, solution to the problem. Notice that this is the solution posed in our use of ⊥ in conjunction with strict functions. Indeed, a more elegant solution has its origins in the early LISP debugging tools. If a computation produced a detectable error, then it was the responsibility of the LISP controller to print an error message and terminate the computation. Such behavior was acceptable for simple computations. As computations became more complex it became clear that the occurrence of one error need not signal the termination of *all* computation. Particularly since the expressions were available as data structures, the opportunity for self-correcting programs existed in LISP. Thus LISP needed a mechanism for more selective control of error messages.

The early LISP systems supplied a pair of functions named *errset* and *err*. The function *errset* evaluates its first argument in the current context. If no error occurs in that evaluation, the result is *concated* onto ( ) and returned. If an error does occur then the value of the *errset* is f. Notice that in either case the *errset* terminates. We can test the success of our calculation by sampling the value of *errset*: f implies failure; otherwise the *first* element of the result is the true value.

The user can also force the occurrence of an "error" by calling *err*. The unary function *err* returns the value of its argument to the dynamically enclosing *errset* or, if there is no such *errset*, the value is returned as the final value of the computation. For example if *err* is restricted to returning values in a set disjoint from those returned by a non-"error" computation, then the user can test the value of *errset* to discover the type of "error".

The freedom allowed by the *errset-err* combination soon became exploited in ways not originally intended. The use of *errset* and *err* in non-error-handling contexts often became quite confusing. The MacLISP ([Moo 74]) dialect includes a pair of constructs named *catch* and *throw* to be used in these situations.

catch and *throw* are both binary functions. Both first arguments are expressions; both second arguments are interpreted like *prog* labels.

catch[<form>;<label>] evaluates its first argument in the current context, and returns that value, except that if during that evaluation, a *throw*[<form>;<label>] with the same <label> is evaluated, then the value of *throw*'s <form> is returned immediately as the value of the corresponding *catch*.

For example [11]:

$$catch[mapfirst[function[\lambda[[x][x<0 \rightarrow throw[x;negative];t \rightarrow f[x]]]];$$
$$y];$$
$$negative]$$

Assuming y is a list of numbers, this expression will return a list of f applied to each element of y if each element of y is non-negative, otherwise it will return the first negative element of y.

The *catch-throw* pair are the control analog of the *function-funarg* application pair for access. A general implementation of *catch-throw* introduces a very non-recursive control regime. The ususal implementation corresponds to allowing functional *arguments* only; if we wish to *throw* into procedure activations which have already been exited, then we must implement a control tree similar to the environment trees generated for functional values. The next few sections will develop implementation techniques which will support such tree-like implementations.

As motiviation for those techniques, recall the the "value" of a *prog* label is essentially a pointer to a segment of text in the *prog* body. The label which appears in a *catch* is evaluated similarly; in this case the "value" is a pointer just prior to the return mechanism implemented in the call to *catch*. The action of *throw* searches the control tree for a matching label and jumps to that saved value, thus returning from the *catch*. If the value which a *throw* returns is a *catch* label, then we have a handle into the control tree similar to that created by a functional value when it creates a handle into an environment tree.

4.6 *eval* with Explicit Access

There are two major portions of the evaluation schemes which we should scrutinize before we discuss implementations: the access and binding structures, and the description of recursive control. This section will look at access and binding.

The Weizenbaum environments give a nice graphical representation of the access structures, but it would be instructive to express these ideas in terms of LISP functions. This would give us an algorithm, suitable for implementation, and would describe the mechanisms of LISP at a more

---

[11][Moo 74]

detailed level than that in the evaluators of Section 3.5. The description will involve primitive notions just as the prior *eval*'s do, however the level of detail which they capture will be more readily transcribed to implementations. As we have previously mentioned, the Weizenbaum environments leave much of the detail of access and binding implicit; it will be a goal of this section to fill in these details.

Recall that a Weizenbaum environment was created at function-entry time. As we evaluated the arguments to a function, we saved the results in some internal data structure. When all arguments were evaluated we formed a new local block, linking it onto the front of the existing environment. The resulting structure became the new environment. An analysis of these steps highlights several points. We need space to contain the evaluated parameters, and those results are then moved into a environment block; therefore, if we construct the space which is to contain those evaluated parameters like an environment block then the linking operation need only attach that new object. This strategy is possible since the space requirements for the evaluated parameters is known: the block must be as long as the number of formal parameters expected. [12] This requirement can be ascertained by examining the definition of the function being called. Once the block is allocated, the actual parameters are evaluated and the results are sent to the proper slot in the allocated block. Such a block will be called a **destination block**; and the operation of placing a result in a destination will be called **sending**. Once all the evaluated parameters have been sent, we link the completed block into the front of the current environment. The ideas expressed in this section are an embellishment of those on page 124. The innovation is to allocate space for the evaluated arguments before beginning their actual evaluation. The evaluator sends the values to the allocated block.

Here are the primitive routines:

1. *alloc_dest*: This unary function is supplied with the formal parameter list of a function, and supplies a new destination block with the formal parameters placed in the name-section of the block. An internal pointer is initialized to the first slot in the block. Thus:

---

[12]Some LISP systems allow discrepancies between the number of actual parameters and formal parameters. The current scheme will accommodate that generality.

a destination block

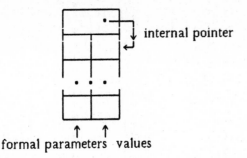

formal parameters values

2. *send*: This is a binary function whose first argument is a destination block and whose second argument is a value to be sent. The value of *send* is the destination block. The effect of *send* is to send its second argument to the current destination slot. The internal pointer is *not* updated; that is the business of *next*.

3. *next*: This function takes a destination block as argument and moves the internal pointer of the block to point to the succeeding slot. The value of *next* is the destination block. Thus *next* is an identity function with a side-effect.

4. *link*: *link* takes a destination block and an environment as arguments and links the destination block onto the front of the environment. The resulting environment is the value of *link*. Since the internal pointer is only used during the filling of the dest-block, we can assume that *link* replaces that pointer with a pointer to the previous environment.

5. *receive*: Sometimes we will wish to examine the result of a computation before making a decision on how to proceed. In particular, in conditional expressions we must evaluate the predicate position before knowing how to handle the rest of the conditional. The unary primitive *receive* lets us look at the result of a computation. The argument to *receive* is a destination block, and the value returned is the value in the current slot.

Problem

Give a full LISP representation of destination blocks and supply the corresponding implementations for the primitive routines, 1 through 5.

In the following evaluators we will freely use the extended conditional expressions and λ-expressions introduced on page 194 and page 196. The first evaluator is named *deval*, with the "*d* coming from "destination".

deval <= λ[[*exp;env;dest*]
  [*isconst*[*exp*] → *send*[*dest;denote*[*exp*]];
  isvar[*exp*] → *send*[*dest;lookup*[*exp;env*]];
  t → *deval*₁[*func*[*exp*]; *arglist*[*exp*]; *env*; *dest*]]]

*deval*₁ <=
λ[[*fun;args;env;dest*]
  [*atom*[*fun*] →[*iscond*[*fun*] → *devcond*[*args;env;dest*]
          isprim[*fun*] → *execute*[*fun*;
                    link[*evalargs*[*args*;
                            env;
                            alloc_dest
                              [*createvars*[*args*]]];
                          env];
                        dest];
        t → *deval*[*fun;env;dest*];
          *deval*₁[*receive*[*dest*];*args;env;dest*]]
  islambda[*fun*] → *evalargs*[*bodylist*[*fun*];
                link[*evalargs*[*args*;
                        env;
                        alloc_dest[*vars*[*fun*]]]];
                    env];
                  dest]
  t → *deval*[*fun;env;dest*]; *deval*₁[*receive*[*dest*];*args;env;dest*]]]

evalargs <= λ[[*args;env;dest*]
      [*null*[*args*] →*dest*;
      null[*rest*[*args*]] → *deval*[*first*[*args*];*env;dest*];
      t → *deval*[*first*[*args*];*env;dest*];
        next[*dest*];
        evalargs[*rest*[*args*];*env;dest*]]]

execute <= λ[[*fun;env;dest*]*send*[*dest;apply*[*fun;vals*[*env*];( )]]]]

Note that *execute* resorts to *apply* to handle primitive application.

devcond <= λ[[*args;env;dest*]
      deval[*pred*[*first*[*args*]];*env;dest*];
      [*receive*[*dest*] → *evalargs*[*condbody*[*first*[*args*]];*env;dest*];
      t → *devcond*[*rest*[*args*]; *env;dest*]]]

This new evaluator must be supplied with an initial destination as well as being supplied with an initial symbol table. Also, since the result of any calculation is a destination block rather than just a simple value, we should supply a selector to extract the desired value. For example, if we designate *val* as such a selector, and designate the atom *TLB* as the repository for the top level binding then:

$$eval <= \lambda[[exp;env]\ val[deval[exp;env;alloc\_dest[(TLB)]]]]$$

More of the details of argument handling should now be understandable: when a function application has been recognized, the evaluator sets up a block to hold the results of evaluating the actual parameters. If the function is a primitive function then the name slots are filled with some system-created names, otherwise the λ-variables are used.

Problem

Using the new evaluator, sketch the evaluation of $f[A]$ where: $f <= \lambda[[x]\ eq[x;A]]$.

Notice that for most of the evaluation process, *dest* is a passive element. A new destination block is created on function applications, but that *dest* is passed around as an argument through most of the pieces of the evaluator without explicit modification. That is, in most λ-bindings *dest* simply gets rebound to the same object. Since the λ-binding process is not inexpensive it is tempting to make variables like *dest*, which change infrequently, into non-local variables; they would be initialized at the outside layer and modified by side-effects during the evaluation. However the current value of *dest* does need to be saved occasionally. Those occasions correspond to the places where *dest* gets rebound to something other than *dest*. We will supply two new primitives to handle explicit saving and restoring of values:

1. *save*: This binary function would be implemented as a special form. Its first argument is a name *old*, and its second argument is a value *new*. The current value associated with *old* is saved, and the value *new* becomes the value of *old*.

2. *restore*: This is a unary function; its argument is a name *name*. The latest value which was saved for *name* is restored. The value which *name* had on entry to *restore* is lost.

Using *save* and *restore* we could express the evaluation of a λ-application something like:

$eval[\Re[\![\; \lambda[[x;y]\xi][a;b] \;]\!];\; env] = save[x;a];$
$\qquad\qquad\qquad\qquad\qquad\quad save[y;b];$
$\qquad\qquad\qquad\qquad\qquad\quad eval[\Re[\![\xi]\!] \; ;env'];$
$\qquad\qquad\qquad\qquad\qquad\quad restore[y];$
$\qquad\qquad\qquad\qquad\qquad\quad restore[x];$

The implementation details of *save* and *restore* will not be needed for most of our discussion, however we include some of them here for completeness. The information which is *saved* and *restored* is accessible through a global variable named *control*. A *save*[<name>;<value>] has the effect of *concat*-ing the current value of <name> onto the front of *control*; it then sets the new value of <name> to <value>.

That is:

$\qquad control \leftarrow concat[eval[<name>;env];control];$
$\qquad set[<name>; eval[<value>;env]];$

Then   *restore*[<name>] performs:

$\qquad\qquad set[<name>;first[control]];\; control \leftarrow rest[control]$

The manipulation of *control* by *save* and *restore* is stack-like in LISP. That means that only the *first* element of *control* is accessible; to access elements in the interior of *control* requires *restore*-ing down to them by sequence of "*control* ← *rest*[*control*]". Once we have removed elements from *control* there is no way to access that information again. The *control*-structure is not accessible as a data structure to the same degree of generality as is the access structure. The closest analogy to *function-funarg* is the *catch-throw* pair. However now that *control* is explicit we can begin to describe extensions to LISP which *will* allow us to capture *control* like *function* captures *env*.

Given *save* and *restore* we can rewrite *deval* and its subfunctions to access non-local representations of variables used in the current *deval*. Thus the evaluator becomes a function of no arguments; it *knows* where to find the values and it knows how to save and restore those variables. The result is an evaluator which has even *fewer* implict operations than *deval*.

$deval' <= \lambda[[]\; [isconst[] \rightarrow send[denote[]]];$
$\qquad\qquad\qquad isvar[] \rightarrow send[lookup[]];$

$\qquad\qquad t \rightarrow save[fun;func[]];$
$\qquad\qquad\qquad save[args;arglist[]];$
$\qquad\qquad\qquad deval_1[];$
$\qquad\qquad\qquad restore[args];$
$\qquad\qquad\qquad restore[fun]\;]]$

A few points should be noted now. We will be using the same names as we did in *deval* for all subfunctions of *deval'*. The difference will be that here those functions will *know* where their arguments are to be found; they need not be explicitly passed in. Thus *send*[*denote*[]] means that *denote* extracts a value from the representation in *exp* and *send* knows that it is to send its value to *dest*.

With this new evaluator we can define *eval* as:

$$eval <= \lambda[[x;y]\,fun \leftarrow ();$$
$$args \leftarrow ();$$
$$exp \leftarrow x;$$
$$env \leftarrow y;$$
$$dest \leftarrow alloc\_dest[(TLB)];$$
$$deval'[];$$
$$val[dest]]$$

Here is the remainder of *deval'*:

$deval_1 <= \lambda[[]\,[isatom[] \rightarrow \quad [iscond[] \rightarrow devcond[];$

$$isprim[] \rightarrow \quad save[env;env];$$
$$save[dest;alloc\_dest[createvars[]]];$$
$$evalargs[];$$
$$link[];$$
$$restore[dest];$$
$$execute[];$$
$$restore[env];$$

$$t \rightarrow deval_2[]\ ]$$

$$islambda[] \rightarrow save[env;env];$$
$$save[dest;alloc\_dest[vars[]]];$$
$$evalargs[];$$
$$link[];$$
$$restore[dest];$$
$$save[args;bodylist[]];$$
$$evalargs[];$$
$$restore[args];$$
$$restore[env];$$

$$t \rightarrow deval_2[]\ ]]$$

$deval_2$ <= λ[[ ] *save[exp;fun]*;
　　　　　　　　deval"[];
　　　　　　　　restore[exp];
　　　　　　　　save[fun;receive[]];
　　　　　　　　$deval_1$*[]*;
　　　　　　　　restore[fun]]

We introduced $deval_2$ to capture the computation to be performed when the function-position is not recognized as either a λ-expression, a conditional, or a primitive. Note that we perform *save[env;env]* in a couple of places in $deval_1$. This is necessary to save the current value of *env* since *link* modifies *env*. Indeed, the sequence: save *env* and *dest*, *evalargs*, *link*, and restore *dest* can be simplified to: save *dest*, *evalargs*, followed by *link"*. where:

$$link" <=λ[[] set\_int[dest;env];rotate[env;first[control];dest]]$$

and *set_int* sets the internal pointer of the dest-block to the current environment, and *rotate[x;y;z]* moves the contents of *x* to *y*, contents of *y* to *z*, and contents of *z* to *x*.

evalargs <= λ[[] *[emptyargs[] → ( )*;
　　　　　　　　singlearg[] → save[exp;first[args]];
　　　　　　　　　　　　　deval"[];
　　　　　　　　　　　　　restore[exp];
　　　　　　　t → *save[exp;first[args]]*;
　　　　　　　　deval"[];
　　　　　　　　restore[exp];
　　　　　　　　next[];
　　　　　　　　save[args;rest[args]];
　　　　　　　　evalargs[];
　　　　　　　　restore[args]]]

　　The discussions surrounding this evaluator tacitly assume that a deep binding strategy is being implemented. That assumption is not necessary. The final shallow binder of Section 3.11 can be incorporated in the framework of these latest evaluators. The key alterations involve the rebinding of the value cells inside $deval_1$ when *islambda* is true. We leave the modifications as a problem for the reader; and we postpone the treatment of *function* until Section 5.19 and Section 5.20.

　　Note also that we are never interested in the value returned from a call on a sub-function in the evaluator; all values are passed explicity from their creator to a destination. We might say that *deval"* never returns a value. In the next section we will build an evaluator which never returns at all.

Problems

1. Write the new version of *devcond*.

2. Examine the *save-restore* sequences in *deval'* and its sub-functions for possible inefficiencies. That is, are all the saves and restores necessary or could explicit assignments to some of the non-local variables speed things up?

3. Using the new evaluator, sketch the evaluation of *f[A]* where: *f* <= λ[[*x*]eq[*x;A*]].

4. Revise the new evaluator to use shallow binding. You may restrict your solution to the case of simple function application without *function*.

4.7 *eval* with Explicit Control

Recursion and call-by-value are used to guide the flow of control in a LISP evaluator. We have started to explore the implementation of call-by-value, and now we wish to discuss the implementation of recursion. It is not necessary to understand *how* recursion works to understand recursion; that understanding *is* necessary when we wish to implement recursion. The mechanisms used in the implementation of any concept must be of a higher level of detail than the mechanism being implemented. We cannot use recursion to implement recursion. The basic purpose of recursive control in the evaluator is to describe what computation to perform next and to describe where to go when finished. The evaluator of this section will rely on explicit directions to tell it what to do next. The idea is closely related to the logical notion of **continuations** ([Str 74a], [Rey 72], [Fis 72], [Hew 76]) and thus we will use that terminology here. In the evaluators of this section we will use the destination to tell where the result of the current computation is to be put, and use the continuation to tell what the next computation will be.

Note that the computations in *deval* are basically of two categories:

1. Simple transformations like sending, building *dest* blocks, or selecting components of expressions. These computations are non-recursive, requiring a bounded amount of computation.

2. Recursive calls on the evaluator or its subfunctions. These computations can be arbitrarily complex.

It is the recursive computations which we wish to examine. One of the implications of a function call is that we have further computation to be performed *after* the call is completed. It is the responsibility of the evaluator to remember where a computation has been interrupted so that it may pick up where it left off, after completing the call. One of the major problems in implementing evaluators is "how to remember". If the function being called is a simple calculation of type 1. above, then we could replace the call with a

copy of the body of the definition where we have replaced each occurrence
of a formal parameter with the appropriate actual parameter; this works
nicely. Indeed making such formal substitutions at runtime is sufficient for
computations of type 2. as well. However the solution in this case is not
sufficiently efficient.

Previous evaluators "remembered" what was to be done either by using
recursion, as in *eval* (Section 3.5), or by explicit sequencing as in *deval*. We
now propose to explicitly **pass along** information about what to do after the
current computation is completed. This information is called the
continuation.

The first evaluator of this section is *ceval*; [13] it is a modification of
deval' of page 204. It takes a single argument *c* which is a continutation.
The continutation is passed along as a funarg structure until *ceval* has
completed its current computation. At that time *c* is executed. For example
we transform *deval'* into *ceval* by forming a continuation from that portion
of *deval'* which follows the call on $deval_1$. Thus:

$ceval <= \lambda[[c]\ [isconst[] \rightarrow send[denote[]];c[];$
$\qquad\qquad\qquad isvar[] \rightarrow send[lookup[]];c[];$

$\qquad\qquad\qquad t \rightarrow save[fun;func[]];$
$\qquad\qquad\qquad\qquad save[args;arglist[]];$
$\qquad\qquad\qquad\qquad ceval_1[function[ev1]]\ ]]$

$ev1 <= \lambda[[\ ]\ restore[args];\ restore[func];\ c[]\ ]]$

For the simple cases we just execute the continuation after the *send*; when we
have a function application we make up a new continuation. When $ceval_1$ is
finished with the function application it executes *ev1*; that does the *restore*
operations and then performs the saved continuation.

Note the use of *function*. The non-local variable *c* in *ev1* represents the
continuation passed into *ceval*. Therefore *c* must be found in the
environment of the body of *ceval* not in the environment which is current
when *ev1* is applied.

As before, *eval* is expressible with the new evaluator:

$eval <= \lambda[[x;y]\ fun \leftarrow ();$
$\qquad\qquad\quad args \leftarrow ();$
$\qquad\qquad\quad exp \leftarrow x;$
$\qquad\qquad\quad env \leftarrow y;$
$\qquad\qquad\quad dest \leftarrow alloc\_dest[(TLB)];$
$\qquad\qquad\quad ceval[function[\lambda[[\ ]\ val[dest]]]]\ ]$

Transforming the sub-functions of *deval'* is reasonably straightforward: the
segment of program below a call on one of the recursive parts of the
evaluator is given a name; a new continuation is made, similar to the process

----

[13]*c* for control or continuation

of creating *ev1*; then the transformation process is applied to each new continuation. For example, here's *ceval₁*:

$ceval_1 \;<= \; \lambda[[c] \; [isatom[] \; \rightarrow \; [iscond[] \; \rightarrow \; devcond[c];$
$\qquad\qquad\qquad\qquad\qquad\quad isprim[] \; \rightarrow save[env;env];$
$\qquad\qquad\qquad\qquad\qquad\qquad\qquad save[dest;alloc\_dest[createvars[]]];$
$\qquad\qquad\qquad\qquad\qquad\qquad\qquad evalargs[function[ev2]];$
$\qquad\qquad\qquad\qquad\qquad\qquad t \; \rightarrow \; ceval_2[];$
$\qquad\qquad\qquad\quad islambda[] \; \rightarrow save[env;env];$
$\qquad\qquad\qquad\qquad\qquad\qquad save[dest;alloc\_dest[vars[]]]$
$\qquad\qquad\qquad\qquad\qquad\qquad evalargs[function[ev5]];$
$\qquad\qquad\qquad\qquad t \; \rightarrow \; ceval_2[]] \;]]$

$ceval_2 \;<= \; \lambda[[\;] \; save[exp;fun]; \; ceval[function[ev3]]]$

$ev2 \;<= \; \lambda[[\;]link[];$
$\qquad\qquad restore[dest];$
$\qquad\qquad execute[];$
$\qquad\qquad restore[env];$
$\qquad\qquad c[]]$

$ev3 \;<= \; \lambda[[\;] \; restore[exp];$
$\qquad\qquad save[fun;receive[]];$
$\qquad\qquad ceval_1[function[ev4]]]$

$ev4 \;<= \; \lambda[[\;] \; restore[fun]; \; c[]]]$

$ev5 \;<= \; \lambda[[\;] \; link[];$
$\qquad\qquad restore[dest];$
$\qquad\qquad save[args;bodylist[]];$
$\qquad\qquad evalargs[function[ev6]]]$

$ev6 \;<= \; \lambda[[\;]restore[args];$
$\qquad\qquad restore[env];$
$\qquad\qquad c[]]$

Problems

1. Continuations can also be used as general programming tools. For example, evaluate $fact_2[2]$ where:

$fact_2 \;<= \; \lambda[[x] \; fact_2'[x;function[\lambda[[x] \; x]]]]$

$fact_2' \;<= \; \lambda[[n;f] \; [zerop[n] \; \rightarrow \; f[1];$
$\qquad\qquad\qquad t \; \rightarrow \; fact_2'[sub1[n];$
$\qquad\qquad\qquad\qquad function[\lambda[[x] \; f[times[n;x]]]]]]]$

2. Write the new version of *devcond* and *evalargs*.
3. Using the new evaluator, sketch the evaluation of $f[A]$ where:
$f \;<= \; \lambda[[x]eq[x;A]].$

The final transformation step is analogous to that which we performed in moving from *deval* to *deval'*: we remove the argument to *ceval* and pass the continuation explicitly in a non-local variable named *cont*. This new evaluator is named *ceval'*:

$ceval' <= \lambda[[\ ]\ [isconst[] \to send[denote[]]];\ cont[];$
$\qquad\qquad\quad isvar[] \to send[lookup[]];\ cont[];$
$\qquad\qquad\quad \mathbf{t} \to save[fun;func[]];$
$\qquad\qquad\qquad save[args;arglist[]];$
$\qquad\qquad\qquad save[cont;function[ev1]];$
$\qquad\qquad\qquad ceval_1[]\ ]]$

$ev1 <= \lambda[[\ ]\ restore[args];\ restore[func];\ restore[cont];\ cont[]\ ]]$

We can remove more control structure from the evaluator by noting that executing the continuation, "$cont[]$", and executing the explicit calls on the evaluator's subfunctions are two manifestations of the same phenomenon. In the first case we restore to a variable and then execute the variable as a function application; in the second, we execute a known call. We can replace these two actions by a common action if we always execute from the variable $cont$ and replace calls like "$ceval_1[]$" with the sequence:

$$save[cont;function[ceval_1]];\ cont[]$$

Notice that when we make this last $save$ we know that the current value of $cont$ is $ev1$. Notice also that when we execute $cont[]$ we enter $ceval_1$ and therefore within this call on $ceval_1$, $cont$ is $ceval_1$. All this discussion can be simplified if we think a bit about the purpose of continuations: we will need to make note of what the continuation should be *after* the current computation is finished; and we will need to set $cont$ to designate which computation to perform now. We therefore introduce a binary primitive $save\_cont$ which will save its first argument such that $restore$ can restore it to $cont$ at the appropriate time; $save\_cont$ will set $cont$ from its second argument.

$$save\_cont <= \lambda[[x;y]\ cont \leftarrow x;\ save[cont;y]]$$

We can remove the calls $cont[]$, and perform the execution outside $ceval'$ using a simple loop:

$\qquad loop <= \lambda[[]\ prog[[]$
$\qquad\qquad\qquad\qquad l\ cont[]$
$\qquad\qquad\qquad\qquad go[l]\ ]]$

Each function executed by $cont[]$ will perform some simple operations like $send$ or $alloc\_dest$, and then will exit, setting $cont$ to a function name. The next pass around, $loop$ will execute the new $cont$. After slight reorganization to eliminate some $save\text{-}restore$ operations on $cont$, we have:

$ceval'' <= \lambda[[\ ]\ [isconst[] \to send[denote[]];\ restore[cont];$
$\qquad\qquad\qquad\ isvar[] \to send[lookup[]];\ restore[cont];$
$\qquad\qquad\qquad\ \mathbf{t} \to save[fun;func[]];$
$\qquad\qquad\qquad\quad save[args;arglist[]];$
$\qquad\qquad\qquad\quad save\_cont[quote[ev1];quote[ceval_1]]\ ]]$

$ev1 <= \lambda[[\ ]\ restore[args];\ restore[func];\ restore[cont]\ ]]$

Notice the use of *quote* rather than *function*. In the previous evaluators we used *function* since we had to save the current environment; but the continuation *c* was the only free variable which was in jeopardy. In *ceval"* we have explicitly saved the continuation using *save_cont*, and thus *quote* plus the proper use of *restore* can replace *function*. We will also introduce an abbreviation, writing *'xx* for *quote[xx]*. [14]

Finally, here's *eval*:

$$eval <= \lambda[[x,y]\ catch[\ prog[[\ ]\ fun \leftarrow ();$$
$$args \leftarrow ();$$
$$exp \leftarrow x;$$
$$env \leftarrow y;$$
$$dest \leftarrow alloc\_dest[(TLB)];$$
$$save\_cont['\lambda[[]throw[val[dest];\ out]]];$$
$$'ceval"];$$
$$loop[]];$$
$$out]]$$

What has been gained by these transformations of the original *eval*? We have made the mechanisms which were implicit in LISP very explicit. We have described the implementations of LISP's access and control requirements in terms of very simple computations. We now have developed enough detail that we can give a faithful implementation description of all of LISP including the *function* and *prog* constructs.

Problems

1. Could we use statements like *save_cont[evl;eval₁]* rather than *save_cont['evl; 'eval₁]* ?

2. Using the new evaluator, sketch the evaluation of *f[A]* where:
   $f <= \lambda[[x]\ eq[x;A]]$

4.8 An Evaluator for *prog*

The evaluator in this section will be the definitive interpreter for LISP throughout the rest of this book. It will handle the applicative subset of LISP as well as handling *prog* related constructs.

We need to add more mechanism to handle *prog*. For example the execution of the *return* statement requires that we locate dynamically surrounding *progs*. The *go* must also locate the latest *prog* which surrounds the *go* and contains the desired label. The evaluator needs to know when we are evaluating a conditional expression and when we are evaluating a

---

[14]This abbreviation is used in several implementations of LISP. See page 280.

conditional statement; if we are (immediately) in a *prog* then it's a conditional statement, otherwise it's a conditional expression. All of this information could be discovered by the evaluator using the currently supplied information, however the evaluator can be made more efficient by adding a bit more explicit information. Most of the additions involve *prog*-entry, *go*, and *return* and will therefore be presented when we discuss that part of the evaluator. The only addition we will make now will be introduction of a variable *type* which is set to *PROC* when we begin an evaluation of an application, and is set to *PROG* when we enter a *prog*.

We will also rework some of our current sub-functions to improve readability. Since sequences of *saves* happen frequently in the evaluators we introduce a new procedure named *save'* which acts like a sequence of calls on *save* for arguments other than *cont*. In this latter case, a call on *save_cont* is simulated. Similarly we introduce an iterated version of *restore* named *restore'*.

Problem

Write *restore'* and *save'* as macros which expand to calls on *save* and *restore*.

Here's the new *peval*:

$$peval <= \lambda[[\ ]\ [isconst[] \to send[denote[]];restore[cont];$$
$$isvar[] \to send[lookup[]];restore[cont];$$
$$t \to save'[fun;func[];$$
$$args;arglist[];$$
$$cont;\ 'evl;\ 'peval_1]\ ]]$$

$$evl <= \lambda[[\ ]\ restore'[args;func;cont]\ ]]$$

It is the responsibility of *peval* to recognize the occurrence of one of the basic forms: a variable, a constant, or a function application. Discovering the structure of an application is the business of *peval*$_1$. We need to know whether the function position represents a call-by-value function or a special form. So far the only special form we recognize is *cond*; [15] however many of the constructs which *prog* introduced are special forms. We could add a collection of recognizers *issetq*, *isgo*, *isprog*, etc., to augment the existing *iscond*. Instead we would rather add a device similar to *isprim* but instead of handling the call-by-value primitives with the underlying evaluator, we wish to handle special forms with our own pieces of *peval*. We need a predicate

---

[15]Actually *quote* is also a special form which we recognize, however its recognition is handled within *isconst*.

named *isspec* to recognize occurrences of special forms and will need to add functions to *peval* to execute the appropriate programs when *isspec* is true. We will do this by introducing a global table called *spectbl*. The name components of the table will be the names for special forms; the value components of *spectbl* will be the names of functions which will evaluate the corresponding special form. [16] Then we can write:

$$isspec <= \lambda[[\ ][null[nassoc[fun;spectbl]]] \rightarrow f; \ t \rightarrow t]$$
$$nassoc <= \lambda[[x;l] \ [null[l] \rightarrow (\ );$$
$$eq[x;name[first[l]]] \rightarrow first[l];$$
$$t \rightarrow nassoc[x;rest[l]]]]$$

To execute the appropriate routine we need only put the name in the variable *cont* and *loop* will do the rest. We can load *cont* by:

$$cont \leftarrow valspec[\ ]; \ where: \quad valspec <= \lambda[[\ ]value[nassoc[fun;spectbl]]]$$

For example, with *spectbl* bound to *((COND DEVCOND))*, our previous *ceval*$_1$ would work quite nicely as:

$$ceval_1 <= \lambda[[\ ] \ [isatom[] \rightarrow [isspec[] \rightarrow cont \leftarrow valspec[\ ];$$
$$isprim[] \rightarrow save[env;env];$$
$$... \ ] \ ... \ ]]$$

Before introducing *peval*$_1$ we should say a bit about the inefficiency involved in the *isspec-valspec* pair. We already noted that the linear search encoded in *assoc* is unnecessarily inefficient. However the present predicate-function pair is even more wasteful; if *isspec* is true we perform *nassoc[fun;spectbl]* twice. A more efficient computation might save the result of the first call on *nassoc* in a temporary variable *tl* and if *isspec* is true, move the *value*-part of *tl* to *cont*. Thus:

$$isspec <= \lambda[[\ ] \ tl \leftarrow nassoc[fun;spectbl]]$$
$$[null[tl] \rightarrow f; \ t \rightarrow t] \ ]$$

with: $valspec <= \lambda[[\ ] value[tl]]$

This is a useful programming trick but does not add to the clarity of the program. In Section 5.5 we shall see a more subtle, but related trick.

What follows is the remainder of the evaluator interspersed with commentary. The main function is *peval*$_1$; it handles function applications. The application is either a call-by-value application or it is a special form. An instance of the first requires evaluation of the argument list and then evaluation of the procedure body. If the application is a special form then the evaluation is handled by a special piece of the evaluator, using the mechanism described above. The call-by-value applications are either

---

[16]In the next chapter we will see a more efficient way to recognize and execute special forms.

primitive applications or are anonymous function applications. If the form is not recognizable then the function-position is evaluated until a function object *is* recognized. At that time, the function is applied to its argument list.

The anomalous situation involves the application of a *funarg*; though it is possible to handle this case as a primitive, it is more instructive to present it in detail. Here is $peval_1$:

$$peval_1 <= \lambda[[\ ][isatom[] \to [isspec[] \to \quad cont \leftarrow valspec[\ ];$$

$$isprim[] \to save^*[env;env;$$
$$dest;alloc\_dest[createvars[]]];$$
$$cont;\ 'ev2;\ 'evalargs];$$

$$t \to save^*[exp;fun;cont;\ 'ev3;\ 'peval];$$

$$islambda[] \to save^*[\ env;env;$$
$$dest;alloc\_dest[vars[]];$$
$$cont;\ 'ev5;\ 'evalargs];$$

$$isfunarg[] \to prog[[x;y]$$
$$x \leftarrow args;$$
$$args \leftarrow bodylist[second[fun]];$$
$$y \leftarrow env;$$
$$env \leftarrow third[fun];$$
$$save^*[env;env;$$
$$args;x;$$
$$dest;alloc\_dest[vars[second[fun]]];$$
$$env;y;$$
$$cont;\ 'ev7;\ 'evalargs]];$$

$$t \to save^*[exp;fun;\ cont;\ 'ev3;\ 'peval]\ ]]$$

The functions *ev2* through *ev8* handle the control in $peval_1$:

$$ev2 <= \lambda[[\ ]\ link[];\ restore[dest];\ execute[];\ restore^*[env;cont]]$$

This function passes the evaluation to the body of the primitive.

$$ev3 <= \lambda[[\ ]\ restore[exp];\ save^*[fun;receive[];cont;\ 'ev4;\ 'peval_1]]$$

ev3 is the return point if we have to evaluate the function position of a form. When *ev3* is called the result of that evaluation is in the current dest-slot. A *receive* gets the value; we then pass the new form back to $peval_1$.

$$ev4 <= \lambda[[\ ]\ restore^*[fun;cont]]$$

$$ev5 <= \lambda[[\ ]\ link[];\ restore[dest];\ save^*[args;bodylist[];\ cont;\ 'ev6;\ 'evalargs]]$$

ev5 handles the evaluation of the body of a λ-expression. Since we are allowing multiple-bodied λ-expressions (page 196), we pass the *bodylist* to *evalargs*. If we were restricting ourselves to single-bodied expressions, then passing *body* to *peval* would suffice.

$$ev6 <= \lambda[[\ ]\ restore^*[args;env;cont]]$$

The next four functions handle the evaluation of a sequence of expressions. If the sequence is empty, then there is nothing to do. If there is a single argument then evaluate it and restore the continuation. Otherwise evaluate the first one using *peval* (sending its result to *dest*) and then execute *ev11*. At *ev11* we update the destination block using *next* and get set to evaluate the next argument.

evalargs <= λ[[] [*emptyargs*[] → *restore*[*cont*];

$\qquad\qquad$ t → *save*[*exp*;*first*[*args*]];

$\qquad\qquad\qquad$ *cont* ← '*ev9*]]

ev9 <= λ[[ ][*singlearg*[] → *save_cont*['*ev10*; '*peval*];

$\qquad\qquad$ t → *save_cont*['*ev11*; '*peval*]]]

ev10 <= λ[[ ] *restore°*[*exp*;*cont*]]

ev11 <= λ[[ ] *next*[];

$\qquad\qquad$ *args* ← *rest*[*args*];

$\qquad\qquad$ *exp* ← *first*[*args*];

$\qquad\qquad$ *cont* ← '*ev9*]]

Problem

Using the new evaluator, sketch the evaluation of *f*[*A*] where: *f* <= λ[[*x*]*eq*[*x*;*A*]].

The combination of *evcond* and *cond1* handle conditional expressions. [17] *evcond* sets up the evaluation of the predicate position such that the computation will continue at *cond1*. When that evaluation is completed *cond1* receives the result. If t is received then the consequent part of that conditional clause is evaluated. Note that we use *evalargs* here since we allow extended conditionals (page 194). If f is received we go back to *evcond* with the remaining part of the conditional.

evcond <= λ[[ ][*emptyargs*[] → *err*[*NO_TRUE_COND_CLAUSE*];

$\qquad\qquad\qquad$ *cont* ← '*ev1*;

$\qquad\qquad$ t → *save_cont*['*cond1*; '*peval*];

$\qquad\qquad\qquad$ *exp* ← *pred*[*first*[*args*]]]]

cond1 <= λ[[ ][*receive*[] → *args* ← *conseq*[*first*[*args*]];

$\qquad\qquad\qquad$ *save_cont*['*ev1*; '*evalargs*];

$\qquad\qquad$ t → *args* ← *rest*[*args*];

$\qquad\qquad\qquad$ *cont* ← '*evcond*]]

---

[17]See the problem on page 219.

The next four functions deal with functional arguments. If the argument is a primitive, then we just *quote* it; the assumption is that primitives only access local variables and therefore don't need to save the environment. An expression which is already *funarg*-ed is passed as is since it is aready closed and therefore has no free variables. If it is a λ-expression, we make a *funarg*; otherwise we evaluate the function until we discover its character.

evfunction <= λ[[ ] *fun* ← *first*[*args*];
                            [*isprim*[] → *send*[*mkquote*[*fun*]];*restore*[*cont*];
                            islambda[] → *send*[*mkfunarg*[*fun*;*env*]];*restore*[*cont*];
                            isfunarg[] → *send*[*fun*];*restore*[*cont*];
                            t → *save_cont*['*fun1*; '*peval*];
                                exp ← *fun*]]

fun1 <= λ[[ ] *send*[*mkfun*[*receive*[ ]]; *cont* ← '*ev1*]

The functions *ev7* and *ev8* control the application of a *funarg*.

ev7 <= λ[[ ] *restore*[*env*];
         link[];
         restore°[*dest*;*args*];
         save_cont['*ev8*; '*evalargs*]]]

ev8 <= λ[[ ] *restore*°[*env*;*cont*]]

Special functions are needed to handle explicit calls on the evaluator: *eval*[<form>;<env>]. We set up a destination to receive the values of <form> and <env>, and ask *evalargs* to evaluate these arguments. The results of the computation are seen by *ev12*; this function sets up the call on *peval*.

eveval <= λ[[ ] *save*°[*env*;*env*;
                  dest;*alloc_dest*[*createvars*[(G1 G2)]];
                  cont; '*ev12*; '*evalargs*]]

ev12 <= λ[[ ] *exp* ← *first_dest*[];
          env ← *second_dest*[];
          restore[*dest*];
          save_cont['*ev13*; '*peval*]]

ev13 <= λ[[ ] *restore*°[*env*;*cont*]]   (≡ *ev8*)

There is a second form of call on *eval* which is useful. If we write *eval*[<form>], then the <form> is evaluated in the environment which exists at the point of call. See problem on page 220.

    The remainder of the evaluator involves the *prog* related constructs. Several new ideas are involved. As we discussed on page 211, we must be able to determine whether or not we are executing within a *prog*: we introduced *type* to handle this. Also every expression or statement in LISP has a value. Since we are always *send*-ing values, we must have a destination to receive the values created by *prog* statements: we will introduce a dummy destination which will always receive the value of any statement. This destination is named *bb*, for "bit bucket". Finally, we must handle assignment statements. The innovation here is that the *send* goes to some pre-existing destination and destroys the current value: we use a primitive *mkdest* whose effect is to generate a destination pointer to the slot which is to receive the value of the right-hand-side of the assignment. In *evsetq* we use a function *lookup'* which is similar to *lookup* except that it returns a pointer to the slot containing a value, rather than returning the value in the slot.

Here are the evaluators for *setq* and *set*:

$$evsetq <= \lambda[[\ ] \quad save'[dest;mkdest[lookup'[first[args]]];$$
$$cont; \ 'setq1; \ 'peval];$$
$$exp \leftarrow second[args]]$$

$$setq1 <= \lambda[[\ ]\lambda[[x] \quad restore[dest];$$
$$send[x];$$
$$cont \leftarrow 'ev1 \ ][receive[\ ]]$$

$$evset <= \lambda[[\ ] \quad save'[args;args; \ cont; \ 'set1; \ 'peval];$$
$$exp \leftarrow first[args] \ ]$$

$$set1 <= \lambda[[\ ] \quad restore[args];$$
$$args \leftarrow mkass[receive[];rest[args]];$$
$$cont \leftarrow 'evsetq \ ]$$

The *prog* evaluator, *evprog*, must handle all of the control structures which can occur within a *prog*. Besides ordinary recursion, we can have *gos* and *returns*. The *go* must be able to search the control chain for the appropriate label, and the *return* must find the dynamically enclosing *prog*. To handle either of these eventualities, we *save* some additional information when we enter a *prog*. First we save the current state of the computation; this will allow the *return* to *restore* everything as it leaves the *prog*. Next we make a new *env* which has bound all the *prog* variables to ( ). We save *that* *env*, since a non-local *go* will want to restore that *env* as it returns for execution. Finally we create a *golist* which is a list of all points in the *prog* which have labels. This construct allows us to discover quickly which labels are present in the *prog* and where they are. [18] After all this is done we are ready to execute the first line of the *prog* body.

---

[18]If it weren't for the existence of anonymous *progs* and function-modifying functions, we could put the responsibility of making the go-list on "<=".

$evprog <= \lambda[[\ ]\ save^{*}[exp;exp;$
                               $env;env;$
                               $dest;alloc\_dest[prog\_vars[args]];$
                               $fun;fun;$
                               $args;prog\_body[args];$
                               $type;PROG];$
                    $link[];$
                    $save^{*}[env;env;$
                               $golist;mkgolist[args]];$
                    $cont \leftarrow 'line\ ]$

$mkgolist <= \lambda[[body]\ prog[[z]$
                    $a\quad [null[body] \rightarrow return[z];$
                               $islabel[first[body]] \rightarrow\quad z \leftarrow concat[body;z]\ ];\ ^{19}$
                               $body \leftarrow rest[body];$
                               $go[a]\ ]]$

The actual execution of each line of a *prog* body is controlled by the pair *line* and *linel*. Their behavior is similar to that of *evalargs*. *line* examines the next expression; if there is no next statement, we exit with ( ) using *prog_exit*; if the next statement is a label, it is ignored; otherwise we prepare to evaluate the expression, setting the destination to *bb*.

$line <= \lambda[[\ ]\ [null[args] \rightarrow prog\_exit[(\ )];$
                    $islabel[first[args]] \rightarrow\quad args \leftarrow rest[args];$
          $t \rightarrow exp \leftarrow first[args];$
                    $dest \leftarrow bb;$
                    $save\_cont[\ 'linel;\ 'peval]\ ]]$

$linel <= \lambda[[\ ]\ args \leftarrow rest[args];$
                    $cont \leftarrow 'line\ ]$

Note that we don't change *cont* in *line* when we see a label; we just leave it at *line* and *loop* does the rest.

We call *prog_exit* to return ( ) when the body of the *prog* is empty. Thus the discussion of *prog_exit* involves the semantics of *return*. Of the two control mechanisms, *return* is simpler than *go*. Recalling the discussion of *save* on page 204, we need to look through the *control*-list for the last block designating a *prog* entry. We *restore* to that saved state and set *control* to that prior point.

$evreturn <= \lambda[[\ ]exp \leftarrow first[args];$
                    $save\_cont[\ 'retl;\ 'peval]\ ]$

$retl <= \lambda[[\ ]\ prog\_exit[receive[]]]$

---

[19]Note that this program handles multiply-labeled statements.

$prog\_exit <= \lambda[[val] \, control \leftarrow find\_prog[control];$
$\qquad\qquad\qquad restore^{\bullet}[type;args;fun;dest;env;exp;cont];$
$\qquad\qquad\qquad send[val] \,]$

The *go* statement is a bit more complicated. When a *go* statement is recognized, we look back through the dynamic chain to find the first occurrence of the desired label. If we are in a *prog* we check the current *golist*; if the label is not found, or if we are not immediately in a *prog*, we look for the latest *golist* and search it. We continue this process until we discover the label. At that time we restore the environment to that which encloses the label, reset *control*, and continue the computation at that point.

$evgo <= \lambda[[\;]exp \leftarrow first[args];$
$\qquad\qquad [isconst[] \rightarrow err[BAD\_PROG\_LABEL];$
$\qquad\qquad not[isvar[]] \rightarrow \; save\_cont[\,'gol;\,'peval]$
$\qquad\qquad t \rightarrow \; control \leftarrow prog\_go[control;exp] \,]]$

$prog\_go <=$
$\lambda[[cntrl;exp]$
$\qquad prog[[\;] \, a \; \; [eq[type;PROG] \rightarrow [check\_go[exp;golist[cntrl]] \rightarrow restore[env];$
$\qquad\qquad\qquad\qquad\qquad\qquad\qquad\qquad\qquad\qquad\qquad\qquad\qquad\qquad cont \leftarrow 'line;$
$\qquad\qquad\qquad\qquad\qquad\qquad\qquad\qquad\qquad\qquad\qquad\qquad\qquad\qquad return[cntrl];$
$\qquad\qquad\qquad\qquad\qquad\qquad\qquad t \rightarrow \; cntrl \leftarrow find\_go[rest[cntrl]]; \, go[a] \,];$
$\qquad\qquad\qquad t \rightarrow \; cntrl \leftarrow find\_go[cntrl]; \, go[a] \,]]]$

$check\_go <= \lambda[[lab;glist][null[glist] \rightarrow f;$
$\qquad\qquad\qquad\qquad eq[lab;first[first[glist]]] \rightarrow \; args \leftarrow rest[first[glist]];t;$
$\qquad\qquad\qquad\qquad t \rightarrow check\_go[lab;rest[glist]] \,]]$

The origins of the interpreter presented here can be traced from several sources: [Bla 71], [Con 73]. [Sus 75], [Ste 76b].

Problems

1. This problem involves the *escape* expression discussed in [Rey 72] and implemented in the University of Paris's LISP [Gre 75]. We introduce the form:

   $$escape[<function>; <form_1>; ...;<form_n>]$$

   with the following semantics: we evaluate the <form$_i$>'s from left to right, returning the value of <form$_n$> unless we encounter an application involving <function>. If such an application *does* appear we perform that application and immediately return the resulting value as the value of the *escape* expression.

   Extend our latest evaluator to recognize and execute the *escape* expression.

2. The semantics of *go* specified that the argument would be evaluated if it were a function application, however the current *peval* does not handle this case. Correct that oversight.

3. Extend *evcond* to handle conditional statements.

4. On page 204 we discussed the implementation of *save* and *restore*. Implement *save* and *restore* for *peval*.

5. Write *find_go* and *find_prog*.

6. Revise *eveval* to handle calls on *eval* with either one or two arguments. See page 216.

7. Refer to the problem involving multiple *setq*'s on page 193. There you were asked to implement that feature using macros. Either implement a macro facility in *peval* or explicitly introduce such a multiple assignment feature. You may implement that feature as either a sequential assignment or a parallel assignment.

8. Recall our discussion of the general *catch-throw* pair on page 199. Implement these functions in *peval*.

4.9 Alternatives to *eval*

We have seen a lot of evaluators for LISP. We should at least look a bit at other possibilities for describing computational behavior. Indeed, what is "computation"? When we are given an expression to evaluate we are really simulating the application of simplification and substitution rules. The simplification rules tell us when an expression can be replaced by another expression; typically we think of the replacing expression as being "simpler" than the replaced expression. Thus $car[(A \cdot B)]$ can be replaced by A, or $[t \to 2; ...]$ can be replaced by 2.

The substitution rules typically allow us to replace a procedure call with an appropriately instantiated copy of the procedure body. Thus a computation involving $append[(A\ B);(2\ 3)]$ is identical to that obtained by replacing the occurrence of $append[(A\ B);(2\ 3)]$

with $$[null[(A\ B)] \to (2\ 3);\ t \to concat[first[(A\ B)];$$
$$append[rest[(A\ B)];$$
$$(2\ 3)]]]$$

The result of such a substitution is usually a candidate for further substitutions and simplifications. The collection of simplification and substitution rules is called the reduction rules for the language. Given an expression, a computation is said to terminate when there are no further reduction rules applicable and the reduced expression is a constant of the language. That reduced expression is the value of the original expression.

The difficulties with these schemes come from both practical and theoretical considerations. The direct application of reduction rules is quite inefficient: making textual substitutions is expensive. Instead we developed the ideas of symbol tables to contain the bindings of the variables, rather than perform the actual substitutions.

The theoretical difficulty appears since, at any time in a computation, there may be more than one reduction rule which is applicable. A further difficulty is that one sequence of reductions may terminate, while another sequence of reductions is non-terminating. We have seen this phenomenon in previous discussions of call-by-value versus call-by-name, inner-most versus outer-most, and normal order reductions versus applicative order reductions.

Though LISP opted for the call-by-value interpretation of expressions, it is possible to develop a call-by-name evaluator. Call-by-name implies that we substitute the unevaluated actual parameters for the formal parameters. As in *eval*, we need not make explicit substitutions; appropriate use of symbol tables will simulate the action, but now, when we build a symbol table on entry to a λ-expression we bind the actual expressions to the λ-variables. When we encounter a variable in the body of the expression we evaluate the actual parameter. The difficulty is that an actual parameter itself may contain variables, and those variables need to be interpreted in the binding environment. This means that we must bind *funarg*-like expressions to the formal parameters.

Most of $eval_{name}$ is like *eval* of Section 3.5, so we only sketch the interesting parts. Assume the *funarg*-expression we manufacture has two components, the *expr*-component, and the *env*-component.

We can implement $eval_{name}$ by simply changing the symbol table orgainzation, supplying new versions of *lookup* and *mkenv*. See page 124 and page 152.

$alloc <= \lambda[[vars]\,()]$

$send <= \lambda[[var;val;dest]\,concat[mkent[var;val];dest]$

$link <= \lambda[[dest;env]\,concat[dest;env]]$

$lookup <= \lambda[[var;env]\,l''[var;first[env];rest[env]]$

$l'' <= \lambda[[n;bl;env]\,[null[bl] \rightarrow l''[n;first[env];rest[env]];$
$\qquad\qquad\qquad eq[n;name[first[bl]]] \rightarrow eval[expr[value[first[bl]]];$
$\qquad\qquad\qquad\qquad\qquad\qquad envir[value[first[bl]]]];$

$\qquad\qquad t \rightarrow l''[n;rest[bl];env]\,]]$

One advantage of such an evaluator is that it will not evaluate a parameter until it actually needs it, whereas *eval* evaluates all parameters at function entry time. If an actual parameter is not used in the computation and the computation of that parameter fails to terminate, then $eval_{name}$ will terminate while *eval* will not. There are disadvantages to $eval_{name}$. Every occurrence of a variable within the body of the function will involve a re-evaluation of the corresponding actual parameter. If there are no side-effects in the computation then these repeated computations are an unnecessary expense. Several people ([Wad 71], [Vui 74], [Pac 73], [Hen 76], [Fri 76a]) have suggested modifications to $eval_{name}$ to reduce the inefficiency. The basic idea, described as **call-by-need**, is to proceed in the $eval_{name}$ style until the first use of a variable. At that time we evaluate the actual parameter, and modify the symbol table, *replacing* the actual parameter with its value. Further references to that variable simply get the value. Obviously the scheme will not work correctly if side-effects are present. We leave it to the reader to supply the details of $eval_{need}$; see page 224.

We now explore a different kind of modification to LISP. This one is grounded more in practical experience with the programming language, though the results do have theoretical interest. It has been noted that programmers frequently wish to return more than one value as the result of a function application. The standard alternatives in LISP are either to make global assignments from within the body of the function, or to return a list of the desired values making it the responsibility of the calling program to select the proper components. Neither alternative is particularly compelling. Programming with extensive side-effects tends to lead to obscure programs and may incur unnecessary complications in debugging; see Section 6.23. Passing lists back as values requires much additional computation: someone must build the list; someone must tear it apart. It is also disturbing that the operation being modelled, --multiple-values--, is not recognizable as a construct. This is a similar complaint to that we raised in discussing labels-and-*gos* versus an iterative construct.

Our goal is realizable by a slight extension of the re-interpretation of conditional expressions and multiple-bodied λ-expressions (page 194, page 196). We will interpret the form:

$$p_i \rightarrow e_{i1}; \ldots e_{in}$$

to return the e_{ij}-values to the calling function in a left-to-right order. If the calling program is single-valued then the value it sees is the value of e_{in}. This is compatible with our current interpretation. The evaluation of:

$$\lambda[[\ldots] f_1[\ldots]; \ldots; f_n[\ldots]]$$

will be interpreted similarly.

For example [Fri 76b] discusses a multiple-valued function named *sigmasum*. This function is to take a list of numbers and return three items: the length of the list, the sum of the numbers in the list, and the sum of the squares of the numbers in the list. In our notation *sigmasum* can be expressed as:

$$sigmasum <= \lambda[[x][null[x] \rightarrow 0;0;0;$$
$$t \rightarrow \lambda[[z_1;z_2;z_3]add1[z_1];$$
$$plus[first[x];z_2];$$
$$plus[times[first[x];first[x]];z_3]]$$
$$[sigmasum[rest[x]]]]]$$

Notice that we use an anonymous λ-expression to spread the multiple values at the level of the caller.

Another example is a solution to the *samefringe* problem [Hew 74]:
determine whether or not the terminal nodes of two trees are the same,
respecting order, but irrespective of tree structure. [20] Thus:

$$samefringe[(A \ (B \ (C))); (A \ B \ C)] = \mathsf{t}$$

but $\qquad\qquad samefringe[(A \ (B \ C)); (A \ C \ B)] = \mathsf{f}$

$samefringe <= \lambda[[x;y] \ [null[x] \rightarrow null[y];$
$\qquad\qquad\qquad \mathsf{t} \rightarrow \lambda[[z_1;z_2;z_3;z_4][eq[z_1;z_3] \rightarrow samefringe[z_2;z_4];$
$\qquad\qquad\qquad\qquad\qquad \mathsf{t} \rightarrow \mathsf{f}]]$
$\qquad\qquad\qquad [fringe[x];fringe[y]] \ ]$
$fringe <= \lambda[[x][atom[first[x]] \rightarrow first[x]; \ rest[x];$
$\qquad\qquad \mathsf{t} \rightarrow \quad \lambda[[y;z] \ y; \ [null[z] \rightarrow rest[x];$
$\qquad\qquad\qquad\qquad\qquad \mathsf{t} \rightarrow cons[z; \ rest[x]] \ ] \ ]$
$\qquad\qquad [fringe[first[x]]] \ ] \ ]$

In this solution, *samefringe* is single-valued but uses values from a
multiple-valued function. The two values from *fringe*[x] are spread into z_1
and z_2 and the values from *fringe*[y] are spread into z_3 and z_4.

It is easy to write an evaluator for such multiple-valued expressions.
Here is a sketch of the basic parts:

$meval <= \lambda[[x;e] \ [isconst[x] \rightarrow list[denote[x]];$
$\qquad\qquad\quad isvar[x] \rightarrow list[lookup[x;e]];$
$\qquad\qquad\quad iscond[x] \rightarrow mevcond[condbody[x];e];$
$\qquad\qquad\quad \mathsf{t} \rightarrow mapply[fun[x];mevlist[arglist[x];e];e] \ ]]$

$mapply <= \lambda[[fn;args;e][isprim[fn] \rightarrow list[apply[fn;args;e]]$
$\qquad\qquad\qquad islambda[fn] \rightarrow mevlist[\ bodylist[fn];$
$\qquad\qquad\qquad\qquad\qquad\qquad\qquad mkenv[vars[fn];args;e] \ ]$
$\qquad\qquad\quad \mathsf{t} \rightarrow mapply[eval[fn;e];args;e] \ ]]$

$mevlist <= \lambda[[l;e] \ [null[l] \rightarrow ();$
$\qquad\qquad\quad \mathsf{t} \rightarrow append[meval[first[l];e]; \ mevlist[rest[l];e]] \ ]]$

$mevcond <= \lambda[[l;e] \ [null[l] \rightarrow ();$
$\qquad\qquad\quad first[meval[pred[first[l]];e]] \rightarrow mevlist[\ conseq[first[l]];$
$\qquad\qquad\qquad\qquad\qquad\qquad\qquad\qquad env];$
$\qquad\qquad\quad \mathsf{t} \rightarrow mevcond[rest[l];e] \ ]]$

---

[20]There are many "solutions" to this problem; the simplest is to flatten
the trees first, then use *equal*. Indeed, there are many "problems"; the most
accurate formulation requires that no *cons* operations be done. For more
details and interesting discussions see [Gre 76], [Hen 76], [And 76a], and
[Fin 76].

Problems

1. Complete the specification of $eval_{name}$.

2. Complete the specification of $eval_{need}$. To do this, you may assume the existence of a binary function named *stuff* whose first argument x is the a name in the symbol table, and whose second argument y is a value. *stuff* is to replace the current binding of x with y.

3. Modify *peval* to handle multiple-valued functions.

4. Recall problem 2 on page 154 dealing with the analysis of *lookup*. Include call-by-name and call-by-need in your analysis.

5. Using the results of the previous problem, make up a table whose rows are labeled with the binding implementations: "deep", "shallow", "Weizenbaum", "need", and "name"; and whose columns are labeled with the prmitives: *alloc*, *link*, *send*, and the primitives for *lookup*. Supply the entries.

4.10 Function Definitions

Now that we have developed these more explicit evaluators, we should exploit some of this additional detail. In particular, more of the detail of "<=" should be understandable. The effect of $f <= \lambda[[x]\; \xi]$ is to put the definition of f in the global environment, whereas *label* creates a new dest-block with f bound to a *funarg* consisting of ξ and that constructed environment. Once we leave the environment containing the *label* definition, that definition is effectively destroyed. The effect of "<=" is to be global. A "<="-definition could be temporarily superseded by a *label*-definition to the same name and therefore our search for a binding for f may not short-circuit the environment chain.

Our search strategy is encoded in the *lookup* function; using the current environment, we find the latest active binding for a variable. The *prog* evaluator, $peval_1$ of page 214 is a bit more complicated. Besides finding the definition we must also determine whether the arguments are to be evaluated. The device of *isspec* (page 212) is sufficient for the evaluators, but has some difficulties if we wish to allow user-defined special forms. We will develop a syntax for expressing special forms at the user level, and then discuss problems of implementation.

We will define "$<_f=$" to mean "..is defined to be a special form...". A special-form definition is also called a **fexpr**; and a call-by-value definition is called an **expr**.

A fexpr is defined with either one or two formal parameters. The first parameter is always bound to the list of *unevaluated* actual parameters. If the definition has a second formal parameter, then the environment at the point of call is assigned to the second parameter. This distinction needs to be made if we expect to perform some evaluation of the formal parameters within the fexpr. Using the implementation of *eval* discussed on page 216 we can write either *eval*[<form>;<env>] or *eval*[<form>]. In the latter case the environment that is used is the environment which was current when the *eval* is performed. Sometimes this is not the desired environment. Consider:

$$f1 <_f= \lambda[[x] \ prog[[y]$$
$$y \leftarrow 2;$$
$$return[eval[first[x]]]]]$$

If we execute *f1*[0], *x* will be bound to the list (0) and *eval*[*first*[x]] will return 0 as expected. But if we execute:

$$y \leftarrow 0;$$
$$f1[y];$$

then *x* gets bound to (Y), and *eval*[Y] will find the value associated with Y to be 2, and the value of *f1*[y] is 2, rather than the expected 0.

The problem is that the call on *eval* takes place in the *prog* environment. We can correct this by making the definition with *two* arguments, binding the second to the environment at the point of call to the fexpr:

$$f2 <_f= \lambda[[x;a] \ prog[[y]$$
$$y \leftarrow 2;$$
$$return[eval[first[x];a]]]]$$

$$y \leftarrow 0;$$
$$f2[y];$$

The call on *f2* will use the environment with *y* being 0 rather than 2.

As a final example:

$$f3 <_f= \lambda[[x;a] \ prog[[z]$$
$$y \leftarrow 2;$$
$$return[eval[first[x];a]]]]$$

$$y \leftarrow 0;$$
$$f3[y];$$

would return 2.

As we have just seen, special forms must be used with care. However, they are useful in several contexts. Recall that we restricted LISP call-by-value functions to have a fixed number of arguments. For example if we wish to add four numbers or append three lists we have to write something like:

$$plus[x_1;[plus[x_2;plus[x_3;x_4]] \quad \text{or} \quad append[append[l_1;l_2];l_3]$$

Since *plus* and *append* are associative operations we would rather write:

$$plus[x_1;x_2;x_3;x_4] \quad \text{or} \quad append[l_1;l_2;l_3]$$

We discussed the macro implementation of these constructs in Section 3.12. Using a special form, we could write *plus* as:

plus <$_f$= ·λ[[*l;e*] *prog*[[*sum*]
        sum ← *0;*
      a [*null*[*l*] → *return*[*sum*]];
      sum ← *plus*[*sum;eval*[*first*[*l*];*e*]];
      l ← *rest*[*l*];
      go[*a*]]]

Notice that we could have used *eval* with one argument unless the variables *l* or *sum* appeared as constitutents of the actual parameters.

Recalling Section 3.12, we can use <$_f$= to extend the evaluator. For example, *and* could be defined as:

and <$_f$= λ[[*l;e*] *evand*[*l;e*]]   where   *evand* is defined on page 155.

The implementation of *g* <$_f$= λ[[*x*] **ξ**] requires that we represent the fact that *g* is a fexpr rather than an expr. The implication of *isspec* of page 212 is that we have two tables: one for exprs, one for fexprs. This complicates the search strategy unnecessarily. Indeed there should only be one definition or value associated with a name at any one time, so a single table should be both necessary and sufficient. We *do* need some way of determining the calling style to be used when applying the definition. One way is to revise the *isspec* technique slightly: we use *lookup* for *all* searches, but also have a table relating function-name with its calling style. One difficulty with this scheme is that we could not handle anonymous fexpr definitions. Therefore some versions of LISP replace the character "λ" with another special character when making fexpr definitions. For example:

$$g <_f= \lambda[[x;y] \text{ ξ}] \equiv g <= \beta[[x;y] \text{ ξ}]$$

We would translate such β-expressions into S-expr form, and extend the evaluator to recognize such constructs.

We could use a similar technique to recognize macro definitions. The next chapter will discuss some alternative implementations.

Problems

1. Define *list* as a special form.
2. Write a version of *peval* to handle β-expressions.
3. Define two special forms, *de* and *df*, which will implement <= and <$_f$= respectively. The format of these special forms is identical. For example:
        de[<name>;<formal parameters>;<body>]
will implement
        <name> <= λ[<formal parameters> <body>]

4.11 Rapprochement: In Retrospect

As with the review section of the previous chapter, this section is a mixture
of the practical and the theoretical. That is a healthy attitude to cultivate
when discussing programming languages. For example, in the first section of
this chapter we claimed that a theoretically expected relationship between
call-by-name and call-by-value breaks down in the presence of side-effects.
The idea of side-effects is a decidedly practical one, based on the "practical"
notion of a "variable" as a "box which contains a value", rather than the
mathematical notion of a "variable" as a description for an anonymous, but
fixed, element of a domain.

Consider the following expression:

$$prog\ [[\ ]\ y \leftarrow 0;$$
$$\lambda[[x]\ prog[[\ ]$$
$$loop\ [eq[y;0] \rightarrow go[loop]]$$
$$[y \leftarrow 1]]]]$$

If this expression is evaluated using call-by-value, we bind y to 0, and
evaluate the anonymous λ-expression. That entails evaluation of $y \leftarrow 1$, *before*
entering the *prog*. The computation of the *prog* body terminates, returning
NIL. Call-by-name evaluation would not evaluate $y \leftarrow 1$ and the
computation would not terminate.

The issue of side-effects highlights an important distinction between
"variables" in the mathematical sense and "variables" in the programming
sense. In mathematics, we use the term, variable, to designate a fixed, but
anonymous, object: "let x be a real number ...". In programming languages, an
object is "variable" as opposed to a "constant", meaning that the quantity
associated with the object may vary. Thus the idea of "box which contains a
value" arises again. The manipulation of variables in languages leads to
further distinctions.

Applicative languages, modelled after the λ-calculus, simulate the
reduction rules by associating an environment or symbol table with an
expression. What is being simulated is a "copy rule" which says that the
reduction is to be done by making a copy of the expression, substituting the
actual parameters into the copy wherever one of the λ-variables appeared in
the original expression. The effect of the symbol table is to *share* a common
instance of the actual parameter. The idea of sharing becomes central when
we discuss assignments and the behavior of side-effects. If *copies* of values
are made, the issue of side-effects vanishes. Important distinctions arise
when we are able both to *share* values and to destructively *change* values.
This combination of properties is present in the general assignment
statement. Because of the close relationship between assignment and LISP's
λ-binding, λ-binding is sometimes called a "pushdown" assignment
([New 61]), as compared with a "destructive" assignment. The adjective,

"pushdown", refers to the λ-binding's ability to save the prior binding of a λ-variable in such a way that it may be restored after the computation is completed.

Differences in binding are highlighted by the implementation of *function*. In the applicative subset, *function* is satisfactorily implemented by the *FUNARG* triple, where the substitution is represented by a pointer to the binding environment. In the presence of assignment statements, this equivalence breaks down.

Consider the following example due to H. Samet:

$$f <= \lambda[[x] \ prog \ [[]$$
$$a \leftarrow a+1;$$
$$return[[eq[a;1] \rightarrow x; \ t \rightarrow -x]]]]$$
$$g <= \lambda[[x;fun] \ prog[[]$$
$$a \leftarrow 0;$$
$$return[fun[x]]]]$$

Now evaluate $h[1]$ where $h <= \lambda[[a] \ g[3;function[f]]]$

If we implemented *function* as a direct substitution of values for free variables, then $h[1]$ would yield -3. The implementation of *function* as a pointer to the binding environment yields 3. It is clear where the problem lies; we have assigned to a non-local variable after the substitution would have been carried out. However, compare the current situation with the example on page 145. The lesson to be learned is that assignment statements do not fit well with the substitution model.

We enriched the LISP subset to allow such constructs as iteration and assignment; therefore, we wished to provide an evaluator which adequately reflected the implementation, or pragmatics, of these facilities. We could have modelled them directly in the initial LISP subset, but the representation would not convey the intended implementation. As a result, we developed an interpreter which directly modelled the assignment statements, *return* statements, and non-local *go* statements. These are some of the most troublesome areas to reflect in an applicative model.

The result of our investigations was *peval*. This evaluator expresses the implementation of the enriched subset of LISP; it is self-explanatory in the sense that any construct which *peval* uses has a data structure representation which is recognizable by *peval*. That is, *peval* can interpret expressions involving representations of *peval*.

The process of developing *peval* exposed the control structure of LISP just as the development of *eval* in Chapter 3 exposed the access structure. A data structure model for access environments was necessary since the implementation of *function* demanded it. Traditional LISP does not allow such generality in the area of control structure. The appearance of non-local *gos* and *returns* requires control behavior analogous to that of functional arguments, but control regimes analogous to that of functional *values* do not appear in LISP. More recent demands from LISP users have prompted development of generalized control structures in LISP-like languages ([Hew 72], [Pre 72], [Pre 76a], [Bob 73a], [Con 73]). Now that we have developed the data structure representation for control, we could extend LISP to allow manipulation of control structures. We resist that temptation, leaving such experimentation to the reader.

As we have just seen there are alternatives to some of the LISP-techniques and there are some things which, in retrospect, LISP could have done better. There are some conceptual difficulties with LISP evaluation. We have seen some computational schemes which will give values when LISP's call-by-value does not terminate. Whether these schemes are better is a debatable point. Programmers tend to think "call-by-value," but it is not clear whether that is habit, training, or a fundamental point of view towards computation. [21]

The practical and the theoretical aspects of programming languages have much common ground. As we have seen, the notion of "function" in mathematics is different from the notion of "LISP function." The former is a set-theoretic notion, the latter is an algorithmic notion. With the introduction of iteration, a further discrimination is needed. A useful classification of "recursive" appears in [Hew 76].

1. "Recursive" in the sense of recursive function theory ([Rog 67]) meaning that there is an algorithm which specifies the function. This involves a precise study of the concepts of algorithm and computability.

2. "Recursive" in the sense of self-referential. The definition of an algorithm makes reference to the algorithm itself. The idea of "self-reference" needs to be handled carefully. The definition may involve mutual recursion: f calls g, and g calls f. Also, we saw on page 149 that a function may be dynamically self-referential, while the static text is not.

---

[21]Compare [And 76] in discussing call-by-name versus call-by-value: "programs which don't terminate usually have bugs, and programmers would rather find out sooner (call-by-value) than later (call-by-name)".

3. Finally, "recursive" is used meaning "non-iterative". This is the usual interpretation imposed in programming languages. This sense implies some assumptions about the evaluation implementation. Basically, it is to mean that a recursive evaluation will require more bookkeeping than the iterative evaluation. A problem on page 193 asked for an iterative evaluation of *fact*[2]; fewer environments were created there than we required for the evaluation of the "recursive" (in the sense of 2) version. This third use of the word "recursive" is the least well defined and understood. It is frequently believed that "recursive" in the sense of 2 implies the third "recursive." The third sense is more a property of the implementation of the evaluation scheme than a property of the algorithm. Techniques are know for evaluating several classes of "recursive" algorithms using iterative storage requirements; [Hew 76], [Sus 76], [Gre 76a].

Since the ideas involved in "recursive" are so important to LISP and programming languages in general, we want to explore the ideas further. We will be most concerned with "recursive" in sense 2; we want to understand what is involved in giving a recursive definition. We now have three ways to define functions: the *label* operator, the "<="-operator, and the assignment statement. We need to understand the differences between these operations.

To begin with, we were able to give counterexamples to interpreting:

$$f <= \lambda[[x] \xi] \quad \text{as} \quad f \leftarrow \lambda[[x] \xi]$$

The discussion of binding and environments made $f \leftarrow function[\lambda[[x] \xi]]$ a more likely candidate; however this interpretation is also not adequate.

We might implement $fact <= \lambda[[x][x=0 \to 1; t \to *[x; fact[x-1]]]]$ as:

$$fact \leftarrow function[\lambda[[x] \ldots fact[x-1] \ldots]]$$

Consider an initial environment with *fact* defined:

$$E_i$$
$$E_c \mid E_a$$

$$\overline{fact \mid \lambda[[x] \ldots fact[x-1] \ldots] : E_i}$$

We will demonstrate the inadequacy of two natural interpretations of function values: direct assignment of value, and assignment of *funarg*. We execute *foo* ← *fact* and *baz* ← *function*[*fact*], giving:

$$E_i$$
$$E_c \mid E_a$$

$$\overline{\begin{array}{l} fact \mid \lambda[[x] \ldots fact[x-1] \ldots] : E_i \\ foo \mid \lambda[[x] \ldots fact[x-1] \ldots] : E_i \\ baz \mid fact : E_i \end{array}}$$

Things don't look quite right; the "intent" of both *foo ← fact* and *baz ← function[fact]* was to make *foo* and *baz* synonymous with *fact*. That clearly is not the case though the right thing happens if we were now to evaluate an expression involving *foo* or *baz*. The problem is that it happens for the wrong reason even though the occurrence of *fact* in the body of *foo* will find the right definition of *fact*; an application of *baz* will find the definition of *fact*.

One more step will lead to disaster: $fact ← \lambda[[x]\ x]$

$$E_i$$
$$E_c\ |\ E_a$$

$fact|\ \lambda[[x]x]$
$foo\ |\ \lambda[[x]\ ...\ fact[x\text{-}1]\ ...\ ]:E_i$
$baz\ |\ fact:E_i$

Now we are really lost. Though it is reasonable to redefine *fact* -- it is only a name -- our intent was to keep *baz* and *foo* as realizations of the factorial function. This intent has not been maintained.

$fact\ <=\ \lambda[[x]\ ...\ fact[x\text{-}1]\ ...\ ]$ is quite different from:

$$foo\ <=\ \lambda[[x]\ ...\ fact[x\text{-}1]\ ...\ ]\quad [22]$$

To understand what has happened we look at assignments to *simple* variables rather than functional variables. It is clear how the environment should change during the execution of the sequence:

$x ← 3$
$y ← x$
$x ← 4$

Let's try something slightly more complicated:

$x ← 1$
$x ← x^2 - 6$

Here we first assign *1* to *x*; then we evaluate the right hand side of the next statement. We look up the current value of *x*, perform the arithmetic computations, and finally assign the value *-5* to *x*. Compare *this* to the *fact* definition; there we made a point of not "evaluating" the name *fact* in the right hand side of "<=".

Notice that *after* an assignment like $y ← x$ has been executed, then equality holds between the left-hand and right-hand quantities. Let's look more closely at the relationship between "←" and "=". Consider $x ← x^2 - 6$.

---

[22]In LISP 1 ([McC 60]) considerations were given to representing recursive definitions as circular structure, instead of referring to the name. That would have solved the current problem.

After the assignment is made, equality does *not* hold between left- and right-hand sides. Now consider $x = x^2 - 6$. Interpreting this expression as an equation, not as an expression whose value is true or false depending on the current value of x, we find two solutions: let x have value *-2* or *3*. If we examine our "definition" of *fact* in *this* light, interpreting "<=" as being related to "=" rather than "←", then we are faced with an equation to be solved, only now the form of the solution is a *function* which satisfies the equation. There may be many solutions; there may be no non-trivial solutions. In our case there is at least one solution: the usual factorial function. So what we *should* write is something more like:

fact ← a solution to the equation: $f = \lambda[[x][x=0 \to 1; t \to *[x; f[x-1]]]]$.

That is, the *real* intent of the recursive definition of *fact* was to define a function to effect the computation of factorial and then to *name* that function *fact*. Questions of when solutions exist, how many, and which are the "best" solutions is a topic of much current research ([Man 74]).

We have seen a related result in the problem on page 183; we were to show that *fact* = $\tau[fact]$. That is, *fact* is a solution to the equation $\tau[x] = x$. Solutions to such equations are called **fixed points**.

The *fact* result is an instance of a more general result:

(Y)

for any τ, define $h <= \lambda[[g]\ \tau[function[\lambda[[x]\ g[g[x]]]]]]$

then $h[function[h]] \equiv \tau[h[function[h]]]$

We shall not prove this result but we can give some insight into its justification as we develop the mathematical properties of *label*; we continue our discussion of Section 3.13. Recall Δ_e and Δ_a from page 232. In any environment Δ_a should map *label*[f;g] in such a way that the denotation of f is synonymous with that of g. That is, f is a mapping satisfying the equation $f(t_1, ..., t_n) = g(t_1, ..., t_n)$. So:

$$\Delta_a [\![\textit{label}[f;g]]\!](I) = \Delta_a [\![g]\!](I)$$

This will suffice for our current λ-definitions; we need not modify I since the name f will never be used within the evaluation of an expression involving g.

We must be a bit careful. Our treatment of non-local variables in LISP (on page 127 and in Section 3.8) requires that these variables be evaluated when the function is *activated* rather than when the function is defined. Thus a λ-definition generally requires an environment in which to evaluate its non-local variables. So its denotation should be a mapping like: **env** → $[S^n \to S]$ rather than simply $[S^n \to S]$. This is consistent with our understanding of the meaning of λ-notation. It is what *function* was attempting to describe. What we previously have called an open function is of the form: $[S^n \to S]$. Given a name for a function in an environment we can expect to receive a mapping from **env** to an element of **Fn**.

A modification of our handling of *label* is required to describe the case for recursion:

$$\Delta_a [\![label[f;g]]\!](I) = \Delta_a [\![g]\!](I : <f, \Delta_a [\![g]\!]>)$$

Interpreting this equation operationally, it says: when we apply a *label* expression in an environment it is the same as applying the body of the definition in an environment modified to associate the name with its definition. This is analogous to what the LISP *apply* function will do. Since this interpretation of *label* is inadequate in general contexts, we should look further for a general reading of *label*. Our hint comes from our interpretation of "<=" as an equality. Recall:

fact ← a solution to the equation: $f = \lambda[[x][x=0 \rightarrow 1; t \rightarrow *[x;f[x-1]]]]$

What we need is a representation of an "equation-solver" which will take such an equation and will return a function which satisfies that equation. In particular we would like the *best* solution in the sense that it imposes the minimal structure on the function. [23] This request for minimality translates to finding the function which satisfies the equation, but is least-defined on other elements of the domain. This discussion of "least" brings in the recent work of D. Scott and the intuition behind this study again illuminates the distinction between mathematical meaning (denotational) and manipulative meaning (operational).

Consider the following LISP definition:

$$f <= \lambda[[n][n=0 \rightarrow 0; t \rightarrow +[f[n-1];*[2;subl[n]]]]]$$

When we are asked what this function is doing, most of us would proceed operationally; that is, we would begin computing $f[n]$ for different values of n --what is $f[0]$?, what is $f[1]$, ... It is profitable to look at this process differently: what we are doing is looking at a *sequence* of functions, call them f_i's .

$f_0 = \{<0,\perp>,<1,\perp>, ... \}$	when we begin, we know nothing.
$f_1 = \{<0,0>,<1,\perp>, ... \}$	now we know one pair.
$f_2 = \{<0,0>,<1,1>, ... \}$	now two
$f_3 = \{<0,0>,<1,1>,<2,4>, ... \}$	now three

   ...   thinks   ...   **Eureka!!**

When or if, we realize that the LISP function denotes the "squaring function" for non-negative integers, then we have moved from pragmatics to semantics. The process of discovering the denotation may be likened to a limiting process which converges to a function satisfying the LISP definition.

---

[23]Like a free group satisfies the group axioms, but imposes no other requirements.

That is:

$$\lambda((n) \; n^2) = \text{limit of the } \; f_i\text{'s}$$

where f_i may also be characterised as:

$$f_i(n) = \begin{array}{l} n^2 \text{ if } 0 \le n \le i \\[1em] \perp \text{ if } i<n \text{ or } n<0 \end{array}$$

We may think of our "equation-solver" as proceeding in such a manner. As with simpler equations, there may be several solutions. For example, we have seen that a function, g, defined to be $n!$ for $n \ge 0$ and 0 for $n<0$ also satisfies the LISP definition of *fact*. The expected solution for *fact* is undefined for $n<0$, and is therefore "less defined" than g. We would like our equation solver to produce a minimal solution, if possible.

That is, Y applied to a term τ gives a function f satisfying $f = \tau(f)$.

$$Y(\tau) = \tau(Y(\tau))$$

Also f should be minimal in the sense that any other function which satisfies the equation is more defined than f. Compare this with page 232. That result can be interpreted as saying: for any τ

$$Y(\tau) = h(h) \quad \text{where} \quad h = \lambda((g)\tau(g(g)))$$

Such an equation solver *does* exist; it is called the **fixed-point operator**. It is designated here by Y. To comprehend Y we generalize from the previous example.

In terms of our example we want a solution to $f = \tau(f)$, where:

$$\tau(g) = \lambda((n) \; \text{if}(n=0, \, 0, \, g(n-1)+2*n-1))$$

Our previous discussion leads us to believe that $\lambda((n) \; n^2)$ for $n \ge 0$ is the desired solution.

How does this discussion relate to the sequence of functions f_i? Let's look at the behavior of τ for various arguments. The simplest function is the totally undefined function, $\perp$.[24]

$$\tau(\perp) = \lambda((n) \; \text{if}(n=0, \, 0, \, \perp(n-1)+2*n-1))$$

but this says $\tau(\perp)$ is just f_1. Similarly,

$$\tau(\tau(\perp)) = \lambda((n) \; \text{if}(n=0, \, 0, \, f_1(n-1)+2*n-1))$$

is just f_2. Writing τ^i for the composition of $\tau...\tau$, i times, [25] we can say

$$f_i = \tau^i(\perp) \quad \text{or,}$$

$$\lambda((n)n^2) = \lim_{i \to \infty} \tau^i(\perp)$$

---

[24]This $\perp$ is the totally undefined function in $[\text{Fn} \to \text{Fn}]$.
[25]Define τ^0 to be $\perp$ in $[\text{Fn} \to \text{Fn}]$.

It can be shown that the least fixed-point of an equation $f = \tau(f)$ satisfies the relation:

$$Y(\tau) = \lim_{i \to \infty} \tau^n(\bot)$$

So the denotation for *label* might be better described by:

$$\Delta_a[\![label[f;g]]\!](I) = Y(\lambda(h)\Delta_a[\![g]\!](I : \langle f,h \rangle))$$

rather than:

$$\Delta_a[\![label[f;g]]\!](I) = \Delta_a[\![g]\!](I : \langle f, \Delta_a[\![g]\!] \rangle)$$

The characterizations are not equivalent. The behavior of $\Delta_a[\![label[car;car]]\!]$ will exhibit a discrepancy. The fix-point characterization reduces *label[car;car]* to the minimal solution of the equation **car** =**car**; that solution is $\bot$. The LISP interpretation of *label[car;car]* gives **car**. The general question of the correctness of the denotational semantics which we are developing is the subject of [Gor 73].

In summary, LISP has two ways of assigning values to functions: *label* and <=. The use of *label* manufactures a new "knotted" environment but does not always find the mimimal solution [Gor 73]. The evaluation of $f <= \Phi$ is interpreted as $f \leftarrow \Phi$, where the assignment is made in the global environment. LISP's solutions are sufficient for most definitions, but a more general treatment of the ideas involved in function definitions is needed from both practical and theoretical considerations.

A mathematical treatment of the imperative features of programming languages requires an extension of our model. An essential ingredient of imperatives is their ability to produce side-effects. This is usually modelled by including some notion of "the state of the machine". In such a development, the Δ function is specified in terms of an expression, an environment, and a state.

Problems

1. The *foo-fact-baz* example of page 230 is not described directly in LISP. Can you write a LISP program, without *prog*s which will also exemplify this difficulty?

4.12 LISP Machines

"in the beginning was the Word"

John, *1:1*

"in the beginning was the Word all right, but it wasn't a fixed number of bits"

R. S. Barton, *Software Engineering*

The LISP definitions and expressions which we have been writing are expressed in a language called the **meta-language**, and the LISP expressions are called M-expressions or M-exprs. The most primitive data structures of LISP are called S-expressions. We have seen that it is possible to represent M-expressions as S-expressions, and indeed, that significant results are obtained from such a mapping. The **programming language**, LISP, uses the S-expr translation of the LISP algorithms. As we move from the more formal aspects of LISP to the practical details of implementations, we should reflect on some of the features of LISP which make it a unique programming language.

The arguments to LISP programs are S-exprs and since we are writing LISP programs in S-expr form, then data and program are indistinguishable. Programs must have a very special structure, but program and data are both S-exprs just as in most hardware machines the contents of locations which contain data are not distinguishable from locations which contain instructions. [26] On a typical contemporary machine it is the way in which a location is accessed which determines the interpretation given to the location. If a processor accesses the location via the program counter, the contents are executed as an instruction. That same location can usually be accessed as part of a data manipulating instruction. In that case, the contents are simply taken to be data. LISP is one of the few high-level languages which also has this property [27] It gives the programmer exceptional power.

Since the next three chapters delve more deeply into implementation details and machine organization, it is useful to illuminate the similarities between LISP machines and traditional computers; The similarities are striking. A contemporary machine is a computer which executes well-behaved programs segments referencing very well-behaved data structures. A LISP architecture, catering to program debugging, has a different emphasis. We will see the traditional design as a specialization of a LISP design.

---

[26] A few machines *have* been built to enforce a dichotomy between data and program; the HP3000 and several of the Burroughs machines ([Org 73], [Dor 76]) follow this approach.

[27] The IPL series of languages ([New 61]) had this property, however those languages were more reminiscent of assembly language.

Our discussion will be restricted to common features of contemporary computers; we will not single out one specific architecture. [28] The basic item of information in the computer will be the **word**; That word will consist of binary bits, zero and one:

```
┌──────────────┐
│  01 ... 10   │
└──────────────┘
```

The number of bits in a word will not be too relevant for this discussion, however we will assume that each word contains the same number of bits. The "word" is our basic unit of data. Since programs will be specified as collections of words, it will be convenient to introduce an information unit for program representation.

In most machines, the words are not simply scattered about like loose paper on a desk top. Rather, they are arranged neatly like the pages in a book. Each word has an associated number called a its **location**. We will call a sequential collection of computer words a **vector**. For example:

```
100    ┌──────────────┐
       │  10 ... 1    │
101    ├──────────────┤
       │  01 ... 1    │
       ├──────────────┤
              ...
       ├──────────────┤
111    │  11 ... 0    │
1000   ├──────────────┤
       │  10 ... 1    │
       └──────────────┘
              ...
```

The numbers preceeding the words are the locations of the words. In this example we have sketched the vector from locations 4_8 through 10_8. [29] A program will be stored in memory as a vector of numbers.

Over this simple matrix of words and vectors the computer industry has presented a myriad of representations for instructions and data items. A ubiquitous feature is the execution cycle of a stored program machine.

For simplicity, we will assume that the architecure is a single-address instruction machine. This implies that each instruction of our machine will

---

[28]Readers who are familiar with computer architecture may find much of this discussion too simple; however our discussions *will* show relationships between LISP and other architectures, and raise some interesting questions about machine design.

[29]The notation "i_8" denotes the base eight, or "octal", representation of i. In the remainder of this section, any numeral is an octal numeral.

specify two parts; an operation, and a single operand. Since many operations we wish to perform expect two operands, the address format may reference an implicit operand. That operand, named **AC**, is a special register in the machine. For example, an instruction *ADD 100* would mean form the sum of the number represented in location 100 and the number represented in AC, and place the summation back in AC.[30] Thus the result of the addition is "accumulated" in **AC**; **AC** is also called the "accumulator." Or *JMZ 101* might mean "begin execution at location *101* if the contents of **AC** is a representation of zero; otherwise execute the instruction following the *JMZ*." We will postpone more detailed examination of specific machine instructions until Chapter 6. We wish to concentrate on the mechanisms which a computer uses to execute a program.

The **program counter**, denoted by **PC**, is used to control the execution path of a program. If **PC** references an instruction like the *ADD* above, then the machine executes the addition and then prepares to execute the next instruction in the sequence. The details of the *JMZ* are a bit more complicated. If the contents of the **AC** is (a representation of) zero then the machine will place *101* in the **PC** so that it can execute the instruction in location *101*; otherwise the instruction following the *JMZ* is executed. Our intent should be clearer now, but we can do better with a diagram. Something like:

$$
\begin{aligned}
\text{l:} \quad & C(IR) \leftarrow C(C(PC)) \\
& C(PC) \leftarrow C(PC) + 1 \\
& \text{execute } C(IR) \\
& \text{go to l}
\end{aligned}
$$

The notation, $C(x)$, is read "contents of x"; the arrow "$\leftarrow$" is read "replaced by". The **IR**, or **Instruction register**, is an internal register used to hold the instruction we are to execute. So step-by-step the diagram reads: "the contents of **IR** are replaced by the contents of the contents of **PC**"; that gets the next instruction. Next, "contents of **PC** are replaced by contents of **PC** plus *1*. Note that **PC** is incremented *before* execution of the instruction. If we incremented **PC** *after* the execution of the instruction, and the instruction were a *JMZ*-type instruction, then the **PC** might get a spurious incrementation. Finally we execute the instruction and then go back to fetch the next instruction. Embellishments of this basic cycle will get us to a LISP machine.

We will assume that any such word can contain an instruction or data, and the interpretation of a word depends on the way the execution mechanism of the machine accesses the word. For example, the contents of a

---

[30]Actually the operation "*ADD*" will not appear in the memory; rather, a bit-pattern will appear there and the computer must interpret that pattern to mean "*ADD*".

location can be used both as an instruction and as data; if location *101* contained the representation of the instruction *ADD 101*, then the execution cycle for that instruction would involve location *101* in both roles; instruction *and* data. This dual role of instruction and data occurs in less ad hoc situations. An assembler converts an external string of characters into a vector of bit patterns which a loader finally converts into real machine instructions. Many of the bit patterns which the loader receives from an assembler are simply machine "instructions", however the loader acts on them as data items; it does not execute them.

Several machines allow certain embellishments of the operand field of an instruction; indirect addressing is one example. If an operand is fetched indirectly, that means that contents of the operand field are not used directly as data, but are interpreted as a further address and the contents of that further address are examined. If the machine allows arbitrarily deep indirect addressing, that further address is examined to see if it specifies additional indirection. This chain of indirect addressing must terminate with a "real" address if the instruction which instigated this mess is ever to complete its execution.

For example, let a modifier *i* indicate indirect addressing; then *ADD 10 i* means don't add the contents of location *10* to AC but look at the contents of location *10* to determine the address. If the contents of location *10* is *2*, then the contents of location *2* will be added to AC. If location *10* contained *2 i*, then indirect cycle continues and the contents of location *2* would be inspected for an address. However if the contents of location *10* is *10 i*, then we will continue to fetch the contents of location *10*, looking for an operand which will not be forthcoming.

We should examine several of the conventions of this machine, asking if they are fundamental to the architecture or are more whims or historical accidents. After all the original Von Neumann machines were numerically oriented. [31] Why should data be numerical? Why should the instructions be sequential? Why do we need accumulators? Let's examine indirect addressing more closely.

Indirect addressing is actually a special case of an interesting idea: instead of requiring that the operand be a data item, let the operand specify a further operation. There are several problems with this scheme, none of which are insurmountable as we shall see. However, the most important problem for our current concerns is: if an operand may specify a further operation, then we must have a way of terminating the "get-new-operand" fetch. We saw two solutions in the indirect address paradigm:

1. An instruction will not invoke indirection if the *i* modifier is not present in the instruction.

---

[31][Car 75] is interesting paper on the practical design proposed by Alan Turing (of the theoretical Turing machine fame); Turing's machine had a much more non-numerical flavor.

2. An indirect addressing cycle will terminate the operand fetch when it comes across a reference which does not contain the *i* modifier.

These two solutions generalize nicely:

1. Have operations which look no further. That is, their operand may look like an operation, but it is not to be taken as such in the current context. This is the effect of the *quote* operator.

For example:

```
   loc      ┌───────────────┐
            │ ADD     loc   │
            └───────────────┘
```

When we execute loc, we also access loc as data.

2. Supply each word with an indicator that distinguishes data from instruction. The operand fetch would terminate when a "real" operand was fetched.

As we have already noted, some machines do supply a data-instruction indicator (though not for the purpose we have ascribed to it); and as we have further noted, we do not plan to follow this policy. The freedom to move freely between data and instruction is very powerful, albeit dangerous. We would like uniform access to program elements and data elements. That is, an instruction can reference either data locations or instruction locations. In terms of our current machine this means:

If a location is referenced by the PC then its contents is decoded as an instruction. If a location is referenced as an operand then its contents is taken as data.

We want similar flexibility in a LISP machine. What "arbitrary" decisions in the current architecture should we replace? The data items are particularly puny. As an initial generalization, we might consider a "vector" machine. Here, the basic data units would be vectors of numbers. The would lead to an interesting generalization: the *ADD* operation might now specify the component-wise addition of two vectors, etc... . Also programs would be representable as data items, since they are vectors. That's some improvement. [32] But data and programs are still represented linearly, and the data items are all representations of numbers. Surely we can do better.

First, realize that most programs are *not* linear; they typically have jumps and subroutine calls. A linearity is imposed on program structure because of the gratuitous incrementation of the program counter. That linearity becomes particularly bothersome when one has to patch machine language programs. Note also that much data is non-numerical in nature;

---

[32]This generalization is similar to that available in APL.

and much of that information has more complex structure than that supplied by a "vector" machine. "Ah, Hah!", you exclaim; we might want vectors, of vectors, of ... vectors, because that's a more general structuring of data and could be used to reflect the non-linear structure of programs, and ...

Excellent! Now you're ready for a LISP machine!

The processor of a "LISP machine" is *eval*. [33] If *eval* references an S-expr via its "program counter", then that S-expr is decoded via the internals of *eval*. If an S-expr is referenced as an argument, then it is taken as data. [34] The identity of program and data is not fixed even within the execution; a LISP program can create a data structure which can then be executed either explicitly, by appearing as an argument to *eval*, or implicitly, by appearing in the function-position of an application. A LISP machine is a generalization of the simple computer. The operations which get the next instruction or get the next data object, are more complex since neither program nor data is sequentially related. The next chapters will discuss implementations of LISP structures on traditional computers.

The simplest way to communicate with such a machine is to read an S-expr translation of a LISP expression into memory, evaluate the expression, and print the result. Several implementations of LISP use a variant of this "*read-eval-print*" loop:

$$prog[[]$$
$$a\ print[eval[read[]; (\ )]];$$
$$go[a]]$$

Note the similarity with *loop* on page 210 and the basic execution cycle of our simple computer. [35]

A LISP machine is a calculator using list-notation input and converting the output from LISP programs to list-notation wherever possible. But internally, all manipulations are done on the S-expression representation. LISP will allow you to manipulate the *representation* of the lists. The LISP S-expr operations like *car*, *cdr*, and *cons* operate without complaint on lists, even though we have repeatedly said that these functions are S-expression functions. LISP's attitude toward *car* and *cdr* is similar to its treatment of *gos* and labels: these are useful primitives from which to build tools.

One effect of this generality is to present the unwary LISP user with an incredible potentiality for generating programming errors. The alternative, to require declarations for all data objects and disallow run time modifications to programs offers a debugging tool of some power. If we

---

[33]Several "LISP machines" have been proposed or actually built including: [Got 74], [Gre 74], [Deu 73], and [Bar 71]

[34]This goes for *funargs* as well: until they're applied, they're data.

[35]The details of *read* and *print*, two of the input and output operations in LISP, are discussed in the next chapter.

write programs such that the type of each data object must be given, [36] and if we write each function such that the process of binding arguments to values must check that the type of the actual parameter agrees with the type of the parameter of the function, then a very large number of programming errors can be located almost as soon as they occur. You can think of the parameter-passing mechanism as a "fire-wall," which will help contain the deviant behavior to within the particular function.

Any function which gets called has a right to expect that it will be called with reasonable values. Part of being reasonable is having the correct number of arguments given to it; *cons[A; B; C]* is as bad as *cons[A]*. Part of being reasonable is having the right kind of arguments; we don't expect results from *sub1[A]*. We should not expect that the functions are sufficiently omniscient to convert an argument of the wrong kind into a proper one. If a function is written to expect an argument of type *polynomial* then it should complain if it receives an argument of type *list* even though the current representation for polynomials might be special instances of lists.

Many programming languages *do* offer such omniscience. Fortran calls this service "conversion"; Algol68 calls it "coercion". However if each function accepts whatever argument it is given and attempts to use it in its computation, then the first indication of trouble will occur when a primitive function is called and causes some error deep within the implementation. Typically this indication of error is way past the actual source of the difficulty. The alternative is to explicitly code tests into the entry code of each function definition; but that's an expensive use of the programmer's time and computation time. What typically happens is that the tests are left out and intensive debugging soon follows.

As with most areas of programming, coercion is not a black-or-white issue. A strong type structure can hinder as well as help. Requiring explicit declarations and directions for conversion is frequently annoying. Several important programming tasks are type-free. In particular, the debugging programs must be able to freely access all parts of the representation of program and data without regard for type. To make debugging meaningful, such programs must *modify* existing structures, changing data structures and programs. When dealing with large complex computations, it is not acceptable to edit programs, recompile them, and reinitialize the whole computation. More sophisticated debugging techniques must be developed.

LISP's position is that it is the user's responsibility to handle all type restrictions by programmed tests. LISP has no capability to maintain abstract data structures; in fact, the implementation of LISP itself is open to programmer modification. However people have begun investigations of "typed LISP" [Car 76], and some implementations of LISP [Int 75] give some aids in constructing and maintaining typed data structures.

---

[36]For example, in Section 2.3 the types of the arguments to *diff* should be <poly> and <variable>, *not* list and atom.

Symbolic expressions are the only real data structure; we almost have sequences as a data structure, and the necessary ingredients are there to build abstract data structures. But the question of integrity in using such defined data structures is left in the hands of the programmer. In summary, LISP is an excellent tool for building more complex systems; as a tool, it has the ability to cause injury, and since it is a tool it has few preconceptions. These are some of the reasons that LISP has maintained its position as the "machine language" for Artificial Intelligence.

The Static Structure of LISP

5.1 Introduction

The material in the previous chapters has been rather abstract. This chapter begins a discussion of the mechanisms which occur in implementations of LISP. However the importance of the techniques we will describe extends far beyond the implementation of this particular language. Most of the ideas involved in our implementation are now considered standard system programming techniques and are common tools in language design. LISP is particularly well-suited to the task of explicating these ideas since many find their origins in the first LISP implementation.

We will begin our discussion of implementation with an analysis of storage regimes for S-expressions. As with the more abstract discussions of representations, the "concrete" representation which we pick for our data structures (S-expressions) will have direct bearing on the implementation of the primitive constructor (*cons*), selectors (*car, cdr*) and predicates (*atom, eq*) of LISP. We must also consider the efficiency of the implementation and we must include input and output mechanisms to translate this representation back and forth between the external S-expr notation.

The present chapter will develop a picture of the *static* structure of an implementation, or to be more graphic, this chapter describes the memory of a LISP machine. The next chapter discusses the *dynamic structure* of LISP;

that is, the control structures necessary to evaluate expressions involving recursive functions and other LISP control constructs.

Throughout these discussions we will remain as abstract as possible without losing too much detail. We will describe the "logical" structure of a LISP machine, even though a more efficient implementation might map differing logical structures onto the same physical structures by utilizing machine-dependent techniques.

5.2 Representation of S-expressions

We previously have expressed the dotted pair *(A . (B . C))* as:

or occasionally (see page 9) as:

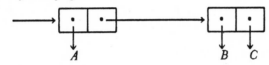

This second style of graphical representation has a direct representation in the storage layout of our machine. Each "double-box" will be represented as a machine location and each arrow will be represented as a pointer to a machine location. Notice that each box contains two pointers; therefore each corresponding machine location, loc, will be interpreted as containing two machine addresses. [1] The left-hand address will represent the *car*-branch; the right-hand address will represent the *cdr*-branch:

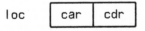

The pointers will either reference atoms or point to two-pointer boxes. Literal atoms -- like *A, B, C* -- will also be represented in machine locations,

---

[1] An actual hardware machine may not be of sufficient word-size to accomodate two addresses; in this case, several real words may be needed to represent one LISP word. For example, the PDP-11 (16 bit words) implementations typically use two machine words ([Har 75]), and micro-processor versions (8 bit words) may use four words ([Pag 76]). In Section 7.13 we discuss a special compact representation of LISP cells.

only here the contents of each location will be an encoding of the name of the atom. The contents of such a location must not be interpreted as pointers.

loc | rep. of literal atom

To help keep track of the different uses of machine locations we will partition our machine's memory into two disjoint spaces: **pointer space**, which will contain two-pointer cells; and **atom space**, which will contain information like atoms which should not be interpreted as pointers. Thus if the first box in our example were represented by location 100 and the second were represented by location 405, and the atoms A, B, and C were represented by the numbers 40, 41, and 42, and were to be found in locations 710, 762, and 711, respectively, then the following picture beginning at location 100 could represent the dotted pair $(A . (B . C))$.

| 100 | 710 | 405 |

. . .

| 405 | 762. | 711 |

. . .

| 710 | | 40 |
| 711 | | 42 |

. . .

| 762 | | 41 |

The left half of location 100 points to the representation of the atom A and the right half points to the representation of the dotted pair $(B . C)$. Notice too, that given the entry point into the representation --location 100 in the example-- we can discover the S-expr being represented.

This representation of S-exprs is a special case of a scheme called **linked list structure**. The term "linked" refers to the fact that to find succeeding elements in the representation we must follow the explicit pointers as opposed to, say, merely incrementing an array pointer. The phrase "list structure" describes an arbitrary interconnection of these two-pointer nodes, including self-referential structures. We will discuss such general structures later; for the moment we restrict such constructions to LISP trees: no intersecting branches.[2]

The particular brand of linked list structure which we have demonstrated is called **singly linked**. The adjective "singly" means that only *one* pointer is stored as the representation of the arrow, →. This means that the representation only tells us how to find successor elements in the structure. For example, if we were looking at location 405 the representation tells us how to find the *car* or *cdr*; they're at 762 and 711 respectively. But if we wanted to find the *predecessor* of 405 in this representation it would require some further calculation. We would have to start at the beginning of the S-expr representation and look for a location such that its *car* or *cdr* is the desired cell. If a particular application required frequent discovery of such predecessors then we might consider a more complex representation which would also contain information about the predecessor of each node, essentially representing → as ↔.

For example:

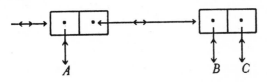

A   B   C

One such representation is called **doubly-linked list structure**. In this representation of LISP trees we could store *three* pieces of information with each node:

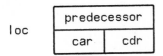

Note that LISP trees always *do* have unique predecessors. In the case of list-structure, unique predecessors do not always exist. Compromises exist in some applications: some data structures can be doubly-linked, allowing fast traversal but requiring more space; while other data structures are singly linked, requiring less space, but requiring more time to traverse ([Gua 69]); still other structures may have more compact representation as arrays or numbers. For example, a typical representation of a vector, or sequence of fixed length, is to store the elements sequentially in memory.[3] Since each element in this structure has at most one successor we can use the sequential addresses as implicit pointers to retrieve successive elements. A general S-expr has two successors, thus the implied linear addressing scheme of most

---

[2]The implementation of lists using linked addresses was introduced by the IPL series of languages; [New 61].

[3]We will discuss these more detailed representations in Chapter 7.

machine memories is insufficient as it stands; LISP uses linked allocation. Again there are compromises. For example, the following memory representation is valid for LISP trees: for any location n, find its successors at locations $2n$ and $2n+1$; note that the predecessor of any cell is unique. Each location must contain an indication of whether or not it is an atom. The remaining contents of a location is available for data; see [Ber 71].

We will frequently refer to several different S-exprs simultaneously; for example, when we are talking about the implementation of the function *cons* we will be manipulating the representations of two S-exprs. Similarly we will want to refer to several pieces of a single complex S-expr; for example we might wish to "put a finger" at a specific point in a structure and then, depending on the result of a computation on some sub-part, move the "finger" either left or right. To facilitate such discussions we will assume the existence of a set of pointer registers: $Pt_1, Pt_2, ..., Pt_n$. Thus, using the above example, the following represents Pt_1 pointing at $(B . C)$ and Pt_2 pointing at the atom A:

$$Pt_1 \qquad\qquad\qquad\qquad Pt_2$$

$$\boxed{405} \qquad\qquad\qquad\qquad \boxed{710}$$

Implicit in our representation is the assurance that we can differentiate between locations in atom space and locations in pointer space. For example, assume each of our locations can hold six digits and assume we will store a numeric atom as its corresponding number. Then the atom 762711 would be stored as:

$$\boxed{762711}$$

Since this is exactly the contents of location 405 [4] some confusion is possible: is the contents a number or is it two pointers? A typical trick is to partition memory such that particular portions of the address space correspond to each of the logical spaces: atom space or pointer space. In our example we could assume that addresses less than 700 are locations for pointers, while addresses greater than or equal to 700 contain atoms. Thus the representation of 762711 would appear in a location with address 700 or greater.

Though our memory system is not completed yet, we *do* have enough structure to begin a discussion of the implementation of some of the primitive LISP operations.

---

[4]The vertical bar doesn't appear in the machine's memory.

Problems

1. What problems do you foresee in using the double-linking scheme for representing LISP's S-exprs?

5.3 Representation of LISP Primitives

Now that we have some of the representational problems for S-exprs reasonably well in hand we will look at the implementation of the LISP primitives. We will examine *car, cdr, eq,* and *atom* in this section, leaving *cons* for later.

We must understand how these primitives obtain their parameters and how they are to return their values. Recall our discussion of environments and destinations in Section 4.6. An environment chain was constructed by linking destination blocks whose value slots have been filled. A dest-block was created when we recognized a function application. [5] The name components of a block are either the λ-variables in the case of a λ-application or are system-generated names in the case of primitive application; the value-slots of a dest-block received the evaluated actual parameters. When a dest-block was filled, it was chained onto the front of the environment and we were ready to call the function. Thus the first block on the environment chain was the local symbol table. The function was expected to return its value to a designated dest-block, and then return to the interrupted computation. So, on entrance to a primitive we have access to at least two structures: a destination block and the environment chain.

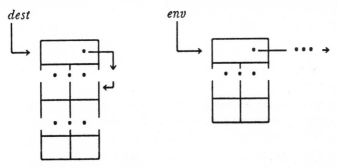

---

[5]If the application supplied an incorrect number of arguments no dest-block is built; the debugging routine is called. Several implementations supply missing arguments with *NIL* or evaluate and discard extra arguments. This treatment of improper calling sequences ignores one of the most common sources of bugs in LISP programs ([Mot 76]).

Here is how *car* uses these structures:

> Let *val* be the value-part of the first entry in the local table. If *val* is an atom then *car* is undefined; the implementation should send a message to the debugging package (see Section 6.23). If *val* is *not* atomic, it has a left- and right-hand side. We should send the *left*-hand side of *val* to the value part of the slot pointed to in the dest-block.

For example:

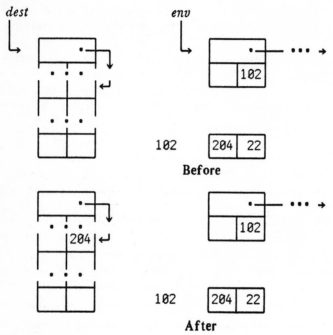

Example for *car*

For successful completion *car* expects that its actual parameter represents a node in pointer space; otherwise we get an error. If the operation is successful then the dest-slot is changed to point to whatever was pointed to by the left-hand side of the selected cell. The description of *cdr* is sufficiently similar that we leave it to the reader.

On page 248 we described the internal structure of LISP atoms. Using that representation we can give a simple implementation for the predicate *atom*:

> Does the actual parameter point into that area reserved for atom names? If so, send a representation of truth as value, otherwise send a representation of false.

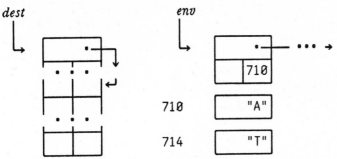

We are writing "A" instead of the numeric encoding. Thus "A" is really 40.
Before

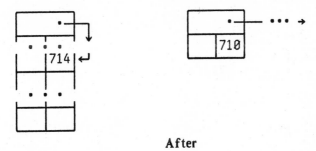

After

Example for *atom*

Notice that we did not need to examine the contents of location 710, thus saving one storage reference. It was sufficient to know that the location was between predetermined bounds. If the actual parameter was not pointing at an atom we would have returned a pointer to a location containing "NIL".

Finally we describe an implementation of *eq*:

Do both actual parameters point into atom space? If not the result is undefined. If they *do* then do they reference the same atom? We can determine this latter condition in two ways: first, they might point to two different locations in atom space; we would have to examine the contents of those locations; if they agreed then *eq* should return a representation of truth. A more satisfactory solution is to store each atom *uniquely*; one location will be reserved for "A", etc. Now all *eq* need do is make sure that both slots point into atom space *and* point to the same location. Thus no additional memory reference is required. From now on we will require that all atoms are stored uniquely.

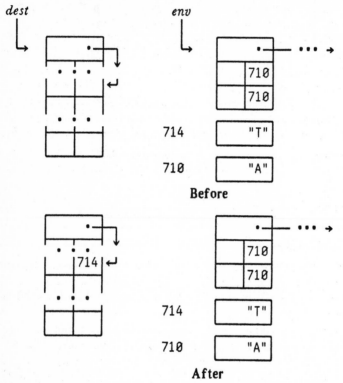

Example for *eq*

We still have a ambiguity to resolve if we represent the number *40* as 40 and represent the atom *A* as 40. Section 5.6 resolves this conflict.

5.4 AMBIT/G

Before investigating the implementation of atoms, we should explore other possible descriptions for LISP's primitives. We have described the primitives by example; it would be more pleasing if we could describe each primitive in more general terms. Fortunately we can, using a micro-version of a graphical language called AMBIT/G. [6]

When developing a complex structure-manipulating program, we draw pictures. In LISP we frequently describe data structures graphically and in the previous section we gave graphical descriptions of the LISP primitives using examples. AMBIT is an extension of both of these ideas; it is a graphical language for the description of both data and algorithms.

The basic statements of the language are **pattern-match** and **replacement** rules. Several programming languages have complex pattern matchers; AMBIT's uniqueness is its graphical presentation of the patterns. Patterns are described as combinations of shapes and solid arrows. If an instance of a pattern can be found in the current state of the computation, then we will replace that instance with a new pattern. The only kind of replacement we will allow is the **swinging** of an arrow so that its head moves from one node to another; the tail of the arrow is immovable. Thus the new pattern differs from the old only in the positioning of some of the arrow heads. Where the arrow head strikes a node is immaterial. Dashed arrows show replacements to be made if the pattern matches. Portions of the shapes marked with "?" are "don't-care" conditions.

For example, here's *car*:

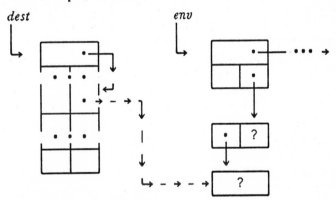

Algorithm for *car*

This AMBIT diagram contains equivalent information to the previous

---

[6]AMBIT/G is an acronym for Algebraic Manipulation By Identity Transformation/Graphical.

example of *car*, but the extraneous details of specific addresses have been stripped away. We will use such diagrams occasionally when they will contribute to clarity.

Problem

Give an AMBIT diagram for *eq*.

5.5 A Few Programming Techniques

There are a few useful and practical LISP programming techniques which take advantage of the implementation. These tricks are supported in most implementations and are useful enough that they should be documented as programming language features.

1. In most implementations of *eq* the check for atom-ness is suppressed and a simple address comparison is made. Non-atomic S-expressions are not usually stored uniquely;[7] Thus in most implementations

   $eq[(A . B);(A . B)]$ is usually false, but
   $eq[x;x]$ is usually true for any *x*.

We are *not* changing the definition of *eq*; it is still undefined for non-atomic arguments. The preceding remarks deal only with the usual implementation of *eq*.[8]

2. The implementation of the truth values t and f is usually simplified, mapping f onto *NIL*, but allowing anything *but NIL* as a representation of t. This allows several related tricks:

   a. Any expression may be used as a predicate, and
   b. Used as a predicate, *not[null[l]]* has the same effect as *l*.

For example, consider the following extended version of the predicate *member*.

$mem^* <= \lambda[[x;l]][null[l] \rightarrow f;$
$\qquad\qquad equal[x;first[l]] \rightarrow l;$
$\qquad\qquad t \rightarrow mem^*[x;rest[l]]]]$

This "predicate", *mem**, will return f if no matching element is found, otherwise it will return the list beginning at the match. The non-empty list can be used as an indication of truth, and can also supply the calling function with the match if a match is found.

---

[7]See the problem on hash consing on page 287.
[8]Formally, the implementation *is* wrong in not satisfying the definition. Pragmatically, the implementation is convenient.

3. Several implementations of conditional expressions allow "p_i" as an abbreviation for "$p_i \rightarrow p_i$". The computational effect is the same, but p_i is only evaluated once.

Using this feature, *mem'* could be written:

$$mem' <= \lambda[[x;l][null[l] \rightarrow f;$$
$$equal[x;first[l]] \rightarrow l;$$
$$mem'[x;rest[l]]]]$$

This feature is more useful in contexts where we wish to test for the existence of an object and, if a match is found, do something with the object. For example, the trick of page 213 could be written:

$$[cont \leftarrow isspec[fun;spectbl];$$
$$isprim[] \rightarrow ...; ...]$$

where:

$$isspec <= \lambda[[x;l] [null[l] \rightarrow (\ );$$
$$eq[name[first[l]];x] \rightarrow value[first[l]];$$
$$isspec[x;rest[l]]]]$$

Since the result of *value* will be a function name, and never f, there will be no ambiguity in using *isspec* as a predicate.

Problem

1. The application of these tricks may give rise to some unaesthetic programs. Typically we have to test for existence then, assuming an instance was discovered, we have to perform further computation on that instance. [9] Constructs like:

$$[it \leftarrow test[object] \rightarrow smash[it]; ...]$$

arise. The objectional aspect involves the variable *it*. The variable *it* is not local to the conditional expression. Either *it* is global: an unnecessarily gratuitious side-effect; or *it* is bound by an enclosing λ-expression or a *prog*. In either case the binding is too far removed from its usage. Sussman and Steele [Sus 76] suggest the construct:

$$test[<form_1>; \lambda[[x] <form_2>]; <form_3>]$$

with the following semantics: evaluate $<form_1>$; if it gives a value other than f then apply the second argument, a unary function, to that value. Otherwise evaluate $<form_3>$.

Recast the *isspec*-argument of page 213 in terms of *test*. Give an implementation of *test* by extending one of our evaluators.

---

[9]If no further computation is necessary, trick No. **3** suffices.

5.6 Symbol Tables and Property-lists

Since we are examining implementation details, and since manipulation of symbol tables is such a central issue in evaluation, we should also scrutinize symbol tables and their organization. We have seen two fundamentally different symbol table organizations: deep binding and shallow binding. We should examine the implications of these organizations, and probe deeper into their implementation. If the number of entries associated with an atom is small then shallow binding may be advantageous. If the number of entries associated with an atom is very large then the shallow binding technique may be too costly and deep binding or yet another organization may be required ([McD 75]).

Recall our discussion of *getval*, *addval*, and *getval_cell* in Section 3.11. These functions were developed to describe shallow binding, but they are illustrative of a more general idea. In symbol manipulation and symbolic programming, we often want to be able to associate a set of data with an item. For example, an algebraic simplifier would like to know whether a specific operator is commutative; if so, certain simplifications are valid. We could maintain a list of all commutative operations and require that the simplifier check that list. But since commutativity is a property of the operator it seems more natural to associate the property with that operation. Search considerations also arise if the list of operations is long.

We generalize the idea expressed in *getval* and *addval*, allowing the association of an arbitrary collection of **property-value** pairs with an atom. With each atom we will associate a list called the **property-list** or **p-list**. [10] The names, **attribute** or **indicator**, are sometimes used as synonyms for property. An atom is frequently called a **carrier** of the properties.

A property list is a table of properties and property values. The size of the property list is not fixed, but can shrink and grow during a computation.

prop1	val1
prop2	val2
• • •	
propn	valn

We have seen an identical diagram in Section 2.5; property lists are a very effective tool for modelling data bases. [11] Thought of as abstractions, property lists are symbol tables. The name-entries are properties and the value entries are the property values.

---

[10]Property lists were introduced to programming languages in the IPL series of languages [New 61].

[11]They are by no means the *only* or *best* way of representing a data base. See [McD 75].

We identify an atom with its property list. For example, if we wished to represent the "+"-operation as the atom *PLUS* and wished to signify that the operation is commutative and binary, the atom *PLUS* might be represented as:

PLUS

commu	T
arity	2

In these kinds of applications, we are using the atom as a data structure and attaching properties to that atom rather than thinking of the atom as a representation of an identifier.

For example:

CAR

MFGR	BUICK
YEAR	1959

These same techniques are applicable when we consider atoms as representations of variables as used in the evaluation process. In fact, an atom can simultaneously be used as a carrier of a value and can also have a property list:

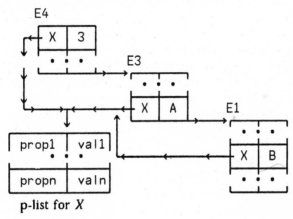

p-list for *X*

All instances of X share a common property list, but the value, or binding of x is found using the environment chain. This example is described in terms of deep binding, but the property-list idea is also directly applicable to the shallow binding schemes. To adapt p-lists to the first shallow binding scheme of page 151, we introduce a property named *VAR* whose property value will be the collection of environment-value pairs:

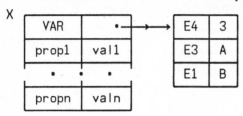

Similarly, the second shallow binder could use:

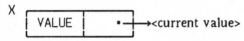

In summary, property lists are a language feature which is independent of the binding strategy we have implemented. A property list can contain all the aspects of an atom which we wish to consider; the class of attributes need not be fixed, but can vary during the execution of the program. Those properties need not involve the fact that atoms are used to represent identifiers when we map the meta language onto data structures. The deep binding implementation emphasizes that the value of a variable is associated with the environment in which that value is created. However a shallow binding organization associates values with variables, and thus it is natural to think of property-lists when thinking of shallow binding.

We wish to look more closely at the value aspects of atoms. We have seen three properties related to the value of a variable: simple value, call-by-value function (expr) and call-unevaluated function (fexpr). We were able to distinguish between exprs and fexprs: either place the fexpr name in a special list; or store the fexpr as a β-expression, rather than as a λ-expression. We made no explicit distinction between simple values and function values; if a simple value appeared in the function position of an application, we evaluated that expression until we *did* discover a function object. [12] If a function appeared in a position expecting a simple value, then the data structure interpretation of the function object was taken.

---

[12] It may be a bad idea to distinguish between the evaluation of an argument position and the evaluation of a function position.

Since "<=" and "<$_f$=" were defined to place the appropriate function definition in the global table, we can interpret these operations as associating the definition with the atom. That is, being an expr or fexpr is a property of the atom. Similarly, globally bound variables like t and nil play the roles of constants and therefore can be interpreted as having a value associated with them. Primitive functions like car, and primitive special forms like $cond$ should also be considered constants. Their "values" are fixed procedures for specific call-by-value and call-unevaluated operations, respectively. [13]

This discussion exemplifies five value-like properties which are properties of an atom, rather than properties of a particular environment: [14]

CONST	simple value; used as a constant
EXPR	call-by value definition
FEXPR	call-unevaluated definition
SUBR	call-by-value primitive
FSUBR	call-unevaluated primitive

In Section 6.18 we will introduce another protocol for assigning values to variables, but at any one time an atom may have at most one of these value-related indicators. [15]

For example, car might be represented as:

| SUBR | • —→To machine language code for car |

Part of the atom-structure for CAR

----

[13]Many implementations are less restrictive: 1. T and NIL can be redefined; 2. car, cdr and the other primitives can be redefined. Allowing 1 will always lead to grief. 2 is justified only for debugging calls on these functions; however, if one programs abstractly, there will be no need to debug such low level calls.

[14]We will discuss the VAR and $VALUE$ properties later. That will be the intent of Section 5.19.

[15]Several implementations allow atoms to have several of these system properties. Thus expressions like $car[car]$ are executable. The implementation uses context to determine which car is a simple variable and which car is the primitive procedure. The current *eval will* operate correctly on this example since a recognizer for the function car is explicitly encoded in *apply*, but such tricks lead to unnecessarily mysterious programs. For the same reason, the LISP obscenity λ[[*lambda*] ...] will work. Notice its S-expr representation is *(LAMBDA (LAMBDA) ...)*. Context is used by an evaluator in slightly less obnoxious ways. For example, an evaluator for *prog* can tell a reference to the label x from the *prog*-variable x in ... $prog[[x;y]$ ... x $f[..]$ ... $g[x$ ...] ... $go[x]$. See page 189.

When *apply* recognizes *CAR* as a representation for the function *car*, the machine-dependent code will be executed, but *CAR* can also be used as an atomic data structure. For example:

in *eval[(CAR (QUOTE (CAR BMW)));( )]* both uses of *CAR* will appear.

As a further example, consider the representation of:

$$fact <= \lambda[[x][x=0 \rightarrow 1;\, t \rightarrow times[x;fact[sub1[x]]]]]$$

The right-hand side would be:

```
(LAMBDA (X) (COND ((ZEROP X) 1)
                  (T (TIMES X
                     (FACT (SUB1 X)))))))
```

To represent the intention that *fact* is to be defined as the above recursive function, we might store the S-expr representation on the property-list of the atom *FACT* and use *EXPR* as its indicator. The occurrence of the atom *FACT* in the λ-expression is represented as a pointer to the atomic structure of FACT.

Here is part of the atom-structure for *FACT*:

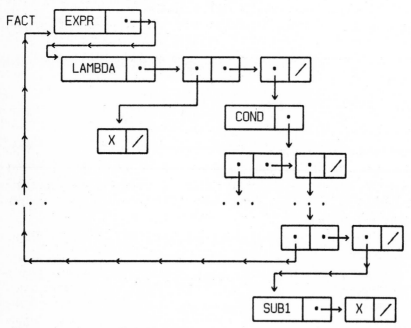

Atom-structure for *FACT*

Every occurrence of an atom --EXPR, LAMBDA, and so forth-- is actually a reference to the appropriate atomic structure. Note that both instances of X are actually pointers to the representation of *X*, but that two representations of *(X)* will typically be distinct. Also keep in mind that we are storing the data structure *representation* of the *fact* function.

$$(LAMBDA\ (X)\ (COND\ ((ZEROP\ X)\ 1)$$
$$(T\ (TIMES\ X\ (FACT\ (SUB1\ X)))))\ )$$

is a perfectly good list. If we attached it to the indicator *VALUE* then we would have represented the list as the *simple* value of *fact*.

Representations of special forms like *COND* and *QUOTE* give rise to the indicator *FSUBR*. When an instance of such a special form is recognized, the argument list is passed to the primitive without any evaluation. In a similar manner we introduce the indicator *FEXPR* to designate the occurrence of a "$<_f=$" definition.

Our discussion of property lists as carriers of values has centered on the representations of constants; many identifiers in LISP are constants. Even though we can redefine functions using a version of "$<=$", most such definitions are relatively constant. [16] The primitive functions are also constant. Shallow binding tries to capitalize on this observation, by associating all of the value aspects of a variable with the property list, and we will soon see that for several interesting subsets of LISP, we can significantly simplify the handling of shallow binding. Before discussing that, we will show how an evaluator might use such property-list information. This requires the introduction of property-list manipulating functions.

5.7 Property-list Functions

There are four functions for manipulating the property-list:

putprop[a;v;p] will put the value *v* under the property *p* on the property-list of the atom *a*. If the property *p* already appears on the p-list then the *v* over-writes the old value; otherwise a new property-value pair is added to the front of the p-list of *a*. The value returned by *putprop* is *v*. [17]

get[x;i] will search the property-list of the atom *x* looking for the indicator *i*. If *i* is found the value associated with that indicator is returned by *get*.

If *x* does not have the indicator then f is returned. Thus *getval[x]* could be defined as *get[x;VAR]*.

---

[16]To define a temporary function we use *label*.

[17]In some implementations, the old pair is removed and the new pair is added to the front of the p-list. The idea is that since short p-lists are usually searched linearly, one should have the most popular properties near the front of the list. This reorganization of the table can even be extended to include *references* to properties, always moving the last referenced property pair to the front of the list [Riv 76].

getl[*x*;*l*] will search the property-list of the atom *x* for the *first* occurrence of any indicator which appears in the list, *l*, of indicators. If such a match is found, then the *remainder* of the p-list, beginning with the matching indicator, is returned. If no match is found, f is returned. The virtue of *getl* is that it can distinguish between an atom which has an indicator with value f and an atom which does not have the indicator. *get* cannot communicate this distinction. The disadvantage of *getl* is that it gives access to the internal structure of the p-list, and therefore access to the representation of the atom. Such p-list functions are useful but dangerous ([Sam 75]).

remprop[*n*;*p*]: The final function in this class is used to remove property-value pairs from the p-list of an atom. The function is named *remprop*. *remprop* has two arguments: *n*, an atom; and *p*, a property. If the property is found on the p-list of the atom, then *remprop* removes the property-value pair and returns t; otherwise it returns f.

5.8 An *eval* for Property-lists

The evaluators in this section do not reflect typical implementation policies, but illustrate the use of property lists and introduce the first non-trivial application of LISP's ability to interchange program with data. Though this chapter is mostly concerned with the *static* organization of LISP, the ideas involved in the evaluator are sufficiently important and demonstrative of the power of property lists that we include them here rather than later.

The first evaluator uses property names like *CONST* and *EXPR* as representations for functions *const* and *expr*. Discovering that an atom has the *CONST* property, the evaluator *applies* the function named *const* to perform the evaluation. In this case, the evaluation is simple: return the represented constant. We will assume a shallow binding implementation and therefore variables are handled by recognizing the property *VAR* and passing the evaluation to the function *var*. In the case of an application, we have more work to do; *expr* handles that. The actual application, is handled using LISP's computed function facility discussed on page 158.

We will describe a sequence of evaluators based on property list manipulation. We will not express all of the details of this family of evaluators, but leave many of the details to the reader.

$$eval \ <= \ \lambda[[exp;env]$$
$$[atom[exp] \rightarrow form\_name[getl[exp;$$
$$(VAR\ CONST)]]\ [exp;env];$$
$$atom[first[exp]] \rightarrow form\_name[getl[first[exp];$$
$$(EXPR$$
$$FEXPR)]]\ [exp;env];$$
$$...\ ]]$$

$$var \ <= \ \lambda[[form;env]\ lookup[form;env]]$$
$$const \ <= \ \lambda[[form;env]\ denote[form;env]]$$
$$expr \ <= \ \lambda[[form;env]\ \lambda[[def]\ eval[body[def];$$
$$mkenv[\ vars[def];$$
$$evlist[args[form];env]]\ ]$$
$$[get[func[form];EXPR]]]$$

No substantial benefit is apparent after all this work. With a slight change, we could extract a small improvement: replace the explicit lists *(VAR CONST)* and *(EXPR FEXPR)* with *idprop* and *appprop*. Bind these variables globally to the respective lists. Then if we wished to define a new kind of calling sequence, say *gexprs*, we could add *GEXPR* to *appprop* and write a function named *gexpr* to handle the evaluation of *gexpr* forms. However with further analysis, we can do much better.

Consider simple variables. Each instance of a simple variable has the same value property; when we see *x* we apply *lookup* through *var*; when we see *y* we apply *lookup* through *var*. However the association of a value property with each *instance* of a variable is discomforting. The value property is more a property of the class of variables than it is a property of an instance. That is, an instance inherits a property by being a member of a certain class.

Let the atom *VAR* represent the class of variables; let the atom *EVAL* represent the property name describing value properties. The function *lookup* is therefore a property value of the atom *VAR*, and should be associated with the property name *EVAL*.

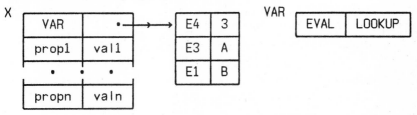

Now the evaluator should do a double *get*, looking down the property list of an object, for a class name which has an *EVAL* property. Finding *EVAL*, the evaluator applies the associated property value to the object and the environment.

Before presenting the next evaluator we should settle one more point. In the preceeding *eval* we ignored the question of anonymous λ-expressions; we assumed that the function-part of an application was an atom. We did this becaue we have implied that only atoms have property lists. We will remove this restriction for the next evaluator and assume that any object can have a property list. A λ-expression will have a property list with (at least) property name *LAMBDA* and property value of the repesentation of the λ-expression. The atom *LAMBDA* will have an *EVAL* property whose value is the function *eval_λ*; this function will evaluate applications whose function-parts are λ-expressions.

Finally, since *eval_λ* handles most of the evaluation of an application, there is no need to make *eval* do it too. In fact, our previous distinction between *VAR* and *EXPR* is unnecessarily restrictive. We should be able to return functions as values just as we can return constants or simple values. So *EXPR* should be a property name, with property value being the λ-expression, but *EXPR* should now have an *EVAL* property which is just *lookup*.

For example:

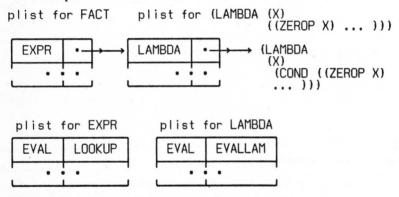

With all this extra mechanism in place, *eval* does absolutely nothing!

$$eval <= \lambda[[exp;env]\ getget[exp;EVAL]\ [exp;env]],$$

where *getget* looks at property names associated with *exp* until it finds one which itself has a property list containing *EVAL*.

Now real progress has been made. The evaluation of any expression is controlled by a function associated with the class to which that expression belongs. It is trivial to modify or extend such an evaluator: supply the class name and the appropriate *EVAL* property value.

The technique is applicable to more general kinds of computation than just evaluation. With a class name we can associate arbitrary pairs of properties and functions. For example, we might wish to define special input or output conventions for classes; to do this we simply associate a *READ* property and a *PRINT* property with the class name and supply routines to perform the special reading or printing. Similarly, we can associate a compile property, and a function describing how to compile instances of this construct. [18]

The net effect of this reworking of evaluation is to expose a much more general scheme for handling computation. Such a distributed *eval* is an example of a LISP technique called data-driven programming ([San 75a]). [19]

Property list representations have also found extensive use in data base applications (Section 2.5; see [San 75a].

5.9 Representation of Property-lists

In discussing representations, we must keep the essential characteristics of property lists well in mind. A property list is similar to a local environment block; each property list is a sequence of names and values. However a property list can grow and shrink dynamically, whereas an environment block is created at a fixed size. Since we cannot predict the size of the block, a natural representation is that of a list.

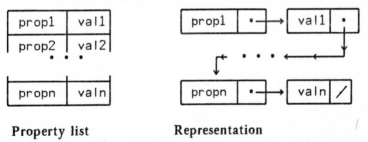

          Property list   Representation

The elements of the p-list are associated in pairs. The first element of a pair is the property, the next element is the property value. But atoms can't be represented as just any arbitrary list. We must be able to recognize the occurrence of an atom so that we can implement the predicate *atom*.

There are at least two alternatives. We might partition memory as we began to do on page 248 with pointer space and atom space. Then the test of atom-ness is a test on the location being referenced. We might also preface the property list with an "atom header" which will signal the

---

[18]The language EL1 ([EL1 74]) incorporates a similar scheme, however only five designated properties can be associated with any class name. The techniques of syntax-directed input-output, developed in Section 9.4, are also applicable to such an evaluator.

[19]The author first saw this technique used in a non-trivial way in [Dif 71] in the Stanford LISP compiler.

beginning of the atom. Here the test for atom-ness is a test on the contents of the location being referenced. In the first case we dedicate a section of memory for the storage of atoms; [20] in the second case we require an extra memory reference.

A related efficiency consideration involves the use of property lists in the implementation of LISP. Since the evaluator will be making frequent examination of the p-list, it is often useful to store the system-related properties in specific positions relative to the beginning of the p-list; this will eliminate a search.

Using a separate "atom space", an atom would be represented by its property list. In this case, property lists need not be stored in pointer space. Chapter 7 examines some of these techniques. In the text we will describe atoms using the "atom header" since it makes it clearer in pictures. Atoms will be special lists whose *car*-part contains an indicator used exclusively for the beginning of atoms. We will use ɣ to designate the beginning of an atom. The *cdr* of the representation of the atom is the representation of the property list. Such locations in pointer space containing ɣ in their left-half and a pointer to a p-list in their right-half are called **atom headers**.
For example, here is part of a representation for the atom for *car*:

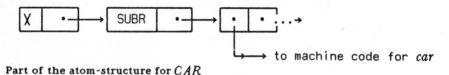

to machine code for *car*

Part of the atom-structure for CAR

An example of the distinction between *get* and *getl* in our representation may be useful.

$getl[FOO;(BAZ)]$
$\parallel$
$getl[FOO;(PNARF\ BAZ)]$ $get[FOO;PNARF]$

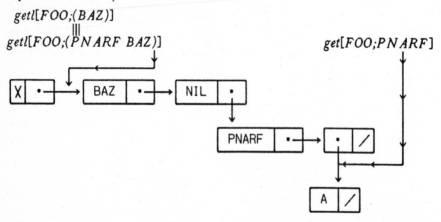

---

[20]We need not dedicate a whole section of the machine to "atom space". Several techniques are available for "mapping" a conceptually contiguous space onto a scattered memory.[Ste 73], [Nor 76], [Pre 76a].

and $get[FOO;BAZ] = get[FOO;BAR] = NIL$. Notice how both *get* and *getl* allow free access to the internal representation.

The simple atom is becoming much more complex. It has a whole substructure attached to it. Thus each atom is like a word in a dictionary; many words can be used as different parts of speech and their dictionary entries will reflect this by having several alternative meanings. Similarly, an atom can have several different "meanings" attached to it and depending on the context, we will be interested in one of those interpretations. Just as we will find all meanings of a specific word in one location in the dictionary, our implementation of LISP becomes much simpler if we store each atom and its associated p-list uniquely. Every reference to the atom A is actually a pointer to the same location in memory. This location has a *car*-part which is the special atom indicator Χ, and a *cdr*-part which is the p-list for the atom A.

Thus $(A \cdot A)$, which we have been writing as:

might be represented as:

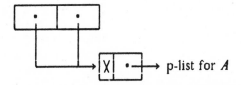

The internal structures of this implementation of LISP are *not* L-trees, but list structure; that is, there are intersecting and circular branches. LISP implementations therefore involve binary list structure since each non-terminal node in our representation has exactly two branches.

Assume we have the above dotted pair as a value of a variable x and we wish to print the value of x. We would expect that an output routine would be given a pointer to the dotted pair and we would hope to see "$(A \cdot A)$" appear on the output device. The LISP output routine, named *print*, can recognize that "$(A \cdot A)$" is a dotted pair since its *car* is not Χ. But how can *print* distinguish $(A \cdot A)$ from $(B \cdot B)$? The pointer in the preceding diagram will point to A in one case and to B in the other, but nothing about the atom tells us *what* to print. The simplest thing to do is to store a representation of the name on each p-list. This is done with another indicator called $PNAME$, standing for **print-name**. Each atom is guaranteed to have a print-name or "p-name". The print-name of the atom is what the LISP output routine will print as the name of the atom.

For example, the atom *BAZ* will have at least the following: [21]

PNAME	"BAZ"

where "BAZ" means a representation of the string of characters, *B, A, Z.*

When we represent such a property pair we must deal with representational problems of character strings. We desire strings of unbounded length, but must represent them in a machine with fixed word size. We will discuss a more general representation in Section 7.3, but here we will represent the print name by using the basic dotted-pair data structure.

p-name representation for *BAZ*

BAZ□□ means a memory location containing some encoding of the letters B, A, and Z. The symbol, □, represents some non-printing character; we are therefore assuming that a location can contain five characters.
We represent the print-name as a list so that we may allow atoms with p-names of unbounded length. The p-name for *BLETCH*, would be:

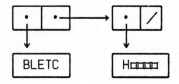

P-name structure for *BLETCH*

With such print-names on each property-list *print* can now operate. The *print* routine needs the print name and, as we shall see shortly, the input routine also needs the print name, but otherwise all LISP calculation is done using the internal pointers to the property lists. Several implementations exploit this observation by placing the print names in slower memory than that used for the main computation. Since access to print names is infrequent,

---

[21]Since *every* atom is guaranteed to have a print name, many implementations separate this property from the general p-list.

we can afford to spend more time in retrieving them. We will discuss more of the details of LISP input and output in Section 5.11.

The print-names BAZ□□, BLETC, and H□□□□, should be stored in atom space since their encodings should not be interpreted as pointers. Since "atom space" is no longer an appropriate descriptor for that space, we will give it a new name. We will call that area of memory which contains information *not* to be interpreted as pointers, **Full Word Space**, and abbreviate it as FWS.

In summary, we have discussed the details of a typical implementation of the class of S-exprs. Our non-atomic S-exprs have their branching structure stored in pointer space. Our initial discussion of atoms supposed a particular simple representation: simply store the encoding of the atom in a memory location in a separate space called atom space. Upon further reflection we decided that atoms should play a more active role in the implementation. Since identifiers are to be represented as atoms, we needed some way to represent those properties typically associated with identifiers. Identifiers in LISP are, among other things, used for names of functions and names of variables. We needed the ability to represent at least these two kinds of "values" with a LISP atom. We introduced the general scheme of property-lists and associated such a p-list with each LISP atom. All the things we know about a specific atom are stored on the p-list. We stored each atom uniquely; then to examine the properties of an atom only one structure need be located. Since all of our LISP programs must be read into the memory, we required that the input function keep atoms stored uniquely. On reading a literal atom, the program checks the current table of atoms. If the atom appears, the program returns a pointer to the entry. If the atom does not appear it constructs a new table entry consisting of the print name. One effect unique storage was to turn our abstract LISP-trees into list structure. Indeed, the representation of a LISP expression is a complex net of pointers; even atoms are now pointers. The only LISP objects we have represented which are *not* pointers are the actual print-names like BAZ□□.

To reinforce our discussion we illustrate the abstract picture of *NIL* and, on the next page, one implementation of the atom *NIL*. In all of the resulting worms there are only three elements in Full Word Space; everything else is a pointer.

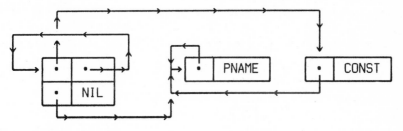

.1 A Picture of the Atom *NIL*

We have been writing the atom *NIL* as:

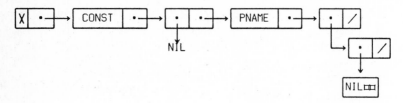

where the atoms for *PNAME* and *CONST* are represented as:

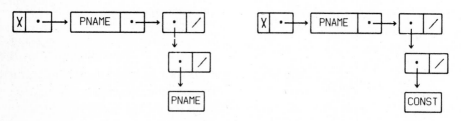

In full detail, *NIL* is represented as:

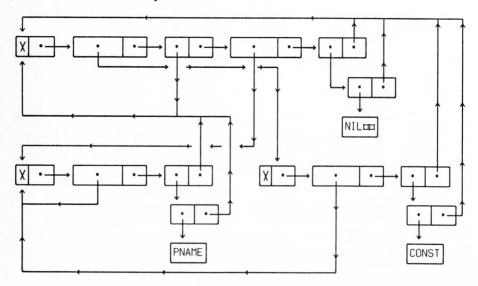

5.11 Input/Output: *read* and *print*

"...*Thus syntax is the servant of sematics, an appropriate relationship since the substance of the message is conveyed with the semantics, variations in syntax being an inessential trimming added on human-engineering grounds. ...*"

Vaughan Pratt, [Pra 73]

The implementation of LISP is simplified dramatically since a very large part of that implementation can be written in LISP itself. We have already seen that the evaluation process is expressible this way, and we will exploit this property again in dealing with compilers (Chapter 6).

In this section we will show that the majority of the LISP input and output routines can be written as LISP functions calling a very few primitive routines. The primitive routines are also described in LISP, though they would normally be coded in machine language.

The primitive functions are *ratom* and *patom*.

ratom[ ] is a function of no arguments. It reads the input string, constructing the next atom or special character (left paren, right paren or dot). It looks up that object in the atom table and returns a pointer to that table entry. [22] If no entry is found an appropriate entry is made. *ratom* skips over spaces and commas, only recognizing them as delimiters. It returns only atoms or special characters to *read*.

patom[*x*] is a function of one argument expecting an atom, left paren, right paren, blank, or dot as the value of its argument. It will print the p-name of that object on the output device.

To simplify matters, we need to refer to atoms whose print-names are the characters ")", "(", ".", and " " (blank). We will assume that *RPAR*, *LPAR*, *PERIOD*, and *BLANK* denote such atoms. For example, if the next input character is "(" then

eq[*ratom*[ ];*LPAR*] is true (and the input pointer is moved to the next character!).

patom[*PERIOD*] will have the effect of printing a "." on the output device.

The LISP scanner is *ratom*. A scanner must negotiate with the actual input device for input characters. The scanner builds the most basic

---

[22]Numerals are typically not stored uniquely; also they are given a simpler structure than the atomic p-list. See Section 7.9 for more details on LISP numbers.

ingredients, like identifiers or numbers, and only after such a basic block has been recognized is the next level of syntax analysis attempted. The units, also called tokens, which the scanner has built are passed to the **parser**.

A parser determines whether or not the input stream is a well-formed expression. The LISP parser is *read*; it builds a tree-representation of the input string, recognizing both S-expression and list-notation.

$$read <= \lambda[[\ ] \ \lambda[[j] \ [atom[j] \to j;$$
$$is\_lpar[j] \to read\_head[\ ];$$
$$t \to err[\ ]]$$
$$[ratom[\ ]]]$$

The call on *err* will terminate the input scanning immediately.

read_head will translate strings α acceptable in the context "(α". Thus α being "*A)*" or "*A (B . C))*" would be suitable for *read_head*; (A) and (A (B . C)) are S-exprs or lists. *. A)* would not be acceptable since (. A) is neither an S-expr nor list.
Therefore, if *read_head* sees:

an atom, then α is <atom>β);

a left parenthesis, then α is (β) δ);

a dot, then α is . β); this is an error;

a right parenthesis, then α is)

$$read\_head <= \lambda[[\ ]\lambda[[j] \ [atom[j] \to cons[j;read\_tail[]];$$
$$is\_lpar[j] \to cons[read\_head[\ ];$$
$$read\_tail[\ ]];$$
$$is\_rpar[j] \to NIL;$$
$$t \to err[\ ]]]$$
$$[ratom[\ ]]]$$

read_tail is looking for legal α's in the context "(<sexpr> α". The structure of this function is that of *read_head* except for recognition of dots. ". β)" is plausible in the context "(<sexpr> α". It is up to *read_cdr* to see if its expectations are fulfilled.

$$read\_tail <= \lambda[[\ ]\lambda[[j] \ [atom[j] \to cons[j;read\_tail[]];$$
$$is\_lpar[j] \to cons[\ read\_head[\ ];$$
$$read\_tail[\ ]];$$
$$is\_dot[j] \to read\_cdr[];$$
$$is\_rpar[j] \to NIL;$$
$$t \to err[\ ]]]$$
$$[ratom[\ ]]]$$

The only input legal after a dot is a S-expr or list followed by a right parenthesis. Therefore:

$read\_cdr <= \lambda[[\ ]\ \lambda[[j]\ [is\_rpar[ratom[\ ]] \rightarrow j;$
$$t \rightarrow err[\ ]\ ]]$$
$$[read[\ ]]]$$

Finally, here are some of the primitive recognizers which these functions use.

$$is\_dot[x] <= eq[x;PERIOD] \qquad is\_lpar[x] <= eq[x;LPAR]$$

The printing of an internalized LISP expression is straightforward.

$$print <= \lambda[[x]\ prin0[x];\ terpri[\ ];\ x]$$

terpri initiates a new output line.

$prin0 <= \lambda[[x][atom[x] \rightarrow patom[x];$
$$t \rightarrow patom[LPAR];\ prinbody[x]]]$$
$prinbody <= \lambda[[x]\ prin0[car[x]];$
$$[null[cdr[x]] \rightarrow patom[RPAR];$$
$$atom[cdr[x]] \rightarrow patom[BLANK];$$
$$patom[PERIOD];$$
$$patom[BLANK];$$
$$patom[cdr[x]];$$
$$patom[RPAR];$$
$$t \rightarrow prinbody[cdr[x]]]]$$

Notice that we have used the extended λ-expressions and conditional expression as described in Section 4.3. [23]

The basic *print* routine allows us to print data structures and program representations. However the printer will print duplications for a list structure which has shared branches and, worse yet, will not terminate if it is given a circular structure. Some implementations of LISP remedy this ailment; see [Ter 75] or [Int 75].

---

[23]Notice too that $print[(A .(B . C))]$ prints as $(A\ B . C)$. This is because *print* doesn't know that the structure is not a list until it sees the last dotted-pair. There are two ways of handling this: either require a type-code, telling whether the structure is a dotted pair or a list, represented as a dotted pair. Then *all* dotted pairs are printed in dot notation, and *all* lists are printed in list notation. The other alternative is to first examine the structure; if it is a list representation, then print it that way, otherwise print it as a dotted pair. This problem is another indication of "object vs. representation".

The output format is a simple linear string of atoms, numbers, spaces, and parentheses. For example a *print*-based program for printing function definitions might output the following as the definition of *member*:

(MEMBER (LAMBDA (X L) (COND
((NULL L) NIL) ((EQ X (FIRST L))
T) (T (MEMBER X (REST L)))))))

The print routine can break the text at the end of any atom; [24] the only restriction we place on printing of expressions is that what is *print*-ed must be *read*-able.

Even with a small definition like this, we have difficulty deciphering the structure. When functions or lists become large and deeply nested then readability becomes impossible. Most implementations of LISP supply formatting programs called "pretty-printers" or "grinders" to supplement the basic print routine.

A pretty-printer might print *member* as:

(MEMBER
(LAMBDA (X L)
(COND ((NULL L) NIL)
((EQ X (FIRST L)) T)
(T (MEMBER X (REST L)))))))

See Section 9.2 for a more detailed description of such formatting functions.

So far we have thrown all the I/O back on *ratom* and *patom*. Clearly *ratom* will be more interesting. All *patom* need do is get the p-name and print it. *ratom* should perform an efficient search of the atom table and if the atom is not found, add it to the table. All *ratom* has to work with is the actual character string which will be the p-name of some atom. What *ratom* could do is look at the p-name of each atom currently in the table of atoms; when it finds a match it returns a pointer to that atom; this is essentially the linear search scheme of *assoc*. If the appropriate atom is not found it can build a new one consisting of the p-name, add it to the table, and return a pointer to this new entry. In the next section we will introduce an alternative scheme called hashing.

---

[24]Some implementations even allow the printer to break in the middle of an atom. This is accomplished by designating a special character for carriage control, and the *read* routine knows to ignore the immediately following end-of-line sequence.

Problems

1. You might have noticed that the definitions of *read_head* and *read_tail* are almost identical: the difference involves treatment of dots. Write new versions of these functions utilizing a common routine and functional arguments.
2. Write a set of BNF equations that generate the same set of sentences that *read* parses.
3. Write a version of *read* which only accepts list notation.

5.12 Table Searching: Hashing

Table lookup is analogous to the problem of looking up words in a dictionary. The scheme of *assoc* is analogous to beginning at the first page of the dictionary and proceeding linearly, word-by-word and page-by-page, through the book until the word in question is found. More usually, we look at the first character of the word and go immediately to the subsection of the dictionary which has the words beginning with that character. We know that if we cannot find the definition of our word in that subsection we need look no further. We delimit our search even further by keying on subsequent characters in the word. Finally we may resort to linear search to locate the word on a specific page or column. A machine might mimic the dictionary search and subdivide the table into 26 subsections. [25] However, since it is the machine which will subdivide and index into the table, there may be schemes which are computationally more convenient for the machine. The scheme should also result in rather even distribution of atoms in the subsections. If the majority of the atoms end up in the same partition of the table we will have gained little improvement in the search efficiency.

An algorithm used to determine which partition a particular element belongs in is called a **hashing algorithm** or hashing function. One obstacle in such schemes is the management of each partition. If more than one element "hashes" to a partition then we have a **collision**. There are two basic strategies available to resolve such a collision. The first, called **open addressing** involves re-hashing the element, thus refining the partition, until no collision exists. In the second, called **bucket hashing**, the hashing function hashes to a "bucket". All the elements with the same hash number are stored in the same "bucket"; a separate search, perhaps linear search, is used to discover if an element is in the bucket; and an element will appear in at most one bucket. Since most LISP implementations use bucket hashing, we will describe that scheme in more detail.

The search algorithms are applied within *ratom* after an identifier has

---

[25] That is, a base 26 sort.

been delimited. All *ratom* has at that time is the encoding of the actual name of the atom; call that string *chr_str*. The hashing function will use *chr_str* to determine which bucket must contain the atom. Given the bucket number, we examine the list of atoms in that bucket, comparing each print-name against *chr_str*. If a print-name matches, we return a pointer to the property list of that atom. If the atom with print-name *chr_str* does not appear in that bucket we are assured that it does not appear anywhere in the table. In this case we create a new atom structure, add it to that bucket, and the value of *ratom* is a pointer to that new structure.

Here is a simple hashing function:

1. Assume that we have N+1 buckets, numbered 0, 1, 2 ... N.
2. Take the numeric representation of *chr-str* and divide that number by N+1.
3. Look at the remainder. It's a number between 0 and N.
4. Use that remainder as the index to the appropriate bucket.

The LISP atom table, usually called *OBLIST* (for object list), is a list of buckets. Each bucket is a list of the atoms which 'hash' to that bucket. We actually represent the object list as an array named *oblist*. Arrays are discussed in full in Section 7.2, but basically are an efficient storage representation for sequences of fixed length. In this case we can allocate a block of sequential cells and use the addressing structure of the hardware to do a rapid subscript calculation. The hash number will give us the array subscript and we can go to the correct bucket immediately; we won't have to *cdr* down the object list to locate the bucket.

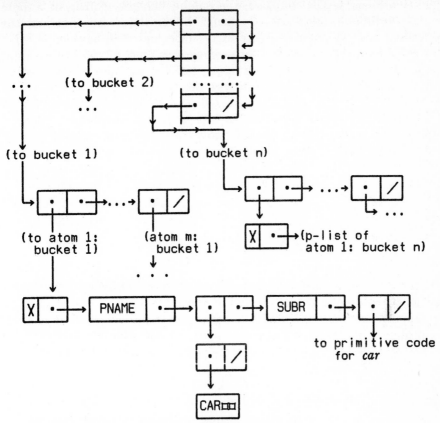

Partial Object List; where atom 1:bucket 1 is *CAR*

Note: Though the top level of *OBLIST* is stored sequentially for fast access by the hasher, the *cdr*-parts are chained together in a sequential list so that the table will have the same structure as any other list. The chained representation is used by any LISP process other than the hasher.[26]

---

[26]In particular, the garbage collector uses this linking. As a further implementation note, the implementors of MACLISP noted the frequent use of single character atoms and added a special section to the top-level of the object list. A contiguous block of cells, of size equal to the number of

Whether a linear search and storage technique, like *assoc-pairlis*, or a more complex technique like hashing should be employed depends on the application, and the speed and size of the machine. The hash table takes extra space both for storage and for program, but gives a faster search time. The linear technique requires less space, but can be quite slow. Several books cover searching and sorting in great detail ([Gri 71], [Knu 72]).

MACLISP embellishes the basic *OBLIST* idea in an important way. That system will allow several object lists to exist simultaneously This is useful since several cooperating LISP subsystems may exist; for example the LISP editor, debugger, and compiler are all written in LISP and may all be used within the same interactive session. There is a potential difficulty since each of those subsystems may use names which conflict with names in the user's programs. Multiple object lists are a way to overcome this problem. [27] Only one object list is current at any time, but several may exist in the system. Object lists are swapped by λ-binding to the identifier *obarray*. [28]

Consider: $\lambda[[obarray]\xi][ob_1]$

Assuming that ob_1 is bound to an object list, then within the evaluation of ξ the symbols and bindings of ob_1 would be accessible.

Finally, we want to present a version of *ratom* which uses a hash organization. In this discussion, we will restrict ourselves to literal atoms, leaving the reader to supply the necessary parts for recognition of numbers.

We will recognize three classes of characters:

1. The class of letters will include the alphabetic characters.
2. The class of delimiters consists of those characters which signal the end of an atom. For this scanner we assume space and carriage control are delimiters.
3. The special characters will consist of "(", ")" and "." .

Special characters also act as delimiters in LISP and this results in a slight complication. Consider the partial string "AB)C". Our scanner should scan the "A", scan the "B", and scanning the space, should recognize a delimiter. It should recognize the AB as an atom, and signal *read*. The string will be reduced to ")C". The next time *read* calls *ratom* the right parenthesis will be seen, recognized as a special character and an indication of that will be returned to *read*.

Now consider the string "AB)C"; *ratom* will scan "A" and "B" as before. It will then scan the ")". It now needs to do *two* things; it must signal *read*

---

characters, was added. On reading a single character atom, the corresponding entry in the table is examined. A *NIL* says the atom hasn't been seen before; otherwise its p-list representation resides there.

[27]Static binding is another way to handle the problem.

[28]An object list is called object array in MACLISP since the table is represented as an array. We discuss arrays in Section 7.2.

about the atom it has seen, but it must also remember the ")" so that the *next* time *read* asks for information, it sees the ")" and not the "*C*". We handle this problem by using a global variable named *lst_chr*. This variable is initialized to *NIL* and remains that way until our anomalous situation occurs. At that time the special character is placed in *lst_chr*, and *ratom* exits normally. So, whenever *ratom* is called, the first thing it does is check the contents of *lst_chr*. If it is non-empty, its contents is returned, as *lst_chr* is set empty again.

$ratom <= \lambda[[]\ prog[[chr]$
$[lst\_chr \rightarrow swap[lst\_chr;chr];return[chr]];$
$a\ chr \leftarrow readch[];$
$[is\_let[chr] \rightarrow stuf\_buf[chr];return[ratom_1[]];$
$is\_delim[chr] \rightarrow go[a];$
$is\_spec[chr] \rightarrow return[chr]]]]$

This procedure uses tricks advertised in Section 5.5; it uses *lst_chr* as a predicate, knows that *prog* variables are initialized to *NIL*, and knows that the representation of Ⲧ is *NIL*. With that knowledge, *swap* swaps the contents of *chr* and *lst_chr*.

The routine *readch* gets the next character, and *stuf_buf* is used to save the character string which is to become an atom. The character string is built up in *buf*.

$ratom_1 <= \lambda[[]\ prog[[chr;chr\_str]$
$l\ chr \leftarrow readch[];$
$[is\_delim[chr] \rightarrow return[intern[chr\_str]];$
$is\_spec[chr] \rightarrow lst\_chr \leftarrow chr;\ return[intern[chr\_str]];$
$Ⲧ \rightarrow stuf\_buf[chr];\ go[l]]]]$

If *ratom_1* sees a special character it is saved in *lst_chr*.

$intern <= \lambda[[l]\ prog[[bucket]$
$bucket \leftarrow oblist[hash[maknam[l]]];$
$a\ [null[bucket] \rightarrow return[insert[l]]];$
$[right\text{-}one[get[first[bucket];$
$PNAME];l] \rightarrow return[first[bucket]]];$
$bucket \leftarrow rest[bucket];$
$go[a]]]$

maknam takes our character string and converts it into an appropriate numeric representation; for example, the input string might exceed one machine word. *hash* returns the bucket number of its argument, and *insert* builds the atom and inserts it into a bucket. *right-one* is a predicate used to check if an atom has the right print-name.

An implementation of *ratom* may be generalized so that the class of special characters and delimiters can be varied. This is done using a representation of a character table whose name entries are characters, and whose value entries determine the *ratom* properties. This allows LISP users to define their own parsers and scanners. LISP's modifiable input routine, coupled with its data structures and extendible evaluator make LISP an excellent tool for building more sophisticated language systems.

On page 211 we introduced the abbreviation $'x$ for *quote[x]*. This *quote* facility is an instance of a device called a *read* macro; it is the duty of *ratom* to recognize such constructs. Whenever *ratom* sees the prefix $'$ it reads the next S-expr α and returns the list $(QUOTE\ \alpha)$ as value. In some systems ([Moo 74]) users may define their own *read* macros. For example a definition like:

$$'\ <_r = \lambda[[]\ list[QUOTE;read[]]]$$

would signal LISP to change the character table entry for $"\ '\ "$ to be a *read* macro. If $"\ '\ "$ appeared during an input operation, then the body of the *read*-macro would be evaluated; that would call *read*, and then form a list with $QUOTE$ and the result. The resulting list would be returned to within the original input process.

MACLISP also defines a comment facility using a *read* macro. The occurrence of a semi-colon signals the beginning of a comment; all characters to the end of the line are taken as commentary.

Several implementations also include abbreviations to decrease the number of parentheses needed. For example "[" and "]" are often defined to be "super-parentheses". The "[" acts like a "(" but its scope runs to the next "]", constructing sufficient ")" to balance the intervening expression. Similarly, the scope of a "]" extends to the prior matching "["; if none exists, the expression is completed by supplying sufficient ")" to balance.
For example:

$$((A\ B)\ ((C\ D\ E)))\quad = ((A\ B)\ ((C\ D\ E))]$$
$$= [(A\ B)\ ((C\ D\ E))]$$
$$= ((A\ B)\ ((C\ D\ E]$$

and
$$(A\ [B\ (C]) = (A\ (B\ (C)))$$

Regardless of the specifics of the implementation, the input routines will read a list representation of a LISP expression and convert it into an S-expr. For example, let's see what happens if we want to evaluate

$$eq[x;A]$$

This will be presented to the machine as:

$$(EQ\ X\ (QUOTE\ A))$$

That input will be recognized with the *read-eval-print* loop:

$$prog[[]$$
$$a\ print[eval[read[];(\ )]];$$
$$go[a]]$$

read will begin parsing the sequence of characters; it will depend on *ratom* to return indications of the special characters, and will depend on *ratom* to properly represent each occurrence of an atom. The parser knows about the representation we have chosen for lists and will use *cons* to build up the S-expression form:

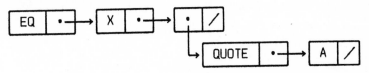

The references to the atoms *EQ, X, A,* and *QUOTE* are actually pointers to the atoms. Each atom is located only once by the reader. After that we have direct access to atom and its property list.

Since the input routines perform several *cons* operations; we should look at the details of *cons*.

5.13 A First Look At *cons*

The *cons* operation is quite different from the other LISP primitives. The other primitives manipulate existing S-expressions, whereas *cons* must construct a new S-expression from two existing S-exprs. Given representations of two S-exprs, say x and y, *cons*$[x;y]$ must get a new cell, put a pointer to the representation of x in the *car*-part of the cell and a pointer to the representation of y in the *cdr*-part and return a pointer to the new cell:

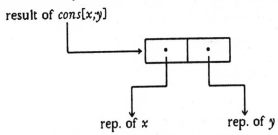

result of *cons*$[x;y]$

rep. of x rep. of y

Before computation is begun, only the atomic structure for the initial LISP system table uses cells in the pointer area. The remaining pointer cells are linked together and form the **free space list** or **FS list**. [29] Whenever *cons* needs a cell, the first cell in the FS list is used and the FS list is set to the *rest* of the FS list.

---

[29]LISP free space is an instance of "heap storage" ([Alg 75]). The rationale for heap storage is that storage usage is not sufficiently disciplined that its allocation and deallocation can be predicted. Therefore some more global management scheme is required.

For example the following represents the effect of *cons[A;B]*

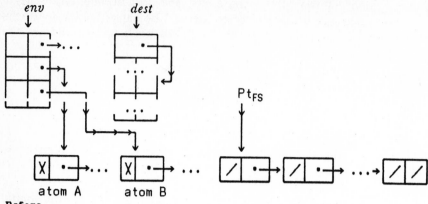

Before

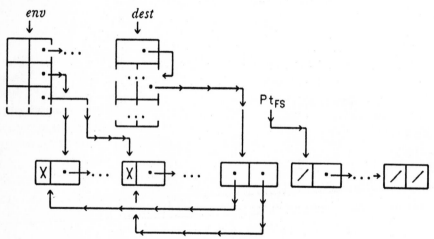

After

As the computation continues, cells are taken from the FS list. When a *cons* operation needs a cell and the FS list is empty, the computation is suspended and a **storage reclaimer** is called. The reclaimer is often known by a more colorful name: the **garbage collector**. The job of the garbage collector is to locate cells for a new FS list.

5.14 Storage Management: Garbage Collection

During the course of a computation, contents of cells which were taken from the FS list often become unnecessary. For example, if we ask LISP to evaluate something as simple as:

(CONS (QUOTE A) (QUOTE B)), many cells are used:

1. At least seven cells are needed just to read in the expression:

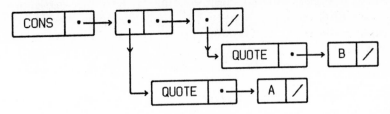

If some of the atoms are not present in the atom table, more cells will be needed.

2. One cell will be needed to perform the *cons* operation. See the previous example.

After the computation is completed, LISP will print "(*A . B*)" and wait for more input. After the *print* statement is completed none of the eight mentioned cells are needed. They are garbage. In the current example, these "garbage cells" could have been explicitly returned to the free list, but in general it is difficult to know exactly which cells *are* garbage.[30] In Section 7.7 we will see how these difficulties can arise.

The responsibility for reclamation is therefore passed to the LISP system. The *cons* procedure removes cells from the FS list, and its FWS counterpart *fwcons*, removes cells from the FWS list when making numbers or print-names. These two functions are the only functions allowed to manipulate the free storage lists. When either list becomes empty, the garbage collector is called.

The fundamental assumption of garbage collection is:

At any point in a LISP computation, all cells which contain parts of the computation are reachable (for example, through *car-cdr* chains) from a fixed set of known cells or base registers.

The first phase of the garbage collector, called the **marking phase**, marks all of the list structure which is currently active. By definition, a cell is active if it is reachable from the base registers. The base registers include: pointers to the beginning of the atom table and the environment chain; a pointer to the control chain is also included since partial results are stored there. Active cells therefore include all the atoms in the atom table and all the associated elements on property lists. Any partial computations which have been generated will also be marked.

---

[30]Experiments have been performed in which LISP programmers were allowed to return "garbage" to the FS list themselves. The results were disastrous; list structure thought to be garbage was returned to the FS list even though the structure was still being used by other computations.

In terms of our implementation, we mark from the object list, from *dest*, and from *control* (see page 204). If deep binding is used, we mark the elements reachable through *env*. If shallow binding is used, then marking of *oblist* would capture all the values; even the ones which may not be accessible as λ-values. What we should do instead is mark the non-value properties on atoms using *oblist*; we then mark the values separately using the current *env* skeleton tree.

A structure might be referenced several times in the marking process, since we allow shared structure, and since the implementation will be referencing structures also referenced by the user's program. We must take this into account since, though naive marking of an already marked structure is at wasteful, it is fatal if the structure is self-referential. Once all the active structure has been marked, we proceed to the **sweep phase**.

The sweep phase proceeds linearly through memory, collecting all those cells which have *not* been marked. [31] These unmarked cells are chained together via their *cdr*-parts to form a new FS list. The FS pointer is set to the beginning of this list. The unmarked cells in FWS comprise the new FWS list.

If there is sufficient room in a full word to contain a pointer, then we chain the words together; otherwise we must designate the FWS list some other way.

Garbage collection is a very general storage management technique. It has become a standard tool for implementors of complex systems. It was invented by the original LISP implementation team. The basic ideas have been embellished over the years to account for larger real memories, virtual memories, different implementations of LISP data, and different machine architectures; but the basic ideas are simple. More complex algorithms will be discussed in Section 7.3 and on page 397.

5.15 A Simple LISP Garbage Collector

We will now write a garbage collector in LISP to mark and sweep nodes in FS and FWS.

---

[31]The sweep phase is sometimes a good place to unmark the marked cells. This depends on the implementation. If each word carries a "mark bit" then, perform the unmarking; if the marked flags are all localized in a separate bit table (Section 7.5) then there is no advantage to doing the unmarking now.

The algorithm will have three main functions:

initialize[x;y] initializes the marking device for each cell in the space between
    x and *y*. *initialize* will be called twice; once for FS and once for FWS.
    The next algorithm does the actual marking.

mark[l] will be called for each base register *l* which points to active list
    structure. If the word is in FWS *mark* will mark it and return; if the
    word has already been marked it simply return, since we are assured
    that any cells further down the structure have already been marked.
    Otherwise the word is in FS and thus has a *car* and a *cdr*; mark the
    word; recursively mark the *car*; recursively mark the *cdr*.

sweep[x;y] collects all inaccessible cells in the space delimited by *x* and *y*.
    sweep will be called twice; once to generate a new free space list and
    once to generate a new full word space list. Elements of these free lists
    will be chained together by their *cdr* parts. The initialization and
    sweep phases of this garbage collector are very similar and, as we
    mentioned above, can sometimes be combined. Both these phases must
    be assured of reaching every node in the space.

These main functions use several other functions and predicates:

fwswrdp[x] is true just in the case that *x* is a word in FWS. This is used as
    one of the termination conditions of *mark*.

markA[x] marks word *x* as accessible.

markNA[x] marks word *x* as not accessible.

Ap[x] is true if word *x* is marked "accessible".

up[x]: If *x* is at location n then *up[x]* is location n+1.

rplacd[x;y] modifies *x* by replacing its *cdr*-part with *y*. The value returned is
    the new *x*.

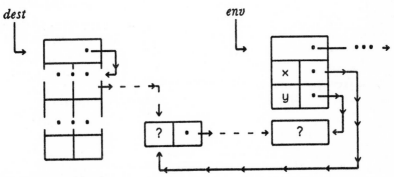

Algorithm for *rplacd*

Can you write *rplacd* as a LISP function?

$initialize <= \lambda[[x,y]\ prog[[]$
$a\quad markNA[x];$
$x \leftarrow up[x];$
$[eq[x,y] \rightarrow return[t]];$
$go\ [a]]]$

$mark <= \quad \lambda[[l]\ [Ap[l] \rightarrow t;$
$fwswrdp[l] \rightarrow markA[l];$
$t \rightarrow markA[l];$
$mark[car[l]];$
$mark[cdr[l]]\ ]]$

$sweep <= \lambda[[x,y]\ prog[[z]$
$a\ [not[Ap[x]] \rightarrow\ z \leftarrow rplacd[\ x;z]];$
$x \leftarrow up[x];$
$[eq[x,y] \rightarrow return\ [z]];$
$go[a]]]$

As indicated previously, there are alternatives to garbage collection. If the data-structure manipulations are particularly simple one might leave storage management to the programmer.[32] There is an intermediate area between garbage collection and explicit management. First notice that storage management becomes quite simple if there is no sharing of sublists. However sharing substructures can save space and careful modification of shared structures can communicate global information between algorithms. A rich class of symbolic data manipulations fall into the category of shared, but non-circular, structures. In this case, storage can be managed by the **reference counter** method.

Instead of using a garbage collector, we might associate a counter, called a **reference counter**, with each list when it is built. In that counter we will store the number of references to that list. The counter will be initialized to 1 when the list is created. Whenever the list is shared we increase the counter by 1; whenever the list is no longer to be shared by some list structure, we decrease the counter by 1. When the count goes to 0 we can put the cells of the list in the free space list.

A difficulty with the reference counter scheme is the inability to collect

---

circular lists. A circular list is a list structure which is self-referential. [33]
Consider the following sequence:

1. Manufacture a list, x: $x \leftarrow (B\ I\ G\ L\ I\ S\ T)$. Reference count is 1.

2. Circularize it: $x \leftarrow circle[x]$;. Reference count is now 2.

3. Delete all references to x: $x \leftarrow NIL$. Reference count reverts to 1.

The list is no longer referenced, but it is not on the free space list, and has thus been lost to the system.

Two less serious considerations should be mentioned in conjunction with reference counters. First, each node which is to be collected with this scheme must have an associated reference field to contain the count. That requires extra space, and usually imposes a maximum size for the reference count. If that maximum is reached, either an additional space is allocated, or the filled count may never be decremented and the associated structure must be garbage collected.

The second problem involves decrementing counts. Whenever a count goes to zero the counts associated with its immediate successors must also be decremented. This process is applied recursively until non-zero counts are encountered. The bookkeeping for such a task is non-trivial.

There are significant storage management problems which are amenable to reference counting. LISP generates very intertwined structures; therefore these alternative methods are insufficient in general. However, some parts of LISP implementations could use reference counting; we will discuss some of these aspects in Section 5.20. For an excellent discussion and analysis of storage management schemes see [Mul 76].

Problems

1. This problem deals with what is known in LISP as **hash consing** ([Got 74]). We have been storing atoms uniquely, but it should be clear from the behavior of *cons* that non-atomic S-exprs are *not* stored uniquely. Storing single copies of any S-expr would save space. For example, the non-atomic structure of $((A \cdot B) \cdot (A \cdot B))$ could be represented with two cells rather than three. Unique storage is not without its difficulties. What problems do you foresee in implementing such a scheme?

2. We said on page 267 that many LISP computations generate list structure rather than true LISP-trees. Give an example.

3. Can you write a LISP function $circle <= \lambda[[x] ...]$ which will take a list x and make it circular. Thus:

---

[33]LISP 1 ([McC 60]) disallowed circular list, but succeeding LISP dialects have allowed arbitrary binary structure.

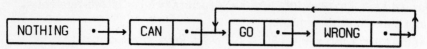

This list is circular on its "last two" elements. Printing such structures is not possible using the *print* function.

4. What LISP operations generate structures such that a reference counter implementation would not suffice?

5.16   A Review of the Structure of the LISP Machine

We have a good portion of the storage conventions for LISP set out. A difficult area involves the organization of the data structures to perform the correct binding and unbinding of variables. Before we tackle that, we give a diagram showing the basic structure of LISP memory.

```
••• THE SUBCONSCIOUS •••
eval and friends
read and print
the garbage collector
the base registers for marking;
   these include:
 FS pointer
 FWS pointer
 atom table(OBLIST) pointer
 registers for partial results
    dest, control
 the access chain
```

```
••• POINTER SPACE •••
the free space list
those parts of S-exprs containing
   car- and cdr-parts.
```

```
••• FULL WORD SPACE •••
the full word space list
atom print names
numbers
```

Structure of LISP memory

5.17   Implementations of Binding

In Section 3.5 and Section 3.11 we discussed deep binding and shallow binding respectively. That discussion took place at a reasonably abstract level. The next few sections discuss these binding implementations in more detail. We first examine some of the possible pitfalls in the implementation of LISP; then we give deep and shallow implementations for an important subset of LISP. Finally, we sketch some of the methods available for implementing the full language in an efficient manner.

Though much of this discussion deals with the binding stategies of

LISP, and therefore with control structure, we are restricting ourselves to the data structure requirements. The next chapter shows how the control structures of LISP implementations manipulate these data structures.

Consider the evaluation of a form: $f[a_1; \ldots ;a_n]$

where: $f <= \lambda[[x_1; \ldots ;x_n] \ldots g[\ldots] \ldots ;i[\ldots]],$

$g <= \lambda[[\ldots] \ldots h[\ldots]],$

and $i <= \lambda[[\ldots] \ldots j[\ldots]]$

Typically a picture like the following occurs, where the instance of function name means a block of λ-bindings necessary to begin evaluation of that function:

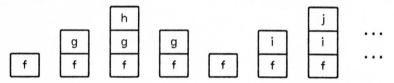

We build up a stack of λ-binding blocks as we continue to enter procedures, and as we leave a procedure we remove that block of bindings from the stack. When we wish to know the value of a variable we look down the stack for the first occurrence of that variable; the associated binding is the desired value. However, LISP allows functional arguments and functional values; these constructs require modification of the behavior modelled in this simple blocks world.

When we recognize a functional argument, we note the block which is currently on the top of the stack. When we apply that functional argument, intervening blocks will have been stacked; we change the environment such that the lookup of non-local variables takes place beginning with the saved block, rather than with the top of the stack.

However, if h say, generated a functional value which is to be applied in the context of j then we must retain those values in the f-g-h stack in such a way that they may be used to restore the enviroment when we desire to apply the functional value in the f-i-j stack.

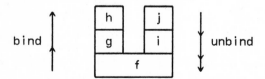

We will discuss data structure requirements for implementation of these three LISP subsets: first, simple function application; then, functional arguments; and finally, functional values.

The mechanism which we described in the initial blocks model occurs quite naturally in computer science. It is called a stack. [34] The important characteristics of stacks are that they are lists such that additions and deletions can only be made at the front of the list.

What is of interest to us now is that stacks have a particularly efficient implementation; due to the very regular way in which stacks are manipulated, the linked allocation implementation is not usually necessary. [35] Instead a stack can be implemented as:

1. A sequence of contiguous locations.
2. A pointer initialized to point *before* the first of these locations.
3. An operation, typically called **push** which places a new object in the stack. This can be accomplished by adding 1 to the value of the stack pointer, and then putting a representation of the object in the cell currently referenced by the pointer.
4. An operation called **pop** which gets the first value in the stack and then decrements the pointer by 1.
5. Though the abstract structure of a stack does not involve limitations on the length of stack-space, any representation should include techniques for assuring that the stack pointer stays within its allotted space. See the preceding footnote.

Notice that the *concat* operation can be interpreted as *pushing* and the *rest* operation as *popping*. Indeed our earlier manipulations of symbol tables effectively used such stack operations. This is particularly apparent in the representation of symbol tables given on page 124.

---

[34]Stacks are closely related to a theoretical device called a push-down automaton. There, only the top element of the stack is accessible. We take a more pragmatic position, allowing access to elements within the stack, and indeed modification of elements within the stack; but removal of elements from within the stack is not allowed. To remove an element, we must first remove the elements above it.

[35]The typical model for a stack is a contiguous block of memory but that ignores the question of exceeding the bounds of that memory allocation. A stack can be implemented in a discontinuous fashion ([Bis 74]) as long as the stack manipulating functions are able to cope with such behavior. The degenerate case of such discontinuous stacks is a linked allocation scheme.

We will discuss the binding process in terms of a sequence of three events:

1. *bind* describes what the implementation does when we are ready to call a procedure. The actual parameters are evaluated and we are ready to add them to the environment and evaluate the body of the procedure.

2. *lookup* will determine how values are located in the current environment.

3. *unbind* will describe what has to be done as we prepare to exit from a procedure.

5.18 Stack Implementation of a LISP subset: Deep Bound

The stack implementation of simple function application is a straightforward implementation of our blocks picture. We have two stacks which operate synchronously. One stack is called the **name stack**; the other is called the **value stack**. The name stack maintains the λ-variables (and generated names, if a primitive is called). The top of the name stack defines the origin of the environment. When the value of a variable is requested *lookup* proceeds down the name stack, looking for the first occurrence of the variable. The corresponding position in the value stack contains the desired value.

When we recognize a function application, we begin the evaluation of the actual parameters. As each parameter is evaluated, the result is pushed into the value stack. When all the parameters have been evaluated, we are ready to evaluate the body of the expression. At that point *bind* pushes the λ-variables onto the name stack. When we complete the evaluation of the body of the expression *unbind* pops the λ-variables from the name stack, and pops their values from the value stack.

Since the λ-variables are removed from the stack as a group we can sometimes speed up the operation by storing block sizes in the stack. Also, the word size of the machine may allow using one stack for both names and values. For example:

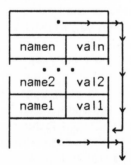

where val1 is furthest down the stack since it was pushed on first, and

where all references to name i and val i are really pointers to appropriate
S-expressions (atoms or dotted pairs). The "back pointer" is used for
removing blocks of bindings, but it is also a representation of the control link
discussed in Section 3.8.

A slight modification of this scheme is sufficient to support
implementation of functional arguments. An additional piece of information
is added to guide *lookup* in its search for the next block of bindings. Instead
of proceeding linearly down the stack, *lookup* proceeds linearly through a
block and at the end of each block is information telling *lookup* where the
next block of bindings is to be found. Recall that information is called the
access link (Section 3.8).

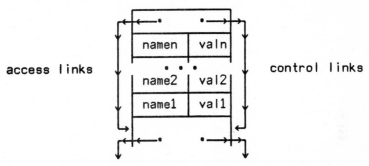

access links   control links

In simple function application, the access links and control links are
identical. The evaluation of a functional argument will generate an access
link, pointing to the current stack. That is, the *function*-construct is
responsible for saving the binding environment by saving a pointer to the
current top of the name and value stack. When a functional argument is
applied, the access link will be set to that saved binding environment
(page 146). Since we are restricting attention to functional arguments, we are
assured that the application of that argument will occur within an expression
which dynamically surrounds the creation of the functional argument. This
means that our environment pointer will indeed be a pointer down the stack.
The use of functional values invalidates that assumption. Before examining
that problem we will discuss shallow binding for these same LISP subsets.

5.19 Stack Implementation of a LISP Subset: Shallow Bound

A stack implementation of shallow binding allows some elegant economies.
We can use a stack implementation for the first shallow binder of
Section 3.11. There we had a collection of bindings associated with the
identifier. Without loss of generality, we can organize *mkenv* such that the
new binding is added in front of any previous binding. Now if we are only
evaluating simple function applications, *lookup* will find the desired binding

provided the unbinding operation removes the first binding as it exits the procedure. In this way, binding and unbinding act on the value entries in a stack-like fashion. Instead of associating a separate stack with each variable and accessing the value through the top of the stack, we associate a single value cell with each variable and store the saved values of all variables on a common stack. The "shallowest" of the shallow schemes, which only used the value cell, can also be extended to handle functional arguments.

The implementation of *lookup* will be simple for either shallow scheme: take the value in the value cell. Since the value cell will be maintained to *always* contain the proper binding of a variable, the distinction between local and non-local variables vanishes. The contents of the value cell is *the* current value for any variable.

We first review the process of shallow binding with the value cell, including the details we added in Section 4.6. When an application is recognized we allocate a block to contain the values of the actual parameters; that is the *dest* block. As the arguments are evaluated, the results are sent to the appropriate slots in the *dest* block. [36] When all the arguments are evaluated, we link the *dest* block onto the front of the environment, but as we do that we *swap* the current contents of the affected value cells with the new values. This establishes the new values in the value cells while saving the prior bindings. We are now ready to evaluate the body of the application. When evaluation is completed we swap *back*, using the first block of the saved environment chain; then we remove that first block from the chain. Since we are assuming a simple function call, that old *dest* block is no longer accessible and can be collected. [37] The allocation and de-allocation process is stack-like; we will develop our implementation using a stack called the Special Pushdown stack. This stack will be referenced by a stack pointer called SP or called ENV when we wish to reinforce its relation to the more general environment structures.

In the spirit of the evaluator of Section 4.6, we would evaluate $\lambda[[x;y]\ \xi][C;D]$ as follows:

1. Allocate space for the parameters x and y. This space is reserved on the top of the ENV stack, and is referenced by a pointer named DEST.
2. Evaluate the actual parameters and send the results to the *dest* block.
3. Swap the contents of the value cells for x and y with the contents of the *dest* block. Move ENV to point to the *dest* block.

---

[36]This scheme will also work with multi-valued functions.

[37]Since the *dest* block is no longer accessible, it was unnecessary to *swap* back; we could have simply *restored* the value cells. The swap was described in preparation for more general implementations.

4. Evaluate ξ. Within ξ, *lookup* will go to the value cells for all variable references.
5. Restore the old environment. Swap the contents of the first block of ENV with the contents of the appropriate value cells.
6. Set ENV to point at the prior block.

To reinforce these notions we supply a more detailed implementation. We will implement our value cells as elements of the property lists. The property name will be $VALUE$, and the corresponding property value will be the value cell. Assume x and y are currently bound to A and B respectively; and assume we wish to evaluate:

$$\lambda[[x;y]\;\xi][C;D]$$

We assume ENV is in some well-defined state:

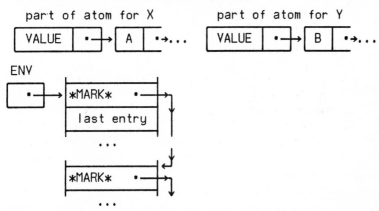

In this implementation, the stack is organized in blocks. The allocation operation claims space from the top of the stack and puts a special mark in the top of the ENV stack to delimit the block of λ-rebindings; that marked entry will also contain the *dest* pointer. The implementation will indicate the new block by pointing to it by DEST. The allocation routine is also responsible for filling the name-entries of the *dest* block. Those entries will be represented as pointers to the value cell entry on the property list of the atom.

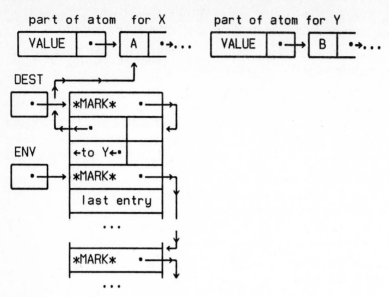

The *send* operation will fill the *dest* entries for *x* and *y*. The *next* operation will increment the *dest* pointer so that after all entries have been made to the *dest* block, the *dest* pointer will indicate the next block of saved bindings.

With *x* and *y* bound to C and D in the *dest* block, we are ready to swap the value cells. After the swap the picture is:

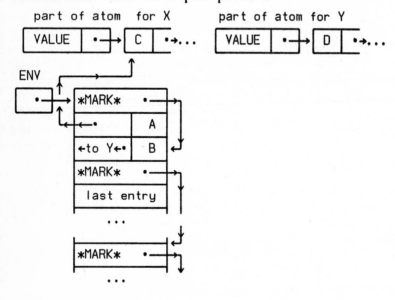

Now x and y have values C and D respectively and the previous bindings are saved on the ENV stack. We may now begin the evaluation of ξ assured that we will get the expected values for x and y. We have also saved sufficient information to restore the previous values afterwards. Since we are assuming simple function composition, the unbind operation can simply "pop" entries off of the top of ENV into the value cells rather than swap them with the value cells.

The unbinder restores the first block of saved values using the pointers to the value cells as destinations for the values.[38] This stack of previous values is also visited by the garbage collector; it may be that the only copy of some value is accessible only through the ENV stack. It would be most unfortunate if the garbage collector neglected to mark that entry and the unbinding mechanism later tried to restore the value.

This implementation works quite well for simple λ-binding and lookup. Changing environments is a bit of work, but the access to the values of variables is relatively rapid, particularly if we make sure that the value cell is always stored at a known position relative to the beginning of the property list. In describing this implementation we have used more representation than might seem appropriate. In particular the representation of the value cell as a linked list seems unnecessarily explicit. This was done to illuminate the pointer modifications involved in binding and unbinding.

We would like to implement functional arguments in this shallow binder. Recall how deep binding coped. When we recognized an instance of a functional argument we saved a pointer to the current environment. When we *applied* the functional argument we restored the symbol table in such a way that global variables were accessed in the saved environment while local variables were found in the current environment. We must try to do the same with the shallow-binding. The action taken when a functional argument is recognized is quite similar to our previous solution: when *function* is seen, save the current ENV pointer. This setting of ENV establishes the binding environment, and is therefore callled the **binding context pointer**. The action therefore, manufactures a triple $(FUNARG$ <function> <binding context pointer>$)$.

However, the action required when we wish to apply the functional argument is much more complicated. In the deep binding implementation we just set up a new access chain such that the local table referred to binding environment saved by the $FUNARG$ construction. The problem with the shallow-binder is that ENV only reflects the *incremental* changes in the environments during the computation. To retrieve the environment current

---

[38]An alternative implementation would only store the saved values, without explicitly saving the locations, and without marking the stack. In this implementation the unbinder would require an argument describing which variables needed restoring.

when the functional argument was bound, we must unwind ENV back to the binding environment; we must also save the current activation environment so that we may return to *it* when finished with the functional argument. Since we are dealing with a functional argument, rather than a functional value, we can easily locate the binding context pointer. The pointer is *below* the current ENV in the stack. We search down the stack for that saved pointer, swapping back the saved value cells. When we reach the binding context pointer we stop. At that time the value cells have been restored to the binding environment and the segment of the stack between the activation environment and the binding environment accurately reflects the bindings which were made between binding and activation; that is, that segment of the stack is deep bound. That stack segment must be saved so that the activation environment can be restored, thus ENV is not restored to the binding context, but remains where it was.

This process is complex enough to warrant an example.

An example of shallow binding and *FUNARG*

I Assume that x initially has value *1* and the SP pointer is at location SP1,

II then assume that a λ-binding rebinds x to *2*;

III in this new context, assume a functional argument, g, is to be bound to a function-variable f.

IV-V As the computation continues x is rebound first to *3* and within *that* context rebound again to *4*.

VI Finally f is applied; this will resurrect g [39] requiring a restoration of the environment current at step **III**.

---

[39]From the value cell of f as *(FUNARG G SP2)*.

Steps **I** through **V** would lead to the following sequence.

X: 1

SP1 →| *MARK* | =II=>   X: 2

SP2 →| X | 1 | =III=>   F: (FUNARG G •)
X: 2

     |*MARK*| SP2 →| X | 1 |

SP1 →| . . . |

X: 3   X: 4

=IV=> SP3 →| X | 2 | =V=> SP4 →| X | 3 |

SP2 →| X | 1 |

Now to apply the functional argument: *(FUNARG G SP2)*. This is accomplished by tracing down the SP stack with a pointer SP*, moving from SP4 --the current stack pointer-- down to SP2 --the *FUNARG* pointer--, reversing all the intervening bindings on SP and putting the saved values back into the value cell. The pattern of these reversals must be saved; we do this by swapping the values back into the stack segment between SP4 and SP2.

Thus, steps **VII** and **VIII**:

X:3   X: 2

     SP4 →| X | 4 | SP4 →| X | 4 |

=VII=> SP3 →| X | 2 |← SP* =VIII=> SP3 →| X | 3 |

     SP2 →| X | 1 | SP2 →| X | 1 |← SP*

Now we are in a position to evaluate the call on *g*; when we are finished with *g* we will use the unbinding mechanism to reinstate the world as it existed at SP4. This process will restore the value cells using the areas of the stack between SP2 and SP4.

Functional arguments are more difficult since there is only one symbol table, not the stack of tables implicit in the deep binding implementation. True, the information necessary to recover an environment is present in SP, but now it is more expensive to retrieve it.

Though the stack implementation of shallow binding *will* perform for functional arguments, it will involve even more complexity if we wish to handle functional values. The difficulty is the same as that for the stack implementation of deep binding: the *FUNARG* will point "up" the SP stack rather than "down". A straightforward application of the technique used for functional arguments will not work. At the time we wished to apply the functional value its saved SP-pointer will be pointing into a section of the SP stack which no longer reflects the proper state. For when we leave the environment which created the functional value the current unbinding mechanism will cut the stack back to the point which existed when we entered that environment.

The generalization of this shallow binding scheme to functional values is possible. There are two problems to be solved. First, the storage for ENV and DEST must be generalized to be tree-like rather than stack-like. This generalization is not simply a problem of shallow binding. The deep binding scheme builds a tree isomorphic to the shallow tree; only the information saved in the respective trees differs. The problem which the shallow binder must solve is how to rebind from the activation environment to the binding environment. The functional argument case was simplified since the binding environment was on the same branch of the environment tree. In the more general case the binding environment will be on a different branch. We will investigate some solutions to this problem in the next section.

5.20 Strategies for Full LISP Implementation

The discussion of the last three sections should be related to the earlier discussion of binding strategies, Weizenbaum environments, functional arguments and the non-recursive evaluators. Our mapping of the binding implementations (shallow or deep) onto a stack is sufficient for the great majority of LISP programs. However as the LISP community explores new ways of using the language, they expect that the full power of functional values be available; and have proposed extensions in the LISP control structure to allow non-recursive control. Since these topics are of current research interest it is not clear how lasting their impact will be. We will sketch a few of the ideas involved and indicate how the techniques we have discussed in this chapter can be applied.

In the implementation of *eval* of Section 3.5 we represented symbol tables as list-structure. Later, when we introduced the *function* construct, this generality became necessary. As long as a *FUNARG* construct accessed a table, then that table was retained; symbol tables were then a garbage collectible commodity. Essentially we had removed the stack-like behavior of symbol-table accesses which occurs most of the time and replaced it with a general scheme which works for all cases but incurs a significant overhead in even the most simple of function calls.

We would like an intermediate solution: one which works for all cases and minimizes overhead in the typical call. Such a scheme can indeed be implemented. Recall our discussion of garbage collection in Section 5.14. There we said that a garbage collector was used in LISP since the interrelationships which we generated in the data structure manipulations were sufficiently intertwined that it was not possible to use less sophisticated methods to determine whether a structure was still active.

Symbol tables *are* data structures; the discussion of Weizenbaum environments in Section 3.8 should have convinced you of that. They are chained together in a manner reminiscent of that of our implementation of S-exprs; indeed as we have just mentioned LISP's attitude toward management of such tables was to garbage collect them. However the *behavior* of tables during the execution of a program is much less complex than that of arbitrary list structure. As we have just seen, the behavior is predictable except for procedure-valued variables. A solution giving a reasonable implementation based on the alternative storage management scheme of reference counters, which we described on page 286, is described in [Bob 73a]. Several other generalized control schemes have been proposed; for example [Con 73], [Gre 74], [Mon 75], and [Wegb 75]. The intent of all these schemes is that minimal overhead be experienced if a program does not use the more exotic features: a stack-like device results. A larger toll is paid for use of more general control regimes.

It *is* possible to combine the use of the value cell with either shallow or deep strategies. We have *both* a value cell and either name-value trees or shallow bound p-lists. We will try to use the value cell as much as possible. We associate an extra piece of information with each value attached to any value cell, telling the binding time of that variable. We have a global indicator telling the current context which we are using: $E_{current}$, say. When we want the value of a variable, we first go to the augmented value cell; if the binding time indication is that of $E_{current}$, then the value is correct and we take it. If the indicators disagree, we use the full *lookup* strategy; when we find the variable we update the value cell and change the binding time indicator to $E_{current}$. This way we only search the stacks for the first access to a variable; after that we can justifiably use the value cell until we change context again. This scheme, called **cache value cells**, has been implemented in [Mud 75].

Finally, we describe a full shallow binding implementation of functional values ([Gre 74]). We identified the critical problem as that of discovering the path between the activation environment and the binding environment.

Let us call the two nodes E_{act} and E_{bind}. With any node in the tree is associated a flag named *active*; only nodes on the currently active branch are marked *active*. It will be the responsibility of the binding and unbinding routines to maintain this flag. In the current situation, E_{act} is on the active branch and E_{bind} is not. We go to the node E_{bind} and search back down its branch, looking for a node marked *active*. Call this node E_{inter}. E_{inter} represents the intersection of the active branch with the branch tipped in E_{bind}.

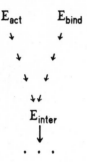

We now go E_{act} and unbind down to E_{inter}, swapping the value cells as we go. At E_{inter} we bind up to E_{bind}, still swapping value cells. When we reach E_{bind} the binding environment has been restored, and the path from E_{bind} through E_{inter} to E_{act} contains the necessary information to allow us to rebind to E_{act} if desired.

The winding and unwinding of value cells is a time consuming process, much more so than the context swap used in a deep binding scheme. One objection to this implementation of the shallow scheme is that it optimized for the case that many of the references in the new environment will be to free variables: those variables which are non-local, but are not globally bound. If a variable is local or global, its access is trivial. If there are no free references in the new environment, then this shallow swap is not needed. Alternative schemes exist which allow the fast access of shallow binding and allow the fast context swap of deep binding.

5.21 Epilogue

Most programming languages are much less complex than LISP; they are far less flexible in their control regimes or their symbol accessing mechanisms. In Fortran there is a simple relationship between variables and memory locations which will contain their values; a Fortran evaluator can assign fixed locations to the variables in a program. In Algol, there is a simple relationship between variables and positions in the run-time stack; an Algol evaluator cannot assign fixed locations, but it can replace the variable lookup with a simple address calculation. This is partly due to Algol's use of static binding [40] and partly due to its restrictions on procedure-valued variables. These kinds of restrictions allow Fortran and Algol compilers to produce efficient code.

In the most general uses of LISP, both the quality and the quantity of variables can change. Arbitrary properties can be associated with atoms at run-time. Indeed, the symbol table mechanism of LISP is more reminiscent of that associated with the compilers for other languages. For these languages it is the compiler which performs the mapping from source language to running machine code. It is the compiler's responsibility to discover the properties associated with each variable. The compiler can do this because the semantics of the language is such that at compile time all, or almost all, of the properties of the variables are known. This is not true for LISP. In general you cannot tell until run time what the attributes of a particular atom are. The situation is really even worse than this. Since programs and data are indistinguishable, we can construct a list using the data structure facilities and the turn right around and evaluate that list as a representation of a LISP expression.

However, a large majority of LISP computations fall into a much more disciplined set, and for those computations, some of the ideas available for Fortran or Algol translators are applicable. If we don't use all of the generality available in the language, we can reduce some of the run-time overhead. For these kinds of computations, it might be appropriate to compile out the unneeded generality. There are LISP compilers, typically written in LISP. They can make many decisions at compile time about the properties of variables; and given comparable information about a program's characteristics can produce code comparable to that produced by Algol and Fortran ([Fat 73]).

In the most general cases, the compiled code may be interspersed with calls on *eval*. This implies that compiled and interpreted code must be able to communicate with each other. A piece of compiled code can call a λ-expression or conversely. The execution of the program should be totally transparent as to whether any, or all, or none of the functions are compiled. This means that the calling sequences for both kinds of functions must be compatible. Less obvious and by far more troublesome, is the communication of the values of free variables. The next chapter discusses the run-time behavior required for implementations of LISP-like languages including a discussion of LISP compilers.

---

[40]This is another benefit of referential transparency (page 171).

The Dynamic Structure of LISP

6.1 Introduction

We have now developed the basic static structure of a LISP machine consisting of *eval* and its subfunctions; we have discussed the I/O routines, the garbage collector, and the organization of a symbol table. This table contains the primitive functions, constants like T and NIL, and a collection of utility functions like *append*, and *reverse*. We have also isolated two areas of memory: pointer space, and full word space.

Expressions are read in, converted to list structure, and evaluated by *eval*. The evaluator traverses the S-expression representation of the form, interpreting the information found there as LISP "instructions". We have discussed some basic data structures for implementation of λ-bindings and evaluation, but we have said little about how the actual execution of the expression takes place. The essential ingredient involved here is the handling of control -- the dynamics of LISP execution. For example, how can we implement call-by-value, parameter passing, recursion, and conditional expressions? At an abstract level, the original *eval-apply* pair of Section 3.5 describes the evaluation mechanism. Given the data structure representation of an expression, we can mechanically perform the transformations implied in the *eval-apply* pair. Even more of the detail is made explicit in the later evaluators of Section 4.6 through Section 4.8. However we must still implement these evaluators on a "real" machine and, unless the evaluator is built into the hardware, we must express the evaluator in terms of more primitive operations. For example, we cannot "implement" recursion by *using* recursion; we must express that idea in terms of lower level operations. Obviously this decomposition must stop somewhere. As J. McCarthy once said: "Nothing can be explained to a stone"; we must assume certain primitives are known.

In this chapter we will discuss two layers of "primitive operations" or **instructions**. One layer will correspond to traditional hardware, and another layer will correspond to the primitives which we derive from the evaluator of Section 4.8. Here we discuss the primitives of that section as the basis for a machine which executes LISP expressions. We can describe the evaluation of a LISP expression as the execution of a sequence of these instructions. Both operations are equivalent: either evaluate the expression or execute the instruction sequence.

There are common instances in which the execution of the instructions can be considered "more efficient" than the evaluation of the expression. For example, consider the access to a local variable. Each such access is to the same location relative to the local environment. That relative location can be computed easily, but the evaluator will use a version of *lookup* for every access. We resort to *lookup* for non-local variables, since LISP uses dynamic binding and the activation environment will typically effect which binding is accessible, but since the location of any local variable is computable, we should exploit that knowledge when executing our programs.

Several examples also arise in the evaluation of a *prog*. For example a loop typically consists of a static [1] sequence of statements. Each time around the loop an evaluator will execute the same sequence of instructions. It would be faster to simply execute the sequence of instructions rather than re-interpret each expression. A related efficiency involves the execution of *go*. We assumed in Section 4.8 that the evaluator will either lookup the label by searching the body of the *prog* or, perhaps more efficiently, searching a computed *go_list*. Either case requires a search. If we can replace the body of a loop with a sequence of primitive instructions, then we can replace a *go* with a transfer of control to the beginning of an appropriate block of instructions. Such a transfer operation should be one of our instructions. [2]

---

[1]By static we mean that the actual expressions do not change during execution. Using the fact that LISP programs are data structures and using some marginal programming techniques *rplaca* and *rplacd* (Section 7.7) we can in fact write self modifying programs. However, such practice is not common.

[2]A problem related to the execution of loops is the *recognition* of a loop. The extent of --or even the presence of-- a loop which the user is controlling by tests and *go*'s may be difficult to discover. If a loop is

The translation of an expression into a sequence of instructions is not without cost. If we wish to evaluate a simple expression only once, then direct evaluation is may be less time-consuming than translation plus execution. However expressions subjected to repeated evaluation can profitably be translated into instructions and then executed.

The translation part of the process which we have been describing is called **compilation**; the translator is called a **compiler**. The compiler is a mapping from the LISP expressions to a sequence of instructions. A compiler is a useful tool for increasing the speed of execution. J. McCarthy says a compiler allows you to look *before* you leap; we will show that we can look *as* we leap. That is, we can compile instructions as we evaluate expressions; if the expression is evaluated again then we execute the faster compiled version.

The relationship between compilation and interpretation should be more apparent now: the interpreter performs the evaluation; the compiler emits instructions which when executed produce the same computational effect as the evaluator. Since the code produced by the compiler is either in machine language or in a form closer to the machine than the source program, we can execute the code much faster. A speed-up factor of thirty to fifty is not uncommon. Compilation may also reduce storage requirements; interpreted programs are stored as S-expressions, but compiled code will be machine language. The machine code will require significantly less space than the interpreted version, the S-expr storage may be reclaimed, and garbage collection time will be decreased since the compiled code is not in free space.

Why not compile all programs? We already have seen that we can *cons*-up new expressions to be evaluated while we are running. Even so, we can compile those expressions before execution. [3] The answer, rather, is that for debugging and editing of programs it is extremely convenient to have a structured representation of the program in memory. This structured representation also simplifies the discussion of compilation. It is true that compilers can translate directly from M-expression representation to internal machine code. [4] Conventional compiler discussions include description of the

---

controlled by language constructs (*while, do, repeat,* etc.) then the interpreter should have some chance of improving the execution of the loop. This, perhaps, is reason for removing control of iteration from the hands of the programmer.

[3]There are, however, programs which simply *cannot* be compiled. The most obscene examples involve self-modifying programs; that is, programs which modify their representation in order to affect the course of interpretation. An example is reluctantly given on page 388.

[4]The compilers which perform in this manner are called sytnax directed compilers. They are an instance of a computational scheme called

syntax analysis problems, for we cannot compile code until we know what the syntactic structure of the program is. However, syntax analysis is really irrelevant for a clear understanding of the behavior of a compiler. Assuming the existence of the structured representation, the compiler is conceptually very simple. The S-expr representation in LISP and resembles the parse tree of other language processors. When we wish to run the program at top speed, we can compile the programs. The compiler can then translate the abstract representation of the program into machine code. We shall say more about this view of programming later.

We shall exploit the analogy between compilers and evaluators when we write the function, *compile*, which will implement the compiler. We will also abstract from the specific compiler, the essence of all LISP compilers. We will have to separate two representations from the specific compiler; we are representing one specific compiling algorithm, and we are also dealing with the representation of a specific machine. The task is worth pursuing since we wish to write different compilers for a specific machine and also would like a single compiler capable of easy transportation to other machines.

The input to *compile* is the representation of a LISP function; the output is a list which represents a sequence of machine instructions. Assume that we have LISP running on **Brand X** machine, and we have written *compile* which produces code for **Brand X** machine. Then perform the following sequence of steps:

1. Create the S-expression form of *compile*.
2. Introduce this translation into the machine, defining *compile*.
3. Ask LISP to evaluate: *compile[COMPILE]*.

Since *compile* compiles code for **Brand X** machine, it translates the S-expression representation of its argument into machine code. Therefore the output of step 3 is a list of instructions representing the translation of *compile*. That is, step 3 compiles the compiler.

A technique called **bootstrapping** is closely related to the process just described. To illustrate this idea, assume that we have LISP and its compiler running on **Brand X**, and we wish to implement LISP on **Brand Y**. If we have been careful in our encoding of the *compile* function then *most* of *compile* is machine independent; that is, it deals mostly with the structure of the LISP expression and only in a few places deals with the structure of a particular machine architecture; this is not an unrealisitc assumption. Notice that this is one of our early programming admonitions: encode algorithms in

---

syntax directed computation; the idea is based on the observation that many algorithms parallel the underlying data structure. We have seen this behavior frequently in our data structure algorithms. For application to compiling and parsing see [Gri 71] or [Aho 72].

a representation-independent style and then include representation-dependent routines as the interface. Changing representations simply requires changing those simpler subfunctions. Here the representations are machines and the algorithm is a compiling algorithm for LISP functions.

Let us call those parts of the compiler which deal with the machine, the code generators or instruction generators. Now if we understand the machine organization of brands X and Y then for any instruction on **Brand X** we should be able to give a sequence of instructions having the equivalent effect on **Brand Y**. We can change the instruction generators in *compile* to generate instructions which run on **Brand Y**. We would have a *compile* function, call it *compile*∗, running on X and producing instructions for Y. Take the S-expr representations of *eval, apply, read, print, compile*∗,... etc. and compile these with *compile*∗; we will generate a large segment of code for a LISP system which will run on Y. Certain primitives will have to be supplied to run these instructions on Y, but a very large part of LISP can be bootstrapped from X to Y.

Given a compiler and interpreter for a language Λ_1 we can often bootstrap Λ_1 to a language Λ_2. We express the interpreter for Λ_2 as a program in Λ_1. We can then execute programs in Λ_2 by interpreting the Λ_2 interpreter. We can improve efficiency by compiling the Λ_2 evaluator. Perhaps we can express the Λ_2 compiler in Λ_1 or Λ_2; in either case we can then compile that compiler. [5]

The purpose of this chapter is to discuss implementation of control structures for LISP, yet most of this introduction has been a description of compilers. These positions can reconciled easily.

1. The instructions generated by the compiler will reference the control primitives of the machine. The control structures of the evaluator will also be implemented from these primitives. The machine code produced by an implementor might be more highly optimized than that produced by a compiler, by the essential structure of the code will will be quite similar. We are initially interested in understanding. It is easier to understand an abstract general algorithm than to understand the implementation of one specific evaluator.

2. It will clearly show the relationship between compilation and evaluation. That is, the LISP function representing the compiler will very closely parallel the structure of the interpreter, *eval*. If you understand *eval*, then the compiler is easy.

The design of the compiler will also illustrate another non-trivial application of abstract computation, showing how simple it is to describe an

---

[5]The first bootstrapped compiler was the LISP compiler for the IBM 704. Bootstrapping is a common practice in A.I. now, using LISP as a base language and extending it to any number of specialized A.I. languages.

apparently complex algorithm. As in the previous chapter, we will remain as abstract as possible without losing the necessary details. A meaningful description of compilers entails an understanding of a machine, so before the actual construction of the compilers, we will describe a simple machine with a sufficient instruction set to handle the control structures of LISP. First we will review and expand the primitives of Section 4.8, emphasizing their interpretation as machine instructions.

6.2 Primitives for LISP

In our discussion of the evaluators in Section 4.6 through Section 4.8 we uncovered more details involved in evaluation of LISP expressions. In the final evaluator we identified a dozen or so actions. The underlying idea was to remove recursion and replace that implicit control structure with very explicit actions, controlled by a simple loop:

$$loop <= \lambda[[]prog[[]$$
$$l \quad cont[]$$
$$go[l] \ ]]$$

The variable *cont* was a functional variable, bound to states and set to the next state by the action of the current state. This observation marks the beginning of a traditional machine description. It remains to separate the actions of the machine from the instructions it is executing. That is, some of the details of the state transformations deal with the bookkeeping which the machine is doing to discover what the expression is, and some of the transformations perform the actual evaluation of the expression. For example, the manipulation of *fun* and *args* is part of the activity to discover the form of the expression. The execution of *send* and *receive* are involved with the evaluation. The parts of the evaluator involved with the execution of the expression will become the instructions of the machine. Supplied with an appropriate execution device, a sequence of these instructions captures the meaning of the evaluation of an expression. It is the business of this section to review the evaluators and extract a sufficient set of instructions. We begin that task with some examples, using *peval* of Section 4.8 as the basic interpreter.

First, the evaluation of a constant *A* involves the recognition that we have seen a constant; that is part of the control of the evaluator. We evaluate that constant by *send[denote[]]*. The *denote* operation is still part of the evaluator, but the *send* operation is an instruction. The execution of *send[A]* performs the evaluation. The *restore* operation returns the evaluator to its previous state. We must allow for some state-saving in our repertoire of instructions. The evaluation of a function application, like *g[A]*, involves the evaluation of *A*, the calling of *g*, and a means of returning to the computation surrounding $g[A]$. Function calls involve several things: we need space to contain the evaluated arguments; we need a control mechanism to describe which argument is being evaluated; we need to suspend a computation such that we can execute the function with the evaluated arguments; and we must be able to return to the suspended computation when the function has completed its task.

The necessary ingredients are already present in *peval*; we need only extract and package them. Clearly *alloc_dest* is involved in getting new space for the evaluated arguments. There is a second required activity since *alloc_dest* always occurs in conjunction with a *save* of the current *dest*. Therefore we define an instruction named *alloc* which saves the current destination *and* intitializes a new *dest* block.

Each slot of the destination block is filled by an appropriate *send* operation. Examination of the sub-states of *evalargs* (page 215) reveals another machine instruction: *next*[] is used to increment the destination pointer.

Finally, after all the arguments are evaluated, the destination block must become the local environment, and the function can be called. Thus two more instructions: *link* will attach the destination block as the local environment and restore the previous dest block; *call* will call the function after saving sufficient control information so that we may return after execution of the function is completed.

For example, consider $f[g[A];h[B]]$. Assuming f and g are λ-definitions with formal parameters $[x,y]$ and $[z]$ respectively, and h is a primitive, then an instruction sequence might be:

$alloc[(X\ Y)]; alloc[(Z)]; send[A];$
$link[]; call[G]; next[];$
$alloc[(G1)]; send[B]; link[];$
$call[H]; link[]; call[F]$

There are two classes of instructions to break the sequential flow of a machine program: we transfer control when we call or return from a function; and we transfer control when we execute a conditional expression.

Examination of *ev2*, *ev5*, and *ev6* (page 214) reveals some of the details of a function call-return sequence. After saving the current environment, restoring the saved destination, and saving a continuation point, we passed control to the body of the function. The instruction sequence, representing the body of the function, will be terminated by a call on *ret*. This instruction will restore the saved environment and return control to the instruction immediately following the *call* instruction. The saved information is governed by the variable named *control*, with *call* adding information, and *ret* removing information. Before showing how instructions are executed and how *control* is manipulated, we will describe the primitives for conditional expressions.

Examination of the details of *evcond* and its associated functions (page 215), exhibits more instructions. We use the evaluator to evaluate a predicate; we then *receive* the result from the *dest*-block. If that answer is true, we evaluate one path; otherwise we evaluate another path. We see two instructions here: a test and jump instruction, which we shall call *receive_test*, which tests the contents of the current destination slot and jumps to one instruction sequence if the result is true, and jumps to (usually) another instruction sequence if the result is false. The second instruction is a means of jumping unconditionally to a prescribed instruction sequence. This second instruction is named *goto*.

For example, a conditional expression $[p_1 \rightarrow e_1; ...; p_n \rightarrow e_n]$ has a code sequence like:

```
<instructions for p₁>
[receive_test[] → <code for e₁>;goto[a0]]
<instructions for p₂>

    ...

<instructions for pₙ>
[receive_test[] → <code for eₙ>;goto[a0]]
err[NO_TRUE_COND_CLAUSE]
a0 ...
```

Whenever *receive_test* is true we execute a sequence of instructions and then transfer out of the conditional using the *goto*. We could have treated conditional expressions like special function calls, saving *a0* as the continuation and restoring it from *control* instead of using *goto*. However conditional expressions don't require that extra generality. [6]

We can now give a more detailed picture of a device which can execute this instruction set. A program will be represented as a sequence of instructions. Some of these instructions may be prefaced with labels. These labels either represent function names or names used within a conditional expression. Given a sequence of instructions named *inst_seq*, we expect that they be executed in sequence, unless some transfer of control occurs. For example, the following program suffices for the execution of such instruction sequences:

---

[5]Our treatment of conditionals is an instance of "open coding" a function call. That means we replace a possible *call-ret* with the "in-line" instruction sequence which makes up the body of the function. This trick gives faster execution, but takes more space. We will see another instance of "open-coding" when we compile macros in Section 6.18.

$$loop <= \lambda[[inst\_seq]prog[[i\_s;pc]$$
$$i\_s \leftarrow inst\_seq;$$
$$l \ [null[i\_s] \rightarrow return['halt]];$$
$$pc \leftarrow first[i\_s];$$
$$i\_s \leftarrow rest[i\_s];$$
$$[not[is\_label[pc]] \rightarrow pc[]];$$
$$go[l] \ ]]$$

If *loop* returns *HALT*, then the result of our computation is found in *dest*. Labels are not executable instructions, and are therefore ignored. The effect of *goto* is to replace the current instruction sequence with the sequence which begins immediately after the label which is the argument to the *goto*. The effect of *call-ret* is a bit more complex. We describe *only* the control aspects of *call*, leaving the other details until later. Let an instance *call[fn]* be the current instruction; and let *is'* be the current instruction sequence. Note that *is'* is the sequence immediately after the call. We save *is'* on *control* by *control* ← *concat[is';control]*; then we set *i_s* to the sequence beginning at *fn*. Execution of *go[l]* sends us to label *l* and we begin executing the body of *fn*.

We leave *fn* by executing *ret*. This instruction performs

$$i\_s \leftarrow first[control]; \ control \leftarrow rest[control];$$

and we are back at the instruction following the *call*.

Part of the execution of *call* and *goto* involves locating the desired label. Since we have saved the original instruction sequence we can search that list for the desired label. We will see more effective ways for locating labels in Section 6.5.

6.3 SM: A Simple Machine

This section describes a simple machine which has a sufficient instruction set to describe the LISP primitives in terms of a more conventional machine. [7] Note that this machine is *not* necessary for our understanding of *eval*. The evaluator is self-descriptive. We need describe a machine only to discuss lower level implementation and compilation. Indeed, this is an objection to describing meaning of programming languages in terms of a compiler: you must then understand *two* things, the language *and* a machine.

The simple machine, SM, has a slight similarity to the organization of the PDP-10 [DEC 69], however we need very few features to illuminate the interesting facets of our primitives. If we were to implement a production LISP, many more instructions would be necessary. Similarly, our SM suffices for a description of compilation algorithms, but if we wished to perform

---

[7]See also [Deu 73].

highly efficient compilation for a production LISP system, we would require a full instruction set. The point now is to understand basic algorithms. When that is accomplished it is reasonable to examine problems of efficiency and details of implementation. We address some of the techniques available for optimization of compiler code in later sections.

SM has a conventional addressable main memory, including registers, $AC1$, $AC2$, ..., ACn addressable as memory locations 0 through n. These registers, called **accumulators**, will be used as pointer registers. Each memory location is assumed to be large enough to contain two addresses. For sake of discussion, assume the word size is 36 bits. One mapping of a dotted-pair onto an SM location is straightforward: the *car* maps to the left-half of the word; the *cdr*, to the right. The addressing space for dotted pairs is therefore 2^{18}. A memory area is set aside to contain such dotted pairs. A memory area is also dedicated to full-word space; all p-names and numbers are stored there.

Parts of SM memory can be designated as stacks. Each stack is a contiguous area of memory, and the current top of a stack is referenced by one of the registers, $P1$, ..., Pj; these registers are called **stack-pointers**. [8] The stacks will be used to contain the partial results of calculations and will contain the information necessary to implement the function exit sequence. In our compilers, a single stack will suffice for saving partial computations, environments, as well as control information. This single stack will be referred to by P.

There are only three classes of instructions necessary to describe our implementation: instructions for constant generation, instructions for stack manipulation, and instructions for flow of control.

The control instructions and some of the stack instructions refer to the program counter of SM. This counter is designated as **PC**. In the following, C means "contents of..."; ac must denote an accumulator; loc means any memory location.

Here are the instructions:

MOVEI ac const $C(ac) \leftarrow const$

PUSH P ac $C(P) \leftarrow C(P)+1$ Increment stack pointer.
         $C(C(P)) \leftarrow C(ac)$ Copy contents of ac to top of stack.

POP P ac $C(ac) \leftarrow C(C(P))$ Copy top of stack into ac.
         $C(P) \leftarrow C(P)-1$ Decrement stack pointer.

---

[8]On the PDP-10 a stack pointer must be one of the AC registers.

The next two instructions implement a function calling mechanism.

PUSHJ P loc $C(P) \leftarrow C(P)+1$ Increment stack pointer.

                    $C(C(P)) \leftarrow C(\mathbf{PC})$ Place address following the *PUSHJ*.

                    $C(\mathbf{PC}) \leftarrow loc$ in the stack. Then change control to location *loc*.

POPJ P $C(\mathbf{PC}) \leftarrow C(C(P))$ Copy top of stack into **PC**.

                  $C(P) \leftarrow C(P)-1$ Decrement stack pointer.

We have ignored some of the details of stack operations; each stack operations must consider boundary conditions on the storage allocated for the stack. Any condition which would violate these bounds must be detectable. If a stack is allocated in a discontinuous fashion ([Bis 74]) then a storage management decision must be made; if the stacks are of fixed size, then an error must be signaled.

MOVE ac loc $C(ac) \leftarrow C(loc)$ This is an instruction to load a specified *ac* with the contents of *loc*. Note *loc* may be an *ac*; e.g. *MOVE* AC_1 AC_2.

MOVEM ac loc $C(loc) \leftarrow C(ac)$ Copy contents of *ac* into *loc*. For example, *MOVEM* AC_1 AC_2=*MOVE* AC_2 AC_1.

SUB ac loc $C(ac) \leftarrow C(ac) - C(loc)$

JUMP loc $C(\mathbf{PC}) \leftarrow loc$ Go to location *loc*.

JUMPF ac loc   if $C(ac)=\mathfrak{f}$ then $C(\mathbf{PC}) \leftarrow loc$

JUMPT ac loc   if $C(ac) \neq \mathfrak{f}$ then $C(\mathbf{PC}) \leftarrow loc$. Note that *JUMPT* implements the coding trick of Section 5.5 which maps t onto everything which is not false.

These instructions are executed by a machine whose basic execution cycle is essentially:

$$\mathbf{l:}\ \ C(\mathbf{IR}) \leftarrow C(C(\mathbf{PC}))$$
$$C(\mathbf{PC}) \leftarrow C(\mathbf{PC}) + 1$$
$$\text{execute } C(\mathbf{IR})$$
$$\text{go to } \mathbf{l}$$

The **IR**, or Instruction register, is an internal register used to hold the current instruction. Note that the **PC** register is incremented *before* execution of the instruction. If we incremented **PC** *after* the execution of the instruction, and the instruction were a JUMP-type instruction, then the **PC** would get a spurious incrementation.

A critical part of LISP evaluation involves procedure calls and returns. Since we expect to handle recursive calling sequences, the *call-ret* pair (page 310), represented as *CALL* and *RET*, must take this into account. However, there is a more fundamental requirement of this pair: they must make sure that, on completion of a *CALL*, the *RET* can return to the instruction which directly follows the *CALL*. This requirement can be accomplished by a less comprehensive call, say *JSR*, (for Jump SubRoutine), which stores the current value of the PC in a known location. Then the return, *JRTH*, (for Jump THrough), need only pick up that saved value and restore it into the PC. We could implement this instruction on our machine. Recall that in the basic machine cycle the PC was incremented *before* the execution of the instruction. Thus if we were about to execute a *JSR* the PC is already pointing at the next instruction; all we need to do is save the current PC. So let's assume that *JSR loc* stores the PC in *loc* and begins execution in location *loc+1*. Then:

JSR loc	$C(loc) \leftarrow C(\text{PC})$	Save the PC in *loc*.
	$C(\text{PC}) \leftarrow loc + 1$	Jump to location *loc + 1*.
JRTH loc	$C(\text{PC}) \leftarrow C(loc)$	

This pair is sufficient to implement simple non-recursive calling sequences. It's fast and efficient; however it is not sufficient for recursive control. If we always store in a *fixed* location, only the result of the *last* store would be available and previous values set by prior recursions would have been lost. [9] What we need is an implementation of the actions of *control*. For purpose of our discussion we can assume that *control* operates in a stack-like fashion. [10] What the *CALL* will do is *push* the current contents of the PC onto the control stack; and *RET* will pop off the top element and put it into the PC register. [11]

The behavior we have just described is that attributed to the *PUSHJ-POPJ* pair when they are applied to the control stack. We have separated out the *CALL-RET* pair since the calling process is not always as simple as *PUSHJ-POPJ*. Several things impinge on our decision:

1. We want to be able to supply detailed debugging information to the user. How this will be accomplished will be the topic of Section 6.23.
2. We want to be able to freely replace functions with new definitions.

---

[9] The programmer could have saved and restored the return points in an internal stack, but that is wasteful of programmer time, memory space, and succeptible to errors.

[10] Unless we consider extensions of LISP, a stack is sufficient for LISP's control environment.

[11] What will be found on the control stack is a time-sequence of those procedures which have been entered but have not yet been completed. Such information is exceptionally useful in debugging programs.

A *PUSHJ* transfers control to a particular sequence of instructions.

3. We want to be able to intermix compiled and interpreted programs. Compiled programs may call interpreted programs, and vice versa. Indeed we may even wish to replace an interpreted (compiled) definition with a compiled (interpreted) version.

4. In dealing with functional arguments, we must be able to transfer control to a function variable. We cannot know where the *PUSHJ* should transfer.

When an interpreted function calls a compiled (or primitive) function, *eval* will look for the indicator, *SUBR*; then retrieve the machine address of the code and enter via a *PUSHJ*. That code should exit (back to *eval*) via a *POPJ*, after assuring that any internal stacks have been appropriately restored.

Compiled functions call other functions via *CALL*. The *CALL* must discover how to call the function: is it a *SUBR*, *EXPR*, an *FEXPR*, etc? The function is called and on completion control is returned to the address immediately following the *CALL*. For example, *CALL* can be implemented as *(PUSHJ P DECODE)*, where *P* represents the control stack pointer, and *DECODE* represents a routine to decode the actual procedure call. Within *decode* we know that $C(C(P)-1)$ is the actual call instruction; *decode* then can access the function definition associated with *fn*, set up the call, and then return via a *POPJ*.

Within any *CALL* or *PUSHJ* we may call any function, including that function itself. This brings us to one of the most important conventions for *any* stack-like call-return sequence: Whatever we push onto a stack within the body of a function *must* be popped off before we exit from the function body. That is, the state of any stack must be transparent to any computations which occur within the function. This is called **stack synchronization**.

Usually the effect of *RET* is identical to *POPJ*, however it is conceivable that we might expect that complex returns require special care. The basic idea in this discussion is that we will supply two similar, compatible, but not identical call-return sequences: *PUSHJ-POPJ* is fast and simple; the other, *CALL-RET*, is more general but more costly to invoke.

In the next section we will reconcile LISP primitives with the instruction set supplied on SM.

6.4 Implementation of the Primitives

As with any representation problem, several choices are available. We will begin our use of SM with a study of call-by-value function calls; later we will discuss other calling sequences. We will discuss two general implementation techniques. The first is applicable to machines without the special AC's of the SM.

First, we will assume only that we are able to simulate a stack. All the operations occur on the stack. Constants will be generated by pushing the representation on the top of the stack, essentially creating a *dest* block. A function call, $f[t_1; ... ;t_n]$, expects its arguments as the top n elements of the stack, with the value of t_n on the top of the stack, and the other values below. As the function is called, the *dest* block on the top of the stack becomes the local environment. The function replaces the top n elements with the value of the function, thus *send*-ing its value to the destination of the caller. This model is a restricted, but very useful, subset of LISP. It will develop into a more robust example as the chapter progresses. The technique is extendible to support the implementation model we developed in Section 5.18.

Here's an example of the implementation for the expression $f[g[A];C;h[B]]$:

```
(PUSH P (QUOTE A))    ; make argument for call on g
(CALL G)              ; call the function
(PUSH P (QUOTE C))    ; place second argument
(PUSH P (QUOTE B))
(CALL H)              ; h only uses (and removes) B
(CALL F)              ; after the call, f[g[A];C;h[B]] is
                      ;    on the top of the stack.
```

Now we will give implementations of the LISP primitives which result in reasonably efficient code on the SM, and which also reflect several practices applied in current LISP implementations. We will take advantage of the existence of the special AC's; the usual hardware implementation of such special registers allows access to their contents in less time than typical stack references. [12]

Since the creating, saving, and restoring of destination blocks can be expensive, we will try to minimize those kinds of activities. We will use our special registers $AC1$, through ACn to build parameter lists and pass parameters. This entails several conventions. We will try to use the accumulators as the destination block. Our early compilers will be sufficiently weak that this desire can be met. Later we will have to modify our stand slightly.

The actual parameters for a function call, $f[t_1; ... ;t_n]$, will be developed

---

[12]There is a question whether such special registers should be considered good architecture or a trick. The Burroughs 6700-7700 uses special hardware to decrease access time to the initial stack segment. The PDP-10 uses special registers. One can argue that such special tricks belong in the hardware, and that the machine presented to the programmer be correspondingly more uniform [Dor 76].

in *AC1* through *ACn*. In the early compilers we will also pass the evaluated parameters to the called function using the accumulators. Thus values will tend to stay in the *AC*'s unless forced out. They can be forced out by *alloc* since a call to *alloc* is supposed to save the current *dest*. The interplay between *next*, *link*, and *send* requires care.

We will assume that we are compiling for single valued functions, and therefore we must resolve the question of where to put the value of a function. Again consider $f[t_1; \ldots ; t_n]$; we might expect that each t_i be responsible for placing its result in the proper *ACi*. Indeed that is the spirit of the *send* operation; it knows where the result should be placed. This strategy requires some careful register allocation if it is to be carried out successfully. We will postpone this discussion for a while.

There is a simpler solution available: a function always returns its value in *AC1* and leaves the register allocation up to the calling function. There are at least two strategies here:

We try to build the *dest* block in the *AC*'s and also use the *AC*'s to pass parameters and values.

> A function call, $f[t_1; \ldots ; t_n]$, expects its arguments to be presented in *AC1* through *ACn*. We try to compute the values of t_i directly in *ACi*. This is easy if t_i is a constant; if t_i is a function call on *g*, we save *AC1* through *ACi-1*; set up the arguments to *g*; perform the call, returning the result in *AC1*; move the result to *ACi*; and restore the saved values of the *t*'s.

Convention 1

We try to build the *dest* block in the top of the stack, using the *AC*'s for passing parameters and returning values.

> A function call, $f[t_1; \ldots ; t_n]$, expects its arguments to be presented in *AC1* through *ACn*. As we compute each t_i, we store the result on the stack *P*. Thus the execution sequence should be:
>
> compute value of *t*, push onto stack *P*.
>
> . . .
>
> compute value of t_{n-1}, push onto stack *P*.
> compute value of t_n, move into *ACn*.
>
> After this computation the values, $V_{n-1}, \ldots, V_1$, of the arguments are stored from top to bottom in *P* with V_n in *ACn*. Thus to complete the function invocation, we need only pop the arguments into the *AC*'s in the correct order and call *f*. We did not push V_n since we expected to pass the parameters to *f* in *AC1* through *ACn*.

Convention 2

When a function completes evaluation, it is to place its value in *AC1*. Nothing can be assumed about the contents any other *AC*. If an *AC* contains information we need then it must be saved on the stack *before* calling the function.

Instead of referring to *AC1*, *AC2*, ..., *ACn* we will simply use the numbers, *1*, *2*, ..., *n* in the instructions.

General conventions

We now give an example of both conventions for the expression $f[g[A];C;h[B]]$. We use a list representation of the instructions and code sequences in preparation for future discussions.

```
((MOVEI 1 (QUOTE A))     ; make argument for call on g
 (CALL  G)               ; call the function
 (MOVEI 2 (QUOTE C))     ; place second argument
 (PUSH P 1)              ; but now we have to save the values
 (PUSH P 2)              ;  since we must compute h[B]
 (MOVEI 1 (QUOTE B))
 (CALL H)
 (MOVE 3 1)              ; move the result to AC3
 (POP P 2)               ; restore AC2 and AC1 in the correct order
 (POP P 1)
 (CALL  F)  )
```

Example of Convention 1

```
((MOVEI 1 (QUOTE A))     ; make argument for call on g
 (CALL  G)               ; call the function
 (PUSH P 1)              ; save the value
 (MOVEI 1 (QUOTE C))
 (PUSH P 1)              ; save the value
 (MOVEI 1 (QUOTE B))
 (CALL H)
 (MOVE 3 1)              ; don't need to save the value
 (POP P 2)               ;    since this is the last argument
 (POP P 1)
 (CALL  F)  )
```

Example of Convention 2

Neither compiling convention produces optimal code for all occasions. If the parameter list to a function call contains only constants, then the first convention produces better code. If there are many nested function calls then it may produce very bad code. We will worry more about efficiency after we develop the basic compiling algorithms.

At the highest level, our compiler will generate code for the *alloc-link-call-...* machine; but frequently we will express the code in terms of one of our more traditional representations.

The output from the compiler is to be a list of instructions, in the order which we would expect to execute them. Each instruction is a list: an operation followed by as many elements as are required by that operation. We can execute the compiled code by simulating the actions of our machine on each element of the sequence. However it is more efficient to translate this compiler output further, producing a sequence of actual machine instructions, placed in memory and suitable for execution by the hardware processing unit. In preparation for this, we will allocate an area of memory which can receive the processed compiler output. This area is usually called **Binary Program Space** (BPS). The translation program which takes the output from the compiler and converts it into actual machine instructions in BPS is called an assembler.

6.5 Assemblers

In Section 6.2 we gave an abstract description of an algorithm for executing sequences of instructions. In this section we discuss the mechanism for translating the LISP list, which represents instructions, into machine instructions in Binary Program Space. Part of the process involves the actual instructions; before a machine can execute an instruction it must be transformed into a numerical code which the machine understands. Part of the process involves establishing a link between the BPS code and the LISP evaluator; before the evaluator can call the compiled code, it must know where to find it. A program which performs these operations is called an **assembler**.

There are two alternatives available to solve the first problem. We might add the assembly phase to the end of the compiler. Then the output from the compiler would go directly to locations in BPS. The alternative is to compile the functions onto an external medium, and perform the assembly phase later; this has some advantages. The assembly phase is significantly less time consuming than the earlier phases of a compiler. Therefore several programmers may take advantage of assembly code without the necessity of recompilation. In either case, the assembler must complete the translation to machine code and link that code into the object list such that it may be accessed.

One of the arguments to the assembler is the representation of the program. One of its arguments should describe where in BPS we wish the assembled code to begin loading; this second argument becomes the initial value for the **assembly counter**. The assembler can sequence through the program list, looking up each definition, manufacturing the numerical equivalent of each instruction, and then depositing that number in the location referenced by the assembly counter. The assembley counter is incremented, and the next element of the program list is examined.

We must also have access to an initial symbol table, describing the pre-defined symbol names. These pre-defined names include information about the actual machine locations for the utility functions, the values of special stacks or registers which the compiler uses internally. We must also have an instruction list which gives a correspondence between the names like *ALLOC* or *PUSHJ* and the actual numbers which the hardware uses in interpreting the instruction. [13]

Below is a low level representation of a code sequence for $f[g[A];h[B]]$ assuming that h is a primitive routine.

```
((MOVEI 1 (QUOTE A))      ; make argument for call on g
 (CALL  G)                ; call the function
 (PUSH P 1)               ; save the value
 (MOVEI 1 (QUOTE B))
 (PUSHJ P H)  ¹⁴
 (MOVE 2 1)
 (POP P 1)
 (CALL  F) )
```

The machine representations of these instructions are encodings of specific fields of specific machine locations with specific numbers. For example, the operation *PUSH* is represented as a certain number, called its **operation code** or **op code**, and which will occupy a certain area of a machine word so that the CPU can interpret it as an instruction to push something onto a stack. Other fields in the instruction are to be interpreted as references to stacks, to memory locations, to accumulators, constants or external references to other routines.

We must exercise a bit of care in handling *QUOTE*d expressions. Assembling a construct like *(MOVEI 1 (QUOTE (A B C)))* should have the effect of constructing the list *(A B C)* in free space and placing an instruction in memory to load the address of this list into *AC1*. We must notice that this list is subject to garbage collection and, if left unprotected, could be destroyed. The garbage collector could look through compiled code for any references to free-space or full-word-space; or we could make a list of all of these constants and let the garbage collector mark the list. Looking through compiled code is expensive; that expense can be minimized by compiling referneces to constants into an initial block in in the prolog of the code.

---

[13]A hardware machine is just another interpreter like *eval*. It is usually not recursive, but performs more like *loop* in the *prog*-evaluator.

[14]Note that we use P; this assumes we use P to save *both* value and control information.

```
            (JUMP loc)
            <const1>
            <const2>
              . . .
            <constn>
      loc   <code>
              . . . )
```

Then the garbage collector need only search well-defined positions.

Keeping a *QUOTE*-list is a compromise; it is a compromise since that strategy might retain unnecessary structures in case functions were redefined or recompiled.

The assembler also needs to recognize that there are different instruction formats. That is, some instructions use an opcode and a memory reference: (*JUMP L*); some use an opcode, accumulator, and an address: (*PUSH P 1*); and some use a LISP construct: (*MOVEI 1 (QUOTE A)*). Therefore, the assembler has to have an initial symbol table of opcodes and stack numbers.

Here is a sample op-code table with their machine equivalents:

symbol	value
MOVE	*200*
MOVEI	*201*
SUB	*274*
JUMP	*254*
JUMPE	*322*
JUMPN	*326*
PUSH	*261*
POP	*262*
PUSHJ	*260*
POPJ	*263*
RET	*263*
CALL	*034*
P	*14*

And here's what the code for $f[g[A];C;h[B]]$ might resemble after being assembled:

201	1	405
034		1107
261	14	1
201	1	406
260	14	11121
200	2	1
262	14	1
034		1051

(100 labels the first row)

where A is located at 405; the atom F begins at 1051, and the instruction sequence for h begins at 11121, etc.

6.6 Compilers for Subsets of LISP

We will examine compilers for increasingly complex subsets of LISP; we begin with functions, composition and constant arguments, and gradually include more features. Though each subset is a simple extension of its predecessor, each subset introduces a new problem for the compiling algorithm. If the corresponding evaluator (*tgmoaf*, *tgmoafr*, and the most simple *eval*) is well understood, then the corresponding additions to the compilation algorithm are easy to make.

The first compiler will handle representations of that subset of LISP forms defined by the following BNF equations:

<form>   ::= <constant> | <function>[<arg>; ...; <arg>]
<arg>   ::= <form>
<constant> ::= <sexpr>
<function> ::= <identifier>

This LISP subset corresponds closely to that of *tgmoaf*, handling only function names, composition, and constant arguments. In the interest of readability and generality, we will write the functions using constructors, selectors, and recognizers and supply the necessary bridge to our specific representation by simple sub-functions.

All the compilers we develop will be derived from the second compiling convention, saving the results on the top of the stack. Our compilers will incorporate some knowledge of the SM machine, and we will try to note places where substantial assumptions about machine structure have been made. The remainder of this section describes the main components of the first compiler.

compexp expects to see either a constant or a function followed by a list of zero or more arguments. The appearance of a constant should elicit the generation of a list containing a single instruction to *send* back the representation of that constant; *mksend[dest;exp]* is a call on the constructor to generate that instruction. Since values are always found in *AC1*, that should be the destination for the *send*. Since we are assuming the expression is a constant, the operation can be a *MOVEI*. If the expression is not a constant, we can assume it is a call-by-value application. We should generate code to evaluate each argument, and follow that with code for a function call.

$$
\begin{aligned}
compexp <= \quad &\lambda[[exp][isconst[exp] \rightarrow list[mksend[1;exp]]; \\
&\qquad t \rightarrow \lambda[[z]compapply[func[exp]; \\
&\qquad\qquad\qquad\qquad complis[z]; \\
&\qquad\qquad\qquad\qquad length[z]]] \\
&\qquad [arglist[exp]]]]]
\end{aligned}
$$

complis gets the representation of the argument list; it must generate a code sequence to evaluate each argument and increment the destination. After we have compiled the last argument we should not increment the destination. Notice that we have used *append* with three arguments; this could be justified by defining *append* as a macro (Section 3.12).

$$
\begin{aligned}
complis <= \lambda[[u] \quad &[null[u] \rightarrow ( ); \\
&null[rest[u]] \rightarrow compexp[first[u]]; \\
&t \rightarrow append[compexp[first[u]]; \\
&\qquad\qquad list[mkalloc[1]]; \\
&\qquad\qquad complis[rest[u]]]]]
\end{aligned}
$$

compapply has a simple task: it generates code for allocation of the values; it takes the list of instructions made by *complis* and adds instructions at the end of the list to generate a function call on *fn*. Here's *compapply*:

$$
\begin{aligned}
compapply <= \lambda[[fn;vals;n] \quad &append[vals; \\
&\qquad mklink[n]; \\
&\qquad list[mkcall[fn]]]]
\end{aligned}
$$

Finally, here are the constructors, selectors, and recognizers:

Recognizer

isconst <= λ[[x] or[numberp[x];
                            eq[x;t];
                            eq[x;f];
                            and[not[atom[x]];eq[first[x];QUOTE]]]]

Selectors

func <= λ[[x] first[x]]
arglist <= λ[[x] rest[x]]

Constructors

mksend <= λ[[dest;val] list[MOVEl;dest;val]]

mkalloc <= λ[[dest] list[PUSH;P;dest]]

mkcall <= λ[[fn] list[CALL;fn]]

mklink <= λ[[n][eq[n;1] → ( ); t → concat[mkmove[n;1];mklink1[sub1[n]]]]

mklink1 <= λ[[n][zerop[n] → ( ); t → concat[mkpop[n];mklink1[sub1[n]]]];

mkpop <= λ[[n] list[POP;P;n]]

mkmove <= λ[[dest;val] list[MOVE;dest;val]]

Note that *compexp* is just a complex $\Re$-mapping whose image is a sequence of machine language instructions.

The code generated by this compiler is inefficient, but that is not our main concern. We wish to establish an intuitive and correct compiler, then worry about efficiency. Premature concern for efficiency is folly; we must first establish a correct and clean algorithm.

Problems

1. Write *compexp* to generate code for option 1 as discussed on page 318. Compare the two versions of *compexp*; now write a more abstract version which encompasses both as special cases.
2. Write *compexp* and associated functions for a stack-only machine using the techniques outlined on page 317.

6.7 Compilation of Conditional Expressions

Recall *tgmoafr* of Section 2.8; the innovation in *tgmoafr* was the evaluation of conditional expressions. The BNF equations were augmented by:

<form> ::= [<form> → <form> ; ... ;<form> → <form>]

The compilation of conditional expressions will mean an extra piece of code in *compexp* to recognize *COND* and a new function (analogous to *evcond* in *tgmoafr*) to generate the code for the *COND*-body. [15] In fact, the major difference between *evcond* and its counterpart in *compexp*, which we shall call *comcond*, is that *comcond* generates code for each of the branches of a conditional whereas *evcond* only evaluates one branch.

The effect of *comcond* on the form:

COND $(COND\ (\Re\llbracket\ p_1\ \rrbracket\ \Re\llbracket\ e_1\rrbracket\ )\ ...\ (\Re\llbracket\ p_n\ \rrbracket\ \Re\llbracket\ e_n\ \rrbracket))$

can be surmised from the discussion of *receive_test* on page 311. First generate code for p_1; then generate a test for truth, going to the code for e_1 if true, and going to the code for p_2 if not true. The code for e_1 must be followed by an exit from the code for the conditional, and we should generate an error condition to be executed in the case that p_n is false.

We represent the code as:

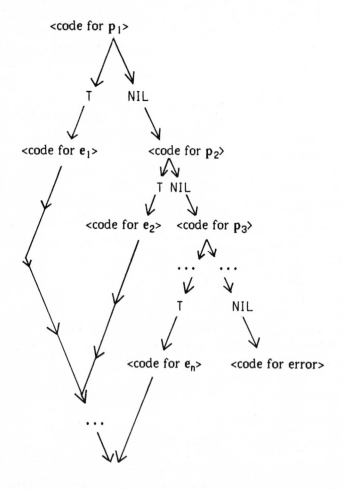

---

[15]If we had designed the compiler like the evaluators in Section 5.8 we would need only attach a compile-property to the atom *COND*, and make the property-value *COMCOND*.

Expressing *comcond* in terms of **SM** primitives requires more conventions in our compiler.

> We must be able to test for t (or f). Previous conventions imply that the value of a predicate will be found in *ACl*.
>
> We can test for the occurrence of t or f using the *JUMPT* or *JUMPF* instruction (see Section 6.3) respectively. [16]

More Compiling Conventions

Since our code is to be a *sequence* of instructions, we must linearize the graph-representation of the generated code. We can generate a sequence representation by appropriately interspersing labels and *JUMP*s between the blocks of instructions for the p_i's and e_i's. We will generate:

```
(       <code for p₁>
        (JUMPF 1 L1)
        <code for e₁>
        (JUMP L0)
L1      <code for p₂>
        (JUMPF 1 L2)
        ...
Ln-1    <code for pₙ>
        (JUMPF 1 Ln)
        <code for eₙ>
        (JUMP L0)
Ln      (JUMP ERROR)
L0      )
```

We need to construct the labels, *Li*. These labels should be atomic and should be distinct. LISP has a function named *gensym* which is used for this task. *gensym* is a function of no arguments whose value is an identifier called a **generated symbol**, or "gensym". Gensyms are not true atoms since they are not placed in the object list; they are usually used only for their unique name. If it is desired to use them as atoms, they must be placed on the object list using the function *intern* (page 279). Gensyms are distinct from each other and will be distinct from all other atoms. [17]

We want to write a recursive version of *comcond*; therefore we must determine what code gets generated on each recursion and what code gets generated at the termination case.

---

[16] In this implementation any value other than f will be considered t. See Section 5.5.

[17] In many versions of LISP, gensyms are of the form *Gn* where n is a four digit number beginning at *0000*. Thus the first call of *gensym*[ ] would give *G0000*; succeeding calls would give *G0001, G0002*, etc.

Looking at the example, we see that the block

$$(\text{<code for } p_i\text{>} \ (JUMPF \ 1 \ Li) \ \text{<code for } e_i\text{>} \ (JUMP \ L0) \ Li)$$

is the natural segment for each recursion and that:

$$((JUMP \ ERROR) \ L0)$$

should be generated for the termination case. Within each block we need a "local" label, Li; and within each block, including the terminal case, we refer to the label $L0$ which is "global" to the whole conditional. We can now add the recognizer for $COND$ to *compexp* and construct *comcond*.

Add the clause:

$$iscond[exp] \rightarrow comcond[args_c[exp];gensym[\ ]];$$

to *compexp* where:

$comcond <= \lambda[[u;glob] \ [null[u] \rightarrow list[mkerror[\ ];glob];$
$$t \rightarrow append[comclause[first[u]];$$
$$gensym[];$$
$$glob];$$
$$comcond[rest[u]; \ glob] \ ]$$

$comclause <= \lambda[[p;loc;glob] \ append[\ compexp[ante[p]];$
$$list[mkjumpf[loc]];$$
$$compexp[conseq[p]];$$
$$list[mkjump[glob];loc] \ ]]$$

Recognizer
$iscond <= \lambda[[x] \ eq[first[x]; \ COND]]$

Selectors
$args_c <= \lambda[[x] \ rest[x]]$
$ante <= \lambda[[c] \ first[c]]$
$conseq <= \lambda[[c] \ second[c]]$ [18]

Constructors
$mkerror <= \lambda[[] \ (JUMP \ ERROR)]$
$mkjumpf <= \lambda[[l] \ list[JUMPF;1;l]]$
$mkjump <= \lambda[[l] \ list[JUMP;l]]$

---

[18]This definition of *conseq* does not allow extended conditional expressions. See problem 2 on page 329.

The partially exposed recursive structure of *comcond* would show:

$comcond[((p_1 \ e_1) \ ...(p_n \ e_n));L0]=$

$$
\begin{array}{ll}
(& \text{<code for } p_1\text{>} \\
 & (JUMPF \ 1 \ L1) \\
 & \text{<code for } e_1\text{>} \\
 & (JUMP \ L0) \\
L1 & comcond[((p_2 \ e_2) \ ...(p_n \ e_n)); \ L0])
\end{array}
$$

We need to extend our assembler to handle the generated labels and jumps which appear in the conditional expression code.

Problems

1. Evaluate: $compexp[(COND \ ((EQ \ (QUOTE \ A)(QUOTE \ B))(QUOTE \ C))$
$((NULL \ (QUOTE \ A))(QUOTE \ FOO)))]$

2. Extend *comcond* to handle extended conditional expressions.

6.8 One-pass Assemblers and Fixups

Compilation of conditional expressions requires that the assembler handle the generated label constructs. On page 327 we illustrated the general form for conditional expression code. The symbols, *L0*, *L1*, and *L2* in that example are generated symbols, representing labels. Though the gensyms are *not* true atoms, they *will* satisfy the test for *atom*. Therefore we can represent the recoginzer *is_label* as the predicate *atom*.

When the assembler recognizes a label, it adds information to a symbol table, associating that label with the current value of the assembly counter. References to that label will be translated into references to the associated machine location. The only problem is that references to labels may occur *before* we have come across the label definition in the program. Such references are called **forward references**. For example, all references in the *COND*-code are forward references. [19]

There are two solutions to the forward reference problem:

---

[19]If we scan the instruction sequence in the order in which the code would be executed, we always refer to a label before we come across its definition. We could skirt the forward reference problem by loading the program in reverse order: rather than beginning with the first instruction and loading *upward* in memory, we could begin with the last instruction and load downward. However, this would only be a temporary expedient: an assembler must also handle *progs*, and the label structure of *progs* is not restricted to such predictable behavior.

1. Make two passes through the program being assembled. The first pass builds a symbol table of pairs, each pair consisting of a label and the value of the assembly counter .which will be assigned to it. No code is generated; a second pass uses this symbol table to assemble the code.

2. The other solution is to make one pass through the input. Whenever we come across a forward reference we update the symbol table with a triple consisting of the label name, the assembly counter, and an indication that the entry is a forward reference. We assemble as much of the instruction as we can, expanding the other fields. When a label is defined, we check the table for forward references pending on that label. If there are entries posted, we **fix-up** those instructions to reference the location now assigned to the label.

Some minor programming restrictions are imposed by one-pass assemblers, but particularly for assembling compiled code, one-pass assemblers are usually sufficient and are quite fast. [20]

There are at least two ways to handle the fixup problem. If the fixups are simple, say only requiring fixups to the address-part of a word, then we may link those pending forward references together, chaining them on their, as yet, un-fixed-up field.

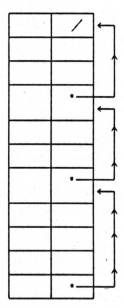

pointer from ⟶
entry in object list

A Simple Fixup Scheme

---

[20]One such restriction requires that any quantities which specify storage allocation, must be resolved before that storage allocation statement is executed.

Each time a forward reference is seen it is added to the linked list; when the label is finally defined and given an address in memory, then the address replaces each reference link. No extra storage is used since the linked list is stored in the partially assembled code. This assumes a word size is sufficient to contain fixup information as well as partially assembled code. If this is not the case, there is an alternative.

Another solution, which is potentially more general is to store the information about each fixup in the symbol table under each label. This solution solves the previous problem and would also allow fixup information for arbitrarily small fields in instructions.

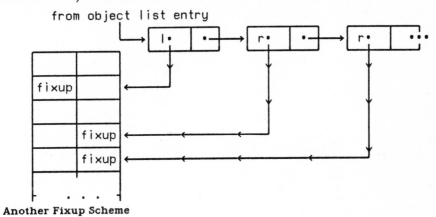

Another Fixup Scheme

The additional information tells the fixup routine how to modify the referenced location.

Both methods are useful. Both have been used extensively in assemblers and compilers. We now sketch a simple one-pass assembler. The assembler will need two functions:

deposit[*x;y*]: *x* represents a machine address; *y* is a list, representing the instruction to be deposited. *y* could be a list of elements: (opcode, accumulator number, memory address) The value of *deposit* is the value of *y*.

examine[*x*]: *x* represents a machine address. The value of *examine* is the contents of location *x* in the form of a list as specified above.

We use our fixup mechanism, combined with *examine, deposit,* and *putprop* and *remprop* from page 261 to write the parts of the assembler which deal with forward references and labels. If the label has been assigned a location then the property list of the label will contain the indicator *SYM* and an associated value representing the assigned location. If the label has *not* been previously defined but has been referenced then the atom will have an indicator $UNDEF$; the value-part will be a list of all those locations which reference that label. Since we will only be doing simple fixups, this will be sufficient. The contents of any location referenced from such a fixup list will be a partially assembled word with the memory address portion set to 0. When the label finally is defined we must perform the fixups, delete the $UNDEF$ pair, and add a SYM pair. There are two main functions.

defloc is called when a label has been defined; if there are no pending forward references then the SYM pair is simply added, otherwise the fixup mechanism is exercised.

$$defloc <= \lambda[[lab;loc] \; prog[[z] \; [null[z \leftarrow get[lab;UNDEF]] \rightarrow go[a]];$$
$$fixup \quad deposit[car[z]];$$
$$fixit[examine[car[z]];loc]];$$
$$[z \leftarrow cdr[z] \rightarrow go[fixup]];$$
$$remprop[lab;UNDEF];$$
$$a \quad return[putprop[lab;loc;SYM]]]]$$

$$fixit <= \lambda[[x;l] \; mkinstr[op[x];ac[x];add[x];l]]$$

gval is called when a label is referenced. If the label is already defined then it simply returns the SYM value; otherwise it adds a forward reference to the list.

$$gval <= \lambda[[lab][get[lab;SYM];$$
$$t \rightarrow putprop[lab;cons[loc;get[lab;UNDEF]];UNDEF];0]]$$

Notes: these functions use lots of tricks.
1. In *defloc* we use *get* as a predicate, relying on our convention that a non-NIL value represents truth (Section 5.5).
2. In that same conditional, we also rely on the fact that the value of an assignment statement is the value of its right hand side. We appeal to points 1 and 2 in the second conditional of *defloc*.
3. In *gval*, there is no e_1; recalling (Section 5.5) that if p_1 evaluates to something non-NIL, then that value is the value of the conditional expression.
4. We also use an extended conditional in *gval*, executing the *putprop* and then returning 0.
5. Note also that *loc* is a non-local variable in *gval*.

6.9 A compiler for Simple *eval*: The Value Stack

The major failing of the previous *compexp* (Section 6.5) is its inability to handle variables. A related failing is its inability to compile code for λ-definitions. This section addresses both problems.
From page 321, we know what *compexp* will do with:

$$f[g[A];h[B]]$$

(MOVE 1 (QUOTE A))	; get *A* into *1*.
(CALL G)	; call the function named *g*
(PUSH P 1)	; save the value
(MOVE 1 (QUOTE B))	; get *B* into *1*
(PUSHJ P H)	; call *h*
(MOVE 2 1)	; restore the arguments in
(POP P 1)	; preparation for
(CALL F)	; calling *f*

No surprises yet. What would we expect to see for a compiled version of:

$$f[g[x];h[y]] \; ?$$

We *should* expect to see the same code except we would have instructions to send the values of x and y into accumulator *1* at the appropriate time. So the first problem is how to find the values of variables. Assume we are really interested in compiling:

$$j <= \lambda[[x;y] \; f[g[x];h[y]]]$$

This added problem makes our question easier. Consider a call on *j*: *j*[*A;B*], for example. We know that the execution of the call occurs after the values *A* and *B* have been set up in *AC1* and *AC2*. Thus at *that* time we do indeed know what the values of x and y are supposed to be. For sake of simplicity, assume that the variables x and y are strictly local. That is, no one within the bodies of either g or h uses x or y free; we will worry about compilation of free references later. Since x and y are local, only *j* needs to find their values. We cannot leave the values in the *AC*s since those registers are needed for other computations. Rather, we will save x and y in the top of the stack *P*.

   Since *P* contains the values of partial computations, and now also contains the values of the local λ-variables, *P* is also called the **value stack**. This is a value stack similar to that described in deep-binding (Section 5.18); however we do not need the name stack here. The compiler will *know* where on the stack values of local variables can be found; it will put them there so it *should* know. This lack of a name stack is a mixed blessing; we save space, but we have lost the names; the names are useful when we are debugging code, and necessary for a full LISP implementation. Note that *P* is not solely a value stack; it also contains the control information. We are not always able to mix access and control information on one stack; in fact, we know that a stack is not always a suffcient vehicle for describing LISP's access requirements. However, a very large subset of LISP *does* allow a single-stack implementation, and we will be compiling within that subset for most of this chapter.

   Addressing the task at hand, the instructions for the body of *j* will be very similar to those displayed for $f[g[A];h[B]]$. We will generate instructions to save the values on the actual parameters by prefixing the *compexp*-code with two *PUSH* operations:

$$(PUSH\ P\ 1)$$
$$(PUSH\ P\ 2)$$

After execution of this pair of instructions, called the **prolog**, the value of y is on the top of the stack, and the value of x is the next element down. [21]

Now that we have saved the values, we need instructions to *send* them to $AC1$ when the value is needed. We will implement *send@* using the $MOVE$ instruction (Section 6.3). In this case our memory reference will be relative to the top of the P stack. Relative addressing is described in our machine as an address field of the form "$n\ P$", where n designates the offset into P and references the nth element, counting backwards from zero. Thus in our current example "$0\ P$" refers to the value for y and "$-1\ P$" refers to x at the time j is entered. Be sure to realize also that our addressing is relative; though "$0\ P$" refers to y at entry time, $0\ P$ will *not* refer to y when we have pushed something onto the stack. Be sure to realize that we *cannot* change our relative addressing to hard machine locations in the assembler. The addressing must always be relative. We will be compiling code for recursive functions. Each recursive call must get a fresh segment of the value stack in which to store its results. A similar problem appeared when we examined the $CALL\text{-}RET$ mechanism on page 314. There we were dealing with control information stored on a stack.

Finally, we cannot leave the code for j as it stands. If the prolog pushes two entries onto the stack then we had better construct an epilog to remove them; otherwise the stack will not be in the state expected by the calling program. As we leave j we subtract 2 from the pointer P to synchronize the stack. The constant 2 is designated as $(C\ 2)$. Finally we exit via RET.

One further embellishment is needed: since we are defining a function and turning it into compiled code, we must preface the code sequence with information to our assembler to designate j as a machine-coded call-by-value function. The assembler will make a new property-value pair consisting of the property name $SUBR$ and an associated value part which is the value of the assembly counter when the assembly was begun. That pair is placed on the p-list of the atom representing the function name.

------

[21]The observant reader will note that the $PUSH$ for x is unnecessary. Since we have assumed that x and y are strictly local, and since no one else needs the value of x except for $g[x]$, we can simply compute $g[x]$ directly. One might also think that we could leave B in $AC2$ while we calculated $g[x]$; we cannot do that, as $g[x]$ might use $AC2$. We must $PUSH\ y$.

```
(LAP J SUBR)        ; says j is a function
(PUSH P 1)          ; save the input args
(PUSH P 2)
(MOVE 1 -1 P)       ; get x
(CALL G)            ; call the function named g
(PUSH P 1)          ; save the value
(MOVE 1 -1 P)       ; get y
(PUSH J P H)        ; call h
(MOVE 2 1)          ; set up the arguments in
(POP P 1)           ;   preparation for
(CALL  F)           ;   calling f
(SUB P (C 2))       ; synchronize the stack by removing
                    ;   the two saved args
(RET)               ; exit with AC1 containing the value of j[x,y]
```

As you read the code and as you study its execution you should remember that the addressing in the code is relative to the top of the stack: *(MOVE 1 -1 P)* gets *x* in one instance and finds *y* in another, because the top of the stack changes. Here is a picture of the execution of the code:

```
AC1: x ; AC2: y                                    AC1: x ; AC2: y
|   |(PUSH P 1)      | x |(PUSH P 2)      | y |(MOVE 1 -1 P)
    =>                   =>               | x|      =>


AC1: x ; AC2: y      AC1: g[x] ; AC2: ?
| y |(CALL G)        | y |(PUSH P 1)      |g[x]|(MOVE 1 -1 P)
| x | =>             | x |    =>          | y |     =>
                     | x |

AC1: y ; AC2: ?      AC1: h[y] ; AC2: ?   AC1: h[y] ; AC2: h[y]
|g[x]| (PUSH J P H)  |g[x]| (MOVE 2 1)    |g[x]|(POP P AC1)
| y | =>             | y |    =>          | y |     =>
| x |                | x |               | x |


AC1: g[x] ; AC2: h[y]    AC1: f[g[x];h[y]]
| y  |(CALL 2  F)        | y |(SUB P (C 2))  =>    (RET)
| x  | =>                | x |
```

6.10 A Compiler for Simple *eval*

Now that we know what the runtime code for local variable references *could* be, we must describe an algorithm which will generate similar code. We shall simulate the behavior of the runtime stack while we are compiling the code. The compiler cannot know what the *values* of the variables will be at run time but it can know *where* to find the values. We will carry this information through the compiler in a manner reminiscent of the *assoc*-style symbol table of the *eval* in Section 3.5. Instead of posting the current values in the stack, the compiler will post information about the positions of the variables relative to the top of the stack at the time we enter the function. The variable-position list, *vpl*, contains this information. If we are to compile a function with λ-variables, [x;y;z] then *vpl* will begin with:

$$((X \ . \ 1), (Y \ . \ 2), (Z \ . \ 3) \ ...$$

When we set up *vpl* we also set the offset, called *off*, to minus the number of arguments added to *vpl*, in this case -3. Now if we come across a reference, say to *Y*, while compiling code, we use *cdr[assoc[Y;vpl]]* to retrieve 2. The offset plus this retrieved value gives us the relative position of *Y* in the stack: -3 + 2 = -1. Thus to refer to the location of *Y* we use *(... -1 P)*.

What happens as we add elements to the stack? Or to be more precise, what happens as we generate code which when executed will add elements to the stack? Clearly we must modify the offset. If we add one element, we would set *off* to -4. Then to reference *Y* now use -4 + 2 = -2; that is, a reference to *Y* is now of the form:

$$(\ ... \ -2 \ P)$$

But that's right. *Y* is now further down in the run time stack. Thus the 'symbol table' is really defined by *off* plus the current *vpl*. Here's a sketch of the proposed *compexp* in its performance of local variable recognition.

$$islocalvar[exp] \rightarrow list[mkvar[1;loc[exp;off;vpl]]]$$

where: $$loc \ <= \ \lambda[[x;off;vpl] \ plus[off;cdr[assoc[x;vpl]]]]$$

and, $$mkvar \ <= \ \lambda[[ac;mem] \ list[MOVE;ac;mem;P]]$$

Next, when will the compiler make modifications to the top of the stack? We push new elements when we are compiling the arguments to a function call. We know that *complis* is the function which compiles the argument list. Thus our new *complis* must know about *off* and *vpl*, and since *complis* changes the state of the stack, then it must change *off* appropriately:

$$complis \ <= \ \lambda[[u;off;vpl] \ [null \ [u] \rightarrow (\ );$$
$$null[rest[u]] \rightarrow compexp[first[u];off; \ vpl];$$
$$t \rightarrow append[compexp \ [first[u]; \ off; \ vpl];$$
$$list[mkalloc[1]];$$
$$complis \ [rest[u]; \ subl[off]; \ vpl]]]]$$

Notice that *complis* compiles the arguments from left to right, following each with *(PUSH P 1)* and recurring with a new offset which reflects the effect of the *PUSH*. This function is analogous to *evlis*.

Here's a brief description of the rest of the new compiler. [22]

compile[fn;vars;exp]: *fn* is the name of the function to be compiled. *vars* is the list of lambda variables. *exp* is the lambda-body.

```
compile <= λ[ [fn;vars;exp]
                λ[[n] append[ mkprolog[fn;n];
                              compexp[exp; -n; prup[vars;1]];
                              mkepilog[n]]]
                [length[vars]] ]
```

mkprolog <= λ[[f;n] concat[list[LAP;f;SUBR];mkpushs[n;1]]]

mkpushs <= λ[[n;m][lessp[n;m] → ( );
                        t → concat[mkalloc[m]; mkpushs[n;add1[m]]]]]]

mkepilog <= λ[[n] list[mksync[n];mkret[]]]

mksync <=λ[[n] list[SUB;P;list[C;n]]]

mkret <=λ[[] (RET)]

prup[vars;n]: *vars* is a lambda list, *n* is an integer. *prup* builds a variable-position list.

prup <= λ[[vars;n][null[vars] → ( );
                        t → concat[cons[first[vars]; n];
                                    prup[rest[vars];add1[n]]]]]]

---

[22]This compiler was adapted from one written by J. McCarthy ([McC 76]), and proved correct by R. London ([Lon 71]) and M. Newey ([New 75]).

compexp[exp;off;vpl]: This function generates the code for constants and for references to variables. If the variable is local, a simple *send* is generated, otherwise a call on *lookup* results. If a conditional expression is recognized, *comcond* is called to produce the code. If *exp* does not fit one of these categories, it is assumed to be an application of a call-by-value function. In this case, *complis* compiles the argument list, leaving the arguments in the stack; *loadac* loads the appropriate *AC*'s. and then we generate a call on the function, and finally generate the *SUB* to synchronize the stack.

$$compexp <= \lambda[[exp;off;vpl]$$
$$[isconst[exp] \rightarrow list[mkconst[1;exp]];$$
$$islocalvar[exp] \rightarrow list [mkvar[1;loc[exp;off;vpl]]];$$
$$isnonlocal[exp] \rightarrow list[mklookup[exp]];$$
$$iscond[exp] \rightarrow comcond[args_c[exp];$$
$$gensym[ ];$$
$$off;$$
$$vpl];$$
$$isfun+args[exp] \rightarrow \lambda[[z] compapply[func[exp];$$
$$complis[z;off;vpl];$$
$$length[z]]$$
$$[arglist[exp]]]]$$

compapply is found on page 324.

comcond[u;glob;off;vpl]: this compiles the body of conditional expressions. *u* is the p_i - e_i list; *glob* will be bound to a generated symbol name; *off* and *vpl* will always be the offset and the variable-position list.

$$comcond <= \lambda[[u;glob;off;vpl] [null[u] \rightarrow list[mkerror[ ];glob];$$
$$t \rightarrow append[comclause[first[u];$$
$$gensym[];$$
$$glob;$$
$$off;$$
$$vpl];$$
$$comcond[rest[u]; glob;off;vpl]]]$$

$$comclause <= \lambda[[p;loc;glob;off;vpl]append[compexp[ante[p];$$
$$off;$$
$$vpl];$$
$$list[mkjumpf[loc]];$$
$$compexp[conseq[p];$$
$$off;$$
$$vpl];$$
$$list[mkjump[glob];loc]]]$$

Here is a partial sketch of *compile* operating on

$$j <= \lambda[[x;y]f[g[x];h[y]]]$$

Compare the code it generates with the code we saw on page 335.

compile[*J* ;(*X Y*);(*F (G X) (H Y)*)]

gives:

$$\textit{append} \quad [((LAP \; J \; SUBR)); \\ (PUSH \; P \; 1) \\ (PUSH \; P \; 2) \\ compexp[(F \; (G \; X) \; (H \; Y));-2;prup[(X \; Y);1]]; \\ ((SUB \; P \; (C \; 2)) \\ (RET))]$$

where: *prup*[(*X Y*);*1*]   gives   ((*X . 1*) (*Y . 2*))

compexp[(*F (G X) (H Y)*);-2;((*X . 1*) (*Y . 2*))]

results in: *append* [*complis*[((*G X*) (*H Y*));-2;((*X . 1*) (*Y . 2*))];
                    mklink[2];
                    ((*CALL F*))]

and *mklink*[2] evaluates to: ((*MOVE 2 1*) (*POP P 1*)).

Thus the code we're getting looks like:

$$((LAP \; J \; SUBR) \\ (PUSH \; P \; 1) \\ (PUSH \; P \; 2) \\ complis[((G \; X) \; (H \; Y)); -2; ((X \; . \; 1) \; (Y \; . \; 2))] \\ (MOVE \; 2 \; 1) \\ (POP \; P \; 1) \\ (CALL \; F) \\ (SUB \; P \; (C \; 2)) \\ (RET) \;)$$

complis is interesting since it actually uses the *vpl* we have been carrying along. It gives rise to:

$$\textit{append} \; [compexp[(G \; X);-2;((X \; . \; 1) \; (Y \; . \; 2))]; \\ ((PUSH \; P \; 1)); \\ complis[((H \; Y));-3;((X \; . \; 1) \; (Y \; . \; 2))]]$$

and the *compexp* computation involves, in part:

$$\textit{append}[complis[(X);-2;((X \; . \; 1) \; (Y \; . \; 2))]; \\ ((CALL \; G))]$$

Finally this *complis* generates the long awaited variable reference using:

compexp[*X* ;-2;((*X . 1*) (*Y . 2*))]   giving, ((*MOVE 1 -1 P*))

So our code is:

```
((LAP J SUBR)
 (PUSH P 1)
 (PUSH P 2)
 (MOVE 1 -1 P)
 (CALL G)
 (PUSH P 1)
 complis[((H Y)); -3; ((X . 1) (Y . 2))]
 (MOVE 2 1)
 (POP P 1)
 (CALL F)
 (SUB P (C 2))
 (RET) )
```

Notice that the offset is different within the call:

$$complis[((H\ Y)); -3; ((X\ .\ 1)\ (Y\ .\ 2))]$$

But that is as it should be: now there is an extra value on the stack.

Problems

1. Complete the code generation for the above example.
2. Extend the compiling algorithm to recognize anonymous λ-expressions.

6.11 Efficient Compilation

"At the risk of slight exaggeration, we must chastize, in today's programming environment, the process of compilation and the very word itself, which is the grand euphemism of computer science. Compilation is like an alchemistic art of transforming gold into lead, to obtain pencils and hence to communicate information. The task of a compiler is to take programs of a high-level, relatively problem-oriented language, and mutilate them beyond recognition, distorting them finally into sequences of unrecognizable codes comprehensible only to elements of electronic circuitry capable of actual execution. Incredibly, the high-level intent is simulated in this world of wires, and the program is executed as desired. The compilation process is magic. A translation has been made between two representations with no apparent similarity of form or content, yet those representations are in a global sense equivalent in their execution."

Mark Elson, *Concepts of Programming Languages* [Els 73]

We have discussed compilation at two different levels: we can translate LISP expressions into sequences of the LISP control primitives of Section 6.2; or we can translate into the instructions of the SM machine of Section 6.3. We conceptualized the compilers in terms of higher level abstractions, but biased many of our choices towards implementation on the SM instruction set. Our choices influenced the efficiency of the resulting compiler.

We should first clarify what we mean by efficiency in this context. If the compiler produces code for the LISP primitives and then we encode the LISP primitives in terms of the SM instruction set, then we get a simple compiler which tends to produce inefficient code; inefficent, in terms of the SM machine, not in terms of the LISP primitives. Such a compiler would be efficient in terms of compilation time and might suffice for debugging runs or student projects.

More likely, efficient compilation is taken to mean production of code which we could expect from a reasonably bright machine-language programmer. It should run reasonably fast, not have obviously redundant instructions, and not take too much space in the machine. It is this second interpretation of efficiency which we shall use. In this interpretation we don't simply implement the LISP primitives, but take a more global view of the underlying machine. We take advantage of more of the hardware features, incorporating them deeper into the structure of the compiler. This process is called optimization. Optimization defies the mismatch between the programming language and the hardware machine. The result is a compiler which is much more machine dependent, may require more processing time, but produces much better code for that specific machine.

Our current compilation algorithm has many opportunities for improvement. A major inefficiency occurs in saving and restoring quantities on the stack. This is a symptom of a more serious disease: the compiler does not remember what will be in the AC's at run-time. Since we are assuming that the arguments to a function call are to be passed through the AC's, and since it is expensive to save and restore these registers, we should make a concerted effort to remember which quantities are in which AC and not reload them unnecessarily. This optimization is dependent on the hardware of our machine; if we had only one AC, the trick would not be applicable.

6.12 Efficiency: Primitive Operations

We should be able to generate references into AC's other that $AC1$. This is particularly useful for compiling constant arguments.

For example, the call on $f[1;A]$ should be generated as:

> *(MOVEI 1 1)*
> *(MOVEI 2 (QUOTE A))*
> *(CALL F)*

There is no reason to save constants in the stack.

We also expect that the LISP primitive operations, *car, cdr, cons, eq,* and *atom* should occur rather frequently in compiled code; [23] and we should expect that a reasonable compiler be cognizant of their existence and compile more efficient code for their execution. In this section we will enlarge the instruction set of our machine, adding plausible operations for some of these primitives. [24]

CAR is an instruction, taking two arguments: an *ac* and a *loc* respectively. The *car* operation is performed from *loc* to *ac*. For example when compiling the call, $f[1;car[x]]$, we want the value *car[x]* in *AC2*. If *x* were in *-5 P* then we could accomplish the loading with: *(CAR 2 -5 P)* instead of:

> *(MOVE 1 -5 P)*
> *(CALL CAR)*
> *(MOVE 2 1)*

Since the second argument to *CAR* can be an accumulator, the second argument to $f[1;car[car[x]]]$ can be compiled as:

> *(CAR 2 -5 P)*
> *(CAR 2 2)*

We will assume the existence of an analogous *CDR* instruction. With these two instructions we can significantly improve the code for *car-cdr*-chains.

Another source of efficiency is available to us. Consider the clause:

$$[eq[x;A] \rightarrow B; ...]$$

_____

[23]Though we program at an abstract level, the code passed to the compiler may have many *car-cdr* references; see Section 6.18.

[24]Some of these instuctions exist on the PDP-10. HLRZ and HRRZ are used for *car* and *cdr*, respectively; and the PDP-6 which was delivered to Stanford had a hardware *cons* operation.

Assuming that *x* were on the top of the stack, our current compiler would generate:

```
(MOVE 1 0 P)
(MOVEI 2 (QUOTE A))
(CALL EQ)
(JUMPF 1 L1)
(MOVEI 1 (QUOTE B))
(JUMP LOUT)
L1 ...
```

The use of predicates in this context does not require construction of the constants t and f. All we need to do is implement the *eq* test as a jump to one of two locations.

We will introduce an instruction *CAME* taking two arguments; first, an *ac* and the second, a *loc*. *CAME* compares the contents of the two arguments, and if they are equal, it skips the next instruction.
Thus the above example could be compiled as:

```
(MOVEI 1 (QUOTE A))
(CAME 1 0 P)
(JUMP L1)
(MOVEI 1 (QUOTE B))
(JUMP LOUT)
L1 ...
```

Notice that we have added an extra piece of knowledge to the compiler; it knows that *eq* is commutative in this instance.[25] We still require some artifacts in the compiler to generate full procedure calls on predicates particularly since predicates may return values other than t and f. But in many instances, particularly within *comcond*, we can generate tighter code.

6.13 Efficiency: Calling Sequences

We want to integrate the new compiling techniques into our compiler. Since LISP depends heavily on procedure calls, the computation of parameter lists and procedure calls is an area of great concern to the designer of a LISP compiler.

Here is the code which the current compiler will produce for the expression $f[1;g[3]; car[x]]$:

---

[25]If there are side-effects in the computation of the arguments, the order can make a difference. However unless explicitly stated our compilers do not have to consider side-effects.

```
(MOVEI 1 1)
(PUSH P 1)
(MOVEI 1 3)
(CALL G)
(PUSH P 1)
(MOVE 1 -2 P)
(CALL CAR)
(MOVE 3 1)
(POP P 2)
(POP P 1)
(CALL F)
```

By way of motivation and introduction, here is what our next compiler does for the same call:

```
(MOVEI 1 3)
(CALL G)
(MOVE 2 1)
(CAR 3 0 P)
(MOVEI 1 1)
(CALL F)
```

Examination of the code shows the results of several optimization techniques. We are using the *CAR* instruction of the last section. We are also doing operations into *AC*'s other than *AC1*. This allows us to remove some of the obnoxious *PUSH-POP* sequences.

The major modification involves an analysis of the arguments being compiled for a function call. The function *complis* is responsible for that analysis. Within our new *complis* we will divide the arguments into two classes: trivial and complex. Since most of our worry is about the optimization of the *AC*'s, we will make *complis* the major state of the compiler. We can define *compexp* as:

$$compexp <= \lambda[[exp;vpl;off] \; complis[list[exp];vpl;off]]$$

complis is the natural place to deal with register allocation since it is responsible for the compilation of the actual parameters. The alternative would be to pass the *AC* destination to *compexp*. That scheme becomes quite complex if dealt with consistently. So *complis* becomes the kernel function and must examine each argument to a function call.

Trivial arguments are those which need make no demands on the runtime stack; the computation they entail can all be done in the *AC* registers. Thus the code that the compiler generates need not involve *PUSH-POP* sequences. For example, references to constants need not be generated and then pushed onto the stack; we can compile the other arguments first and then, just before we call the function, load the appropriate *AC* with that constant. A similar argument can be used for postponing the loading of variable references. [26] The third trivial construct for this *complis* is the handling of *car-cdr* chains. We will use our augmented instruction set to perform computation of *cars* and *cdrs* directly to a specified *AC*. Complex arguments are those which require some non-trivial computation; each non-trivial computation will be prefaced with a *PUSH* to save the current contents of *AC1*.

Besides the compilation of efficient code we would also like to make the compiler efficient. We would like to make the compiling process as one-pass as possible. Our basic tasks in the new *complis* are classification of the arguments and compilation of the code. With a little care we can do both at the same time. There is nothing problematic about the compilation of the trivial code. [27] We thus turn to the complex code.

The old *complis* generated a block <code *arg$_i$*>-*PUSH* on each cycle. That code was followed by a *MOVE* to move the last value from *AC1* to *ACn*. In the previous compiler *compexp* was the major function; it handled the bulk of the code generation. Here *complis* will be the major function. The old *complis* had three states: empty argument list, singleton argument list, and otherwise condition. The new *complis* has two states; this is done to make *complis* shorter. On each cycle through *complis* we generate a *PUSH*-<code *arg$_i$*> sequence. Now we have a spurious *PUSH* on the *front* of the sequence; one *rest* will take care of *that*.

We must also generate a list of *POP*s to suffix to the complex code to get the saved values back into the proper *AC*'s: one pop for each argument. The *last POP* should be modified to be a *MOVE* since we have not generated the corresponding *PUSH*. The memory field of the last *POP* has the needed information; it tells us where the *MOVE* we want to make should go:

$$(POP\ P\ N) => (MOVE\ N\ 1)$$

This modified list of *POP*s is added to the code sequence, followed by any trivial code which we may have generated. Note that this reordering is strictly an efficiency consideration under the assumption that the *AC*'s are being used to simulate a temporary *dest* block, which will immediately become a block of local bindings, and which are subject to local use only. With this introduction, here is *complis* and friends:

complis <= λ[[*u;off;vpl*] *complis'*[*u;off;off;vpl;();();();1*]

---

[26]But note that the argument for variables is shaky; if our compiler handled programs with side-effects then we could *not* be sure that the postponed value would be the same as that fetched at the "proper" time.

[27]That's why it's trivial!

complis' <= λ[[*u;org;off;vpl;triv;cmplx;pop;ac*]
         [*null*[*u*] → [*null*[*cmplx*] → *triv*;

                   t → *append*[*rest*[*cmplx*];
                             list[*mkmove*[*mem*[*first*[*pop*]];*1*]];
                             rest[*pop*];
                             triv]];

         isconst[*first*[*u*]] → *complis'*[*rest*[*u*];
                         org;
                         off;
                         vpl;
                         concat[*mkconst*[*ac;first*[*u*]];*triv*];
                         cmplx;
                         pop;
                         add1[*ac*]];

         isvar[*first*[*u*]] → *complis'*[*rest*[*u*];
                         org;
                         off;
                         vpl;
                         concat[*mkvar*[*ac*;
                                     loc[*first*[*u*];*off;vpl*]];
                             triv);
                         cmplx;
                         pop;
                         add1[*ac*]];

         iscarcdr[*first*[*u*]] → *complis'*[*rest*[*u*];
                         org;
                         off;
                         vpl;
                         append[*reverse*[*compcarcdr*[*ac*;
                                             first[*u*]
                                             off;
                                             vpl]];
                             triv];
                         cmplx;
                         pop;
                         add1[*ac*]];

$$iscond[first[u] \rightarrow complis^*[rest[u];$$
$$org;$$
$$sub1[off];$$
$$vpl;$$
$$triv;$$
$$append[cmplx;$$
$$concat[mkpush[1];$$
$$comcond[args_c[first[u]]$$
$$gensym[];$$
$$off;$$
$$vpl]]];$$
$$concat[mkpop[ac];pop];$$
$$add1[ac]];$$

$$t \rightarrow complis^*[rest[u];$$
$$org;$$
$$sub1[off];$$
$$vpl;$$
$$triv;$$
$$append[cmplx;$$
$$concat[mkpush[1];$$
$$\lambda[[z]\ compapply[func[first[u]];$$
$$complis[z;$$
$$off;$$
$$vpl];$$
$$length[z]]]$$
$$[arglist[first[u]]\ ]];$$
$$concat[mkpop[ac];pop];$$
$$add1[ac]]]$$

$mkmove <= \lambda[[ac;loc][eq[ac;loc] \rightarrow (); t \rightarrow list[MOVE,ac;loc]]]$

$compcarcdr <= \lambda[[ac;exp;off;vpl]$
$$[isvar[arg[exp]] \rightarrow list[mkcarcdr[func[exp];$$
$$ac;$$
$$loc[arg[exp];off;vpl]]]$$

$$t \rightarrow concat[mkcarcdr\_ac[func[exp];ac;ac];$$
$$compcarcdr[ac;arg[exp];off;vpl]]]]$

$iscarcdr <=\lambda[[u]\ [iscar[u] \rightarrow iscarcdr[arg[u]]$
$$iscdr[u] \rightarrow iscarcdr[arg[u]]$$
$$atom[u] \rightarrow or[isvar[u];isconst[u]];$$
$$t \rightarrow f\ ]]$$

$iscar <= \lambda[[x]\ eq[func[x];CAR]]$
$iscdr <= \lambda[[x]\ eq[func[x];CDR]]$
$mkcarcdr <=\lambda[[carcdr;ac;loc]\ list[carcdr;ac;loc]]$

6.14 Efficiency: Predicates

We have already noted in Section 6.12 that some efficiencies are possible when predicates occur within conditional expressions. Here we will examine more possibilities. The first point of contention is that the current *comclause* is *not* good enough. We want to be able to use the Boolean special forms: $and[u_1; ...,u_n]$ and $or[u_1; ...,u_n]$. The definition of these constructs requires they not evaluate any more arguments than necessary. We can exploit this property when *and* and *or* appear as predicates in conditional expressions. We will add recognizers for *and* and *or* inside *comclause* and will add a new section to the compiler to deal with their compilation.

First, here is the structure of typical code sequences:

$and[u_1; ... u_n] \to e;$	$or[u_1; ... u_n] \to e;$
gives:	gives:

\<code for u_1>	*\<code for u_1>*
(JUMPF 1 lint)	*(JUMPT 1 loc)*
\<code for u_2>	*\<code for u_2>*
(JUMPF 1 lint)	*(JUMPT 1 loc)*
. . .	. . .
\<code for u_n>	*\<code for u_n>*
(JUMPF 1 lint)	*(JUMPT 1 loc)*
(JUMP loc)	*(JUMP lint)*
loc	*loc*
\<code for *e*>	\<code for *e*>
(JUMP lout)	*(JUMP lout)*
lint	*lint*

The label *lint* indicates the next clause in the conditional expression. Note the symmetry between the code for *and* and the code for *or*. There is a slight inefficiency in *and* with *(JUMP loc)* immediately followed by *loc*, but we can easily remove that.

Here is a *compclause* which will generate it:

$$compclause <= \lambda[[p;loc;glob;off;vpl]\; append[compred[\; ante[p];$$
$$loc;$$
$$off;$$
$$vpl];$$
$$compexp[conseq[p];$$
$$off;$$
$$vpl];$$
$$list[mkjump[glob];loc]]]$$

$compred$ <= $\lambda[[p;lint;off;vpl][isand[p] \rightarrow compandor[args[p];$
$$off;$$
$$vpl;$$
$$list[mkjumpnil[lint]];$$
$$()];$$
$$isor[p] \rightarrow \lambda\,[[loc]\,compandor[args[p];$$
$$off;$$
$$vpl;$$
$$list[mkjumpt[loc]];$$
$$list[mkjmp[lint];$$
$$loc]]]$$
$$[gensym[]];$$
$$t \rightarrow append[compexp[p;off;vpl];$$
$$list[mkjumpf[lint]]]\;\;]]$$

$compandor$ <=$\lambda[[u;off;vpl;inst;fini]\,[null[u] \rightarrow fini;$
$$t \rightarrow append[compexp[first[u];off;vpl];$$
$$inst;$$
$$compandor[rest[u];$$
$$off;$$
$$vpl;$$
$$inst;$$
$$fini]]\;]]]$$

Problems

1. We should recognize the construct $t \rightarrow e_i$ in conditional expressions and compile special code for it. We should also realize that in the construct:
$$[p_1 \rightarrow e_1\;...\;t \rightarrow e_i;\;...p_n \rightarrow e_n]$$
we can *never* reach any part of the conditional after the t-predicate; therefore no code should be generated. Rewrite the compiler to handle these additional observations about conditionals.

   The second point, above, is a special instance of a general compiling question. How clever should the compiler be? If it can recognize that a piece of program can never be reached, should it tell the user or should it compile minimal code?

2. Write a new *compile* including all the efficiency considerations discussed so far.

3. When we apply the convention that anything non-NIL is a representation of truth, it is often convenient to evaluate *and* and *or* for "value". That is their value is either NIL or non-NIL. Extend our compiler to handle such uses of these functions.

4. Extend the compiler to compile efficient code for compositions of the predicates *and*, *or*, and *not*.

6.15 A Compiler for *progs*

The compiler of this section will not compile all *progs*; it is only intended to demonstrate some of the salient features of a *prog* compiler. They are:

1. Handling of assignments. Since we are assuming local variables, then storage to the value stack is sufficient.

2. The *go*-label pair. We will assume that this can be passed off to the assembler.

3. On leaving a *prog*-body we have to remove the *prog*-variables from the top of the stack. This is done by comparing the current *off* with *vpl*.

$compprog <=\lambda[[locals;body;off;vpl]$
$\qquad\qquad\lambda[[n]append[mkpushlistnil[n];$
$\qquad\qquad\qquad compbody[\ body;$
$\qquad\qquad\qquad\qquad labels[body];$
$\qquad\qquad\qquad\qquad difference[off;n];$
$\qquad\qquad\qquad\qquad pruploc[locals;-off;vpl];$
$\qquad\qquad\qquad\qquad n;$
$\qquad\qquad\qquad\qquad gensym[]]]]$
$\qquad\qquad [length[locals]]$

$pruploc <= \lambda[[locals;off;vpl][null[locals] \to vpl;$
$\qquad\qquad\qquad\qquad t \to pruploc[rest[locals];$
$\qquad\qquad\qquad\qquad\qquad add1[off];$
$\qquad\qquad\qquad\qquad\qquad concat[cons[first[locals];off];vpl]]]]$

$labels <= \lambda[[body] [null[body] \to ();$
$\qquad\qquad islabel[first[body]] \to concat[first[body];labels[rest[body]]];$
$\qquad\qquad t \to labels[rest[body]]]]]$

$compbody <= \lambda[[body;labels;off;vpl;n;exit]$
$\qquad\qquad [null[body] \to list[mkconst[1;NIL];exit;mksync[n]];$
$\qquad\qquad islabel[first[body]] \to concat[first[body];compbody[rest[body];$
$\qquad\qquad\qquad\qquad\qquad\qquad\qquad\qquad labels;$
$\qquad\qquad\qquad\qquad\qquad\qquad\qquad\qquad off;$
$\qquad\qquad\qquad\qquad\qquad\qquad\qquad\qquad vpl;$
$\qquad\qquad\qquad\qquad\qquad\qquad\qquad\qquad n;$
$\qquad\qquad\qquad\qquad\qquad\qquad\qquad\qquad exit]];$
$\qquad isgo[first[body]] \to append[list[compgo[arg[first[body]]];$
$\qquad\qquad\qquad\qquad\qquad\qquad\qquad labels]];$
$\qquad\qquad\qquad\qquad compbody[rest[body];$
$\qquad\qquad\qquad\qquad\qquad labels;$
$\qquad\qquad\qquad\qquad\qquad off;$
$\qquad\qquad\qquad\qquad\qquad vpl;$
$\qquad\qquad\qquad\qquad\qquad n;$
$\qquad\qquad\qquad\qquad\qquad exit]];$

$$isret[first[body]] \rightarrow append[\,compexp[\,arglist[first[body]]];$$
$$off;$$
$$vpl];$$
$$sync[off;vpl];$$
$$list[mkjump[exit]];$$
$$compbody[\,rest[body];$$
$$labels;$$
$$off;$$
$$vpl;$$
$$n;$$
$$exit]];$$

$$issetq[first[body]] \rightarrow append[compexp[\,rhs[first[body]];off;vpl];$$
$$list[mkmovem[1;$$
$$loc[\,lhs[first[body]];$$
$$off;$$
$$vpl]]];$$
$$compbody[\,rest[body];$$
$$labels;$$
$$off;$$
$$vpl;$$
$$n;$$
$$exit]];$$

$$iscond[first[body]] \rightarrow append[\,compcondprog[arg[first[body]]];$$
$$compbody[\,rest[body];$$
$$labels;$$
$$off;$$
$$vpl;$$
$$n;$$
$$exit]];$$

$$t \rightarrow append[\,compexp[first[body];off;vpl];$$
$$compbody[rest[body];labels;off;vpl;n;exit]]]]]$$

$$compgo <= \lambda[[x;l][member[x;l] \rightarrow mkjump[x];\; t \rightarrow err[UNDEFINED\_TAG]]];$$

This *compprog* only handles a subset of the semantics of *prog*. We do not handle any non-local jumps; a new list of labels is made up on entry to a *prog* and only that set of labels is accessible for *gos*. As a further restriction, we also assume that the *prog* variables are used in a strictly local fashion.

Problem

1. Write *compcondprog*.

6.16 Further Optimizations

This section is in the nature of hints and possibilities for expansion of the basic compiling algorithms.

One of the first things to note about the compiling algorithm is its lack of knowledge about what it has in the various AC's. Frequently the compiled code will load up one of the registers with a quantity that is already there. Thus the first suggestion: build a list of what's in various registers. We know what's there when we enter the function; whenever we perform an operation which destroys a register then we have to update the compiler's memory. Whenever we need a quantity, we check the memory. If the object is already in the AC's then we use it. Clearly there is a point at which the complexity of the object stored is too complicated to be worth remembering. However, the idea can be used quite profitably for variable references and simple computations. This idea is a simple form of **common sub expression elimination**. For example, assuming that the compiler knows x is in $AC1$, here's code for:

$$f[car[x];cdr[car[x]]]$$
$$(CAR\ 1\ 1)$$
$$(CDR\ 2\ 1)$$
$$(CALL\ F)$$

This idea can be extended. There is nothing sacred about knowing only the contents of the special registers. We could keep a history of the partial computations in the stack. Then if we need a partial result we might find it already computed in the ACs or stored on the stack. We might also keep track of whether stack or AC contents are still needed. For example, in our compiled function j on page 335 we might have noticed that after the call on g, the value of x was no longer needed; therefore we need not save x. Similarly we don't need the value of y after the call on h. If we build this kind of information into a compiler, we can generate more efficient code. However, many of these ideas must be used with some care. Side-effects can destroy the validity of partial results.

Notice that we are comparing the *symbolic* values in the AC's or stack; we cannot look for actual values. This idea of symbolic processing can be exploited at a much more sophisticated level in LISP compilers. In particular, we can perform program transformations. For example, the compiler can rewrite program segments taking advantage of transformations it knows. These transformations typically involve equivalence preserving operations which might lead to more efficient compiled code.

For example several LISP compilers have the ability to perform recursion removal, replacing recursive programs with equivalent iterative versions. [28] Here's a case:

---

[28]All these transformations should be invisible to the user.

$$rev <= \lambda[[x;y][null[x] \rightarrow y;\ t \rightarrow rev[rest[x];concat[first[x];y]]]]$$

This program is automatically rewritten as:

$$rev <= \lambda[[x;y]\ prog[[]\ l\ [null[x] \rightarrow return[y]];$$
$$y \leftarrow concat[first[x];y];$$
$$x \leftarrow rest[x];$$
$$go[l]\ ]]$$

This second version makes no demands on the run-time stack; it does not stack its partial computation like the recursive version. Each recursive call pushes the values for x and y; the iterative version uses two fixed locations. Typically the second version on rev will execute faster.

A major obstacle to most kinds of optimization is the unrestricted use of labels and gos. Consider a piece of compiler code which has a label attached to it. Before we can be assured of the integrity of an AC we must ascertain that every possible path to that label maintains that AC. This is a very difficult task. The label and goto structure required by *compile* is quite simple. However if we wished to build an optimizing compiler for LISP with *prog*s we would have to confront this problem.

Problems

1. Extend the compiling algorithm to remember what it has in its AC registers. How much of the scheme is dependent on lack of side-effects?

2. Titled: " If we only had an instruction... " We advocate an instruction, *EXCH ac loc*, which will exchange the contents of the ac and the loc. This instruction could be used effectively on the code for j on page 334 to save a *PUSH-POP* pair.

   Here's *EXCH* in action, using the results of the previous exercise:

   ```
   ((LAP J SUBR)          ; says j is a function
    (PUSH P 2)
    (CALL G)              ; call the function named g
    (EXCH 1 0 P)          ; save the value and dredge up y
    (CALL H)              ; call h
    (MOVE 2 1)
    (POP P 1)             ;   preparation for
    (CALL F)              ;   calling f
    (RET))                ; exit. AC1 still has the value from f.
   ```

   Look for general situations where *EXCH* can be used. Try to notice other areas of the compiler which would benefit form new instructions.

3. Write code for the factorial function, and simulate the execution on *2!*.

4. Write a LISP function to take recursive schemes into equivalent iterative ones in the style of the *rev* example on page 353. Your first version need not be as efficient as the one advertized there, but try to make it better as you proceed. See [Dar 73] for this and related transformations.

6.17 Functional Arguments

Function variables add more complication to the compiling algorithms. We will address the simpler cases of functional arguments. There are two issues involved: what to compile when a *function* construct is recognized; and what to do when the function position of an application is a variable.
Consider an example:

$$foo[\; ...;function[\phi];...]$$

We generate $(MOVEI \; 1 \; \phi)$ and compile ϕ if it is a λ-definition; otherwise we essentially generate $(MOVEI \; 1 \; (QUOTE \; \phi))$.
Assume *foo* is defined as:

$$foo <= \lambda[[\; ...;g; \; ...] \; ....g[t_1; \; ...;t_n]]$$

The instance of g in $g[t_1; \; ...;t_n]]$ is a special case of a computed function (page 158); in this case, the computation is only a variable lookup. We will display the more general code for a computed function call of the form:

$$exp[t_1; \; ...;t_n]$$

We get: $append[\; <compexp[exp;off;vpl];$
             $list[mkalloc[1]];$
             $<complis[(t_1; \; ...;t_n);off-1;vpl]>$
             $list[mkalloc[1]];$
             $((CALLF \; n \; 0 \; P))$
             $((SUB \; P \; (C \; 1))]$

The calling structure for a functional argument is slightly different. The arguments are on the stack but, more importantly, note that the call must always be trapped and decoded. We cannot replace that call with a *PUSHJ* to some machine language code for the function because the function referred to can change. We use a *CALLF* instruction to designate a call on a functional argument. Since the value of the expression may very well change during execution we can *never* replace the *CALLF* with a *PUSHJ*.

Often, unneeded generality allowed by the functional notation can be removed by the compiler. Production LISP compilers, like the MACLISP compiler, produce very efficient code for many uses of the mapping functions, like *maplist*.

The problems of compiling efficient code become magnified if generalized control structures are anticipated. The problem is similar to that of recognizing an implied loop construct in a program using labels and *go*'s to control the algorithm. Control constructs like *catch* and *throw* (page 198) have some advantages here; rather than using evaluation relative to arbitrary access and control environments ([Bob 73a]), these constructs do impose some regularity which the compiler and the programmer can exploit.

6.18 Macros and Special Forms

We wish to extend our compiling algorithm to handle macro definitions. Consider the example of defining *plus* of an indefinite number of arguments given on page 156. A compiler can make execution of macros much more efficient than their special form counterpart. Macros usually involve transformations which can be executed at compile time, whereas a special form may involve run time information. For example, consider the case of the macro definiton of *plus*. When *plus* is called we know the number of arguments, and can simply expand the macro to a nest of calls on *plus*. For example:

$$plus[x;add1[y];z] \quad \text{expands to} \quad *plus[x;*plus[add1[y];z]]$$

The second expression may be compiled into machine code which uses the hardware arithmetic unit.

Macros can also be used effectively in implementing abstract data structures and control structures. For example, the constructors, selectors, and recognizers which help characterize an abstract data structure can be expressed as very simple S-expr operations. These operations are performed quite frequently so any improvement in their running efficiency would have dramatic impact. Recall that on page 77 we defined *coef* as *car*. For speed of execution it would be better to use *car* instead of *coef*. Compiled calls on *coef* would invoke the function-calling mechanism, whereas many compilers can substitute actual hardware instructions for calls on *car*; the code executes faster and requires less space. However, good programming style dictates that we stay abstract and use *coef*. Compiled macros can resolve this tension, giving both abstraction and fast compiled code. Define:

$$coef <_m= \lambda[[l] \, cons[CAR;cdr[l]]]$$

The user writes *(COEF ...)*; the evaluator sees *(COEF ...)* and evaluates *(CAR ...)*; the compiler sees *(COEF ...)* and compiles code for *(CAR ...)*. With macros, we can get the efficient code, the readability, and flexibility of representation.

Macros can also be used to perform most of the operations which special forms are meant to do. Since *eval* handles calls on special forms, we should examine the extensions to *compile* to generate such code. We have seen that in compiling arguments to (normal) functions, we generate the code for each, followed by code to save the result in the run-time stack, *P*. The argument to a special form is *unevaluated*, by definition. All we can thus do for a call of the form *f[l]*, where *f* is a special form, is pass the argument, compiling something like:

$$(MOVEI \; AC1 \; (\Re[\![\, l \,]\!]))$$
$$(CALL \; 1 \; (E \; F))$$

We have already mentioned some of the dangers in using special forms; the fact that a compiler cannot do much with them either, makes them even less attractive.

Problems

1. Extend the last *compile* function to handle macros.
2. Define *and* as a macro in terms of *cond*. Compare the code produced in the two cases. How could you improve the compiler to make the two sets of code more nearly alike?

6.19 Compilation and Variables

Our compilers translate the formal parameter list into a block of storage allocated in the stack, P. The body of the function definition references those local variables as the corresponding stack entries. This scheme suffices only for lambda or *prog* variables which are used in a strictly local fashion. We have said that λ-expressions may refer to global or free variables. The lookup mechanism finds the latest active binding of that variable in the current symbol table; this is the dynamic binding strategy. Care is required in extending the compiling algorithms to handle dynamic binding. The problem involves reference to variables which are currently λ-bound but are non-local. Such variables are called **special variables**.

Assume that we are implementing a deep binding algorithm. If all we store on the stack is the value of a variable, then another program which expects to use that value will have no way of finding that stored value. One scheme is to store pairs on the stack: name and value; then we can search the stack for the latest binding. This scheme is compatible with the stack implementation of deep binding given in Section 5.18. The compiler can still "know" where all the local variables are on the stack and can be a bit clever about searching for the globals or special variables.

Shallow binding implementations offer an alternative. We can still store variables on the stack [29] if we are sure that the variable is used in a strictly local fashion. If a variable is to be used as a special variable then the compiled code should access the value cell of that variable. The compiler recognizes a variable as special by looking for the property name *SPECIAL* on the property list of the atom; if the property exists and its value is **t** then the variable is a special variable and the compiler generates different code. When a variable, say x, is declared special the compiler will emit a reference to x as *(GETV AC_i X)* or *(PUTV AC_i X)* rather than the corresponding

---

[29]We assume throughout this discussion that we are compiling code for the stack implementation of shallow binding as given in Section 5.19.

reference to a location on the stack. *GETV* and *PUTV* are instructions to access or modify the contents of the value cell.

When the LISP assembler sees one of these instructions, it will locate the value cell of atom and assemble a reference to that cell. Since the location of the value cell does not change, we can always find the current binding. Any interpreted function can also sample the value cell so non-local values can be passed between compiled and interpreted functions.

Assume a function f calls a function g, and assume that g uses some of f's λ-variables. The usual compilation for f would place the λ-variables in the stack and they would not be accessible to g. Our compiler must therefore be modified to generate different prolog and epilog code for special variables. The code must save the old contents of each special value cell on entry to the function, and the compiler must generate code to restore those cells at function exit. Any references in either f or g to those special variables will involve *GETV-PUTV* rather than references into the stack P. In this scheme, *lookup*[*x;env*] is given by *getv*[*x*].

Non-local variables cause several problems in LISP. The simple mechanism we used for referencing local variables is no longer applicable. Other programming languages allow the use of non-local variables, some, like APL ([Ive 62]), only allow global variables; others, like Algol60 and its successors ([Alg 63] and [Alg 75]), allow free as well as global variables. However, Algol compilers are much simpler to construct than LISP compilers, and we should explore some of the reasons.[30] One simplicity of Algol is its treatment of procedure valued variables. Algol dialects typically restrict themselves to what LISP calls functional arguments. Algol dialects do not allow arbitrary procedures to be returned as values. Their restrictions allow the run time environment to be modelled in a stack, as described in Section 5.18.

The difference between LISP and Algol, which is more to the point here, is their binding strategies (Section 3.11). A typical LISP uses dynamic binding whereas Algol uses static binding. The difference is that Algol translators determine the bindings of variables at the time the definition is made whereas LISP determines bindings at the time the function is applied. That is, definitions in Algol always imply an application of *function*, binding up all non-local variables. The net effect is that Algol does not have free variables in the sense that there is any choice of bindings; all choices have been made when a procedure is declared. That binding decision has dramatic results when we come to implement language translators. As a result, Algol can effectively compile all variable references to be references into the run time stack, and need not retain the name stack for variable look up at run time. It is not at all clear yet which binding strategy will dominate.

_____

[30]For reasons other than those we are addressing here, APL compilers are difficult to construct.

Counterexamples to exclusive use of either strategy exist. Recent work ([Ste 76b], [Sus 75], [Hew 76]) points to the use of static binding in LISP-like languages.

A typical preserve of dynamic binding is that of interactive programming, where programs are created as separate entities to be connected into a cohesive whole at some later time. Frequently one wants the bindings of the free variables to be postponed until such a grouping is made.

6.20 Compiling and Interpreting

We have discussed the similarities between compilers and interpreters. Now that we have seen compilers in some detail we should reexamine the relationships. The compilation of conditional expressions introduces an interesting dichotomy between the action of an interpreter and that of a typical compiler.

We will restrict ourselves to a simple form of the conditional expression: $if[p;then;otherwise]$, where p is a an expression giving t or f; $then$ is the expression to be evaluated if p gives t; otherwise the expression, $otherwise$, is to be evaluated. It is an easy exercise to express a LISP conditional in terms of if expressions.

When an interpreter evaluates a conditional expression or an if, it will evaluate either $then$ or $otherwise$; not both. When a compiler compiles code for an if expression, it compiles $both$ branches. Certainly, we cannot only compile one branch of the if; we expect different input values to use different branches, otherwise the conditional expression should not have appeared. For example, if a particular evaluation $never$ takes the $otherwise$ branch of a conditional, [31] then we need not compile code for that branch; compiling code for program segments which are not executed is disconcerting. At a later date, a different evaluation might take the other branch, and at that time, we should be able to compile the branch.

We will show that it is possible to interpret and compile at the same time. [32] The relevant observation is that large parts of compiling and interpreting algorithms are identical; they deal with decoding the input expression and understanding which constructs are present. It is only after the interpreter or compiler has discovered the nature of the expression that the specifics of compilation or interpretation come into play.

We will build an evaluator/compiler named $evcom$ based on the explicit access evaluator of Section 4.6. It will handle compilation and interpretation of applicative forms involving either primitive functions or named λ-definitions; it will recognize the difference between local and non-local

---

[31] That does not imply that the $otherwise$-branch will $never$ be visited.

[32] See [Mit 70] for a similar idea applied to a different language.

variable references, compiling (and executing) calls on *lookup* for non-local references, and use a faster relative addressing technique for local variables. Finally it will "incrementally compile" *if* expressions, executing (and generating code for) the branch designated by the predicate; and will leave sufficient information available such that if the other branch is ever executed, then code is compiled for it.

Before sketching *evcom*, one other implementation detail is worth mentioning. We cannot simply replace a LISP expression with compiled code; LISP expressions are data structures and we must be able to operate on that data structure representation without being aware that a compilation has occurred. For example the LISP editor (Section 6.22) must be able to manipulate the S-expr representation. So rather than replace expressions with code we *associate* the code with the expression using an association list whose name-entries are LISP expressions and whose value-entries are sequences of instructions. [33] The variable *code* is used to hold the association list or code buffer.

Finally here is the sketch. We have left out many of the subsidiary functions and have left out all of the execution mechanism involved in *xct* and *execute*; *xct* executes a single instruction and *execute* is the combined assembler and execution device.

```
evcom <=
  λ[[exp]
    prog[[z]
          return[ [z ← hascode[exp] → execute[z];
                   isconst[exp] → xct1[list[mksend[exp]]];
                   z ← isvar[exp] → [islocal[z] → xct1[send_code[list[mklocal[z]]];
                                     isfun[z] → send_code[evcom1[def[z];()]]];
                                     issubr[z] → send_code[list[mkpushj[z]]];

                                     t → xct1[send_code[list[mkglob[z]]]]];
                   isif[exp] → send_code[evif[exp]];
                   t → send_code[mkcode[ xct1[list[mkalloc[vars[fun[exp]]]]];
                                 evcomlist[args[exp]];
                                 xct1[list[mkcall[fun[exp]]]] ]]] ]] ]]

evcom1 <= λ[[exp;code] evcom[exp]]
xct1 <= λ[[x] xct[x]; x]
```

Here's the essence of *evcom*: if the expression has code in the current code buffer, then we execute it. A constant is executed and produces code, since that constant may be a subexpression of a larger expression being compiled; we do not save the constant code in the code buffer. Two types of variables are recognized: a local variable is recognized by its presence in the local table;

---

[33]In actual practice, such a representation would be prohibitively expensive and we would substitute a hash array technique; see Section 7.14.

a relative address reference can be given for that entry. If the variable reference is non-local, then we compile a version of *lookup*; the actual form of that code will depend on the binding implementation (shallow or deep). Either type of variable reference saves the code using *send_code*.

If the variable references a function name, then we must compile and execute code for that function definition. [34] We use the function *evcom1* since the code buffer, *code*, must be re-initialized within the compilation of the function body since code in the outer environment won't be valid within the function body. Finally, the variable might be a reference to a primitive function, in which case we just return the call and let the function application execute it.

If the expression is an application, we generate and execute code to allocate space, compile and execute the argument list, and if necessary compile, but always execute, the function call.

$hascode <= \lambda[[exp]\; prog[[z]$
$\qquad\qquad return[\; [z \leftarrow findcode[exp] \rightarrow cdr[z];$
$\qquad\qquad\qquad\qquad t \rightarrow f]]]]$

$evcomlist <= \lambda[[l]\; [null[l] \rightarrow ();$
$\qquad\qquad null[rest[l]] \rightarrow evcom[first[l]];$
$\qquad\qquad t \rightarrow mkcode[evcom[first[l]];$
$\qquad\qquad\qquad\qquad xct1[((NEXT))];$
$\qquad\qquad\qquad\qquad evcomlist[rest[l]]]]]]$

The compilation and execution of *if* expressions is interesting. When compiling the first reference to an *if* instance, we compile the predicate and one of the branches; we associate a structure with the instance; that structure has either the name *ifa* or *ifb* depending on which branch was compiled. If we come across this instance of *if* again (either in a loop or in a recursion) then we find the *ifa* or *ifb* entry in *code*. If we pick the same branch of the *if* then nothing new happens; but if the (compiled) predicate evaluated to the other truth value, then we compile the other branch and associate a completely compiled program with the original *if* expression.

$evif <= \lambda[[exp]\; prog[\; [l\; p\; a\; b]$
$\qquad\qquad l \leftarrow body[exp];$
$\qquad\qquad p \leftarrow pred[l];$
$\qquad\qquad a \leftarrow ante[l];$
$\qquad\qquad b \leftarrow ow[l];$
$\qquad\qquad p \leftarrow evcom[p];$
$\qquad\qquad return[list[\; [receive[] \rightarrow mkifa[exp;p;evcom[a];b];$
$\qquad\qquad\qquad\qquad t \rightarrow mkifb[exp;p;a;evcom[b]]]]]\;]]$

The construction of the completed conditional code is the business of the

---

[34]We assume the variable is being used as a function; we make no attempt to handle funtional objects referenced as data.

next function, *mkifcode*. A call to this function is manufactured within *mkifa* and *mfifb*.

$$mkifcode <= \lambda[[p;a;b]$$
$$\lambda[[l;ll] \ mkcode[\ p;$$
$$list[mkjumpf[l]];$$
$$a;$$
$$list[mkjump[ll]];$$
$$list[l];$$
$$b;$$
$$list[ll]]]$$
$$[gensym[];gensym[]] \ ]$$

Recognizers
$$islocal <= \lambda[[x]in[x;local[env]]]$$
$$isif <= \lambda[[x] \ eq[first[x] \ IF]]$$
$$isprim <= \lambda[[ins] \ get[ins;INST]]$$
$$isfun <= \lambda[[x] \ get[x; \ EXPR]]$$

Constructors
$$mklocal <= \lambda[[var] \ list[SEND@;var]]$$
$$mkglob <= \lambda[[x] \ list[LOOKUP;x]]$$
$$mkalloc <= \lambda[[vars] \ list[ALLOC;vars]]$$
$$mkcall <= \lambda[[fn] \ list[CALL;fn]]$$

We have left out a significant amount of detail and we have only covered a subset of LISP, but the result should be understandable; and it should further clarify the relationships between compilation and interpretation. Typical discussions of compilers and interpreters lead one to believe that there is a severe flexibility/efficiency tradeoff imposed in dealing with compilers. If you compile programs you must give up a lot of flexibility in editing and debugging. With a properly designed language and flexible machine architecture, that is not true.

6.21 Interactive Programming

"... What is actually happening, I am afraid, is that we all tell each other and ourselves that software engineering techniques should be improved considerably, because there is a crisis. But there are a few boundary conditions which apparently have to be satisfied. I will list them for you:

1. *We may not change our thinking habits.*
2. *We may not change our programming tools.*
3. *We may not change our hardware.*
4. *We may not change our tasks.*
5. *We may not change the organizational set-up in which the work has to be done.*

Now under these five immutable boundary conditions, we have to try to improve matters. This is utterly ridiculous. Thank you. (Applause).

E. Dijkstra, *Conference of Software Engineering, 1968.*

We have talked about the constructs of LISP; we have talked about interpreters and compilers for LISP; and we have talked a little about input and output conventions for the language. The combination of these properties leads us to a most interesting practical aspect of LISP: its use as an interactive programming language. A programming language is a tool for building programs. LISP's representation of programs as data structures coupled with the availablilty of display terminals offers the LISP programmer unique opportunities for the interactive construction of programs. Historically, machines have been oriented towards the rapid execution of well-defined numerical algorithms. This perspective over-looks two important points.

First, the actual process of discovering, debugging, refining, and encoding the algorithm is a complex process. In the early days of computation, the programmer performed the analysis on the algorithm on paper, transcribed the algorithm to a programming language, encoded that program on coding sheets and keypunched a card deck. That deck was supplied with data cards and presented to the machine. If some abnormal behavior was detected in the program, an uninspiring octal dump of the contents of memory was presented. Often the state of the machine at the time the dump was taken had only a casual relationship with the actual bug.

Memory dumps were an appalling debugging technique, even then. As higher level languages became more popular, memory dumps became even less attractive; the dump gave little insight unless the programmer knew where the program and data resided in memory, and understood what code was produced by the compiler.

The programmer had a slightly more appealing alternative called tracing. A program could be embellished with print statements whose purpose was to determine access behavior by printing values of variables, and to discover control behavior by printing messages at entry and exit from procedures. This tracing technique was frequently available as an operating system option. Then the programmer would supply control cards which expressed what kind of output was desired. In either case, unless this technique was used with resolute precision, the output would either be voluminous or uninformative, or both.

When the cause of a bug was discovered the offending cards were replaced and the deck was resubmitted for execution. This cycle was repeated until an acceptable program was developed. This approach is still followed by a majority of programmers. What is missed is that much of the detail and tedium of these early phases of program development can be aided by a well-constructed interactive programming system. The major difficulty is the emphasis on program execution rather than program debugging and development. Most architectures and languages assume that a program runs. If one assumes that "programs never run", and designs a "debugging architecture" then a LISP-like machine appears.

The second point which is overlooked is that a large class of interesting problems are not included in the range of "well-defined numerical algorithms". In fact most of the problems which are traditionally attacked by LISP programs fall into this class: language design, theorem proving, compiler writing, and of course, artificial intelligence. In such "exploratory programming" it is often the case that no well-defined algorithm is known, and it will be the final program which *is* the algorithm. Such exploratory programming requires that the programming language be usable as a sophisticated "desk calculator". It requires experimentation with, and execution of, partially specified programs; that is, the ability to develop and run pieces of programs; to build up a larger program from pieces; to quickly modify either the program text or the computational results themselves, before the programmers have lost their train of thought.

An important outgrowth of such exploratory programming is a LISP technique called "throw-away implementation". In developing a large programming system one begins with a few simple ideas and incrementally develops the larger system. If some of the ideas are inadequate they are replaced. At some stage an adequate model is developed; it may be lacking in some aspects, but it does model the desired phenomenon. At that point, the programmer's understanding has been sufficiently improved, that the implementation should be thrown away and a new, more enlightened version, created. Certainly this kind of programming can be accomplished with languages other than LISP; the point is that an interactive LISP environment is sufficiently responsive that an implementation cycle is quite short and relatively painless. The effect is that the programmer does not invest so much effort in an implementation that he feels a compulsion to patch an inferior implementation, rather than start afresh.

The development of an interactive programming system has several important implications. The usual partitioning of program preparation into editing, running, and debugging is no longer adequate. The text editor and the debugger are integral parts of the system. A programming "environment" is established in which all facets of programming are integrated. The tasks which are usually performed by an operating system are subsumed by the programming language. The idea of a separate file system becomes obsolete, and all programs and data are accessible from within the "environment". This has an important advantage in LISP-like representations of programs: the conversion from internal representation to "text file" format is eliminated. The technique puts added burden on naming facilities so that a programmer's definitions are accessible, but are unambigiously addressible. The effect is to structure the interactive environment as a very large data base containing programs and data structures. The programmer has accessing procedures to manipulate the elements in the base. All the items in the base are accessible as data structures; the editor can modify any objects in the base. Some of the objects can be executed as procedures; the evaluator is responsible for this.

A procedure object can be further expanded into machine instructions for faster execution; this may either be done by an explicit call on a compiler or be done invisibly by a compiler/interpreter. If an evaluation is not performing as expected, yet another data structure manipulating program is available. The debugger is able to manipulate both the program structure and the run time data structures which the evaluator has created. Any of these data structure manipulating programs is able to call any other program. The effect is a programming philosophy sometimes characterized as "middle-out" rather than "top-down" or "bottom-up". The emphasis is on the programming process rather than on the final product. [35] This view of program development is in direct conflict with the traditional approach which grew from the card deck philosophy, and assumed that machine time was more valuable than programmer time. Several current research projects are developing along these lines; among them are [Hew 75], [Int 75], and [Win 75]. All of these projects are based on LISP.

---

[35]Compare the term "structured programming". The emphasis is also on the action. The application of a methodology should aid in the development of an object with the desired characteristics. In programming, that implies the existence of a programming environment.

It is not accidental that LISP is the major language for these kinds of programming tasks; it is the features of the language which make it amenable to such programming tasks. In the next two sections we will discuss two of the ingredients of interactive programming systems; this will illuminate the features of LISP which make it important for interactive programming.

First we will sketch some basic features of LISP text editors. This will show some of the benefits of having the program structure available as a data structure. The succeeding section will discuss a few features of a typical LISP debugging system; this will further demonstrate the advantages of having a natural program representation available at run time.

There is no standard LISP editor or debugger. [36] Therefore the next sections will contain general information rather than an abundance of concrete examples. The design of such devices is a subject of very personal preferences and prejudices. Some characteristics are common and those we will stress. A related difficulty is that editing and debugging devices are best done as interactive display programs, rather than as key-punch or teletype programs. [37] Interactive programming is a very visual and dynamic enterprise; teletype-oriented interaction is not sufficient; it results in a presentation more like a comic strip than a movie.

6.22 LISP Editors

A LISP editor is just another LISP program; it operates on a data structure. In this case the data structure represents a program. A simple editor could be constructed along the lines of the *subst* function:

$$subst' <= \lambda[[x;y;z] [atom[z] \rightarrow [equal[y;z] \rightarrow x;\ t \rightarrow z];$$
$$t \rightarrow cons[subst'[x;y;car[z]];$$
$$subst'[x;y;cdr[z]]]]]$$

That is, we would let z be the program; y, the piece of text to be replaced; and x, the new text. Such global editing is useful sometimes, but text editing is a more local and controlled action, better accomplished as a interactive process.

A typical editor will take an expression as input and will then enter a "listen-loop", waiting for commands from the user. The input expression may either be a list representing a constant data structure, or a list representing a (constant) function. There are commands for the selection of a subexpression of the input expression; and there are commands for the replacement of expressions with other expressions.

---

[36]Indeed, ther is no standard LISP. The language is dynamic, flexible, and still developing after twenty years.

[37]That is one of the author's many preferences and prejudices.

The mechanics of presenting list structure to the user are interesting. Since a list may be deeply nested, we need a convenient way of designating subexpressions. A display device might illuminate the selected expression more brightly than the containing expression. More structured representations of text are required, however. A "pretty-printed" (see Section 9.2 or page 274) version of the text may be presented. If the text is too extensive to fit on the display face, then abbreviational devices are available.

If the text is deeply nested it is often difficult to perceive the top level structure even in pretty-printed form. Consider the S-expr representation of the definition of *member*:

```
(MEMBER
 (LAMBDA (X L)
  (COND  ((NULL L) NIL)
         ((EQ X (FIRST L)) T)
         (T (MEMBER X (REST L)))))))
```

In this case the structure of the *COND* is clear; but it is clearer if we express it as:

$$(LAMBDA \ (X \ L) \ (COND \ \& \ \& \ \&))$$

Or given a linear list: $(\alpha \ \beta \ \chi \ \delta \ \epsilon \ \phi \ \gamma \ \eta \ \iota \ \vartheta \ \kappa \ \lambda)$
it may be more instructive to display it as:

$$(\alpha \ \beta \ \chi \ \delta \ \epsilon \ \phi \ \gamma \ \eta \ \iota \ ... \ )$$
or $$(\ ...\delta \ \epsilon \ \phi \ \gamma \ \eta \ \iota \ ... \ ).$$

where the focus of attention is controlled by the user.

There should be commands to move selected subexpressions to different locations within the same structure and move expressions to other structures. Since a common text error in LISP is the misplacing of parentheses, there are commands to move parentheses.

There are at least two reasons for text editors: programmers make errors, and programs which are correct need to be modified to perform other tasks. Particularly in exploratory programming, the "try-it-and-see" attitude must be supported. Thus we demand a flexible editor which can "undo" changes to functions or constant data structure. LISP editors have the ability to save the current edit structure such that an "undo" can restore to that state if needed.

Regardless of the idiosyncrasies of a particular editor the common feature is that LISP editors are structure-oriented editors. They operate on S-expressions, not text strings or card images. A program is not a linear string of characters; it is a structured entity, whose parts are distinguishable as representations of instances of programming language constructs. The editing process should take cognizance of that structure. [38]

6.23 Debugging in LISP

Few areas of computer science field are as primitive as the art of debugging; few areas of the field are as important. The development of a correct program is the point of our programming activity. The power of our debugging techniques has been directly related to the sophistication of the hardware/software interface which is available. Not until the advent of sophisticated on-line systems has there really been any hope for practical "correct-program" construction.

Several pieces of information are required to do interactive debugging. We need an indication of the error condition; we need the current state of the computation; we need to have some indication of how the computation arrived at the error condition; and, if interactive debugging is to be meaningful, we need the ability to modify the computation and resume execution in that modified environment. This last point is quite important; it has implications for programming style. First, we *should* hope to modify an errant calculation rather than restart the entire computation. To start over is like repunching a whole card deck because one card was wrong. We repunch the offending cards and retain the rest. Similarly, we should expect to throw away offending computations and retaining the remainder. Typically, computation is not as local and exciseable as removing a single card; a primary purpose of most computation is to pass a result to some other procedure. However, if we try to localize the effects of each procedure to simple parameter passing and value returning then we have a better chance of discovering a point in the computation history which is prior to the error; return the control stack to that point; modify the erring procedure and restart the computation from that point. This implies that procedures should minimize their use of side-effects; for it is side-effects which spoil the nice applicative behavior and will require the programmer to make explicit modifications in the computational environment before a computation can be restarted. This attention to program interaction is another manifestation of the **modular programming** style; each procedure is a module, or black box, dependent on other procedures only through well-defined input and output considerations. It is this style of modular programming which will enhance the use of interactive debugging tools.

This section will deal only with the primitive mechanisms which underlie LISP debugging techniques. The discussions of more complex tools which are available or are comtemplated are well-documented in other sources; [Int 75], [Moo 74].

---

[38] A case can be made for believing that the program *construction* process should also be driven by that structure [Han 71].

A debugging system for an applicative language like LISP is based on the following kinds of information: which functions are being entered; what are the actual parameters; and what are the values being returned. With an open implementation, like that provided by LISP, such information is readily available.

Assume that we wish to monitor the behavior of the function, *foo*. We will place the real definition of *foo* on another symbol table entry (using *gensym*[]) and redefine *foo* such that, when it is called, it will:

1. Print the values of the current actual parameters.
2. Use *apply* to call the real defintion of *foo* with the actual parameters.
3. Print the value of the call on *foo*.
4. Return control and the value to the calling program.

Since *foo* may be recursive we should also give some indication of the depth of recursion being executed.

Now every call on *foo* will give us the pertinent statistics. This technique is called **tracing**. The current description is similar to many implementations on teletype-like devices. Given an interactive display and a well-defined "LISP machine" description like that in *peval* (Section 4.8), a much more satisfactory trace can be given.

The trace mechanism can be used for both interpreted and compiled function calls, but some care needs be taken. Interpreted calls on *foo* will go through *eval*, and if *(CALL ... FOO)* is being used in the compiled code the *CALL* decoder can pass control to the tracing mechanism. If the call is a *PUSHJ*, control passes directly to the machine language code and we will not intercept the call.

In most implementations of LISP the programmer may selectively replace a *CALL* by a *PUSHJ*. [39] A *PUSHJ* will be executed at machine speed, transfering to known location; whereas the *CALL* is passed to *decode* (page 316) and the function definition is looked up; therefore after a program is debugged, the programmer may replace the *CALL* with the *PUSHJ* and the programs will execute faster. On some implementations this action is reversible ([Ste pc]); a table, relating the *CALLs* to the *PUSHJs*, is built; when tracing is desired, the *CALL* version is made available. [40]

---

[39] As we have seen, *CALLs* to functional variables won't be replaced.

[40] Actually, the scheme is as follows: instead of assembling the *CALL* into a memory location, an XCT is assembled; the XCT references a copy of a table which contains the actual *CALL*. The user may replace the *CALLs* by *PUSHJ*, but also has the original table available to replace the modified version when tracing is desired. This XCT trick has the additional benefit of allowing several users to share a "pure" piece of program, while some people are tracing and some people are not. The added flexibility more than compensates for the slight decrease in speed.

A variant of this tracing scheme can be used to monitor *SET*s and *SETQ*s. We can modify their definitions to print the name of the variable and the new value, perform the assignment, and return. This technique can be lost in some compiled code. If we compile local variables as references into the value stack, we have lost both the names and the ability to trace their behavior. Variable references which use *PUTV* and *GETV* can be traced like *CALL*. In fact, on **SM**, we have an operation analogous to *PUSHJ*, so the *CALL-PUSHJ* technique is open to us. *PUTV* and *GETV* can be implemented as hardware *MOVEM* and *MOVE* instructions.

The trace facility is a debugging feature which has been adapted from the batch-processsing versions of LISP. There is a related, but more interactive, version of this technique called the **break** package. In this mode of tracing, the user can specify that the program should halt on recognition of certain conditions. If that halt occurs, the break package is entered and the user may then type commands which survey the state of the computation. Expressions may be evaluated, which may themselves enter the break package recursively. If desired, the LISP editor may be called either to edit function definitions or to edit an expression on the actual control stack of the current computation.

Since it is difficult to predetermine when a computation may require debugging, several systems supply an interrupt system analogous to that found in hardware machines. Striking certain keys may then cause interrupts to the break package, just as if a break condition were pre-programmed. Such a feature is useful in conjunction with the trace package. If a trace indicates to the user that the computation is not performing according to expectation then an interrupt key can be struck and the computation will be suspended.

User-definable interrupt systems apply to other areas of computation than that of debugging. The most well-developed system is that of MacLISP. The ability to selectively trace the execution, coupled with the ability to interrupt a computation, allows the user to examine computations which are suspected of divergence.

Storage Structures and Efficiency

7.1 Introduction

This chapter reconciles some of the generality of LISP with the realities of contemporary data structures and machine organization. Though any algorithm can be coded in terms of manipulations of binary trees, often there are more efficient organizations of data. For example, our numerical algorithms could be expressed as list algorithms using $(\ )$, $((\ ))$, $((\ )\ (\ ))$, and so on, as representations for $0, 1, 2$, respectively. Most machines supply hardware arithmetic representations and operations, making such list representations unnecessary.

At the next level of data organization are vectors and arrays of numerals. These data structures could also be stored in a list-structure format and individual components could be accessed by *car-cdr* chains. However, most machines have a hardware organization which can be exploited to increase accessing efficiency over the list representation. Sequential storage for elements, often coupled with hardware index registers for fast access to elements, makes a more effective representation.

Similarly, strings can be represented as lists of characters. The string processing operations are expressible as LISP algorithms; again, this is usually not the most reasonable representation. Some machines supply special hardware aids for string operations.

370

Even at the level of list-structure operations, simple binary trees might not be the most expeditious representation. Also many of the algorithms we have presented in LISP are overly wasteful of computation time.

There are no general rules for selecting data representations and chosing programming style. Efficiency must be balanced against generality. The chosen representation must match the machine and the problem domain being studied. If the problem is strictly numerical, then list-structure is overly general. If simple string manipulation is sufficient, then list processing also may be too general. There are many applications of list processing which are so sufficiently well behaved that complex devices like garbage collectors are unnecessary. However, understanding the programming art in a rich environment such as LISP, prepares the programmer to apply these techniques in a meaningful way. Many times a representation in LISP is all that is needed; a "throw-away implementation" may answer the question. A clean representation with comprehensible algorithms is developed. Once a representation is developed, it is easy to get better ones.

7.2 Vectors and Arrays

Vectors. Vectors, also known as one-dimensional arrays, are usually stored sequentially in memory. Simple vectors are usually stored one element to a memory location though this is not a necessity; for example, a vector representation of a complex number may be stored as pairs of cells. If vectors of nonhomogeneous data modes are contemplated, each element would include type information. Also, we have seen a representation of a stack as a (sequential) vector with access made via a global pointer to the vector. In any case, most languages make some restrictions on the behavior of vectors such that efficient accessing of elements can be made. Vectors are an attractive representation when the size of data objects will not vary. Given such a static behavior, machines can perform access and updating of the elements rapidly.

Arrays. Arrays are vectors which allow vectors as elements. For example, a two-dimensional array is a vector, whose elements are vectors of individuals. We will restrict attention to array whose elements are all of the same dimensions; efficient representation of more general arrays, called **ragged arrays**, will be examined in Section 7.13. We will restrict our attention further to two-dimensional arrays, though most of the discussion generalizes very naturally. Since most machine memories are organized as linear devices, we map arrays onto a linear representation. A common implementation stores the array by rows; that is, each row is stored sequentially - first, row 1; then row 2, ... and so on. A simple calculation finds the location of an arbitrary element, $A[i;j]$, given the location of the first element $A[1;1]$ and the length of each row of the array. For an array $A[1:M; 1:N]$,

$$loc[A[i;j]] = loc\ [A[1;1]] + (i-1)*N + (j-1)$$

In languages like Fortran which require that the size of the array be known at compile-time the compiler can generate the accessing code as references to specific memory locations. Languages, like Algol 60 and some versions of LISP, allow the size of an array to be determined at run-time. Algol 60, for example, requires the declaration of the type (real, boolean, etc.) of the array and specification of the number of dimensions in the array, but the size specification of each dimension can be postponed until run-time. To implement this flexibility, a **dope vector** is introduced. A dope vector is a header or **descriptor** associated with the area containing the actual array elements. The information in the dope vector tells the functions which access the array how to treat the data. Type and dimensionality are typical entries in dope vectors.

The compiler can determine the size of the dope vector, but cannot determine its contents. The dope vector is filled in when the array declaration is executed; at that time the array bounds are known. The compiler cannot allocate space for the array elements; the allocation must be done at run-time. At that time we allocate space and complete the dope vector. All references to array elements must use the dope vector.

Assume that the array elements are stored by rows. Look at the calculation of the location of element A[i;j]. For specific execution of an array declaration much of this information is constant; the location of the array elements, in particular, A[1;1] and the number of columns N are fixed.

Thus we rewrite the calculation as:

constant part		variable part
[loc [A[1;1]]-N-1]	+	(i*N+j)

The constant part is stored in the dope vector. When we wish to reference an element A[i;j] we need only compute the variable part and add it to the constant part.

The dope vector for A [1:M; 1:N] perhaps might contain

2	
1	M
1	N
constant part	
. . . array elements . . .	

There is another scheme for storing arrays which is used in some of the Burroughs machines ([Org 71], [Dor 76]). Each row is stored sequentially and access to separate rows is made through a device called a **mother-vector.** The mother-vector is a vector of pointers to the rows.

Thus,

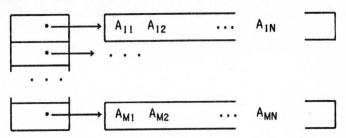

Notice that the accessing computation is very inexpensive. [1] On a virtual memory machine this array organization can be helpful; all rows need not be in memory at once. If an access to a row not in core is made, a "page fault" is raised; the monitor brings the row into memory and the computation continues. The mother-vector scheme generalizes to multidimensional arrays, and can also be used in conjunction with a dope vector.

An implementation of an array facility in LISP might include a declaration:

array[<identifier>;<type>;<bounds>; ... ;<bounds>], where the identifier names
the array; the type could be numeric or S-expr; and finally a declaration
of upper and lower bounds for each dimension would be needed. *array*
is a special form whose effect is to make the array name a *SUBR*,
whose code is the calculation of the dope vector. Thus,

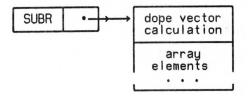

If we are to store S-exprs in the array, then the garbage collector must be able to mark the entries. This is the reason for including type information.

When an array element is to be referenced, the subscripts are evaluated (since the array name was declared as a *SUBR*) and the dope vector code is executed. That computation results in a reference to the appropriate cell.

We also must be able to store information in the array.

store[<name>[<subscr>; ... ;<subscr>];<value>] : *store* is a special form whose
effect is to store the value of <value> in the designated array element.

---

[1]However access by array columns can be expensive. If each row is on a separate page in the machine, the access overhead can be substantial.

We have discussed storage allocation and accessing of array elements. Important distinctions in language design appear in discussing deallocation of array space. Typical Algol-like languages impose a stack discipline on storage management. This imples that the arrray elements may be allocated in the run-time stack. It also implies that the elements become inaccessible once the block which allocated that array has been exited. This is implemented by popping the array from the stack. There are two ways for a language to assure that no references to "inaccessible" elements can occur (such references are called **dangling references**.) Either restrict the semantics of the language such that no such references can occur (Algol 60), or allow constructs which *may* cause dangling references, but declare any occurrence to be an error (Algol 68).

LISP-like languages suppose that data structures are to be retained as long as they are accessible; that treatement is also given to LISP arrays. Therefore arrays are allocated and deallocated in a manner similar to the *cons* operation for S-exprs; sequential blocks are maintained in a free list; we will say more about this in Section 7.13.

The two management philosophies for deallocation of data structures are characterized as the **deletion strategy** and the **retention strategy**; see [Ber 71].

Problem

1. Implement a stack in LISP first using lists or dotted pairs, then using an array. Include implementations of the stack operations.

7.3 Strings and Linear LISP

On page 268 we discussed one representation for LISP print names: a linked list of full words; each full word contained a segment of the atom name. Print names are a special instance of a data structure named strings; our use of strings in LISP has been restricted to manipulating string constants. In this section we will discuss alternative representations for strings, and discuss further operations on string objects. Most production LISP systems have a comprehensive set of string operations. As with numbers and vectors, string operations could easily be represented as operations on S-exprs; however it is frequently more efficient to represent strings as a separate abstract data structure.

Each string object is a sequence of characters. The elements of a string may not be strings; this is the essential difference between sequences and strings. That simplification of data structures introduces some different aspects of storage management. It is these issues which we will emphasize in this section.

The primitive string manipulations -- constructors selectors, recognizers, and equality -- are similar to those for sequences. Therefore we use LISP M-expression syntax when describing the operations; for that reason we call the string language, **linear LISP**. The implementation allows the creation of strings of arbitrary length; it allows the generation of new strings and the decomposition of existing strings. Since arbitrary length strings are to be created, an organization similar to free space will be used. The storage area for strings will be called **string space**.

String space is a linear sequence of cells; each cell can contain one character. A string will be represented as a sequence of contiguous character cells. The value of a string variable will be represented as a pair, containing character count and a pointer to the beginning of the character sequence in string space.

Thus,

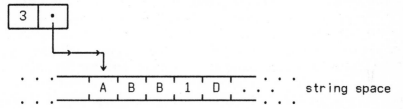

encodes the string *ABB*.

There are two primitive selector functions: *first* and *rest*.

first[*x*] is the first character of the string represented by *x*. *first* is undefined for the empty string, **ϵ**. For example,

$$first[ABC] \text{ is } A; \; first[\textbf{ϵ}] = \bot$$

rest[*x*] is the string of characters which remains when the first character of the string is deleted. *rest* is also undefined for the empty string. For example,

$$rest[ABC] \text{ is } BC$$

There is one constructor primitive.

concat[*x;y*] creates a new string. *x* is a character; *y* is a string. *concat* forms a string consisting of the concatenation of *x* with *y*. For example,

$$concat[A;BC] \text{ is } ABC$$

There are two primitive recognizers:

char[*x*]: is *x* a single character?
null[*x*]: is *x* the empty string?

For example: *char*[*A*] is t
                      char[*AB*] is f

Finally, we include a version of the equality predicate which will determine if two characters are identical.

$$x = y: \text{ are } x \text{ and } y \text{ the same character?}$$

$$AB = AB \text{ is } \bot$$

The implementation of these string primitives is less complex than that of LISP primitives. *first* generates a character count of one and a pointer to the first character of the parent string. *rest* generates a character count of one less than that of the parent and a pointer to the second character of the parent string. Therefore, this implementation shares substrings, just as *car* and *cdr* share substructure.

The implementation of the recognizers and the equality predicate is straightforward. We will blur the distinction between characters and strings of length one. Thus *char* need only check the character count. *null* gives t if the count is zero. To implement equality, we note that characters are not stored uniquely, so we must make an actual character comparison.

As with full LISP, the implementation of the constructor requires more care. Since our implementation requires that string components be contiguous, we must copy the arguments to *concat*. To evaluate *concat*[x;y], we copy x, then copy y so that y follows x in free string space; we generate a character count of one plus the count of y, and generate a pointer to the copy of x. The copies are made in the free string space in a manner similar to that used in *cons*.

The storage management is somewhat different from that of a simple LISP implementation. Since the copying operation within *concat* allocate space, we must include some method for deallocating space. Though simpler methods may suffice we us a garbage collector. [2] The marking phase is much simpler than that for LISP; it is not recursive. We use the descriptor in the symbol table to mark each character string. However, we cannot stop marking simply because we have encountered a previously marked character. Since we are sharing substrings, we must visit each character in the string item.

The sweep phase needs to be more comprehensive for string collection. Since strings are stored sequentially, a fragmented string space is of little use. We must compact all the referenceable strings into one end of string space, and free a linear block for the new free string space. Since we are sharing substrings, a little care must be exercised. When we move a string, the descriptor of any variable referencing any part of that parent string must be changed to reflect the new location. So before we begin the relocation of strings, we sort the string descriptors on the basis of their pointers into string

---

[2]Since string operations are quite well-behaved, a reference counter could be used. We use a garbage collector for its elegance and its pedagogical value for the next section.

space. We then recognize each parent string, moving it down into freed locations and update the address pointers in the descriptors of any substrings. Eventually all strings will be compacted; the string space pointer can be set and the computation continued. Next, we adapt the compacting garbage collectors for use in LISP.

7.4 A Compacting Collector for LISP

We can combine the simplicity of the original mark-sweep garbage collector with the sophistication of the collection phase of string garbage collector and produce a compacting garbage collector for LISP.

There are several motivations for compacting storage. First, besides making the *active* storage contiguous, we also make the *free* locations contiguous. Thus the free lists can be handled as vectors rather than as lists. This simplifies storage allocation: to allocate the next free element, take the next element in the free space vector.

Another reason for concern with compacting is related to hardware. If the underlying machine is using a paging scheme, then we can try to minimize page-faults by keeping the LISP structures localized. In the worst case, we could have every element of a list on a separate page; this could require that the memory manager retrieve a new page for every reference. [3] However, we cannot restrict the operations of the LISP programmer. The underlying hardware must be invisible to the user. The next best thing is to try to keep the structures as local as possible; compaction of spaces is a first attempt at this. We will discuss other lower-level tricks later.

Compaction is important in languages other than LISP. If the language allocates storage in a manner similar to LISP but the constructs allow *different*-sized blocks to be specified (a string processor is a simple example), then compaction may be necessary. [4]

Granted that compaction is a worthwhile endeavor, we proceed. We can't simply mark all the active cells and then move them into unmarked cells to compact the space. We must also maintain the original topological relationships between the elements.

204 | 204 | 204 | is not the same as   100 | 204 | 204 |

Besides moving the cells, we must also update each reference to a moved location:

---

[3]Very little empirical work has been done on the actual storage requirements and running environment of LISP. A start is made in [Cl 76]; much more should be done.

[4]As we shall soon see, the rationale is applicable in LISP as well.

204 | 204 | 204 | *is* the same as   100 | 100 | 100 |

To handle these problems, we expand the sweep phase into two phases: the **relocating** phase and the **updating** phase.

The relocating phase begins after all active structure is marked. Assume we are to compact all active structure *down* to the bottom of the space. First we initialize two pointers: a **free** pointer to the lowest cell in the space; and an **active** pointer to the top of the space. We move the active pointer down until we come across a *marked* location; we move the free pointer up until we locate an *unmarked* cell. We want to move that marked cell down into the free location; but we must also supply enough information to maintain the original relationships in the transformed structure. The cell we move may reference other cells which will be moved.

Here's a picture:

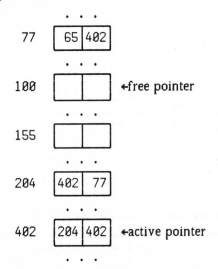

$$
\begin{array}{ll}
77 & | 65 | 402 | \\
100 & | \quad | \quad | \leftarrow \text{free pointer} \\
155 & | \quad | \quad | \\
204 & | 402 | 77 | \\
402 & | 204 | 402 | \leftarrow \text{active pointer}
\end{array}
$$

Cell 77 was active so we left it alone; it references cell 65, which has already been visited; and also references cell 402 which is about to move. We move the contents of cell 402 into cell 100, and to let everyone know where the contents has gone, we leave a forwarding address of 100 in location 402. Thus,

$$
\begin{array}{ll}
100 & | 204 | 402 | \leftarrow \text{free pointer} \\
402 & | \quad | 100 | \leftarrow \text{active pointer}
\end{array}
$$

The active pointer, having writ, moves on; it skips over any unmarked cells, looking for the next marked location. Assume the next marked location is

204. It stops there and waits for the free pointer to discover that location 155 is the next free location. In its search the free pointer will skip over any marked cells. The same relocation operation occurs: the contents of 204 is moved to location 155, and the forwarding address of 155 is placed in location 204. The process continues until the two pointers collide. Call that collision point **col**. When they meet, all locations above **col** either will be free or will contain forwarding addresses. All addresses, **col** and below, will contain marked words or relocated cells. We are now ready to enter the **update** phase.

Here is the picture:

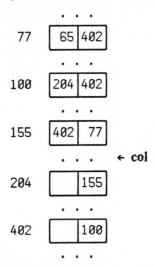

We examine the initial segment of our space from the bottom to **col** looking for any references to that area *above* **col**. A reference to that area must be changed. What is found in the referenced cell is not the desired information, but is the forwarding address of the desired information. What to do is obvious: tell the sender what the change of address is. Thus the *cdr*-part of cell 77 becomes 100; the *car*-part doesn't change. Cell 100 refers to two relocated cells; we find their forwarding addresses, and cell 100 becomes

$$100 \quad \boxed{155 \mid 100}$$

Similar treatment is given to cell 155, modifying the *car*-part. When all cells below **col** are updated, the garbage collection is finished. The cells above **col** are all available for the free-list.

Problems

1. Is col in the free space list after the update phase?
2. Write a LISP algorithm for compacting garbage collection in LISP.

7.5 Bit-tables

In the marking phase of a garbage collector it is necessary to record the visitation of each word. Frequently it is not possible to place a mark in the actual word. This might occur for several reasons:

1. For a word in FS, there is no room if each word contains exactly two addresses.
2. For a word in FWS, the information would be changed if we modified a bit.
3. In structures, more complex than dotted pairs, there may not be room for marking bits.
4. If a mark bit is assigned in each word, then the initialize phase requires that we visit each word. This violates "locality of reference". [5]

An alternative solution designates a separate section of memory called a bit-table. The bit-table is a sequence of binary flags such that there is a one-to-one correspondence between a flag and a markable memory location. Whenever we wish to record the visiting of a word, we set the corresponding flag in the bit table. A bit table is represented as a sequence of machine locations with several flags represented in each word. The initialization phase is improved since it is faster to initialize a whole table rather than initialize single bits in separate words. The mark phase is rapid if there is a simple calculation to relate each bit in a word with its corresponding markable location.

---

[5]Locality refers to the relative distance between memory locations assigned in a particular structure. In some machine organizations, memory is divided into "pages" of a relatively small size. There is significant overhead involved in crossing page boundaries. Therefore memory referencing which entails many scattered references is said to violate "locality of reference."

7.6 Representations of Complex Data Structures

In our discussion of abstract context-free data structures in Section 2.1, we isolated three kinds of structures:

$$\mathfrak{D} ::= \mathfrak{D}_1 \dots \mathfrak{D}_1$$

e.g.,   <seq> ::= (<seq elem>, ..., <seq elem>)

$$\mathfrak{D} ::= \mathfrak{D}_1 \mid \mathfrak{D}_2 \mid \mathfrak{D}_3$$

e.g.,   <seq elem> ::= <indiv> | <seq>

$$\mathfrak{D} ::= \mathfrak{D}_1 \, \mathfrak{D}_2 \, \mathfrak{D}_3 \dots \mathfrak{D}_n$$

e.g.,   <sexpr> ::= (<sexpr> . <sexpr>)

We have discussed the behaviorial characteristics of algorithms which operate on these structures. Now we wish to examine the storage structure aspects of these data structures.

Corresponding to these three data structures are three "natural" storage representations. By "natural" we mean that even though all these structures can be represented as LISP S-expressions, for example, there are representations which might better suit the operations which we expect to perform on those structures. Since "natural" is not a well-defined term, we will clarify its meaning using examples of context-free data structures.

The first type of data structure given above, maps naturally onto a representation which contains information that the object is of type $\mathfrak{D}$ and contains space for the storage instance of this data type. Elements of type $\mathfrak{D}$ are homogeneous, being all of type $\mathfrak{D}_1$; however, the size of a type $\mathfrak{D}$ element is indefinite. Depending on the operations which are to be performed on the representation, either a list representation or an array representation is reasonable for the storage structure. Unless the operations are quite complex, a sequential allocation scheme suffices.

The second type of data structure is frequently represented as a pointer. There really isn't any storage allocated for objects of this type. Instances which satisfy this equation have their storage requirements set by one of the $\mathfrak{D}_i$ alternatives. We will discuss pointer manipulation in LISP in the next section.

This section will discuss the third abstract data structure. The essential characteristic here is that instances of this structure have a fixed number of components, and those components need not be of homogeneous type. Those components are typically referenced by name. These characteristics form a natural distinction between this third class and the first class, even though an appropriate encoding would make it possible to represent either class in the other.

For example, in equations like

<sexpr> ::= (<sexpr> . <sexpr>)

or   <form> ::= <function>[<arg-list>]

we reference components by selectors like *car, cdr, func,* and *arglist.*

LISP represents instances of the above equations as objects of the first and second types of data structure: variable-length lists of pointers. As a result, we have thought of these selectors as operations which might require some nontrivial amount of computation to discover the desired component, but as we saw in Section 1.8 what is algorithm and what is data depends on your point of view. For example, we could think of a dotted pair as an array which has two components, one referenced by *car*, one referenced by *cdr*. We say "array," since the number of components is known; but the element references are done by nonnumerical names.

The natural storage requirements for such objects imply a fixed amount of storage. That storage can be sequentially allocated since the size of the element will not vary. The representation must also encode the scheme for associating external selector with internal representation.

For example,

CAR	
CDR	

Notice that the array-referencing mechanisms have to solve a similar problem. However, array representation is such that the dope vector can perform a *calculation* to locate the element.

The storage element which we are developing is called a **record** ([Pop 68]), or a **structure** ([Alg 75], [EL1 74]), or a **plex** ([Han 69]). [6]

Besides the usual constructors, selectors and recognizers, records may be supplied with a function to modify components of a structure. This function is called an **updater**. Just as we can write $A[43] \leftarrow 56$ where A is an array, an updater function would implement a statement like $car[x] \leftarrow (A . B)$.

Updating of simple variables is called assignment. A discussion of "updating" of more general data structures requires a deeper understanding of the implementation and storage structures. In the case of LISP, it requires a discussion of pointers. That is the topic of the next section.

7.7 *rplaca* and *rplacd*

The discussion in Chapter 5 developed an implementation of the LISP operations in terms of the manipulation of pointers. Those manipulations allowed the creation of new structure or allowed sharing of an existing structure. None of these operations involved the modification of an existing

---

[6]A similar device, called a **hunk**, has been implemented in MacLISP [Ste pc].

structure. In this section we will discuss some LISP coding tricks which do
involve modification operations.
First, consider

$$append <= \lambda[[x,y][null[x] \rightarrow y; \ t \rightarrow concat[first[x];append[rest[x];y]]]]$$

This function copies x onto the front of y. [7] Or recall the *subst* function: it
generates a copy with the correct substitutions made; the substitutions are not
made in the original S-expr. Since it is the constructors which carry out the
copying operations, and since the application of a constructor may initiate the
expensive operation of garbage collection, we should examine the possible
ways of reducing copying.

Consider the expression $append[(A\ B\ C);(D\ E)]$. It appears that we
could get the effect of *append* by *rest*-ing down the list $(A\ B\ C)$ until we
found the terminator; then we could replace that terminator with a pointer to
the list $(D\ E)$. Thus,

The resulting structure does indeed look like one we would have obtained
from *append*. The operation we want to perform *modifies* the existing
structure, instead of *copying* it as *append* would have done. Such
modifications can cause serious difficulties.

Let us call the modifying version of *append*, *nconc*; and consider the
execution of the following sequence of statements:

first $i \leftarrow (A\ B\ C)$

then $j \leftarrow (D\ E)$

and finally, $k \leftarrow nconc[i;j]$

After execution of the third statement, k would have the expected value
$(A\ B\ C\ D\ E)$. However i would *also* have this value since we modified the
structure assigned to i. Also, any value which was sharing part of the
structure of i will also be changed. *nconc* is a pointer modification procedure;
its effect can be quite far-reaching and unexpected. Exclusion of such
features is one solution. However a programming language *is* a tool, and
used carefully, such features are valuable for decreasing storage requirements
and execution time. Inclusion of such features must be done with care,
however. The chance for inadvertent application must be minimized.

With the preceding adminitions, we introduce the LISP pointer
modification primitives. Their appearance at this position in this text

---

[7]Note: y is not copied.

indicates that such operations are not critical to an understanding of programming languages, and also that such features should not be used without a reasonable understanding of that language.

Pointer modification functions for LISP are defined in terms of two primitive operations; *rplaca* replaces the *car* pointer; *rplacd* replaces the *cdr* pointer.

The expression *rplaca[x,y]* replaces the *car*-part of *x* with *y*.

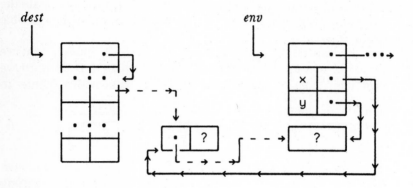

Algorithm for *rplaca*

The AMBIT/G description of *rplacd* was given on page 285.
Now *nconc* can be defined as: [8]

$$nconc <= \lambda[[x,y] \; prog[[z]$$
$$[null[x] \to return[y]];$$
$$z \gets x;$$
$$a \quad [null[cdr[z]] \to rplacd[z,y]; \; return \; [x]];$$
$$z \gets cdr \; [z];$$
$$go[a] \;]]$$

Consider: *prog[[x]*   *x ← (NOTHING CAN GO WRONG);*
                rplacd[cdddr[x];cddr[x]];
                print[x]]

This expression will generate a circular list. Circular lists cannot be generated in LISP without functions like *rplaca* and *rplacd*. See the problem

---

[8] Since we're really involved with the representation we use *car* and *cdr* rather than *first* and *rest*.

on page 287. In general, to circularize a nonempty list, x, $rplacd[last[x];x]$ suffices where

$$last <= \lambda[[x][null[cdr[x]] \rightarrow x; t \rightarrow last[cdr[x]]]]$$

Problems

1. What is the effect of evaluating $rplacd[x;cdr[x]]$?

2. Recall the problem on hash consing on page 287. There we were contemplating unique storage for all S-exprs. Can such a scheme be reconciled (efficiently) with functions like *rplaca* and *rplacd*?

3. It has been pointed out that *rplaca* and *rplacd* are closely related to assignment statements [And 76]. Extend one of our evaluators to recognize expressions like:

$$car[<form>] \leftarrow <form>$$

as abbreviations for:

$$rplaca[<form>; <form>]$$

This extension of assignment is obviously not restricted to *rplaca* but could allow arbitrary forms on the left-hand side of an assignment.

7.8 Applications of *rplaca* and *rplacd*

We begin with rather simple examples. Consider the problem of inserting an element into the middle of a list. For example let x be the list $(A\ B\ C)$. If we wished to insert an atom, say D, between B and C, we could perform

$$x \leftarrow cons[car[x];cons[cadr[x];cons[D;cddr[x]]]]$$

We recopy the initial segment of x, adding D at the appropriate place.

In appropriate circumstances, we can use *rplacd* to insert elements into lists, using fewer *cons* operations. For example, given the list $(A\ B\ C)$ with pointers x and y into it as follows:

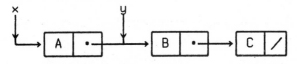

we could insert the element D *after* the first element in y by $rplacd[y;cons[D;cdr[y]]]$, giving: [9]

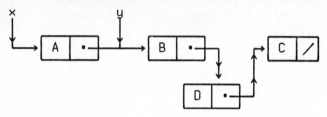

But note that the value of x has also been changed, and any S-expr sharing the list x or y as a sublist has also been affected.

We could delete the element D by

$$x \leftarrow cons[car[x]; cons[car[y];cddr[y]]]$$

We can also use *rplacd* to delete D without using *cons*; we delete not the *first* element of y, but the next element in y by

$$rplacd[y;cddr[y]]$$

Similarly, we can use *rplaca* to modify an element in a list (or S-expr). To change the first element in the list, y, to the S-expr z use

$$rplaca[y;z]$$

Notice that the uses of *rplacd* for insertion and deletion are couched in terms of insert *after* and delete *after*, rather than insert *at* or delete *at*. If you look at a diagram you will see why.

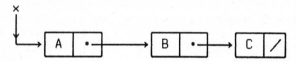

To delete the element B requires modifying the *cdr*-part of the predecessor cell; a similar remark applies to insertion at a specified cell. A simple, perhaps inefficient scheme, to support such modification would be to start a second pointer from the beginning of the list, looking for the cell whose *cdr* pointed to the desired spot; then make the modification.

If these "modification-*at*" functions were to be performed very frequently, then it might be worth starting *two* pointers down the list, one at x, one, say y, at $cdr[x]$, as above. Then testing could be done using y and the modification could be done using x. When we move y to $cdr[y]$, we move x to

---

[9]Notice that *one* application of *cons* is unavoidable.

cdr[*x*]. If we wanted to modify *before* rather than *at*, we could proliferate the "back pointers," but if this kind of generality is required a change of representation is called for. We might resort to the double-linking scheme introduced on page 247; more complex representations are also discussed in detail in [Knu 68] Chapter 2.

A LISP implementation which stores p-lists as list structure would use *rplaca* and *rplacd* heavily; for example, functions which modify properties on the p-lists would use these functions. Here are the two p-list manipulating functions, *putprop* and *remprop*.

putprop was introduced on page 261. Recall that the effect of *putprop* is to attach an indicator-value pair to an atom. If the indicator is already present, then we will simply change its value; if the indicator is not present, then we will add the indicator-value pair to the front of the p-list. In the definition *n* is an atom, *i* is an indicator, and *v* is the value to be stored.

$$putprop <= \lambda[[n;v;i] \; prog[[m]$$
$$m \leftarrow cdr[n];$$
$$a \quad [eq[car[m];i] \rightarrow rplaca[cdr[m];v];return[v]];$$
$$m \leftarrow cddr[m];$$
$$[null[m] \rightarrow rplacd[n;cons[i;cons[v;cdr[n]]]];return[v]];$$
$$go[a] \;]]$$

Note that extended conditional expressions are used in the definition.

remprop was also introduced on page 261. *remprop* is a predicate used to remove attribute-value pairs from the property list of an atom. We will capitalize on the LISP "*NIL*-non *NIL*" trick for predicates and return the removed property value if one is found. The following implementation of *remprop* does that.

$$remprop <= \lambda[[n;i] \; prog[[m]$$
$$m \leftarrow n;$$
$$a \quad [eq[cadr[m];i] \rightarrow return[prog1[\; caddr[m];$$
$$rplacd[m;cdddr[m]]]];$$
$$m \leftarrow cddr[m];$$
$$[null[cdr[m]] \rightarrow return[f]]$$
$$go[a]]]$$

where *prog1* evaluates its arguments from left to right and returns the value of its first argument.

Applications of *rplacd* occur inside *ratom* when p-lists are built and added to the object list. On page 394 we will develop a version of LISP's parser which uses pointer modification to gain efficiency when building the internal representation. Pointer modification is also used inside the garbage collector; examine the *sweep* phase of the collector on page 286.

Finally, pointer modification allows the construction of self-modifying programs. This technique is similar to the machine language tricks of self-modifying code and should be used with similar care. The freedom to hang yourself should not be construed as an invitation to do so, but it again points out the similarities of LISP to machine language and highlights the differences between LISP and its contemporary high-level languages.

LISP's central processor *eval* operates by traversing and interpreting the data structure representation of the program; that data structure is also open for inspection by LISP's data structure manipulating functions. Since we now have list-modifying functions, we could modify a program by changing its internal structure. Indeed we can write a program which modifies its *own* structure.
Here's one:

foo <= λ[[x] *prog*[[y;z]
              z←1;
              y←*sixth*[*body*[*foo*]];
         a *print*[x];
              rplaca[*rest*[y];z←*add1*[z]];
              go[a]]]

The mystery created by *y* is a pointer into the representation of the statement *print*[x]; that representation is *(PRINT X)*. Therefore the effect of the first *rplaca* is to change *(PRINT X)* to *(PRINT 2)*. Subsequent passes through the loop will change the statement to print *3, 4*, and so on. There really isn't much that can be said about such a program.

Problems

1. More on *ratom*. Recall the discussion of *ratom* in Section 5.11 and Section 5.12. Now that you know about *rplaca* and *rplacd* write a more detailed version of *ratom*.

2. On page 48 and page 49 we wrote various styles of *reverse*. All these functions used *concat*; however, we should be able to reverse a list without using any new cells. Express this algorithm as a LISP function. If you use *prog*, don't use any *prog*-variables.

7.9 Numbers

In many implementations of LISP, numbers are stored as very simple kinds of atoms: they are not stored uniquely, and do not need print names. Most implementations allow fixed- and floating-point representation; therefore, indicators for these properties are needed. Thus:

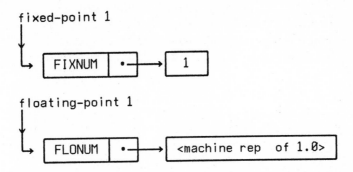

The number is stored in FWS and the type is indicated by a minimal property list. This representation is expensive in space and adds significant overhead to the execution of arithmetic operators. Several techniques have been used to improve LISP arithmetic.

Assume that the addressing space of the machine is 2^{18} and that the usual size of a LISP memory image is N; within the LISP system, all references to memory locations greater than N are illegal. We will use these illegal addresses to encode some of the smaller positive and negative integers, mapping zero on the middle address, the positive numbers to lower addresses and the negatives onto the higher addresses. These smaller integers, called **INUMS**, are represented by pointers outside of the normal LISP addressing space. This trick can considerably decrease the storage requirements for applications which use small numbers extensively.

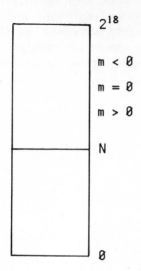

$$2^{18}$$

m < 0

m = 0

m > 0

N

0

Picture of INUM Space

The INUM representation adds some complexity since the arithmetic operators now have to recognize these illegal pointers as encoded numbers.

The MACLISP ([Moo 74]) implementation uses a different representation for numbers. [10] In that implementation, two spaces are allocated for number storage: FIXNUM space and FLONUM space. This makes a more compact representation since the type information is implied in the address of the object rather than being explicitly stored. To those basic spaces we add two temporary stack areas: FIXPDL and FLOPDL. These areas are used for temporary arithmetic computation.

The temporary areas work in conjunction with a type declaration option used to aid the MACLISP compiler. If we know that certain

_____

[10]Much care went into the the representation of numbers in MACLISP. That LISP system is used as the implementation language for MACSYMA ([MAC 74], [Wan 75], [Mos 74]), a large algebraic and symbolic mathematics system. MACLISP's efficient number facilities, coupled with its optimizing compiler, have resulted in the production of compiled code which is more efficient than that produced by DEC's FORTRAN compiler ([Fat 73]).

variables are *always* going to be used as numbers in a particular function, then we can compile better code. Assume x and y are to be used *only* as FIXNUMs within a function f; we would make such declarations for the MACLISP compiler just as we can declare some variables as "special" to other LISP compilers. When we allocate space for x and y, we allocate space on the top of FIXPDL. Within f the arithmetic operations use the hardware arithmetic and reference the stack elements. The stack elements can be passed to other arithmetic functions called within f, and no permanent storage need be allocated in FIXNUM space until later. The efficiency of arithmetic operations is dependent on the existence of special hardware instructions for such arithmetic. However, special hardware also places limits on the arithmetic capabilities of most languages: arithmetic is usually limited by the word size of the machine.

There are several versions of LISP which will automatically change representation when faced with overflow. This scheme is called **arbitrary precision arithmetic** and has been implemented for both fixed-point and floating-point numbers. We will describe a representation for fixed-point numbers called **BIGNUMS**; they could have the following structure:

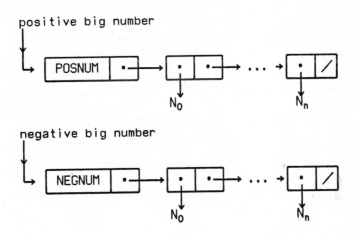

Structure of a BIGNUM

The value of a BIGNUM is given by:

$$\beta(N_0 + \alpha N_1 + \ldots + \alpha^n N_n)$$

where β is either + or - and α-1 is the largest number representable in one machine word. The translations between BIGNUMS and the other numeric representations are done automatically.

On most implementations of LISP, no attempt is made to store numbers uniquely. Thus *eq* will not work on numbers other than INUMs; either *equal* is extended for numbers or a special equality predicate for numbers is provided.

7.10 Stacks and Threading

Though recursive algorithms are usually more illuminating than their machine-oriented counterparts, it is frequently more efficient to encode those algorithms in manners which can take advantage of the hardware. This section will discuss two techniques which "unwind" the recursion and typically lead to faster execution.

Recall the marking phase of a garbage collector in Section 5.14. There we wrote *mark* as a recursive algorithm. We could equally well write *mark* using an explicit stack:

```
mark <= λ[[tr]prog[[st]
            loop  [is_marked[tr] → go[chk_st];
                   is_full_wd[tr] → markA[tr];go[chk_st];
                   is_free_wd[tr] → st←push[cdr[tr];st];
                                    markA[tr];
                                    tr←car[tr];go[loop]];
                   t → go[chk_st]];  11
            chk_st[null[st] → return[t]];
                   tr←top[st];
                   st←pop[st];
                   go[loop] ]]
```

```
push <= λ[[i;st] concat[i;st]]
top <= λ[[st] first[st]]
pop <= λ[[st] rest[st]]
```

Notice that we save only the *cdr*-node in the stack; even at that, the stack grows proportionally to the depth of the tree being traversed. See the

---

[11]This branch of the conditional could be omitted and the effect would be the same.

problem on page 393. The technique of using an explicit stack sometimes is more intuitive and sometimes will lead to faster execution.

The second technique is more tricky but will lead to significant pay-offs in execution time. [12] The technique is called **threading**. The basis for threading is a desire to traverse tree structures in a more efficient fashion than that typically available implicitly in recursion, or explicitly via stacks. Recall that on page 247 we surmised that **double-linking** might be advantageous in moving up and down the "spine" of a tree structure. Double links would allow us to find the successors and predecessors of nodes easily. However the extra link gives us no help if we wish to descend into the substructure. It is this area to which threading addresses itself: descent into tree structure.

Examination of the new *mark* algorithm will reveal that for a *fixed* tree and a *fixed* order of traversal; any two applications of marking will have the same pattern of behavior. The order of visitation to each node will be the same, but more importantly, the dynamic changes in the state of the stack will *also* be the same. Instead of replicating the portion of the stack, it might be possible to store the stack information in the structure itself. Threading hides the control structure in the data structure. Typically, threading requires a more complex data structure since we must store both threads and links. The traversal algorithms also become more complex since we must recognize the difference between control threads and data links. Care must also be taken if we wish to share threaded list structure. See [Knu 68] for a complete discussion of the techniques and tricks.

We do not wish to complicate the LISP structures, but dispensing with a stack, be it implicit or explicit, does influence storage requirements. We can strike a compromise; instead of permanently storing the threads in the structure, we can *temporarily* store threads as we traverse trees. The first application is in the design of a nonrecursive *read* program. The second application we will describe is in the mark phase of a garbage collector.

Problem

1. With a little more testing before stacking we can significantly cut down the number of *push*es we have to do. Namely, if some of the branches point immediately to atoms we might as well mark them at that time and proceed without doing a stack operation. Only when both branches are "nonatomic" do we need stack the *cdr*. Write such an algorithm. Further, is it better to stack the *cdr* nodes or the *cdr* nodes?

---

[12]But there will be a proportional loss in clarity in the code.

7.11 A Non-recursive *read*

The original *read* algorithm of Section 5.11 is a good example of a clear recursive algorithm; it is reasonably straightforward to follow the flow of the algorithm. However, now that we understand what the run-time behavior of such a recursive program is, we see that *read* is a drain on *two* resources: it uses free-space to construct the internal representation of the input; it uses the run-time stack in the implementation of the recursion and for saving parameters and intermediate computations. A deeply nested expression will use a lot of the run-time stack. Clearly, there is nothing we can do about the drain on the free lists, [13] but threading *can* dispense with the run-time stack. We can in fact do so without a proportional increase in the use of free space; indeed we need only *one* additional free cell, regardless of the complexity of the input! The algorithm will be much more complex that the recursive parser, but that's why this section on storage and efficiency is where it is. We now understand the purpose and intent of *read*. Now that the basic algorithm is well understood we can be clever and efficient.

First we describe the basic ideas of the algorithm, then we give the algorithm. The main idea in the algorithm is the realization that we can determine the storage requirements for a complex S-expr or list structure as we read it in. For example, consider the input string "(A (B C) D)". As we start our left-to-right scan of the input, we see "(". This immediately tells us that we need at least one *cons*. We read "A"; that tells us what the *car* of the expression is. Notice that we don't yet know whether the expression is "dotted" or "listed," but the storage requirements will be the same. On reading the next open parenthesis we know we need to add a new level in the developing representation. The "B" and "C" add elements to that level, and the closing parenthesis finishes it off. The closing parenthesis also should signal our parser to return to the prior level and continue scanning the input. The "D" goes on that level and the final closing parenthesis completes the input. To implement this informal idea, we keep a thread in the *cdr*-part of the last cell on every level. When we go down a level we manufacture a new cell with the *cdr* pointing to the cell we just came from in the previous level; this happens when we see a left parenthesis. We go up a level when we see a right parenthesis; that is done by following up the thread in the current level, after doing appropriate cleanup.

There are three basic states in the reader:

1. The next input should go into the *car*-part of the current cell. This state is entered when we go down a level. It is labeled *head* in the following program.

2. The next input should go on the current level. This is the typical state in

_____

[13]We probably will be drawing on the full word area for print name storage as well as on the free space area for list structure storage.

the building of a list-input. Here we add a new cell in the current level and put the input in the *car*-part of that cell; then stay in this state. This state corresponds to label *tail*.

3. The other main state occurs on reading a dot when in *tail* state. [14] In dot state we check the next input; if it is an atom we store it on the thread and follow the thread. If the input is a left parenthesis we add a new cell and go down.

There are some anomalies in the algorithm since it must recognize both S-expr notation and list notation. To handle both kinds of input, we add a parenthesis counter; it increments for left parentheses and decrements for right parentheses. A legal input has been recognized when we are back at the top level and the count is zero.

The final difference between the old parser and the new one involves the scanner *ratom*. We assume a new *ratom* which reads () and returns *NIL*. If the scanner sees an open parenthesis, it looks ahead to the next meaningful character. [15] If the character is a closing parenthesis, the scanner takes it; if the character is not, it is left for the next call on *ratom* and *ratom* returns with an indication that it has seen a left parenthesis.

---

[14]Dots seen in any other context are errors.

[15]It ignores spaces and the like.

With this introduction, here is the new *read*:

```
read <= λ[[] prog[[j;cp;count;top;temp]
                     count←init[]; cp←count; top←cp;
           head      j←ratom[];
                     [or[is_dot[j];is_rpar[j]] → err[];
                     is_lpar[j] → incr[count];
                                     cp←down[cp];
                                     go[head];
                     atom[j] → stuff[cp,j]; go[ckend]]];
           tail      j←ratom[];
                     [atom[j] → cp←insert_move[cp,j]; go[ckend];
                     is_rpar[j] → decr[count];
                                     [eq[top;cp] → go[ck1];
                                      t → cp←stuff_up[cp;NIL]; go[ckend]]];

                     is_lpar[j] → incr[count];
                                     cp←down[insert_move[cp;NIL]];
                                     go[head];

                     is_dot[j] → j←ratom[];
                                     [or[is_dot[j];is_rpar[j]] → err[];
                                     is_lpar[j] → incr[count];
                                                     cp←insert_move[cp;NIL];
                                                     go[head];
                                     atom[j] → cp←stuff_up[cp,j];
                                                     go[ckend]]]];  16
           ckend     [eq[cp;top] → go[ck1];
                     t → go[tail]];
           ck1       temp← cnt[top];
           end2      [zerop[temp] → return[exp[top]]];
                     j←ratom[];
                     [is_rpar[j] → temp←sub1[temp]; go[end2];
                     t → err[] ]]]
```

---

[16]This *go* is superfluous, but makes the flow more apparent.

init <= λ[[] *cons*[*NIL*;0]]
stuff <= λ[[x;y] *rplaca*[x;y]]
incr <= λ[[z] *rplacd*[z;add1*[cdr*[z]]]]

insert_move <= λ[[cp;val] *rplacd*[cp;*cons*[val;*cdr*[cp]]]; *cdr*[cp]]

down <= λ[[cp] *rplaca*[cp;*cons*[*NIL*;cp]];*car*[cp]]

stuff_up <= λ[[cp;j] *prog*[[temp]
$\qquad\qquad\qquad$ temp ← *cdr*[cp];
$\qquad\qquad\qquad$ *rplacd*[cp;j];
$\qquad\qquad\qquad$ return[temp]]]

cnt <= λ[[x] *cdr*[x]]
exp <= λ[[x] *car*[x]]

The development and understanding of this algorithm requires most of what we have covered in the course. We use our knowledge of the parser, *read*; we use our familiarity with S-exprs stored as linked lists; we have to understand the run-time control of recursive calling sequences; we have to understand pointer manipulation; we have to understand pointer modification; and finally we have to be wickedly clever. With that understanding we were able to apply threading at a level higher than a "once only" trick.

Problem

1. Write a version of *read* which uses an explicit stack to remember where it is in the parse.

7.12 More Applications of Threading

A Link-Bending Garbage Collector for LISP

The use of a stack is one of the difficulties associated with garbage collection. Garbage collection is invoked when available space has become exhausted, but here we are asking for *more* space to use for stacking. The usual solution to such a problem is to allocate a separate area for stack storage. This has its drawbacks. If we don't allocate enough stack space the depth of a piece of structure may become too great, and the marker will fail. The amount of stack space can become large - proportional to the depth of a list. We can apply threading here, modifying the structure as we traverse it; as usual the threads will be used as control information. As we finish marking a branch we restore the structure to its original topology. Several versions of such threaded collectors are available; see [Chr 68] for a version written in AMBIT/G; a more traditional description is found in [Sch 67]; [17] and see [Knu 68] for several alternatives.

Binding Implementations

Threading can be used in the shallow binder described in Section 5.20 to remember the path through the environment tree ([Urm 76]). We thread from E_{bind} to E_{inter} when we are looking for E_{inter}. This consists of reversing the access links as we proceed toward E_{inter}. Then, as we swap back the value cells, we will unthread from E_{inter} to E_{bind}.

7.13 Storage Management and LISP

There are two basic areas of LISP which require attention: the implementation of data stuctures, and the implementation of a LISP machine. We will discuss applications in that order.

LISP's typical data object is a dotted pair; however, dotted pairs are frequently used to represent more structured objects. For example, many common LISP programs involve list operations on list representations. But lists, we know, are representations of sequences. From Section 7.2 we now also know that arrays are efficient representations of sequences. Indeed array representations are typically more efficient than the general LISP linked-list. We would like to capitalize on this more efficient representation without jeopardizing the LISP operations.

An analysis of the LISP operations shows that we *share* substructures, and if using *rplaca* or *rplacd*, we *modify* existing structures. Any proposed economies in storage layout must take cognizance of these facts. Fortunately these requirements are compatible.

Consider the typical representation of the sequence:

$$(LAMBDA\ (X)\ (F\ X\ Y))$$

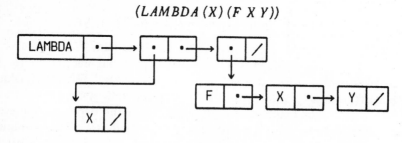

---

[17]The correctness of [Sch 67] has been proved by de Roever.

This representation takes seven words. The *car*-part of each cell contains the information; the *cdr*-part tells where the rest of the expression is to be found. That is, we have dedicated 14 half-words to represent the structure; only seven of which contain the actual information we wish to store. Using some extra encoding we can carry the same information in seven slightly larger cells.

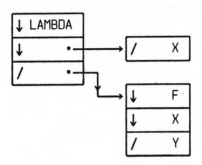

The intent of the special characters is to encode type information about the next cell in the representation. It thus is called *cdr*-**coding**. The ↓ means the next cell is the *cdr*; / means the *cdr* is *NIL*.

The typical LISP cell is a third variety of *cdr*-coding: the code → says the next cell contains a pointer to the *cdr*. With that, we introduce the final code: * means this cell is the *cdr*-half of a LISP word. Thus *(A B)* could be expressed in any of the following forms:

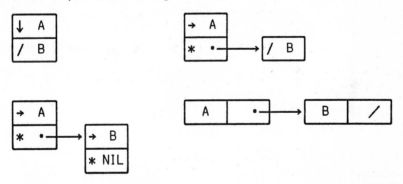

However this encoding scheme is not sufficient as it stands. Consider the following example: Given internal pointers *x* and *z* into

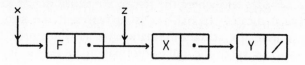

and assume we wish to perform *rplacd*[*x*;(*A B C*)]. Using our standard implementation, we would have:

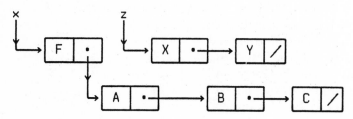

However, a problem arises if (*F X Y*) is represented in its compact form. We can't replace the cell

since the value of *z* would change. The solution is an application of the forwarding address scheme we introduced on page 377 in the compacting garbage collector. We put a forwarding address in the cell referenced by *x*; then allocate a new pair of half-cells, putting *F* in the first and a pointer to (*A B C*) in the second.

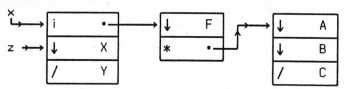

These forwarding addresses are an instance of **invisible pointers** used by R. Greenblatt in his LISP machine; he has also implemented hardware *cdr*-coding. Between invisible pointers and *cdr*-coding, we *can* effect all LISP operations using this potentially more compact representation.

We must be able to maintain that compact representation while the program is running. This requires more care in the management of storage. We cannot simply garbage collect and fragment space; we cannot use the simple compacting garbage collector discussed in Section 7.4 since it does not attempt to maintain the compact representation. Several algorithms with the desired properties exist ([Che 70], [Cla 76]). One feature of this data representation is its use of variable-sized linked blocks of sequential storage. The management of these storage blocks is more complex than that of simple dotted pairs, but the additional overhead may be acceptable if it gives better locality of reference and faster access to list elements. [18]

There is less conflict about the use of more complex storage management techniques in the area of LISP's dynamic implementation. The original versions of LISP 1.5 used dotted pair structure to represent the access environments. [19] This generality gave a correct solution to the implementation of *function*, but experience with LISP implementations has shown that it is quite expensive to maintain this generality when most applications are of a less general nature. Implementation techniques, patterned after our Weizenbaum diagrams, allow some economies without loss of generality. Again, storage would be allocated in sequential blocks; each block would be of a size sufficient to hold the representation of the name-value entries along with the additional areas to link the block to the environment. The storage blocks need not be allocated sequentially; indeed, in the general case blocks cannot be allocated sequentially. The de-allocation problems are somewhat different from those experienced by data structure representations. The environment structures are much more "well behaved" than general list-structures. Therefore an "environment garbage collector" may not be needed.

The most general techniques for management of LISP's dynamic environment are based on [Bob 73a] and succeeding papers. [20]

At a lower level of implementation, LISP has much to say about machine organization. The implementation of efficient environment-swapping algorithms is a problem which any operating system must face. The traditional solutions impose severe restrictions on

---

[18]Notice that the *cdr*-coded representations of *(A B)* and *(A . B)* are equally expensive. In the typical linked-list representation, *(A B)* requires more space than *(A . B)*.

[19]The control information did use a stack implementation coded in machine language.

[20]There is something contradictory about LISP implementors' attitudes toward storage and dynamics. Much effort is expended in attempting to minimize the overhead involved in the dynamic operation of LISP; it is frequently stated that users should not be penalized for access/control constructs which they do not use. However, that attitude is not extended to LISP's data structures. There are very generous subsets of LISP applications in which the data structure operations are suitably well-behaved, that storage reclamation techniques less general than garbage collection are applicable. Analysis of this area of LISP should lead to profitable results.

interprocess communications. The algorithms developed for LISP show promise for giving efficient implementations of more general scope.

LISP's organization of memory also has lessons for machine architecture. The management of large variable-sized memory spaces like [Ste 73] or [Wegb 70] can be supported in hardware. The allocation and de-allocation of such large spaces also require care; LISP implementors have begun to address these problems ([Ste 76a], [Bis 74a]).

7.14 Hash Techniques

One phenomenon of LISP is the sheer size of data structures which a large LISP program generates. Many LISP projects approach 10^7 bits of program and data. Several techniques have been developed to help shrink data representation; *cdr*-coding (Section 7.13) is one technique. Another technique stems from the observation that LISP tends to *copy* structures rather than *share* them. We know that the sharing of structures must be done with great care if modification operations like *rplaca* and *rplacd* are present, but sharing of structure can mean a significant saving in space. In fact, the saving can also improve the algorithms which manipulate the structures. For example if every list structure is stored uniquely, then the time for the equality test *equal* is a constant rather than being proportional to the depth of the structure.

We present two techniques for maintaining unique structure: either maintain list space such that unique representations are always present or supply an algorithm which will "uniquize" structures upon request. The first alternative is usually called **hash consing**; the second technique is called **list condensation** ([Lin 73]). A condensation algorithm must remove all duplicated structure from within a list. Since condensation is a component of many hashed LISP implementations, we will concentrate our attention on hash consing.

Hash consing is an extension of the LISP technique for generating unique atoms. Since list structure is created only by the *cons* operation, [21] we place the responsibility for maintaining unique structure within *cons*. If the result of a pending *cons* is already present, we return a pointer to that structure, otherwise we perform the *cons* and record the result so that it will be retrieved if the same *cons* happens again. The adjective "hash" is applied to this version of *cons* since the typical implementation uses a hashing algorithm to maintain the uniqueness. Hash *consing* imposes restrictions on the programmer's use of list modification operations. If unique copies are available, severe difficulties result if modifications are made. One either may disallow list modification or may supply additional operations to copy

---

[21] However, list structure may be modified by *rplaca* and *rplacd*.

structure, modify it, and "uniquize" the result, or an implementation may supply different kinds of structures, some modifiable and some not modifiable.

A hash *cons* was proposed for LISP 1.75 on the IBM M44, but the implementation was never completed. A limited version of hash *cons*ing was implemented as an extension of LISP 1.6 at Stanford.

Impressive and extensive applications of hashing appear in HLISP ([Got 74], [Ter 75]). That implementation of LISP supplies two different kinds of structures: ordinary list structure and "monocopy" structures. Operations are also supplied for conversion between types. Extensive analysis of hashing effects on algorithm performance has also been done ([Got 76]). HLISP also employs hashing in its implementation of property lists. Property lists are not stored explicitly, but rather the atom name and the property name are used to form a hash index; the property value is associated with that hash index. For example, $get[x;i]$ hashes with both x and i to retrieve the property value.

The other major implementations of LISP also offer specialized operations for dealing with hashed quantities; see [Moo 74], [Int 75], and [Bob 75].

Implications of LISP

Any text which is of the size and extent of this book certainly owes a word of explanation to its readers; after 404 pages it is not fair to turn the page and find the index. This section will try to summarize what we have accomplished in this book and will address some of the current research related to LISP-like languages.

It is the author's belief that LISP should be the first language learned by persons interested in computer science. As a language for studying algorithms for data structures, it is presently without peer. As you have seen, the problems of language implementation and their solutions are describable quite naturally in the implementation of LISP. As a programming language, LISP has powerful features possessed by few languages, in particular the uniform representation of program and data.

We have developed several areas of programming languages and data structures in this book and have hinted at future possibilities in several of those areas:

1. Mathematical models: This refers to some of the theoretical areas which use LISP as the basis for mathematical studies of algorithms, equivalence of programs, and program synthesis from formal specifications. These are not of purely theoretical interest: correctness of non-trivial programs is an important practical problem. The issue of programming language semantics also needs clarification. This branch of semantics seeks a descriptive tool for the meaning of constructs of a language; in particular, a tool of the power and clarity of BNF descriptions of the syntax of languages. We have talked a bit about semantic issues in Section 3.13. The close relationship between LISP evaluators and denotational models is encouraging.

2. Generalized control structures: We hinted at some of the options under consideration for control of algorithms. The work on generalized access and control, also known as "spaghetti stacks" ([Bob 73a]), is of current interest and many of its motivations and implications should be more understandable now. The devices which are required for such general control also come directly from the LISP experience. Devices like "spaghetti stacks" serve for implementation of higher level language constructs like pattern directed invocation.

3. Interpreter/compilers: This is an interesting area which begins to resolve the dichotomy between compilation and interpretation. Work was done in [Mit 70], but little has been done since. Again, LISP is a natural vehicle for discussing this topic.

4. Implementation tricks and machine organization: In the past LISP has been the originator of several, now every-day, programming tricks. Current production versions of LISP continue to develop sophisticated techniques for management of very large spaces, representation of data structures, and execution of complex algorithms. Many of those ideas have direct implications for the development of hardware for LISP like languages.

5. Languages for Artificial Intelligence research: Though LISP is thought of primarily as the language for Artificial Intelligence programming, we have barely touched on those applications. In the last decade, LISP has really become a systems programming language, rather than a research tool. It is the systems language for developing more powerful languages for A.I. They are "more powerful" in the sense of descriptive power, rather than computational power. LISP is also used exclusively as the systems programming language on the M.I.T. LISP machine.

6. Interaction and personal computation. Though LISP developed in the late 1950's, contemporary implementations are finally exploiting the true interactive nature of the language. A LISP machine is a sophisticated and powerful calculator. The language is the most interactive of the major programming languages, and as such, should attract the interest of the personal computer field. This should see the development of sophisticated μ-computer LISP implementations. The combination of LISP, inexpensive hardware, and creative minds should be interesting to watch.

The main purpose of this epilog is to tie together most of the material we have studied. The underlying thread in our study has been the internal and external behavior of LISP. A rather natural vehicle to unify these topics is the design of a new LISP-like language. Language design is not a pastime to be entered into lightly; we will therefore sketch an existing LISP extension named EL1. The name EL1 is derived from Extensible Language/1.

There are two basic views in programming language design: one approach is to design a small language, called a base language, which has suffient expressive power to allow its user to mold a special language from that base. This is called the "core" approach and such base languages are called extensible languages. The alternative, called the "shell" approach, is to design a full language, capable of covering a specific area. That area may only cover a special domain of algorithms or might encompass *all* algorithmic processes.

The "shell" approach to general purpose languages is best exemplified by PL/1. This approach attempts to build a language which encompasses all the Pl/1 is an The approach gives rise to many problems. Of necessity, the language is large; unless care is taken a programmer will have difficulties in learning the language. Even if a small subset is presented to a beginner, the occurrence of bugs in a user program may cause mysterious results if those bugs happen to invoke features outside the subset. Also the language implementor is in for a hard time; language processors will have to be cognizant of *all* the language features even if the user wishes to work within a small subset. The problems of optimization are compounded immensely, since the interaction of language features may well lead to torturous code. Though the "shell" approach presents severe problems, the "core" approach of extensibility is not without flaw. There are non-trivial research areas involved in developing smooth and efficient means of describing the syntax, pragmatics and semantics of user defined data structures, control structures and operations.

An extensible language is designed to supply a base language, which has sufficient handles such that a user can describe new data structures, new operations, and new control structures. These new objects are described in terms of combinations of constructs in the base language. Extensibility is implicitly committed to the premiss that the power of high level languages is primarily notational rather than computational. That is apparent from our experience with high level numerical languages. Their notations allow us to express our problems in mathematics-like statements, rather than coding in machine language.

Like LISP, the extensible language EL1 maps programs onto data structures. EL1 has richer data types including integers, characters, pointers, and structures. Its syntax is described in BNF and a mapping from well-formed syntactic units to data structures is given. The EL1 evaluator is written in EL1 and manipulates the data-structure representation of EL1 programs in a manner totally analogous to the LISP *eval* function.

The syntax of EL1 is similar to that of M-expression LISP. The details are not relevant and are best left to the user's manual, [EL1 74]. What *is* important is the interrelationships between the constucts of the language and their data structure representations. That is, we wish to develop a representation of the abstract syntax of EL1 using the data structures available in EL1. Our approach here is the other way round: to motivate the data structures of a language by the requirements for expressing a realistic evaluator. [1]

Consider this fragment of the LISP syntax from page 17:

<form>   ::= <constant> | <application> | <variable>
<application>   ::= <function-part>[<arg-list>]
<arg-list>   ::= <arg> | <arg-list>;<arg>

These equations demonstrate the three kinds of BNF equations. We will concentrate our attention on the last two equations.

The LISP M-to-S-expression mapping will map an <application> like $f[x;y;z]$ onto $(F\ X\ Y\ Z)$. For all intents and purposes, LISP has little choice; LISP has few representations available and since we wish to use the S-expr representation as the programming language, the representation must be readable. In the typical implementations of LISP, the representation of $f[x;y;z]$ is $(F\ .\ (X\ .\ (Y\ .\ (X\ NIL))))$. That requires a lot of space, and requires some decoding by any program which is to use this representation. If we look closely at the storage requirements for <application>'s and <arg-list>'s, we see that there are differences.

The representation of an <application> has *fixed* storage requirements; it demands space for two components: a <function-part> component, and a <arg-list> component. We have seen such storage structures before in Section 7.6; they are called record structures. The name components of the record structure can be *fun* and *args*, and the selector functions are implemented by matching the name components. Note that the use of record

---

[1]Compare the following discussion with Section 7.6.

structure is a bit freer than LISP's list representation; we need not make a commitment to the position of the *fun* component in the representation.

The requirements for <arg-list> are different. An arbitrary <arg-list> has a variable number of components. Each component has the same characteristic: it's an <arg>. We can represent a homogeneous object like <arg-list> as a sequence whose length is fixed. A natural storage class for such sequences is a linear array, each component of which is an item of the sequence. Information about the length of the sequence, and the class to which elements of the sequence belong, can be stored in the "dope vector" of the representation.

What we are developing is a description of a class of storage representations for language constructs. This class of structures covers the space which LISP covers, but partitions it differently. More information is stored explicitly, and the representations are more discriminating in their storage requirements. Assuming that the resulting structures are made data structures of the language, we can then write a LISP-like *eval* which runs on these data structures.

Our refinement is not without penalty. We are in fact imposing a type structure on the language. We know that such restrictions are not always desireable. The type structure becomes more apparent when we consider the remaining syntax equation:

<form> ::= <constant> | <application> | <variable>

Consistent with our treatment of record structures and sequences, we should develop some representation for <form>. In LISP, no storage was allocated for the representation of such alternative BNF equations; the recognition was done by recognizers embedded in a conditional expression:

$$[is\text{-}const[x] \rightarrow \ldots$$
$$is\text{-}app[x] \rightarrow \ldots$$
$$is\text{-}var[x] \rightarrow$$

$$t \rightarrow \quad \ldots \text{ what to do if } x \text{ is } not \text{ a form } \ldots$$

In EL1, every data item has an associated type. Since we are representing language constructs as data structures they will also have associated types. To determine if something is an <application> requires only that we examine the associated type. The question then arises: what kind of object is to be associated with an object like <form>? At any one time an object of type <form> is one of the three alternatives. The EL1 solution is to assign a pointer-like data object as the representation of such objects. The type of the pointer is constrained to point at one of the alternatives.

Let's compare LISP: Given an application $f[x;A;1]$ we represent it as a constant $(F \ X \ (QUOTE \ A) \ 1)$. That is:

$$\Re_{\mathrm{LISP}}[\![f[x;A;1]]\!] = (F \ X \ (QUOTE \ A) \ 1)$$

We wish to represent this application as a constant in EL1 as well. We need some notation for record structures and sequence constants. A record constant of type t will be represented as $<_t c_1; ... ;c_n>$.[2] A sequence of type t will be represented as $(_t s_1; ... ;s_n)$.

Then $\mathfrak{R}_{EL1}[\![f[x;A;1]]\!] = <_{app} \mathfrak{R}_{EL1}[\![f]\!];$
$$(_{arg\text{-}list} \quad \mathfrak{R}_{EL1}[\![x]\!];$$
$$\mathfrak{R}_{EL1}[\![A]\!];$$
$$\mathfrak{R}_{EL1}[\![1]\!]) >$$

We have suppressed much of the detail because each of the components of the representation must also have type information.

The structured items in LISP are built from dotted pairs; the structured items in EL1 are built from sequences (or lists), from records (or structures), and from pointers (or references). The difference is that the EL1 user has more choice over the underlying representation. This can lead to more efficient utilization of storage and perhaps more efficient programs. Since the evaluator is just an EL1 program, these considerations carry over to the evaluation process. EL1 allows us to *represent* the data structures of the evaluation process in terms closer to actual implementation. Both LISP and EL1 allow us to *express* realistic implementations, however LISP may ultimately represent its structures as dotted pairs.

This realism of representation carries over to the evaluation process which runs on the representation. The language is capable of accurately representing more of the techniques which occur in a language implementation. The language supplies storage management primitives which allow the creation of stack-like objects as well as the heap-stored items of LISP.

The language offers the user the ability to *define* abstract data structures in a manner similar to that we have been advocating informally. Given the finer partition of storage structures, the user can map those structures onto more frugal representations than LISP, and since the type-checking is built into the language, the language processors can check the consistency of the parameter passing. Relating the abstract with the representation requires some care. Supplying a comfortable interface between these two domains is a non-trivial problem. EL1 supplies "lifting" and "lowering" mechanisms to aid in this problem; the result is not completely satisfactory.

We have frequently seen how easy it has been to extend LISP by modifying *eval*. This is particularly easy because we are making modifications at the level of data-structure representation of programs. In EL1 we wish to make the extensions at the level of concrete syntax, rather

---

[2]We have suppressed the explicit naming of each component of the record. We assume that a "template" of each type t is available. That template can be consulted to determine which component is referenced.

than abstract syntax as LISP does.[3] EL1 can do this by using a parser which is table-driven, and operates on a modifiable set of productions. To introduce a new construct into the language we need to supply the concrete syntax for the item, its abstract systax, a mapping from concrete to abstract, and its pragmatics expressed as additions to the evaluator. However there may be wider implications in the language and more general features are required.[4] The field of language design is still quite young and tentative.

Though LISP is a full twenty years old, it is still a fertile research area. Projects are extending LISP in several directions. [Car 76] investigates the possibilities of adding a type-structure to LISP, giving a strong-typed programming language and a precise formalism in which properties of Typed LISP programs can be discussed. This project supplies an Algol-like user language as well as develops interesting theoretical results.

Several people have supplied parsers which give the user an Algol-like syntax ([Mli 73], [Pra 76]). Extensions to the ideas of SDIO Section 9.4 are being pursued.

Programming language semantics is being coupled with the realities of programming language design in a successor of [LCF 72]. This is being built on the LISP experience.

LISP is the direct source of inspiration for two current MIT projects. For several years C. Hewitt has been developing an interesting philosophy of computation. Building on his experience with LISP, he developed PLANNER [Hew 72], and more recently refined thse ideas in a methodology called Actors ([Hew 74], [Hew 76]). One of the aims of these investigations is to develop a self-sufficient description of modern computation much in the way that the λ-calculus gave a foundation to the notion of computable function. The goal therefore is much higher than to develop just another programming language. Along the way, however, these projects have developed some of the most notable ideas of advanced programming languages. From the PLANNER experience, partially implemented in [Mic 71], evolved the ideas of pattern-directed invocation; see Section 2.5. This gave PLANNER a new way to call procedures, and its implementation in Micro-PLANNER gave researchers new power of expression much in the way that LISP improved over machine language several years before. These investigations generated much controversy and stimulated more research in language design for artificial intelligence; see [Bob 74], [Con 73], [QA4 72]. The lessons of PLANNER led to Actors and a study of the control aspects of programming languages. From these investigations Hewitt has developed a

---

[3]To program in the abstract syntax would be possible, but messy. We would be writing constants consisting of pointers, records, and sequences, rather than the list notation of LISP.

[4]For example, if new control structures are desired, major revision of the inner structure of the language may be necessary ([Pre 76b]).

model which looks on control as an activity of passing message between program modules. Recently, Hewitt's efforts have again stimulated others to examine programming languages more closely.

G. Sussman and G. Steele have been developing a language named SCHEME ([Sus 75], [Ste 76b], and [Ste 76c]) which was begun as an experiment to understand and implement several of the ideas of Hewitt. The result is a dialect of LISP which uses static binding rather than dynamic binding. The interpreter is built in the spirit of [Con 73] and is similar to the evaluator of Section 4.8. The result is an interpreter which makes the control aspects of the language much more explicit. Using SCHEME, Steele and Sussman have been able to illuminate many of the control and access problems of programming languages.

In these two projects we see two views of computation: the philosophical and the tool builder. Both are important; together they are developing an impressive array of knowledge.

Finally, LISP is being used as an effective tool for the design of interactive programming systems. The successful development of programming systems which integrate all phases of program creation, debugging and optimization, will be based on LISP user's experience.

Many people find it curious that LISP has survived so long and so well. It is not supported by any organization or computer manufacturer yet it flourishes and continues to attract many of the most exceptional computer science talents. LISP does a lot of things well. As a programming language, it is an exceptional tool for developing sophisticated applications. The artificial intelligence community has always been one of the most demanding and creative builders of programming tools. LISP's treatment of program and data supports this kind of behavior.

Until we can develop a tool which handles any of these areas as well as LISP, LISP will survive.

Projects

This chapter consists of a set of non-trivial projects which either apply LISP or extend LISP by adding new language features.

9.1 Extensions to *eval*

This first project was derived from the syntax of MUDDLE [Mud 75], CONNIVER [Con 73], and MICRO-PLANNER [Mic 71].

We have seen that LISP calling sequences are of two varieties: either evaluate *all* of the arguments; or evaluate *none* of the arguments. To generalize this regime we might allow the evaluation of some selection of the actual parameters; the formal parameter list could specify which parameters are to be evaluated. We have also specified that the number of formal parameters must agree with the number of actual parameters; yet it is sometimes useful in practice to allow such a discrepancy. Some implementations allow a mis-match, supplying default values when too few are given, and discarding the excess actual parameters after their evaluation. We might partition the formal parameters into required parameters, optional parameters, and an excess collector to handle any actual parameters left over. Required parameters *must* have corresponding actual parameters; optional actual parameters are used if present, otherwise default values are used. If there are more actual parameters than the formals encompassed by the first two classes, then they are associated with the excess collector.

412

To be more precise consider the following possible BNF equations:

<varlist>   ::=[<required> <optional> <excess>]

<required>   ::= <par>; ...;<par> | ϵ [1]

<optional>   ::= "optional" <opn>; ...; <opn> | ϵ

<excess>   ::= "excess" <par> | ϵ

<par>   ::= <variable> | '<variable>

<opn>   ::= <par> | <par> ← <form>

1. The formal parameters are bound to the actual parameters from left to right as usual.

2. There must be an actual parameter for each required parameter, and if there is no excess collector there may not be more actual parameters than formals. (There may be fewer if we have optionals.)

3. If a <variable> in a formal parameter is preceded by a "'", then the corresponding actual parameter is *not* evaluated. This is implements the *quote*-ing *read* macro.

4. If we exhaust the actual parameters while binding the optionals, we look at the remaining formal optionals. If a formal parameter is simply a <par> then we bind it to ( ); if a formal is '<variable> ← <form> then we bind the <variable> to the <form>.
   If the formal is <variable> ← <form>, we bind <variable> to the value of <form>, where the evaluation is to take place *after* the required parameters have been bound.

5. Finally, the excess collector is bound to a list of any remaining actual parameters: if <par> is <variable> then using the calling environment, form a list of the values of the remaining arguments; if <par> is '<variable>, bind <variable> to the actual list. If there is no excess, bind to *NIL*.

We will also extend *prog*-variables slightly, allowing them to be initialized explicitly. If a *prog*-variable is atomic, intialize it to ( ), as usual. If it is of the form <variable> ← <form> then initialize it to the value of the <form>.

Here are some examples:

1. In the initialization of *length* on page 186, we could write:

$$... prog[[l ← x; c ← 0] ...$$

2. *list* could now be defined as: λ[["excess" x]x].

---

[1]The symbol "ϵ" stands for the empty string.

3. Consider the following definition:

$$baz <= \lambda[[x; 'y;"optional" z; u \leftarrow 0; "excess" v]$$
$$print[x];$$
$$print[y];$$
$$print[z];$$
$$print[u];$$
$$print[v]]$$

Then a call of:

eval[(BAZ 2 (CAR (QUOTE (X Y))) 4 5 6 7 (CAR (QUOTE (A . B))));
      NIL]

would print: 2
                   (CAR(QUOTE (X Y)))
                   4
                   5
                   (6 7 A)

and return value: (6 7 A).

Similarly, defining:

$$fii <= \lambda[[x;y;"optional" z; u \leftarrow 0; "excess" v]$$
$$print[x];$$
$$print[y];$$
$$print[z];$$
$$print[u];$$
$$print[v]]$$

and calling: eval[(FII 2 (CAR (QUOTE (X Y)));NIL]
prints: 2
                  X
                  NIL
                  0
                  NIL

Problem

Design simple S-expr representations of these proposed constructs. Make the
necessary extensions to *eval*.

9.2 Pretty-printing

This project expands on the basic notion of "pretty-printing" which was
introduced on page 274. [2] This section presents several considerations
involved in designing such a pretty printer. Take these suggestions and

---

[2]Pretty printers are called "grinders" at MIT.

develop a suitable program based on the suggestions and your experience with your locally available pretty printer. In [Gol 73] several pretty printing formats are discussed.

I. **Linear format**: The minimal acceptable output format is that produced by *print*. Acceptability is judged by whether that output can be read back into the machine and have a structure *equal* the the structure printed out.[3]

II. **Standard format**: Given a list $(\alpha \ \beta \ \chi \ ... \ \delta)$ the standard format will assume that we are trying to print a function application and will produce:

$$(\alpha \ \beta$$
$$\chi$$
$$. \, . \, .$$
$$\delta)$$

Thus *(FOO (CAR (CONS (QUOTE A) B)) (G (H A) 4))* would produce:

$$(FOO \ (CAR \ (CONS \ (QUOTE \ A)$$
$$B))$$
$$(G(H \ A)$$
$$4))$$

Note that the "standard format" is recursively applied, and thus may become too wide for the output device. It that case we can resort to the following format.

III. **Miser format**: Write a list $(\alpha \ \beta \ \chi \ ... \ \delta)$ as:

$$(\alpha$$
$$\beta$$
$$\chi$$
$$. \, . \, .$$
$$\delta)$$

Again, the recursive application of this format can overflow the output width. In that case we may have to resort to "linear format".

---

[3]We must hedge that a bit, since *gensym* atoms are not placed on the object list. Also structure made by *rplaca* or *rplacd* may not be re-readable.

Typical pretty printers also recognize certain LISP constructs and "grind" them differently. That is, we build some semantic knowledge into the grinder. Block format is useful in many of these contexts.

IV. Block format: A list $(\alpha_1 \ldots \alpha_{i-1}, \ldots \alpha_n)$ has the block format:

$$(\alpha_1 \ldots \alpha_{i-1}$$
$$\alpha_i \ldots \alpha_n)$$

For example, the list representation of a *prog* might be "ground" with its *prog* variables in block format and special indenting would be used in the *prog* body to emphasize the label and statement structure. The representation of *length* given on page 192 illustrates the special format for *prog*s, though the *prog* variable list is not sufficently long to require block format.

Another list format which is treated specially is the representation of a λ-expression.

(LAMBDA <λ-list ground in block format>
           <body ground as a block>*)*

The example on page 192 also illistrates this. This format will allow multiple-bodied λ-expressions. For example:

(LAMBDA (X Y Z)
          (CONS X
                  (QUOTE A))
          (H 1 2))

Notice that we decided to write *(H 1 2)* in linear format rather than standard format; somehow it "looks better". Personal taste plays a strong role in pretty printing, so several grinders give the users the ability to describe their own formats. We will see a similar, but more general device in Section 9.4. Another possibility for user extension lies with our property list evaluator of Section 5.8. Part of the definition of the various LISP constructs would allow the specification of output conventions for instances of those constructs; thus besides specifying evaluation properties for *LAMBDA*, *PROG*, and *COND*, we would also the grinding routines for outputting instances of those constructs.

Since lists beginning with *COND* are representations of conditional expressions they too are handled specially by the grinding routines.

(COND <grind clause$_1$>

          . . .

          <grind clause$_n$>*)*

These selected formats should give a reasonable idea of the techniques available for pretty printers. More techniques can be extracted from your local grinder.

Your pretty printer may assume the existence of *patom*, *print*, and *terpri* of Section 5.11; and you may assume the existence of the usual class of arithmetic operations. In addition, the following primitives may be used:

1. *linelength*: If *linelength*[ ] is evaluated, the value returned is the number of characters allowed on a line of the current output device. If *linelength* is called with a numeric argument, then the line length of the current output device is set to that number.

2. *chrct*: This is a nullary function, and returns a number representing the number of character positions remaining on the current line. For example, just after *terpri*[] has been executed
   chrct[] = *linelength*[]
   and $prog_2[patom[ABC]; difference[linelength[];chrct[]]] = 3$

3. *flatsize*: A simple count of the atoms and special characters in an expression won't give an accurate picture of the requirements for printing an expression. Special characters take one character position, but literal atoms and numbers may require more. To determine whether or not a special format can be used on an expression requires knowledge of its character count. The number of characters in the atom *x* is given by *flatsize*[*x*]; for example, *flatsize*[*ABCD*] is *4*. Actually *flatsize* is defined for non-atomic arguments, giving the number of character positions required to *print* its argument. Thus, *flatsize*[(*A.B*)] is *7* rather than *5* since *print* will surround the dot with spaces.

9.3 Syntax-directed Processes

This project is only an introduction to the very important area of syntax-directed processes. As the name implies, there is a close relationship between the syntax specification of an object, and the computational rules which we wish to apply. Syntax-directed techniques are used extensively in compiler construction, relating the syntax equations to the code generation. We shall begin by applying syntax-directed techniques to evaluation.

We know that there are alternatives to the call-by-value evaluation scheme; and we know there are alternatives to the prefix notation which we chose to represent function application.

For example, in grade school we all learned infix notation and its implied precedence relations, say for + and *. Simply because infix notation is the first representation we see doesn't mean that it is the most convenient for evaluation either by us or by machine.

Let's take as example the expression: 2+3*5. The grade school precedence relations say that * takes precedence over +. That is, the expression represents 2+(3*5) rather than (2+3)*5. When we write the expression in prefix notation: +[2;*[3;5]], the precedence of operations is made explicit. Similarly, postfix notation (where the operators follow rather than precede the operands) is easy: [2;[3;5]*]+.

Some notational schemes lend themselves to mechanical evaluation better than others. There is a certain amount of implied intelligence required in the usual infix scheme. We have already seen one very mechanical method for evaluating some prefix expressions: the *value* function in Section 2.7.

A strong point of postfix string notation is its ease of evaluation. First, since we know that plus and times are both binary operations, the punctuation,], [, and ; , is redundant (this is also true for prefix notation). Thus the string, 2 3 5 * +, contains the same information as [2;[3;5]*]+.

Using "↓" to point to the current position in the string and using the "| ... |"-notation of page 124 to represent the stack, the following is a trace of the evaluation of the above string, 2 3 5 * +.

```
↓                 ↓              ↓
2 3 5 * + ;|   | => 3 5 * + ;| 2 | => 5 * + ; | 3 | =>
                                            | 2 |


↓             ↓
* + ; | 5 | =>  + ; | 15 | => | 17 |
      | 3 |         | 2 |
      | 2 |
```

It is a very simple task to program this scheme in LISP, and it is quite simple to extend this evaluation scheme to n-ary operators.

Given an arbitrary arithmetic expression involving constants, and the binary operations of plus and times, we have a straightforward mechanical evaluation scheme. It is intuitively clear how to translate infix expressions into postfix notation. If we could mechanize this process then we would have an algorithm for the evaluation of infix expressions. First let's attempt to describe precisely the class of infix expressions which we wish to evaluate. The BNF notation is a good vehicle. Perhaps the following:

> <exp>   ::= <exp><binop><exp>
>   ::= <integer>
> <binop> ::= + | *

There are many difficulties with this grammar. First, many expressions have more than one possible description or parse tree; the grammar is said to be **ambiguous**. Second, this grammar doesn't express our usual precedence relations. The next attempt is successful:

$$
\begin{array}{llr}
\text{<exp>} & ::= \text{<exp>} + \text{<term>} & (1) \\
& ::= \text{<term>} & (2) \\
\text{<term>} & ::= \text{<term>} * \text{<factor>} & (3) \\
& ::= \text{<factor>} & (4) \\
\text{<factor>} & ::= (\text{<exp>}) & (5) \\
& ::= \text{<integer>} & (6) \\
\text{<integer>} & ::= 0 \mid 1 \mid 2 \ldots & (7)
\end{array}
$$

For example the (only) parsing of 2+3*5 is:

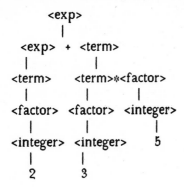

Our next step is based on the following:

Assumption: Given an arbitrary, well-formed, arithmetic expression, e, of our above class, we can find the left-most well-formed subexpression, s, such that s is an instance of the RHS of one of the rules, (1)-(7). Let e′ be the expression obtained from e, by replacing the occurrence of the RHS by the LHS; then our assumption is also applicable to e′.

For example,

e	s	e′	rule
2+3*5	2	<integer>+3*5	(7)
<integer>+3*5	<integer>	<factor>+3*5	(6)
<factor>+3*5	<factor>	<term>+3*5	(4)
<term>+3*5	<term>	<exp>+3*5	(2)
<exp>+3*5	3	<exp>+<integer>*5	(7)
<exp>+<integer>*5	<integer>	<exp>+<factor>*5	(6)
<exp>+<factor>*5	<factor>	<exp>+<term>*5	(4)
<exp>+<term>*5	5	<exp>+<term>*<integer>	(7)
<exp>+<term>*<integer>	<integer>	<exp>+<term>*<factor>	(6)
<exp>+<term>*<factor>	<term>*<factor>	<exp>+<term>	(3)
<exp>+<term>	<exp>+<term>	<exp>	(1)

Now we associate an action with each of the rules (1)-(7) such that whenever we apply one of the rules in the above reduction technique, we will also execute the corresponding action. We will also designate an initialization routine which will be executed at the beginning of the reduction.

Initialization: Let V[0:N] be a vector indexed from 0 to N, where N is at least as long as the input character string. Let i be an integer variable, initialized to 0.

	rule	action
<exp>	::= <exp> + <term>	$V(i) \leftarrow$ '+'; $i \leftarrow i+1$
	::= <term>	do nothing
<term>	::= <term>*<factor>	$V(i) \leftarrow$ '*'; $i \leftarrow i+1$
	::= <factor>	do nothing
<factor>	::= (<exp>)	do nothing
	::= <integer>	do nothing
<integer>	::= 0 | 1 | ...	$V(i) \leftarrow 0 \mid V(i) \leftarrow 1 \mid ...$; $i \leftarrow i+1$

Again performing the reduction of the expression, 2+3*5, but now executing the action routines as well we find the contents of V will contain the following:

```
V: 0 1 2 3 4
   2
   2 3
   2 3 5
   2 3 5 *
   2 3 5 * +
```

That is, the postfix form of the arithmetic expression is formed in V.

So combining the algorithms for infix-to-postfix translation, with postfix evaluation, we could obtain an infix evaluator. However, we can do better. By a simple change to the action routines we can perform infix evaluation as we reduce the expression.

Initialization: Let V[0:N] be a vector and let i be an integer-valued variable, initialized to 0.

	rule	action
<exp>	::= <exp>+<term>	$V(i-2) \leftarrow V(i-1)+V(i-2)$; $i \leftarrow i-1$
	::= <term>	do nothing
<term>	::= <term>*<factor>	$V(i-2) \leftarrow V(i-1)*V(i-2)$; $i \leftarrow i-1$
	::= <factor>	do nothing
<factor>	::= (<exp>)	do nothing
	::= <integer>	do nothing
<integer>	::= 0 | 1 | ...	$V(i) \leftarrow 0 \mid V(i) \leftarrow 1 \mid ...$; $i \leftarrow i+1$

When the arithmetic expression has been recognized, V(0) will contain the value of that expression. Notice that the combination of V and its index i, is performing as a stack in this translator. That is: when we see an integer, we push it into the stack; when we see a binary operator we pop the two operands, perform the operation and push the result back on the stack.

This technique of associating action routines (also called semantic routines) with the BNF (or syntax) equations is extremely powerful. Such processes are called syntax-directed.

Project

Write a LISP program to perform infix to postfix translation; and then modify it to perform infix evaluation. Write your programs two ways: first use an explicit stack; then use recursion to operate with an implicit stack.

Project

As a further example of syntax-directed processes recall the set of expressions evaluated by *tgmoaf*: the five primitives under composition of functions, all with constant arguments. Write syntax equations and action routines to effect the evaluation of such expressions.

9.4 Syntax-directed I/O

It is frequently quite convenient to enter input and receive output in something other than list notation. Recall our diagram on page 56. We wish to mechanize the encoding of the input and the decoding of the output.

Consider for example, the problem of simplification of algebraic expressions. Many rather sophisticated simplifiers have been written ([Hea 68], [MAC 74]). Assume that we have one named *simplify* which expects list input and gives list output. Thus for example:

$$(3+4)*x + x =_I => (PLUS\ (TIMES\ (PLUS\ 3\ 4)\ X)\ X)$$
$$=_{simplify}=> (TIMES\ 8\ X) =_O => 8*x$$

We would like transformations I and O done automatically. M-expr notation is a candidate for such a task. Then we could write algorithms in M-expr notation and have them executed by *eval*.

$$cons[A;B] =_I => (CONS\ (QUOTE\ A)\ (QUOTE\ B))$$
$$=_{eval}=> (A\ .\ B) =_O => (A\ .\ B)$$

Transformation O is the identity in this case.

Frequently, the input and output transformations can be generated automatically. We describe one such program, called SDIO for Syntax-Directed Input-Output ([Qua 68].) It was the forerunner of the

MLISP2 project; see [Mli 73]. We will assume that the input and output syntax is specified in BNF. With each BNF equation we will associate semantics describing the S-expr representation. The input transformation (parser) will use this information to build the representation; and the output transformation (unparser) will map the internal representation back.

Syntax directed I/O is more than a cosmetic. Assume we wish to represent a structure as a particularly horrible list structure. We can give augmented BNF equations specifying the external representation and the translation to the underlying representation. Clearly when outputting these structures we do not want to see the internal representation. This can be particularly annoying when we are debugging; we wish to concentrate on the misbehavior of the algorithm; we do not want to be distracted by incomprehensible output. Syntax directed output, or unparsing, can aid significantly.

The easiest introduction to SDIO is to examine an example. Consider the proposed simplification task above. The "natural" input syntax can be described in BNF. We have given closely related syntax equations on page 419. We will display a few equations augmented by SDIO semantics. For example:

```
<EXP>     ::= <EXP> + <TERM>   =>(PLUS EXP TERM)
          ::= <TERM>           =>*
<TERM>   ::= <NUMBER>          =>*
```

To the input parser the first BNF equation means: whenever the right hand side is recognized, reduce that occurrence to the left hand side and associate with it the list consisting of the atom PLUS, the S-expr associated with the occurrence of <EXP>, and the S-expr associated with the occurrrence of <TERM>. The second equation means reduce <TERM> to <EXP> associating whatever S-expr is attached to <TERM> with that occurrence of <EXP>. In the third equation we assume that <NUMBER> is a syntactic type recognized by the scanner, and return that number as the semantic value. For example, if such a parser were given 2+3+44 it should return the list *(PLUS (PLUS 2 3) 44)*.

The unparser uses these equations in the inverse manner. It will see a S-expr and will attempt to match that to the description of the semantics, outputting an instance of the BNF if successful.

The SDIO program will take such an augmented set of BNF equations and generate a parser and an unparser for the language. This project involves writing such a SDIO program. We describe a basic SDIO program and suggest extensions and improvements.

The best way to describe the format of SDIO input is to give an SDIO description.

```
<RULES>        ::= END                    =>NIL
               ::=<RULE><RULES>           =>(RULE . RULES)
<RULE>         ::= <LFPT><RTLST>          =>(LFPT RTLST)
<RTLST>        ::= ::=<RTPT><SEXPR><RTLST>
                                          =>((RTPT SEXPR) . RTLST)

               ::= €                      =>NIL
<LFPT>         ::= <<ID>>                 =>*
<RTPT>         ::= "=>                     =>NIL
               ::= <RPELEM><RTPT>
                                          =>(RPELEM . RTPT)

<RPELEM>       ::= <<ID>>                 =>*
               ::= <ID>                   =>(SPWD ID)
               ::= ""<CHAR>               =>(QCH CHAR)
               ::= <CHAR>                 =>(CH CHAR)
<SEXPR>        ::= <ATOM>                 =>*
               ::= (<SEXPRLIST>)          =>*
<SEXPRLIST>    ::= <ATOM>                 =>*
               ::= <SEXPR> <SEXPRLIST>
                                          =>(SEXPR . SEXPRLIST)

               ::= €                      =>NIL
```

END

The expressions *(SPWD ID)*, *(QCH CHAR)*, and *(CH CHAR)* are S-expr representations of calls on rountines to process special or reserved words, quoted characters or special characters, respectively.

The input to SDIO is a sequence of augmented BNF equations terminated with END. What the SDIO program sees is a S-expr representation of these equations. The sample equations for <EXP> above would pass the following to the SDIO program:

```
(    (EXP (  ((EXP (CH +) TERM) (PLUS EXP TERM))
             ((TERM) NIL)))
     (TERM (((NUMBER) NIL))) )
```

The SDIO program generates the parser and unparser.

The elements of the BNF equations in SDIO are rather standard: syntactic variables, which are identifiers bracketed by "<" and ">"; and special words, which are identifiers; and special characters, which are preceeded by " if they conflict with the special characters of the BNF.

The elements of the semantics are: unbracketed syntactic variables occurring in the RHS of the associated BNF equation; other identifiers, taken as constants; NIL, the LISP atom; notation for *cons*-ing, (.); notation for making a list, $(e_1 ... e_n)$; the character *, described above.

Project

Write such a SDIO program. You should consult local LISP documentation when building the basic I/O routines like <NUMBER>, <CHAR>, or <ID>.

First Extension

You may have noticed already that the basic SDIO program fails to distinguish two occurrences of the same syntactic variable on the RHS of an equation. Thus an equation like:

<ZIP>   ::= <ZAP> <FOO> <ZAP>   must be replaced by the pair:
<ZIP>   ::= <ZAP> <FOO> <ZAP1>
<ZAP1> ::=<ZAP>

This trick is called stratification. It is a syntactic trick, adding nothing to the semantics.

Add notation to the semantics of your SDIO program to handle RHS with multiple occurrences of syntactic variables. Modify your parser generators accordingly.

Second Extension

Besides building a S-expr representation of the input, it is frequently desirable to generate other information during the input parse. Lists of occurrences of operators or other tables are commonly needed. The additional information could be discovered by examination of the completed parse tree, but that requires reexamination of the tree. It is much more efficient to do as much as possible on a single pass.

Introduce notation which will allow execution of arbitrary LISP code as the parse progresses. That code should be able to manipulate any of the semantic properties associated with the syntactic variables appearing in the RHS of the associated syntax equation.

Third extension

While it is obviously advantageous to produce output in the language described by the BNF equations rather than the S-expr form, formatting of the output can be equally beneficial. We should like to be able to specify formatting information in SDIO such that spacing and line-length are controlled.

One proposal is to embed spacing and line-feed control characters in the BNF equations. The spacing character is "→" and the line-feed is "↓". The "↑" sets the indentation point for the string on its right; and the "→" followed by a digit says space over than number of spaces from the last indentation point if the remaining space on the line is not sufficient to contain all text specified by the remaining RHS of the equation. "0→", meaning go to the indentation point can be written "→".

For example consider the following:

> <EXPR>   ::= <ID>(↓ <EXPR_LIST>)
>   ::= <ID>
>
> <EXPR_LIST> ::= ↑<EXPR> , →<EXPR_LIST>
>   ::= ↑<EXPR>

These equations, when used to drive an unparser, could give:

> *mumf(a,*
> *   foobaz(garp(b)),*
> *   bletch(a,b,c),*
> *   d)*

as the formatted version of:

> *mumf(a,foobaz(garp(b)),bletch(a,b,c),d)*

Extend SDIO to handle formatting of output.

Bibliography

The basic form of an entry consists of three items:

1. A short name which is how the document is referenced in the text.

2. The full bibliographical reference.

3. A sequence of pages in the text which refer to this document. If the document is not referenced the statement [norefs] appears instead; these documents, while not referenced, are relevant to the material covered in the text.

[Aho 72]   Aho, A., and Ullman, J., *The Theory of Parsing, Translation &
           Compiling*, Prentice Hall Inc., Englewood Cliffs, N.J.,
           1972. [4 165 307]

[Alg 63]   Naur, P. et. al., 'Revised Report on the Algorithmic Language
           Algol 60', *Comm. ACM 6*, 1, Jan., 1963. [164 357]

[Alg 75]   van Wijngaarden, A., et. al., eds., 'Revised Report on the
           Algorithmic Language Algol 68', *Acta Informatica*, Vol. 5,
           Fac. 1-3, p. 1-236, 1975. [163 281 357 382]

[Ama 72]   Amarel, S., 'A Set of Goals and Approaches for Education in
           Computer Science', AFIPS Conference Proceedings, Vol 40,
           p. 841-846, 1972. [157]

[And 76a] Anderson, D. Bruce, 'The Samefringe Problem', *SIGART
           Newsletter*, No. 60, p. 4, Nov. 1976. [223]

[And 76]   Anderson, D. Bruce, 'A Brief Critique of LISP', Proc. AISB
           Summer Conference, Edinburgh, p. 14-25, 1976. [229 385]

[Bac 73]   Backus, J., 'Programming Language Semantics and Closed Applicative Languages', IBM Research Lab, R J-1245, San Jose, Cal., July 1973. [156]

[Bar 66]   Barron, D., and Strachey, C., 'Programming', in *Advances in Computer Programming and Non-numerical Computation*, L. Fox, ed., Academic Press, New York, p. 49-82, 1966. [196]

[Bar 71]   Barbacci, M., et al., 'C.ai (P.LISP), A LISP processor of C.ai', Carnegie-Mellon U., 1971. [241]

[Bau 72]   Baumgart, B., 'MICRO-PLANNER Alternative Reference Manual', Stanford Univ. Operating Note No. 67, April 1972. [73]

[Ber 64]   Berkeley, E., and Bobrow, D., eds., *The Programming Language LISP: Its Operation and Applications*, Information International, Cambridge, Mass., 1964. [norefs]

[Ber 71]   Berkling, H., 'A Computing Machine Based on Tree Structures', *IEEE Trans on Comptr.* 20, C-20, 4, p. 404-418, April 1971. [248 374]

[Ber 75]   Berkling,H., 'A Recursive Control Structure for Processing Reduction Machine Languages', Micro Architecture of Computer Systems, Hartenstein, R., & Zaks,R., eds., North Holland, p. 191-200, 1975. [81 108]

[Berr 71]   Berry, D., 'Block Structure: Retention or Deletion?', Proc. of 3rd Annual ACM Symposium on Theory of Computing, p. 86-100, 1971. [norefs]

[Bis 74a]   Bishop, P., 'Garbage Collection in a Very Large Address Space', M.I.T. A.I. Lab, Working paper 111, Sep. 1975. [402]

[Bis 74]   Bishop, P., 'Spaghetti Stacks', unpublished paper, M.I.T., Dec 19, 1974. [291 314]

[Bla 71]   Blair, F., 'The Structure of the Lisp Compiler', unpublished paper, 1971. [219]

[Bob 67]   Bobrow, D., and Murphy, D., 'The Structure of a LISP System Using Two-level Storage', *Comm. ACM 10*, 3, p. 155-159, Mar. 1967. [norefs]

[Bob 69]   Bobrow, D., '(LISP Bulletin)', *ACM Sigplan Notices*, Vol. 1, No. 9, p. 17-45, Sept. 1969. [194]

[Bob 73a]   Bobrow, D., and Wegbreit, B., 'A Model and Stack Implementation of Multiple Environments', *Comm. ACM 16*, 10, p. 591-603, Oct. 1973. [229 301 354 401 405]

[Bob 74]   Bobrow, D., and Raphael, D., 'New Programming Languages for A.I. Research', *Computing Surveys*, 6, 3, p. 154-174, Sep 1974. [410]

[Bob 75]   Bobrow, D., 'A Note on Hash Linking', *Comm. ACM 18*, 7, p. 413-414, July, 1975. [403]

[Boy 75]   Boyer, R., and Moore, J, 'Proving theorems about LISP functions', *Jour. ACM* , 1, p. 129-144, Jan. 1975. [96 160]

[Bur 76]   Burge, W., *Recursive Programming Techniques*, Addison Wesley, Reading, Mass., 1976. [norefs]

[Car 75]   Carpenter, R., & Doran, R., *The Other Turing Machine*, Massey University Computing Unit, Rep. No. 23 Aug 1975. [239]

[Car 76]   Cartwright, R., 'A Practical and Formal Semantics and Verification System for TYPED LISP', Ph.D. Thesis, Computer Science Dept., Stanford Univ., 1976. [96 160 242 410]

[Che 67]   Cheatham, T., *The Theory & Construction of Compilers*, Computer Associates, Wakefield, Mass., 1967. [norefs]

[Che 70]   Cheney, C., 'A Nonrecursive List Compacting Algorithm', *Comm. ACM 13*, 11, p. 677-678, Nov. 1970. [401]

[Che 76]   Cheatham, T., and Townley, J., 'A Look at Programming and Programming Systems', in *Advances in Computers*, Vol. 14, M. Rubinoff, and M. Yovits, eds., Academic Press, New York, p. 45-78, 1976. [norefs]

[Chr 68]   Christensen, C., 'An Example of the Manipulation of Directed Graphs in the AMBIT/G Programming Language', 423-435, in *Interactive Systems for Experimental Applied Mathematics*, Klerer, M., & Reinfelds, J. eds., Academic Press, 1968. [398]

[Chu 41]   Church, A., *The Calculi of Lambda-conversion*, Annals of Mathematics Studies, Princeton University Press, New Jersey, 1941. [110 167]

[Cl 76]   Clark, D., 'List Structure: Measurements, Algorithms and Encodings', Ph.D. Thesis, Carnegie Mellon University, August 1976. [377]

[Con 73]   McDermott, D., and Sussman, G., 'The CONNIVER Reference Manual', M.I.T. A.I. Lab. Memo 259a, Cambridge, Mass., 1973. [74 75 219 229 301 410 411 412]

[Con 74]   Conrad, W., 'A Compactifying Garbage Collector for ECL's Non-homogeneous Heap', Center for Research in Computing Technology, TR. 2-74, Harvard, Feb. 1974. [norefs]

[Cur 58]   Curry, H, and Feys, R., Combinatory Logic, North-Holland, 1958. [173]

[Dar 73]   Darlington, J., and Burstall, R., 'A System which Automatically Improves Programs', Proc. 3rd Int. J. Conf. on A.I., Stanford, 1973. [160 353]

[Dav 76]   Davis, R., 'Deduction, Truth, and Computation', M.S. Thesis, Math. Dept., San Jose State University, 1976. [162]

[DEC 69]   'PDP-10 Systems Reference Manual', Digital Equipment Corporation, Maynard Mass., 1969. [312]

[Deu 73]   Deutsch, P., 'A LISP Machine With Very Compact Programs', Proc. 3rd Int. J. Conf. on A.I., Stanford, 1973. [241]

[Dif 71]   Diffie, W., 'Documentation of the Compiler', unpublished paper, Stanford A.I. Lab., 1971. [265]

[Dij 72a]   Dijkstra, E., 'The Humble Programmer: 1972 ACM Turing Lecture', Comm. ACM 15, 10, p. 859-866, Oct 1972. [norefs]

[Dij 72]   Dijkstra, E., 'Notes on Structured Programming', in Structured Programming, Dahl, O., and Hoare, C., eds., Academic Press, New York, 1972. [53]

[Dor 76]   Doran, R., Architecture of General Purpose Computers, to be published by Academic Press, New York. [236 317 372]

[DSIPL]   Proceedings of a Symposium on Data Structures in Programming Languages, SIGPLAN Notices 6, 2, Feb. 1971. [norefs]

[EL1 74]   Wegbreit, B., 'ECL Programmer's Manual', Center for Research in Computing Technology, TR 23-74, Harvard, Dec. 1974. [265 382 407]

[Els 73]   Elson, M., Concepts of Progranguages, SRA Inc, Palo Alto, Cal, 1973. [norefs]

[Fat 73]   Fateman, R., 'Reply to an Editorial', SIGSAM Bulletin, No. 25, p. 9-11, Mar. 1973. [303 390]

[Fel 68]   Feldman, J., and Gries, D., 'Translator Writing Systems', Comm. ACM 11, 2, p. 77-113, Feb. 1968. [norefs]

[Fen 69]   Fenichel, R., and Yochelson, J., 'A LISP Garbage Collector for Virtual-memory Computer Systems', Comm. ACM 12, 11,

p. 611-612, Nov. 1969. [norefs]

[Fin 76]   Finin, T., and Rutter, P., 'Different Fringe for Different Folk', *SIGART Newsletter*, No. 60, p. 4-5, Nov. 1976. [223]

[Fis 70]   Fisher, D., 'Control Structures for Programming Languages', Ph.D. Thesis, Dept. of Computer Science, Carnegie-Mellon University, 1970. [norefs]

[Fis 72]   Fischer, M., 'Lambda Calculus Schemata', ACM Conf. on Proving assertions about programs, *SIGPLAN Notices*, p. 104-109, Jan. 1972. [207]

[Fri 74]   Friedman, D., *The Little LISPer*, SRA, Menlo Park, 1974. [norefs]

[Fri 76a]   Friedman, D., and Wise, D., 'CONS Should Not Evaluate its Arguments', Proc. 3rd Int. Colloq. on Automata, Languages and Programming, Edinburgh Univ. Press, p.257-284, July 1976. [12 221]

[Fri 76b]   Friedman, D., and Wise, D., 'An Environment for Multiple-valued Recursive Procedures', 2me Colloque sur la Programation, Paris, Springer Verlag, Berlin, 1976. [222]

[Gol 73]   Goldstein, I., 'Pretty Printing: Converting List to Linear Structure', M.I.T. A.I. Lab, Memo 279, Feb. 1973. [415]

[Goo 57]   Goodstein, R., *Recursive Number Theory*, North-Holland Pub. Co., Amsterdam, 1957. [2]

[Gor 73]   Gordon, M., 'Models of Pure LISP', Dept. of Machine Intelligence, Experimental programming reports: No.30, University of Edinburgh, 1973. [175 177 180 235]

[Gor 75]   Gordon, M., 'Towards a Semantic Theory of Dynamic Binding', Stanford A.I. Lab. Memo 265, Stanford University, 1975. [175 180]

[Got 74]   Goto, E., 'Monocopy and Associative Algorithms in an Extended Lisp', University of Tokyo, Japan, May 1974. [46 241 287 403]

[Got 76]   Goto, E., and Kanada, Y., 'Recursive Hashed Data Structures with Applications to Polynomial Manipulations', submitted to SYMSAC 76. [79 403]

[Gre 74]   Greenblatt, R., 'The LISP Machine', M.I.T., Working paper No. 79, Nov. 1974. [241 301]

[Gre 75]   Greussay, P., 'Manuel de Reference Provisoire: LISP T 1600', Universite Paris-Vincennes, Feb. 1975. [219]

[Gre 76a]   Greussay, P., 'Iterative Interpretation of Tail-Recursive LISP Procedures', University of Vincennes, TR-20-76, Paris, Sep. 1976. [230]

[Gre 76]   Greussay, P., 'An Iterative LISP Solution to the Samefringe Problem', *SIGART Newsletter*, No. 59, p. 14, Aug. 1976. [223]

[Gri 71]   Gries, D., *Compiler Construction for Digital Computers*, Wiley, New York, 1971. [278 307]

[Gua 69]   Guard, J., Bennet, J., and Settle, L., 'Semi Automated Mathematics', *JACM 16*, 1, p. 49-62, Jan. 1969. [247]

[Gun 76]   Gunji, T., 'Analysis of Hash Addressing Methods', Department of Information Sciences, TR 76-03, Univ. of Tokyo, Japan, Jan. 1976. [norefs]

[Ham 69]   Hammer, M., 'Formal Definition of BASEL', Mass. Computer Associates, Inc., CA-6908-1511, Wakefield, Mass., 1969. [norefs]

[Han 69]   Hansen, W., 'The Impact of Storage Management on Plex Processing Language Implementation', Stanford Graphics Project, July 1969. [382]

[Han 71]   Hansen, W., 'Creation of Hierarchic Text With a Computer Display', Ph.D. Thesis, Computer Science Dept., Stanford Univ., June 1971. [367]

[Har 64]   Hart, T., and Evans, T., 'Notes on Implementing LISP for the M-460 Computer', p. 191-203 in [Ber 64]. [norefs]

[Har 75]   Howard, F., 'Documentation of Harvard PDP-11 LISP', unpublished documentation, 1975. [245]

[Hea 68]   Hearn, A., 'REDUCE User's Manual', Stanford A.I. Lab Memo 50, Stanford University, 1968. [62 421]

[Hen 75]   von Henke, F., 'On the Representation of Data Structures in LCF With Applications to Program Generation', Stanford A.I. Lab. Memo 267, Sep. 1975. [54]

[Hen 76]   Henderson, P., and Morris, J., 'A Lazy Evaluator', SIGPLAN-SIGACT Symposium on principles of programming languages, Altanta, p.95-103, Jan. 1976. [221 223]

[Hew 72]   Hewitt, C., 'Description and Theoretical Analysis (using Schemata) of PLANNER', M.I.T. A.I. Lab., TR-258, April 1972. [73 229 410]

[Hew 74]   Hewitt, C., et. al., 'Behavioral Semantics of Non-recursive

Control Structures', Proc. Colloque sur la Programmation, B. Robinet ed., in *Lecture Notes in Computer Science, No. 19*, p. 385-407, Springer Verlag, Berlin, 1974. [137 223 410]

[Hew 75]   Hewitt, C., and Smith, B., 'Towards a Programming Apprentice', *IEEE Trans. on Software Engineering*, SE-1, p. 26-45, Mar 1975. [364]

[Hew 76]   Hewitt, C., 'Viewing Control Structures as Patterns of Passing Messages', M.I.T. A.I. Lab, Working paper 92, April 1976. [172 207 229 230 358 410]

[Hoa 69]   Hoare, C.A.R., 'An Axiomatic Basis for Computer Programming', *Comm. ACM 12*, 10, p. 576-580, Oct. 1969. [162]

[Hoa 73a]   Hoare, C.A.R., 'Hints on Programming Language Design', Stanford A.I. Lab Memo 224, Dec. 1973. [norefs]

[Hoa 73]   Hoare, C.A.R., 'Recursive Data Structures', Stanford A.I. Lab Memo 223, Oct. 1973. [norefs]

[Hop 69]   Hopcroft J., and Ullman, J., *Formal Languages and their Relation to Automata*, Addison-Wesley, Reading, Mass., 1969. [25 55]

[Int 75]   Teitelman, W., 'INTERLISP Reference Manual', Xerox PARC, Palo Alto, 1975. [128 194 242 273 364 367 403]

[Ive 62]   Iverson, K., *A Programming Language*, Wiley, New York, 1962. [357]

[Joh 71]   Johnston, J., 'The Contour Model of Block Structured Processes', p. 55-82 in [DSIPL]. [norefs]

[Kan 75]   Kanada, Y., 'Implementation of HLISP and Algebraic Manipulation Language REDUCE-2', Information Sciences Lab., TR 75-01, Univ. of Tokyo, Japan, Jan. 1975. [norefs]

[Kni 74]   Knight, T., 'The CONS Microprocessor', M.I.T., Artificial Intelligence Working paper No. 80, Cambrigde, Nov. 1974. [norefs]

[Knu 68]   Knuth, D., *The Art of Computer Programming, Non-numerical Algorithms*, Vol. 1, Addison-Wesley, Reading, Mass., 1968. [387 393 398]

[Knu 72]   Knuth, D., *The Art of Computer Programming, Searching and Sorting*, Vol. 3, Addison-Wesley, Reading, Mass., 1972. [278]

[Knu 74]   Knuth, D., 'Structured Programming With GO TO Statements', *Computer Surveys 6*, 4, p. 261-301, Dec. 1974. [norefs]

[Lan 64]   Landin, P., 'The Mechanical Evaluation of Expressions', *Computer Journal 6*, 4, p. 308-320, Apr. 1964. [173]

[Lan 66]   Landin, P., 'The Next 700 Programming Languages', *Comm. ACM 9*, 3, p. 157-166, Mar. 1966. [norefs]

[LCF 72]   Milner, R., 'Logic for Computable Functions, Description of a Machine Implementation', Stanford A.I. Lab. Memo 169, 1972. [96 410]

[Leh 73]   Lehmann, D., 'A Direct Proof of the Church-Rosser Theorem', Center for Computer and Information Sciences, Technical Report No. 73-70, Brown University, Providence, R.I., August 1973. [173]

[Lev un]   Levin, M., 'Course notes: 6.542', M.I.T., Cambridge, Mass., undated [181]

[Lin 73]   Lindstrom, G., 'Algorithms For List Structure Condensation', Dept. of Computer Science, Technical Report 73-14, University of Pittsburgh, 1973. [402]

[Lis 74]   Liskov, B., and Zilles, S., 'Programming With Abstract Data Structures', Proc. of Symposium on Very high level languages, *SIGPLAN Notices*, Apr. 1974. [norefs]

[Lon 71]   London, R., 'Correctness of Two Compilers for a LISP Subset', Stanford A.I. Lab. Memo 151, Oct., 1971. [337]

[Lug 73]   Lugger, J., and Melenk, H., 'Darstellung und Bearbeitung Umfangreicher LISP-programme', *Angewandte Informatik*, p. 257-263, June 1973. [norefs]

[MAC 74]   Bogen, R., 'MACSYMA Reference Manual', Project MAC, Mathlab Group, M.I.T., Cambridge, 1974. [62 390 421]

[Man 74]   Manna, Z., *Mathematical Theory of Computation*, McGraw-Hill, New York, 1974. [160 232]

[McB 63]   McBeth, H. 'On the Reference Counter Method', (letter), *Comm. ACM 6*, 9, p. 575, Sep 1963. [norefs]

[McC 60a]   McCarthy, J, et. al., 'LISP 1 Programmer's Manual', Computation Center and Research Laboratory of Electronics, M.I.T., Cambridge, 1960. [norefs]

[McC 60]   McCarthy, J., 'Recursive Functions of Symbolic Expressions and Their Computation by Machine', *Comm. ACM*, p. 184-195, April 1960. [110 185 231 287]

[McC 62]   McCarthy, J., 'Towards a Mathematical Science of

Computation', IFIPS Proceedings of Munich Conference 1962, North Holland, Amsterdam, 1963. [164]

[McC 63] McCarthy, J., *A Basis for a Mathematical Theory of Computation, in Computer Programming and Formal Systems,* North Holland, Amsterdam, 1963. [norefs]

[McC 65] McCarthy, J, et. al., 'LISP 1.5 Programmer's Manual', M.I.T. Press, Cambridge, 1965. [118]

[McC 66] McCarthy, J., 'A Formal Description of a Subset of ALGOL', in *Formal Language Description Languages for Computer Programming,* North Holland, Amsterdam, 1966. [164]

[McC 76] McCarthy, J., *Recursive Programming in LISP,* CS206 notes, Stanford University, 1976. [337]

[McD 75] McDermott, D., 'Very Large PLANNER-type Data Bases', M.I.T. A.I. Lab   Memo 339,   Cambridge,   Mass., Sep. 1975. [75 256]

[Men 64] Mendelson, E., *Introduction to Mathematical Logic,* Van Nostrand, Princeton, New Jersey, 1964. [107 162 174]

[Mic 71] Sussman, G., et al., 'Micro-PLANNER Reference Manual', M.I.T.,   A.I. Lab.   Memo 203a,   Cambridge,   Mass., Dec 1971. [410 412]

[Mil 73] Milner, R., 'λ-Calculus and the Semantics of Programming Languages', Lecture Notes, Computer Science Dept., University of Edinburgh, 1973-74. [173 181]

[Min 70] Minsky, M., 'Form and Content in Computer Science: 1970 ACM   Turing   Lecture',   *JACM 17,*   2,   p. 197-215, Apr. 1970. [norefs]

[Mit 70] Mitchell, J., 'The Design & Construction of Flexible & Efficient Interactive   Programming   Systems',   Ph.D. Thesis, Carnegie-Mellon Unversity, June 1970. [152 358 405]

[Mli 73] Smith, D., and Enea, H., 'MLISP2', Stanford A.I. Lab Memo 195, Stanford Univ., 1973. [410 422]

[Mon 73] Montangero, C., et al., 'An Extended LISP System for Complex Control-structure   Programming',   University   of   Pisa, 1973. [norefs]

[Mon 75a] Montangero, C., et al., 'MAGMA-Lisp: A 'Machine Language' for Artifical Intelligence', Proc. 4th Int. J. Conf. on A.I., Tbilisi, p. 556-561, Sep. 1975. [norefs]

[Mon 75]   Montangero, C. et al., 'Information Management in Context Trees', University of Pisa, N.I. B75-21, Oct. 1975. [301]

[Moo 74]   Moon, D., 'MacLISP Reference Manual', Laboratory for Computer Science, M.I.T., Cambridge, Mass, 1974. [128 148 194 195 198 199 280 367 390 403]

[Moor 74]   Moore, J, 'Introducing PROG to the Pure LISP Theorem Prover', CSL 74-3, Xerox PARC, Palo Alto, Dec 1974. [47 185]

[Moor 75a] Moore, J, 'The INTERLISP Virtual Machine Specification', (in preparation), Xerox PARC, Palo Alto, 1975. [norefs]

[Moor 75b] Moore, J, 'Computational Logic: Structure Sharing and Proof of Program Properties Part II', CSL 75-2, Xerox PARC, Palo Alto, Apr 1975. [96]

[Mor 55]   Morris, C., 'Foundations of the Theory of Signs', *International Encyclopedia of Unified Science*, Vol 1, No 2, University of Chicago press, 1955. [162]

[Mor 68]   Morris, J., 'Lambda-calculus Models of Programming Languages', Project MAC, M.I.T., MAC-TR57, Dec 1968. [22 181]

[Mor 73]   Morris, L., 'Advice on Structuring Compilers and Proving Them Correct', ACM Symposium on Principles of Programming Languages, Boston, p. 144-152, 1973. [norefs]

[Mor 74]   Morris, J., 'Towards More Flexible Type Systems', Proc. Colloque sur la Programmation, Paris, April 1974, p. 377-383, Springer Verlag, Berlin, 1974. [36]

[Mos 70]   Moses, J., 'The Function of FUNCTION in LISP', *SIGSAM Bulletin*, p. 13-27, July 1970. [norefs]

[Mos 74]   Moses, J., 'MACSYMA - The Fifth Year', *SIGSAM Bulletin*, 8, *3*, p. 105-110, Aug 1974. [62 390]

[Mot 76]   Motoyoshi, F., 'A Portable LISP Compiler on a Hypothetical LISP Machine', Dept. of Info. Science, TR 76-5, University of Tokyo, Japan, Jan. 1976. [249]

[Mud 75]   Galley, S.W., and Pfister, G., 'The MDL Language', Programming Technology Division Doc. SYS.11.01, Project Mac, M.I.T., Cambridge, Mass., Nov. 1975. [301 412]

[Mul 76]   Muller, K., 'On the Feasibility of Concurrent Garbage Collection', Ph.D. Thesis, University of Delft, 1976. [287]

[New 61]   Newell, A., *Information Processing Language V Manual*, Prentice Hall, Englewood Cliffs, New Jersey, 1961. [227 236 247 256]

[New 75]   Newey, M., 'Formal Semantics of LISP with Applications to Program Correctness', Stanford A.I. Lab Memo 257, Stanford Univ., Jan 1975. [96 337]

[Nor 70]   Nordstrom, M., et al., 'LISP F1 - A Fortran Implementation of LISP 1.5', Computer Science Dept, Uppsala University, Sweden, 1970. [norefs]

[Nor 76]   Norman, E., 'Documentation for 1100 LISP Implementation', unpublished paper, University of Wisconsin-Madison, 1976. [266]

[Org 71]   Organick, E., and Cleary, J., 'A Data Structure Model of the B6700 Computer System', p. 83-145 in [DSIPL]. [372]

[Org 73]   Organick, E., *Computer System Organization: the B5700/6700 Series*, ACM Monograph Series, Academic Press, New York, 1973. [236]

[Pac 73]   Pacini, G., 'An Optimal Fix-point Computation Rule for a Simple Recursive Language', University of Pisa, N.I. B75-10, Oct. 1973. [221]

[Pag 76]   Page, R., LISP for Fairchild F8, Private communication, 1976. [245]

[Per 67]   Perlis, A., 'The Synthesis of Algorithmic Systems: 1966 ACM Turing Lecture', *JACM 14*, 1, p. 1-9, Jan. 1967. [norefs]

[Plo 74]   Plotkin, G., 'Call-by-name, Call-by-value and the λ-Calculus', *Theoretical Computer Science 1*, p. 125-159, 1975. [norefs]

[Pop 68a]   Popplestone, R., 'The Design Philosophy of POP-2', in *Machine Intelligence 3*, American Elsevier, New York, 1968. [160]

[Pop 68]   Burstall, R., et al., *POP2 Papers*, Oliver & Boyd, Edinburgh, 1968. [160 382]

[Pra 73]   Pratt, V., 'Top-down Operator Precedence', Proceedings of the ACM Symposium on Principles of Programming, p. 41-51, 1973. [162]

[Pra 76]   Pratt, V., 'CGOL - An Alternative External Representation for LISP Users', M.I.T. A.I. Lab, Working Paper No. 89, 1976. [410]

[Pre 72]   Prenner, C., 'Multi-path Control Structures for Programming

Languages', Ph.D. Thesis, Center for Research in Computing Technology, Harvard Univ., 1972. [229]

[Pre 76a]   Prenner, C., 'Data structures for Spaghetti LISP', unpublished notes, University of California, Berkeley, Calif, 1976. [229 266]

[Pre 76b]   Prenner, C., 'Implementation for Spaghetti EL1', unpublished notes, University of California, Berkeley, Calif, 1976. [410]

[QA4 72]   Rulifson, J., et. al., 'QA4: A Procedural Calculus for Intuitive Reasoning', Stanford Research Institute, TN-73, Menlo Park, Cal., Nov. 1972. [74 410]

[Qua 68]   Quam, L., 'SDIO Manual', unpublished paper, Stanford, 1968. [421]

[Qua 72]   Quam, L., and Diffie, W., 'Stanford LISP 1.6 Manual', Stanford A.I. Lab., Operating Note 28.7, Stanford Univ., 1972. [128 194]

[Rey 72]   Reynolds, J., 'Definitional Interpreters for High-order Programming Languages', Proceedings of the ACM National convention, 1972, p. 717-740, ACM, 1972. [137 207 219]

[Ric 74]   Rich, C., and Shrobe, H., 'Understanding LISP Programs: Towards a Programming Apprentice', M.I.T. A.I. Lab, Working paper 82, Dec. 1974. [norefs]

[Ris 73]   Risch, T., 'REMREC - A Program for Automatic Recursion Removal in LISP', Datalogilaboratoriet, DLU 73/24, Uppsala Univ., Nov. 1973. [norefs]

[Riv 76]   Rivest, R., 'On Self-organizing Sequential Search Heuristics', *Comm. ACM 19*, 2, p. 63-67, Feb. 1976. [261]

[Rob 65]   Robinson, J., 'A Machine-oriented Logic Based on the Resolution Principle', *Journal ACM 12*, 1, p. 23-41, Jan 1965. [75]

[Roc 71]   Rochfeld, A., 'New LISP Techniques for a Paging Environment', *Comm. ACM 14*, 12, p. 791-795, Dec 1971. [norefs]

[Rog 67]   Rogers, H., *Theory of Recursive Functions & Effective Computability*, McGraw-Hill, New York, 1967. [22 159 160 229]

[Ros 71]   Rosen, B. 'Subtree Replacement Systems', Ph.D. Thesis, Harvard University, Cambridge, Mass.,1971. [173]

[Rus 64]   Russell R., 'KALAH - The Game and the Program', Stanford A.I. Lab. Memo 22, Stanford University, 1964. [norefs]

[Sam 75] · Samet, H., 'Automatically Proving the Correctness of Translations Involving Optimized Code', Stanford A.I. Lab. Memo 259, May 1975. [185 262]

[San 75a] Sandewall, E., 'Ideas About Management of LISP Data Bases', M.I.T. A.I. Lab., Memo 332, May 1975. [265]

[San 75] Sandewall, E., 'Some Observations on Conceptual Programming', Computer Science Dept., Uppsala University, Sweden, 1975. [norefs]

[San 76] Sandewall, E., 'Programming in an Interactive Environment: The LISP Experience', Linkoping University, Sweden, 1976. [norefs]

[Sau 64] Saunders, R., 'The LISP System for the Q-32 Computer', p. 220-231 in [Ber 64]. [norefs]

[Sch 67] Schorr, H., and Waite, W., 'An Efficient Machine-independent Procedure for Garbage Collection in Various List Structures', *Comm. ACM 10*, 8, p. 501-506, Aug. 1967. [398]

[Sco 70] Scott, D., 'Outline of a Mathematical Theory of Computation', Oxford University Computing Labs, PRG-2, Oxford University, 1970. [175 177]

[Sco 72] Scott, D., 'Mathematical Concepts in Programming Languages', AFIPS Conference Proceedings, Vol 40, p. 225-234, 1972. [161]

[Sco 73] Scott, D., 'Models for various type-free calculi', in *Logic, Methodology, and Philosophy of Science IV*, North Holland, p. 157-187, 1973. [175 177]

[Sik 76] Siklossy, L., *Let's Talk LISP*, Prentice Hall, Englewood Cliffs, New Jersey, 1976. [norefs]

[Sta 74] von Staa, A., 'Data Transmission and Modularity Aspects of Programming Languages', Dept. of Computer Science, Research Report CS-74-17, University of Waterloo, Ontario, October 1974. [160]

[Ste 73] Steele, G., 'BIBOP LISP Memo', unpublished MIT paper, 1973. [266 402]

[Ste 76a] Steele, G., 'Multiprocessing Compactifying Garbage Collection', *Comm. ACM 18*, 9, p. 495-508, Sep. 1967. [402]

[Ste 76b] Steele, G., and Sussman, G., 'LAMBDA: The Ultimate Imperative', M.I.T. A.I. Memo 353, Mar. 1976. [150 172 219 358 411]

[Ste 76c]   Steele,   G.,   'LAMBDA: The   Ultimate   Declarative',
M.I.T. A.I. Memo 379, Oct. 1976. [172 411]

[Ste pc]   Steele, G., private communications. [155 368 382]

[Stei 74]   Steiger, R., 'Actor Machine Architecture', M.S. Thesis, M.I.T.,
1974. [norefs]

[Sto 75]   Stoyan, H., 'Comparison of Two LISP Compilers: Stanford
Versus DOS/ES-LISP', *Elektronische Informationsverarbeitung
und Kybernetik 11*, p. 371-375, 1975. [norefs]

[Str 67]   Strachey,   C.,   'Fundamental   Concepts   in   Programming
Languages', NATO Conference, Copenhagen, 1967. [norefs]

[Str 73]   Strachey, C., 'Varieties of Programming Languages', Oxford
University   Computing   Labs,   PRG-10,   Oxford   University,
1973. [norefs]

[Str 74a]   Strachey,   C.,   and   Wadsworth,   C.,   'Continuations: A
Mathematical Semantics for Handling Full Jumps', Oxford
University   Computing   Laboratory,   Technical   Monograph
PRG-11, Jan 1974. [207]

[Str 74]   Foy, N., 'The Words Games of the Night Bird: Interview with
C. Strachey', *Computing Europe*, p. 10-11, Aug 15, 1974. [97]

[Sug 77]   Sugarman, R., 'Chess Computers Start to Give Humans a
Tough   Game',   *Electronic Engineerging News*,   p. 4, 44, 92,
Apr 18, 1977. [66]

[Sus 75]   Sussman, G., and Steele, G., 'SCHEME: an Interpreter for
Extended   Lambda   Calculus',   M.I.T. A.I. Memo 349,
Dec. 1975. [137 172 219 358 411]

[Sus 76]   Sussman,   G.,   and   Steele,   G.,   'SCHEME   Flash   1',
M.I.T. A.I. Lab., Jan. 1976. [230 255]

[Tei 72]   Teitelman, W., 'Automated Programmering - The Programmer's
Assistant', Proceedings of the Fall Joint Computer Conference,
Dec. 1972. [norefs]

[Ten 76]   Tennent, R., 'The Denotational Semantics of Programming
Languages', *Comm. ACM 19*, 8, p. 437-453, Aug. 1976. [164]

[Ter 75]   Terashima, M., 'Algorithms Used in an Implementation of
HLISP', Information Sciences Lab., TR 75-03, Univ. of Tokyo,
Japan, Jan. 1975. [273 403]

[Urm 76]   Urmi, J., 'A Shallow Binding Scheme for Fast Environment
Changing in a 'Spaghetti Stack' LISP System', Linkoping
University, Sweden, 1976. [398]

[Vui 74]   Vuillemin, J., 'Correct and Optimal Implementations of Recursion in a Simple Programming Language', *Journal of Computer and System Science*, Vol 9, No 3, Dec 1974. [221]

[Wad 71]   Wadsworth, C., 'Semantics and Pragmatics of the Lambda-calculus', Ph.D. Thesis, Oxford University, 1971. [173 174 175 221]

[Wad 74a]   Wadsworth, C., The Relation Between Lambda-expressions and Their Denotations', unpublished paper, Systems and Info. Science Dept, Syracuse Univ., 1974. [173]

[Wan 75]   Wang, P., 'MACSYMA - A Symbolic Manipulation System', Proceedings of International Computer Symposium, Vol. 1, p. 103-109, 1975. [390]

[War 74]   Ward, S., 'Functional Domains of Applicative Languages', Ph.D. Thesis, M.I.T., MAC TR-136, Cambridge, Sep. 1974. [norefs]

[Weg 68]   Wegner, P., *Programming Languages, Information Structures and Machine Organization*, McGraw-Hill, New York, 1968. [norefs]

[Weg 70]   Wegner, P., 'Three Computer Cultures - Computer Technology, Computer Mathematics & Computer Science', in *Advances in Computers*, 10, Academic Press, New York, 1970. [norefs]

[Weg 71]   Wegner, P., 'Data Structure Models for Programming Languages', p. 1-54 in [DSIPL]. [norefs]

[Weg 72]   Wegner, P., 'The Vienna Definition Language', *Computing Surveys*, Vol 4, No 1, p. 5-63, Mar 1972. [42 163]

[Wegb 70]   Wegbreit, B., 'Studies in Extensible Programming Languages', Ph.D. Thesis, Harvard University, Cambridge, Mass.,1970. [402]

[Wegb 71]   Wegbreit, B., 'The ECL Programming System', Proceedings AFIPS 1971 FJCC, Vol 39, AFIPS Press, Mondale, New Jersey, p. 253-262, 1971. [norefs]

[Wegb 72]   Wegbreit, B., 'A Generalized Compactifying Garbage Collector', *Computer Journal 15*, 3, p. 204-208, Aug 1972. [norefs]

[Wegb 74]   Wegbreit, B., 'The Treatment of Data Types in EL1', *Comm. ACM 17*, 5, p. 251-264, May 1974. [norefs]

[Wegb 75]   Wegbreit, B., 'Retrieval From Context Trees', *Information Processing Letters, 3*, 4, p. 119-120, March 1975. [150 301]

[Wei 62]   Weizenbaum, J., 'Knotted List Structures', *Comm. ACM 5*, 13, p. 161-165, Mar 1962. [norefs]

[Wei 63]   Weizenbaum, J., 'Symmetric List Processor', *Comm. ACM 6*, 9, p. 524-544, Sep 1963. [norefs]

[Wei 68]   Weizenbaum, J., 'The FUNARG Problem Explained', unpublished memorandum, M.I.T., Cambridge, Mass., 1968. [131]

[Weis 67]   Weismann, C., 'LISP 1.5 Primer', Dickenson Press, Belmont, 1967. [norefs]

[Win 75]   Winograd, T., 'Breaking the Complexity Barrier (again)', *ACM SIGPLAN Notes 10*, 1, p. 13-30, Jan. 1975. [364]

[Wis 75]   Wise, D., et. al., 'Boolean-valued Loops', *BIT* 15 p. 431-451, 1975. [195]

[Zil 70]   Zilles, S., 'An Expansion of the Data Structuring Capabilities in PAL', M.S. Thesis, MIT, Jun 1970.

Index

SM   312
λ-notation   110
=   376
and   154
append   48
apply   116
array   373
atom   18
BLANK   271
car   13
car-cdr-chains   14
catch   198
cdr   13
cdr-coding   399
char   375
compile   307
concat   29
COND   106, 115
cons   12, 281
deposit   331
eq   19

equal   23
err   198
errset   198
eval   115, 241, 323, 412
evcond   115
examine   331
first   375
FUNARG   146
function   141
gensym   327
go   189
isseq   28
label   136
list   35
LPAR   271
maplist   148
mkent   109
NIL   33, 270
null   28, 375
OBLIST   276
or   154
patom   271
PERIOD   271
PNAME   267
prin0   273
print   273
prog   186
putprop   387
ratom   271, 276, 278, 387
read_head   272
read_tail   272
read   272
read macro   280
remprop   262, 387
rest   29, 375
RPAR   271
rplaca   384
seq   30
store   373
tgmoaf   91, 323
tgmoaf   421

tgmoafr 91, 323
throw 198
α-rule 171
β-rule 171
a-lists 108
access chain 132
access link 132
accumulators 47
activation environment 146
actual parameters 15
AMBIT/G 253
analytic syntax 164
applicative language 15
Assemblers 320
association lists 108
atom header 266
atom space 246
auxiliary function 47
base language 406
Binary Program Space 320
binding 15
binding environment 146
binding strategy 149
bootstrapping 307
bound occurrence 170
bound variable 130
box-notation 9
BPS 320
bucket hashing 275
cache value cells 301
call-by-name 100, 221
call-by-need 221
call-by-value 100
case statement 193
case statement 157
closure 141, 192
code generators 308
coercion 242
collision 275
compiler 332, 335
computed function 158

concrete syntax 165
conditional expression 18, 19, 115
CONNIVER 412
constructor 12
continuation 207
control environment 142
control structures 39
deep binding 152
definition by recursion 43
denotational 167
differentiation 57
discriminator 18
dope vector 372
dotted-pairs 6
double-linking 393
doubly-linked list structure 247
dynamic binding 131
EL1 406
evaluation 13, 97
examples of *eval* 118
expr 224
extensible language 406
fexpr 224
Fibonacci sequence 46
fix-up 330
fixed points 232
fixed-point operator 234
fluid variable 131
form 12, 17, 111
formal parameter 14
forward reference 329
free space list 281
free variable 130, 170
Full Word Space 269
funarg 141
function 111
function application 15
functional argument 137
functional composition 14
functional value 143
FWS 269

garbage collection   282
garbage collector   282, 373, 387
generalized control structures   197
generative definition   3
global variable   129, 131
halting problem   181
hash consing   287, 385, 402
hashing   275
hashing algorithm   275
inductive definition   3
internal lambdas   113
invisible pointers   400
lambda list   111
length   186
lexical binding   150
linear search   108
linked allocation   291
linked list structure   246
LISP machine   289
list terminator   33
list-notation   33
lists   31
literal atoms   5
local binding   129
local symbol table   129
local variable   187
M-expr LISP   107
M-expressions   236
macros   355
mapping functions   148
marking phase   283
match-variable   6
meta-language   107, 236
meta-variables   6
MICRO-PLANNER   412
mother-vector   373
MUDDLE   412
name stack   292
non-local   129
non-local variables   356
non-strict   21

numbers   389
object list   276
offset   336
open addressing   275
open function   232
operation code   321
operational   167
p-list   267
parser   272
partial application   160
partial function   11, 13
pattern directed invocation   73
PL/1   406
pointer   245
pointer space   246
polymorphic functions   29
precedence   417
predicates   18
prefix notation   58
pretty printing   20
print-name   267
property-list   256
recognizer   18, 28
record   382
reduction rule   173
reference counter   286, 301
S-expr LISP   107
S-expressions   5
S-exprs   5
scanner   271
SDIO   421
selector   13
self-applicative   175
self-applicative functions   149
shallow binding   152
singly linked   247
Special Form   154
special forms   115
special variable   356
stack   291
stack synchronization   316

static binding   150
storage reclaimer   282
stratification   424
strict functions   12
string processor   374
sweep phase   284
symbol tables   107
Symbolic expressions   5
syntax-directed   417
table-driven   191
termination conditions   45
threading   393
total function   11
type fault   23
unbound variable   130
universal function   181
value stack   292, 333
value cell   152
variables   128